Choctaw Nation

CHOCTAW

A STORY OF

AMERICAN INDIAN

NATION

◆ ◆ ◆ ◆ ◆ ◆ ◆

RESURGENCE

Valerie Lambert

UNIVERSITY OF NEBRASKA PRESS   •   LINCOLN AND LONDON

Publication of this volume
was assisted by a
University of North Carolina
University Research Council
Publication Grant.

Library of Congress
Cataloging-in-Publication Data
Lambert, Valerie.
Choctaw nation : a story of American
Indian resurgence / Valerie Lambert.
        p.   cm.
Includes bibliographical
references and index.
ISBN-13: 978-0-8032-1105-6
(cloth : alk. paper)
ISBN-10: 0-8032-1105-8
(cloth : alk. paper)
ISBN-13: 978-0-8032-2490-2
(paper : alk. paper)
1. Choctaw Indians—History.
2. Choctaw Indians—Social life
and customs.
3. Choctaw Indians—
Government relations.
4. Southern States—History.
5. Southern States—Social life
and customs.
I. Title.
E99.C81.25 2007
976.004'97387—dc22
2006031812

Set in Trump Medieval by Kim Essman.
Designed by R. W. Boeche.

For Mike

Contents

Acknowledgments

It is impossible to thank adequately the many people who made it possible to write this book. I have benefited enormously from the generosity, support, insight, and kindness of many wonderful people along the way, and my feelings of gratitude and appreciation run deep.

My greatest debt is to the Choctaws. I deeply appreciate the many hours that so many of my people gave to try to ensure the success of this project. At all stages, Choctaws showed a great deal of patience and enthusiasm, contributing time, energy, and other resources in levels that far exceeded my expectations. In order to protect the confidentiality of my consultants, as well as to avoid offending those who might see their friends' and relatives' names but not their own in these acknowledgments, I will thank each of you in person. Let me mention by name, with my sincerest thanks, only the elected leaders of our tribe who provided permission for me to conduct this research: Hollis Roberts, Choctaw chief from 1978 to 1997; Gregory E. Pyle, Choctaw chief from 1997 to the present; and the late Randle Durant, a multiple-term tribal council member who was speaker of the tribal council during the period of my research. When Mr. Durant passed away in 2004, we Choctaws lost a very talented and hard-working leader.

This book was greatly improved by the brilliance and generosity of my colleagues. My wonderful mentor, K. Tsianina Lomawaima, devoted many hours to reading and commenting on each chapter, in addition to offering critical moral support. I was amazed by how important and insightful each of her comments and suggestions were. Her impact on this book has been tremendous, and my debt to her, so great that it can never be repaid.

Another senior female Indian scholar for whom I am eternally grateful is Clara Sue Kidwell, whose extensive knowledge of our Choctaw people is legendary. I was deeply honored to receive so much of her time and attention, and I very much appreciate the many ways that she strengthened every chapter in this book.

Two others who have been mentoring me for years each took time out of their productive academic lives to critique parts of this book and to continue to encourage me to find happiness and satisfaction in all areas of my life. These remarkable individuals are Orin Starn and Cathy Lutz.

I also owe much thanks to Circe Sturm and Phyllis Fast, each of whom used her extensive knowledge of contemporary U.S. Indian life to make insightful comments on several of the ethnographic chapters that enabled me to think about my ethnographic material in new ways. For helping shape the conceptualization of this project and for commenting on early drafts, I would also like to thank Stanley Tambiah, Michael Herzfeld, and Mary Steedly.

Several individuals provided valuable advice about both general and particular features of the manuscript that had an important impact on the final product. They are Vin Steponaitis, Dottie Holland, Judith Farquhar, Peter Redfield, and the fellows in my cohort at the Institute for the Arts and Humanities at the University of North Carolina at Chapel Hill.

I also feel indebted to others who expressed interest in this project and who in many cases read portions of this manuscript prior to its completion. They are Theda Perdue, Mike Green, George Roth, Jason Jackson, Duane Champagne, Tom Biolsi, Jessica Cattelino, Gavin Clarkson, Michelene Pesantubbee, Karla Slocum, Paul Chaat Smith, and Kirk Dombrowski.

Gary Dunham, Director of the University of Nebraska Press, has been a real pleasure to work with and has provided invaluable help and assistance in a number of different areas. I would like to thank him, project editor Sara Springsteen, and my wonderful copyeditor, Colleen Clark. For their efforts and their very helpful suggestions I would also like to thank the anonymous reviewers of my manuscript.

During graduate school, my thinking about Indians was significantly broadened through conversations with Angela Gonzales, Darren Ranco, Bernie Perley, Gabrielle Tayac, Jeff Hamley, Jay Levi, and Bart Dean. I deeply appreciate their important role in my development as a person and a scholar.

Finally, I wish to acknowledge the love and support of my family. Throughout the process of writing this book, my father, Wendell Long, and my sister Kristin Long have been among the most enthusiastic supporters of this project. My mother, my other siblings, my in-laws, my aunts and uncles, and my cousins have also shared an unwavering belief in my ability to complete this book, a belief from which many times I have drawn strength.

My husband, Mike, has seen me in my weakest moments. He and our two beautiful daughters, Jessica and Hailey, have made the greatest sacrifices and have been affected the most by the writing of this book. Many times they have surprised me not only by continuing to love and support me but also by lifting me up during the many points when I became discouraged. In addition, my husband's identity as an anthropologist, as a member of the Eastern Band of Cherokee Indians of North Carolina, and as one of the smartest people whom I have ever met has meant that he has never failed to provide me with innumerable valuable comments and suggestions. I could never ask for a better husband. Or for better children. I don't know how I got so lucky to have these amazing people in my life.

The research and writing of this book were funded by a Wenner-Gren Foundation for Anthropological Research Dissertation Fellowship, a Harvard Department of Anthropology Dissertation Research Fellowship, a Bureau of Indian Affairs Fellowship, a Harvard Department of Anthropology Summer Research Fellowship, a National Academy of Sciences / Ford Foundation Dissertation Completion Fellowship, an Andrew W. Mellon Foundation Woodrow Wilson National Fellowship, a University of North Carolina Institute for the Arts and Humanities Fellowship, a University of North Carolina Research and Study Assignment, and a University of North Carolina Junior Faculty Development Award. Some of the interviews quoted in the text have been reprinted with the permission of the Research Division of the Oklahoma Historical Society or printed with the permission of the U.S. Department of Interior's Office of the Special Trustee for American Indians.

Choctaw Nation

1. Introduction

In the spring of 1995, when I began conducting anthropological field research among members of my own tribal nation, the Choctaw Nation of Oklahoma, I was struck by the extent to which formal membership (or citizenship) in our tribe had become a measure of Choctaw belonging.[1] Citizenship in the Choctaw Nation, one of the most populous Indian tribes in the United States, was creating boundaries that were significantly affecting the lives of Choctaws living within tribal boundaries. Tribal leaders were enforcing a tribal order in which only tribal citizens were deemed entitled to participate in formal tribal affairs, gain access to tribal resources, and attend certain tribal social events. Choctaw citizens were sharing a set of experiences, such as voting in tribal elections and participating in tribal programs, that were separating them from Choctaws who were not enrolled and that were encouraging both the enrolled and the unenrolled to view enrolled Choctaws as somehow "more Choctaw." During my field research, almost every time I engaged in conversation with a Choctaw whom I did not know (both enrolled and unenrolled Choctaws) I was asked whether I was enrolled.

Fortunately for me, the answer was yes. For elected and grassroots Choctaw leaders, my status as an enrolled tribal member meant first and foremost that I was a voter. For tribal bureaucrats, it meant not only that I was a voter but also that I was formally integrated into the Choctaw polity—that I was a Choctaw citizen—and that I was a shareholder in what might be described as the tribal corporation. For Choctaw citizens, it meant that I shared with them formal ties of tribal citizenship that bound us together in a seemingly inextricable way. It also meant that there was a point at which my claims to being Choctaw were unassailable. For unenrolled Choctaws, my status as a Choctaw citizen meant that I likely questioned the legitimacy of their Choctaw identity (which, more often than not, was not the case). For many of the unenrolled, it also meant that I likely naturalized the boundaries that defined the Choctaw citizenry, that is, I did not see these boundaries for what they were and are: as sociopolitical constructions. This, too, was not the case.

During the early days of my seventeen months of field research, I was struck not only by how often I was asked the question of whether I was enrolled but also by how often Choctaws living in the Choctaw Nation asked this question of one another. For example, only a few days after I arrived at the farmhouse of a friend with whom I lived during the first part of my research, my friend received a visit from the tribe's director of agriculture, Randy Bailey. From a big wingback chair in the family's brown-paneled living room, Mr. Bailey, an enrolled Choctaw, told my friend—who also happened to be an enrolled Choctaw—that for health reasons she and her family should no longer use the pond behind their house as their principal water supply. As my friend began expressing concerns about her family's health and the fact that she could not afford to fix the problem, Mr. Bailey interrupted her. "Don't worry," he said. "We [the tribal government] have a program for Choctaws where we'll lay pipe through their land out to the road, where we can [then] hook 'em up to the [local water supply]." Pausing for a moment, he then unclasped his hands, leaned forward in his chair, and asked pointedly, "Are you enrolled?" Only enrolled Choctaws were eligible for this program, as is the case for most present-day Choctaw tribal programs.

In its preoccupation with the boundaries that define Choctaw citizenship, the Choctaw Nation that I encountered in the mid-1990s hardly resembled the Choctaw Nation of my youth. I was reared in Oklahoma, specifically in Oklahoma City. I was born in the mid-1960s, at a time when "the enrolled"—or, as they were sometimes termed, "the enrollees"—meant those Choctaws whose names were listed on the Dawes (Allotment) Rolls of 1906. By the Bureau of Indian Affairs (BIA) and by many Choctaws, all Choctaws born after the rolls were "closed" during the first decade of the twentieth century were termed "the unenrolled." When I was a young child, the Choctaw tribal government was tiny, had little power and few resources, and was headed by a chief whom we Choctaws were not legally entitled to select ourselves. From 1906 to 1970, each of the principal leaders of the Five "Civilized" Tribes, a category of tribes that includes the Choctaws, were appointed by the U.S. president. Furthermore, during the first four years of my life, the Choctaw tribe was slated for the termination of its trust relationship with the federal government. Until the Choctaw termination law was repealed one day before it was scheduled to take effect on August 25, 1970, we Choctaws faced a future in which, in federal terms, our tribe would no longer exist as a tribe. In those days, acts of self-identification as Choctaw were celebrated by other Choctaws as acts of resistance against federal, state, and local pressures to assimilate into the larger, non-Indian society.

I left Oklahoma to attend college in 1984, one year after our tribe ratified the first Choctaw tribal constitution in more than a century. This document expressed, reinforced, and facilitated an intensive period of Choctaw tribal nation building. Against the background of the formal restoration by Congress during the previous decade of our right to select our own leaders, Choctaw leaders reorganized and dramatically expanded the executive branch of our tribal government. They also amplified and redistributed the powers of the tribal executive among two sets of formal political institutions that were formally created in and by the 1983 constitution—the legislative and judicial branches of our tribal government. At the same time, tribal leaders hardened the boundaries around the Choctaw citizenry by defining criteria for tribal citizenship, which were enshrined in our new constitution, and by initiating and carrying out a large-scale issuance of tribal membership cards. Tribal citizenship was limited to those listed as "Choctaw by blood" on the Dawes Rolls of 1906 and to those who could document lineal descent from at least one ancestor listed on these rolls. (The 1906 rolls, it should be pointed out, captured most, but certainly not all, Choctaws who were maintaining Choctaw tribal relations at the turn of the twentieth century.)

With the new tribal political order shaping virtually all aspects of Choctaw social and political life, for me there was simply no question of what I, as an anthropologist, was there to do: I was to document the building of the new order and explore its social, political, and economic consequences. My ability to carry out this work was greatly enhanced by the fact that my status as a Choctaw opened many doors. It was also enhanced by the fact that I had spent the eleven years that preceded my fieldwork living outside Oklahoma. Though I had returned to Oklahoma many times during this period to visit friends and family, my extended absence gave me a certain amount of distance from the transformations and processes that were unfolding in and around the Choctaw Nation, a distance that, I believe, significantly broadened the set of phenomena that I was able to notice and observe. Much of the time I spent away, of course, was spent preparing for the field research that I knew I wanted to conduct among my tribe. While in graduate school at Harvard University, I received formal training as an anthropologist, conducted coursework in and served as a Teaching Fellow for the Department of Government, reviewed the literature about the Choctaws, and read about other tribes. In addition, during and after graduate school I spent sixteen months working as a cultural anthropologist at the BIA in Washington DC. At the BIA I learned much about the complex articulations between Indian tribes and larger legal and political structures. I also learned much about what was happening throughout Indian country, especially as regards the tribal nation building that was taking place on reservations and tribal trust lands across the country. This perspective is especially apparent in chapters 4 through 6, which explore the consequences of the late-twentieth-century period of Choctaw nation building.

The story of the Choctaws' creation of a new political order in the late twentieth century is a story that must be placed in the larger context of the history of our tribe. This is not only because our history is central to our sense of ourselves as a people and critical to understanding who the Choctaws are in the early-twenty-first century but also because it was at least the third time in our history that our tribe experienced a massive rupture followed by a dramatic rebirth. As I chronicle in chapter 2, in the 1500s the ancestors of the modern Choctaw Nation survived the complete disintegration of the great Mississippian chiefdoms of which they were then a part, chiefdoms that dominated the interior of what is now the American Southeast. After likely migrating from their former homes, at the turn of the seventeenth century Choctaws incorporated remnants of other Indian peoples and founded the modern Choctaw tribe. By the mid-1700s the Choctaws had become the premier agriculturalists in what is now the American Southeast. The Choctaw language operated as the lingua franca for most of the region, and, together with only one or two other tribes, the Choctaws held the balance of power in the Southeast. During this period the tribe maintained a cultural distinctiveness that set them apart from other Indian and non-Indian populations in the area, a cultural distinctiveness that was eroded significantly during subsequent periods of Choctaw history.

In the overview presented in chapter 2 of Choctaw culture, history, and society through 1970, I also address the massive leveling of the Choctaw past and the tribal institution building that occurred during the tribe's nineteenth-century history. In 1830 the Choctaws became the first tribe to experience the mass removal of their entire tribe by the U.S. government. The Choctaws were relocated from parts of present-day Mississippi and Alabama to Indian Territory, now Oklahoma, on what is popularly termed the Trail of Tears. This massive rupture devastated the Choctaw people. However, almost immediately upon the resettlement of the first party of Choctaws relocated under the terms of the removal treaty, Choctaw leaders launched a period of intensive tribal nation building and rebirth, creating, among other things, an elaborate set of new formal political institutions in their new home.

For living Choctaws, the success of the Choctaw nation building of the nineteenth century provided and continues to provide much of the inspiration for the nation-building efforts of the late twentieth century. By 1857, less than three decades after the signing of the Choctaw removal treaty, the Choctaws had installed a principal chief to head the tribal government's executive branch, which consisted of tribal, district, and county levels of government, and built a bicameral legislative branch, which consisted of an upper house of delegates based on district representation and a lower house of delegates based on population. A system of county, circuit, and supreme courts comprised the tribal judiciary, dozens of neighborhood schools and more than a half-dozen tribal academies defined a Choctaw-controlled school system, and tribal police, who were called "lighthorse," helped maintain order. This new nineteenth-century political order, like the new political order of the late twentieth century, drew and enforced rigid boundaries around a tribal citizenry, maintaining a set of formal criteria that defined who was and was not a citizen of the tribe. Less than a century after it was built, this political order was almost entirely dismantled by the U.S. government. In an attempt to dissolve the tribe, in 1906 the U.S. government destroyed most of the tribe's formal political structures, stripped the tribal government of much of its powers, and initiated a process of decollectivizing Choctaw tribal assets, a process that, fortunately for the Choctaws, was never completed. Although at no point following this rupture did the Choctaws cease to hold at least some land and monies in common or lose formal recognition of the position of tribal chief, the 1906 razing of Choctaw tribal structures and institutions was extraordinarily far-reaching, as will be seen, and shaped the context for the late-twentieth-century rebuilding that is the focus of this book.

Larger questions about the nature of nation-building projects informed my investigation of the late-twentieth-century rebuilding of my tribe. Broadly structuring my inquiry into Choctaw nation building was a theoretical debate about whether new orders "are erected, like coral reefs, without conscious design" (Sait 1938: 16; see also Leach 1954: 8); or whether their authorship can be discerned (Herzfeld 1992: 67) and characterized as an artifact of political process (Libecap 1989). I began with the working assumptions that the new order was the product of the political actions of certain individuals instead of a creation of the society as a whole, and that political negotiations and processes had shaped the production of the new structures, institutions, and arrangements that together made up the new order. Aware that the vast majority of Choctaws recognized then chief Hollis Roberts as both the founder and architect of the new order, one of the central goals of this part of my research was to critically evaluate this claim.

In seeking to uncover the origins of the new order and document its unfolding, I also drew upon the theoretical insight of anthropology and political science that nationalism plays a central role in nation-building efforts, regardless of whether these efforts are defined by the goal of replacing an existing order or the goal of initiating processes of political centralization. Building upon this work and ethnographies about nationalism, I resolved to explore ethnographically the question of what type of site nationalism emerges from. Anthropologists Stanley Tambiah and Michael Herzfeld provided two different models of the production sites of nationalisms. In an ethnography documenting a large-scale political upheaval in his native Sri Lanka, Tambiah traces the first articulations of the modern variant of Sinhalese nationalism to "militant, chauvinist, and demagogic [Buddhist] monks" (1986: 83). He explains part of the process by which these ideas have been both disseminated and revised in terms of these monks organizing themselves into a corporate group, mo-bilizing "lay supporters," and forming coalitions. According to Tambiah, through these and other political actions, Sinhalese nationalism progres-sively leaked into the political arenas of the Sri Lankan state. In contrast, in an ethnography about nationalist ideologies in Greece, Michael Herz-feld (1992) implies that the work of creating and recreating nationalisms is done not at the periphery of power but rather at its core. Herzfeld argues that elected leaders and their staff construct representations and select icons that they have co-opted from local communities in order to, among other things, calibrate personal and local identities to constructions of "national character." Had Choctaw nationalism emerged from within or outside of the then weak (but still important) Choctaw "state"?

I coupled my interest in pursuing the origins of late-twentieth-century Choctaw nationalism with an interest in critically inspecting its founda-tions. Specifically, I was interested in how the Choctaws had made sense of their history in the context of the upheavals of political centraliza-tion and bureaucratization. What type of narrative of Choctaw nation-hood had fueled the rebuilding that I aimed to document? Had Choctaw leaders, following Arapahoe leaders, cleverly redefined discontinuities as continuities (Fowler 1982) and thus foregrounded the timelessness of the Choctaw polity; or had the new order been constructed as a break from the past? The Choctaw tribal newspapers that I was receiving and con-versations with friends and family strongly suggested that the new order was being framed as a break from the past. However, as with other pre-conceptions that I had of what had been going on in the Choctaw Nation, especially during my absence, I resolved to base my findings on ethno-graphic research, setting aside as much as possible my assumptions about who the Choctaws were and are.

Some of the literature on nation making suggested that the Choctaws may have foregrounded constructions of their nation as timeless during the age of tribal nation building. Benedict Anderson (1991) and Ernest Gellner (1983) treat such constructions as a virtual requirement of na-tion building. The socially ascribed timeless character or quality of the nation is part of the "magic of nationalism," Anderson explains: the na-tion is made to "loom out of an immemorial past" and "glide into a lim-itless future" (1991: 11–12). Hobsbawm and Ranger also note the perva-siveness of group identities that are fashioned as timeless, arguing that groups and nations often use "traditions," which claim to be ancient but which may, in fact, be new or invented, to establish "continuity with a suitable historic past" (1983: 1). They explain that, in the context of "the constant change and innovation of the modern world" there is a need for people to "structure at least some parts of social life . . . as unchanging and invariant" (p. 2). Nash adds that group members find constructions of their group identity in terms of continuity and timelessness attractive because they "give an aura of authority, legitimacy, and rightness to cultural beliefs and practices" (1989: 14). Such constructions help naturalize and legitimize the group not only for group members but also for those located outside group boundaries.

In contrast to these theorists, Samir Amin (1997) describes the "concepts of nationhood" that have been deployed by the world's nations during the modern era as "diverse." He points out, for example, that instead of "the myth of seamless historical continuity" used by Germany and other nations, the French embrace a very different kind of nationalism, a nationalism that is structured around a narrative of rupture and rebirth. He explains that, after the French Revolution in the late eighteenth century, the French adopted a founding "myth of the social contract as the foundation of the nation-state, or of a state or nation existing only by that contract" (p. 9). Thompson (1962) implicitly supports this characterization of French concepts of nationhood, describing the myriad ways by which early postrevolution French leaders foregrounded the event of the birth of their nation and emphasized a leveling of the past. French leaders developed a new system of weights and measures that came to be known as the metric system, devised a new system of measuring time that was based on a ten-day week, and created a "new hierarchy of saints and festivals" (Thompson 1962: ix). Though French nationalism is undoubtedly the archetype of the rupture-and-rebirth narrative of nationhood, British nationalism is also grounded in "the myth of a revolutionary upheaval that dispenses with the past," as Amin points out (1997: 10). In addition, in Africa, there exist surprisingly few nations that have constructed their nation in terms of continuity and timelessness. Most Senegalese, for example, see the nation of Senegal as having been built in the mid-nineteenth century, and many treat a single man, Louis Faidherbe, as the architect of the new order. As I prepared for my research, I treated the two primary possibilities presented in the literature—a foregrounding of continuity, and an emphasis on discontinuity—as equally feasible for the Choctaw case.

The final set of questions that helped frame my inquiries into how, specifically, the Choctaws rebuilt their tribe derived from the historical reality that the social, political, and economic rearrangements that were taking place in the Choctaw Nation during the late twentieth century were occurring at a time when tribes all over the United States were also undertaking intensive institution building, hardening the boundaries around their memberships, and vigorously pursuing tribal economic development. The Choctaws were exploiting legal and political openings for tribal rebuilding and empowerment that were created by the emergence of supralocal social movements such as the American Indian Movement (AIM), shifts in U.S. Indian policy, and the rearrangements of neoliberal economics. Documenting Choctaw rebuilding thus required that I identify the openings that the Choctaws were exploiting and explore how, specifically, these openings were being exploited.

The results of my investigation into the process by which our tribe was rebuilt are presented primarily in chapter 3. Anthropologist Orin Starn is right to point out that if history is understood as a process, determining "an originating moment or person for any turn of events" is "tricky," but that it is critical not "to deny altogether the role of individual decisions and motivating forces" (1999: 65). Interviews and archival research that I conducted strongly suggested that, although many Choctaws played important roles in creating the movement that resulted in Choctaw nation building, the origins of the initial social movement had much to do with the political actions of a single individual, a then young, working-class Choctaw full-blood named Charles Brown who, surprisingly, lived outside the Choctaw Nation in Oklahoma City. In 1969 Brown spearheaded a movement to repeal the Choctaw termination legislation, a movement that swept through the Choctaw Nation—to borrow an analogy used by Smith and Warrior to describe the Indian movement—"like a hurricane" (Smith and Warrior 1996). The Choctaw nationalism that developed as part of this movement was produced outside the then tiny tribal "state" and explicitly challenged, as will be seen, the view of Choctaw history defined by and at the core of formal Choctaw political power and leadership. From sites in the periphery, Choctaws embraced a narrative of Choctaw nationhood that constructed their nation as timeless, and like the Sri Lankan case as described by Tambiah, this narrative of nationhood soon leaked into the Choctaw tribal "state." Through informal and formal tribal political processes, Choctaws negotiated their ideas about nation building and nationhood, instigated processes of reconstituting the tribe, and carried out an ambitious program of tribal nation building. After the passage of the 1983 constitution, the large-scale issuance of tribal membership cards, and the reestablishment of relations of citizenship that formally linked Choctaws to one another and to the reconstituted tribal government, then chief Hollis Roberts revised the narrative of Choctaw nationalism. To legitimize his leadership in the context of the tribe's reinstituted democratic electoral process, Roberts promoted a narrative of the rupture and rebirth of Choctaw nationhood. This narrative, which frames the tribe's reconstitution as a birth, dates its founding to 1983, and treats Roberts as the founding father, is one of many foundation stories that "conceal mixed origins" (Starn 1999: 67) and is a story that is discussed in some detail in chapter 4. This chapter, which describes and analyzes a tribal election that was won by Roberts and that took place during my research, is revealing not only of the content and character of this foundation story but also of its widespread public acceptance among Choctaws at the time of my fieldwork. After I had conducted my fieldwork, Roberts was imprisoned for sex crimes, and his assistant chief, Greg Pyle, became chief, a transformation that, among other things, prompted another revision of the narrative of Choctaw nationhood. In the context of widespread public condemnation of Roberts by Choctaws (and the circulation of rumors among the tribal citizenry that Roberts's victims had covered his portrait in the Choctaw tribal capitol), Choctaw chief Greg Pyle promoted a construction of Choctaw nationhood as timeless and leveled Roberts's stature as founding father.[2] Recent Choctaw history suggests, among other things, that the materials out of which leaders produce the ideas and icons that legitimize and express the nation are sufficiently flexible and polysemous that they can be selected, assembled, and deployed in different ways and with different meanings at different points in time. In addition, such deployments, as the Choctaw case shows, are not fixed, but are best understood as claims that are negotiated and renegotiated, institutionalized and reinstitutionalized, over time.

In addition to tracing the history of the tribe's late-twentieth-century rebuilding, I pursued an exploration of the social, political, and economic consequences of the new order. Analytically, I defined three sets of relations as key: the relations of citizenship that bind together enrolled Choctaws, the relations that formally link Choctaw citizens to the tribal government, and the relations of diplomacy that create interfaces between the tribal government, on the one hand, and the Oklahoma state and U.S.

federal governments, on the other. In the context of the vertical and horizontal entrenchment of the tribal state and large-scale reformulations of the tribal polity, how were these three sets of relations being negotiated and experienced, and how were they helping define what it means to be Choctaw at the turn of the twenty-first century? In addition, how were the rearrangements of power that were being effected by and through Choctaw sociopolitical reorganization and centralization impacting non-Indians in Oklahoma, both those living inside and those living outside Choctaw tribal boundaries?

Following Sally Falk Moore (1987) and others (Gluckman 1958; Barth 1967), I pursued these questions through an event-centered approach. Moore urges anthropologists to center ethnographic description and analysis around events, specifically events that provide evidence of "the ongoing dismantling of structures or attempts to create new ones," that reveal "ongoing contests and conflict and competitions," or that expose the "complex mix of order, anti-order and non-order" that characterizes ethnographic realities (1987: 729–30). She explains that, by and through analyzing such events, anthropologists are best able to explore "what the present is producing" (p. 727) while maintaining a "consciousness of time and the historical moment." (p. 728). Such an approach places the "analytic emphasis on continuous production and construction" and thus helps anthropologists avoid "detemporalizing existing structure." The detemporalization of existing structure, she notes, stems from the long-standing anthropological convention of "removing an abstracted structure from the events that construct it" (p. 729). Moore's event-centered approach most heavily shapes chapters 4 through 6. Each of these chapters revolves around a different event that brings to the fore a particular feature or set of related features of the new tribal political order. Each of these chapters also uses pseudonyms to protect the identities of my consultants. Pseudonyms are not used, however, at any point in this book for Choctaw leaders or for any public officials except petty bureaucrats.

Chapter 4 centers the description and analysis around the event of a tribal election for Choctaw chief. One of the most important ways Choctaws practice their tribal citizenship is by participating in tribal elections. Partly because of this, the actions and rhetoric generated during an electoral season are especially revealing of how Choctaws are experiencing the relations of citizenship that bind together enrolled Choctaws and formally link them to the Choctaw tribal government. Equally important, the content of electoral rhetoric and citizen responses to that rhetoric richly index the present-day meanings of being Choctaw. This was critical, as capturing these meanings ethnographically was one of my highest priorities.

It is in the tribal election chapter that I most fully address the diversity of the Choctaw citizenry, an important characteristic of this citizenry. My choice to broadly cover the Choctaw political landscape helps expose the great variations in class, wealth, skin color, educational background, and political views that today help define the tribe. Social theorists have long noted that the leaders of new, centralized orders often face the problem of how to create a sense of national unity from the diverse assemblage of people, relationships, and social arrangements subsumed under the nation. Through the development in some cases of the kind of "technologies" or forms of control so elegantly described by Foucault (e.g., 1977 [1975]; 1979), nationalist projects, according to some theorists, necessarily produce homogenization. A cornerstone text that promotes this view is Ernest Gellner's polemic *Nations and Nationalism* (1983). According to Gellner, citizens of emerging centralized orders progressively adopt a common set of "idioms," "styles of conduct," and "conceptual currencies" until all citizens are thoroughly assimilated into a "national" culture, and cultural difference disappears. Although Gellner's model is too extreme to accommodate national ethnographic realities, the material I present in the tribal election chapter suggests that Choctaw nation building has had certain limited homogenizing effects. Ideologies produced during and as a part of tribal rebuilding have defined a range of permissible actions and arguments for Choctaw political actors, canalizing their choices in both broad and specific ways. For example, during the electoral season that I studied, contenders for the tribe's highest office adopted a particular style of conduct and drew upon a common set of idioms that had been developed during processes of tribal nation building. In addition, such contenders strongly believed that, to be accorded legitimacy by the Choctaw electorate, they needed to endorse the current course of Choctaw tribal economic development and refrain from publicly calling into question Roberts's status as founding father. Choctaw nationalist ideologies had limited the options for innovation that serious candidates for the position of chief could present to the Choctaw electorate.

Gellner's theories about the homogenizing consequences of nation building have been attacked by, among others, Sally Falk Moore, who argues that within such nations "contrary processes are also strongly at work," "processes that maintain, exacerbate or even lead to new pluralization" (1989: 30). While exploring ethnographically a set of key principles of informal Choctaw political organization, I identify and describe productions of difference that emerged during and through the tribal electoral process, productions of difference that support Moore's argument about nation building's pluralizing effects. As will be seen, some such productions deploy prior ideas about difference used by Choctaws at different points in their history, but substantively repackage and refashion these ideas for new conditions. In this respect, my descriptions and analysis reflect a construct of society and a conceptualization of ethnographic data that Moore develops elsewhere (1986). Moore models society as an assemblage "made out of new and used parts," and defines her investigation as an inquiry in part into "the place of 'used parts' in particular historical sequences" while avoiding "break[ing] up the field of observation into items for a simplified bimodal classification, old and new" (1986: 10; 1987: 728). For the Choctaws, some of these "used parts," as will be seen in the election chapter, are "blood quantum" and ideas about residence.

Chapter 5 moves from the tribal level to the local level, zooming in on the tribal landscape to explore the event of the building of a tribal economic development project in a small, rural Choctaw Nation community. Through an investigation of the local social, political, and economic consequences of this project, which was built during my research, I continue my exploration of the relations of citizenship that bind together enrolled Choctaws and link them to the tribal government. I also critically examine the ways by which the tribal government is negotiating its relationships with non-Indians living in the Choctaw Nation, and the ways by which the Choctaws of a small Choctaw Nation town are negotiating their relationships with local non-Indians in a historical context defined by marked non-Indian denial of the continued existence of Choctaw identity.

I pursued fieldwork in this three-hundred-member community with an eye toward examining what the literature on nation building often presents as a tension between political centralization and the autonomy of the local communities being incorporated into emerging, centralized orders. State leaders necessarily have the task of assimilating local communities as so many constituent units into national-level structures and processes, a course of action that is often resisted by these communities, who experience pressures to cede power and control to those at the emerging center. The erection of a Choctaw tribal-government project in a local community provided an excellent opportunity to explore these tensions. Such a project was an expression of the imperialism of the new order. It was also a likely site through which tribal bureaucrats could extend the reach of, for example, technologies of surveillance among the reconstituted citizenry (Foucault 1977 [1975]).

I found that the building of a tribal economic development project in this town was motivated primarily by tribal-government efforts to generate revenues for tribal programs and services and create jobs for Choctaw citizens. During and after the building of the project, tribal leaders focused on the profits it was expected to and did generate and the jobs it was expected to and did produce. To my knowledge, tribal officials took no actions oriented toward exploiting the opportunities that this project provided for leveling existing social and political structures or even for more fully implementing technologies of surveillance. Even so, the non-Choctaws of this town saw the act of the building of this tribal project in their town as threatening. They expressed fears that the tribe was "taking over" "their" town, and they stepped up their expressions of hostility toward local Choctaws and toward the Choctaw tribal state.

I also found that, almost to a person, Choctaws in this community responded not with resistance to but rather elation at the extension of tribal control and power into their community and the efforts of those at the center to weld together a nation. The response of local Choctaw citizens could be characterized in Godelierian terms as an expression of "the consent of the dominated to their domination" (Godelier 1978: 676). Yet local Choctaws spoke only of their own empowerment and even their liberation—via the development project and Choctaw nation building—from oppressive local praxes, structures, and ideologies that had been developed and institutionalized by non-Choctaws during the years that followed the dismantling of most tribal political structures in 1906.

Choctaws in this community spoke most often, as will be seen, of their recent economic empowerment through the new jobs created by and through this project. In their descriptions of their community's past, however, they also told a heartbreaking story of how, specifically, non-

Choctaws had attempted to erase the Choctaw history of their community and legitimize white control and ownership of the town. In this connection, the new tribal economic development project was fashioned as the latest expression of a reinstated Choctaw presence and an effort by Choctaws both at the center and at the local level to reclaim the Choctaw identity of this town and other towns within tribal boundaries. To bring into relief the ways by which this has shaken up social relations, I trace the history of transformations in the local meanings of being Choctaw in this town from the late nineteenth century to the present. I also address the experience of present-day unenrolled Choctaws and the experience of enrolled black Choctaws.

While the Choctaw case represents a somewhat unusual case of nation building—a case of nation building by a nation within a nation—it points to the necessity of analyzing community responses to the incorporative efforts of centralizing polities in terms of the question of who stands to gain and who stands to lose from an institutional reordering. Resistance can be expected of those who stand to lose much, such as local leaders. In contrast, community members who, as is the case for the local Choctaws of this study, stand to lose little or gain much from a large-scale political transformation may endorse or even promote the efforts of centralizing orders to extend the reach of the state into their community.

It goes without saying that the greater part of this book is about the ways by which living Choctaws are exercising Choctaw tribal sovereignty. Living Choctaws exercised the sovereignty of our tribe when they rebuilt our tribe in the late twentieth century. Today, in the aftermath of the rebuilding, they exercise tribal sovereignty when they hold tribal elections, when they create new tribal businesses, and even when they refer to our homeland as the Choctaw Nation rather than southeastern Oklahoma. In chapter 6, the last chapter in this book, I describe and analyze a Choctaw tribal sovereignty assertion that was and is of great sociopolitical, symbolic, and economic significance: the assertion that the Choctaws own of all of the water in southeastern Oklahoma. This conflict engendered a protracted battle between the tribe and the state of Oklahoma. It also produced significant discord between the Choctaws and the federal government. As such, this event was well suited for exploring the third set of relations that I identified as key in analyzing the aftermath of Choctaw tribal rebuilding—the relations of diplomacy that create interfaces between the Choctaw tribal government, on the one hand, and the Oklahoma state and U.S. federal governments, on the other.

Documenting this conflict involved field research in domains at a remove from that which tends to be the traditional domain of anthropologists—the on-the-ground domain inhabited by the groups that most often
serve as the subjects of anthropological investigation. Because the Oklahoma state government played such a critical role in the Choctaw water
conflict, and because my goal was to document both tribal-government
and Oklahoma state perspectives on the conflict, I spent much time in the
state's capitol city talking with and observing state leaders and lawmakers, as well as collecting data that permitted me to place Choctaw water
within the larger context of regional and statewide water resources and issues. This research revealed, among other things, that I had grossly overestimated the degree to which Oklahoma state actions and perspectives
were coherent, unified, coordinated, and consistent. It also revealed that
I had grossly underestimated the level of hostility and resistance on the
part of the Oklahoma state government to Choctaw water rights.

By extending my field research into domains that included the state,
I have followed a growing number of anthropologists who, like David
Nugent, have been exploring the cultures and workings of the governments that help shape conditions and possibilities at the local level, and
who, like Orin Starn, have made field research among state leaders and
bureaucrats a critical part of their investigation of local realities. For example, in "Governing States" (2004), Nugent provides a fascinating, remarkably comprehensive, and eye-opening account of the internal operation and transformations of the Peruvian state and an entity (the Popular
American Revolutionary Alliance) that poached from the state a wide
range of its functions, attributes, and even legitimacy. In so doing, Nugent launches a powerful critique of Max Weber's once normative model
of the state. In his outstanding ethnography *Nightwatch: The Politics of
Protest in the Andes* (1999), Orin Starn conducted interviews with state
officials and bureaucrats that yielded surprising findings about the rondas, an institution that was part of a larger set of institutions produced by
a grassroots Andean social movement. Starn found, for example, that the
Peruvian government had been a coproducer of the rondas. He also found
much that exposed the illusion of the state's wholeness and the inaccu-
racy of characterizations of the government as monolithic. Starn uses this
material, together with other material, to shed light on the many consequences that state actions and processes have had on the local level that
is the focus of his descriptions and analysis.

My descriptions and analysis of the 2001 water-rights conflict bring into relief three important aspects of tribal sovereignty. The first is the construction of tribal sovereignty as "a bundle of inherent powers" (see especially Wilkins and Lomawaima 2001: 123). The legal construction of tribes as political bodies with a bundle of inherent sovereign powers is enshrined in treaties, in the U.S. constitution, in federal law, and in federal Indian policy. By virtue of their sovereignty, tribes are entitled to, among other things, elect their own leaders, determine their own memberships, maintain tribal police forces, levy taxes, regulate property under tribal jurisdiction, control the conduct of their members by tribal ordinances, regulate the domestic relations of their members, and administer justice. Under the same set of founding American charters and laws, the federal government is legally obligated to, among other things, protect tribes against encroachments upon their sovereignty, protect tribal property, and foster conditions that permit tribes to more fully exercise their sovereignty. The bundle-of-inherent-powers construction of tribal sovereignty is the construction of tribal sovereignty that tribal leaders most often emphasize. By foregrounding this construction, tribal leaders seek to maximize their political leverage in battles with American state governments and with the federal government. Several different parts of chapter 6 foreground the bundle-of-inherent-powers construction of tribal sovereignty, including my overview of the history of tribal water rights in the United States, which provides essential background for understanding the Choctaw water-rights conflict, and my descriptions of how, specifically, Choctaw tribal leaders launched and pursued their claim that the tribe has sovereignty over southeastern Oklahoma water.

The water conflict also brings into relief an aspect of tribal sovereignty that complicates the neat circumscription of the sovereign powers of tribes that is outlined above. A second aspect of tribal sovereignty—a critical, inescapable aspect—is the fact that American Indian tribes exercise their sovereignty in a larger, national context over which a more powerful centralized federal government also exercises sovereign powers, as do fifty subnational or state governments (Wilkins and Lomawaima 2001). This political reality is a fundamental aspect of tribal sovereignty. Whether at the local, regional, national, or international level, tribes exercise their sovereignty in political arenas defined by overlapping and competing sovereignties (see especially Biolsi 2005).

The conditions of multiple and overlapping sovereignties help produce a third aspect of tribal sovereignty that the Choctaw water conflict brings to the fore. This aspect derives from the fact that, even when certain tribal rights, such as Choctaw tribal water rights, appear legally well-established, the exercise of such rights is often not a fait accompli for tribes. Instead, it is very often the case that tribes must negotiate their right to exercise these "rights," "rights" that become, in the negotiation process, merely rights-claims. It is often only after and through processes of negotiation—usually with state governments and/or the federal government—that tribes are able to legitimately exercise certain of their "rights" (see Cattelino 2004 for another conceptualization of tribal sovereignty as a process of negotiation, with a different emphasis). Moreover, in the end, these rights may or may not bear much resemblance to the rights that tribes claim inhere in federal law, case law, or treaties. Tribal governments tend to frame such processes of negotiating their rights as processes through which their preexisting rights are merely affirmed; non-Indian American governments (especially state governments) sometimes view such processes as processes through which tribes acquire "new" rights. The Choctaws and other Indian tribes in the United States are not alone in having to negotiate certain aspects of their sovereignty. All nations must (and do) negotiate certain aspects of their sovereignty. Indeed, a critical aspect of sovereignty is that, for the most part, it cannot simply be claimed. It is a product in part of processes of negotiation (Clara Sue Kidwell, personal communication; see also Cattelino 2004).

This entire book, in fact, can be viewed as an exploration of the ways by which the Choctaws have negotiated their sovereignty over time—through periods of great despair, dispossession, and upheaval, and through periods of great triumph, creativity, and regeneration. Assertions of Mohawk national self-determination fundamentally constitute Mohawk identity, history, culture, and society, as Mohawk political scientist Gerald R. Alfred has shown in *Heeding the Voices of Our Ancestors: Kahnawake Mohawk Politics and the Rise of Native Nationalism* (1995). Such assertions are also key to understanding the history of the Choctaws, as scholars Clara Sue Kidwell and Duane Champagne have shown. In the following chapter, I provide a brief overview of Choctaw history and culture during the period that preceded the period of tribal rebuilding that is the focus of this book. This history is an essential part not only of the late-twentieth-century rebuilding but also of what it means to be Choctaw at the turn of the twenty-first century.

2. The Journey Has Been Long and Hard

Choctaw Culture, Society, and History through 1970

The Choctaws and Chickasaws, say Choctaw leaders and storytellers, come from a land far to the west of the homeland in which we lived when Europeans first encountered our two tribes. At that time, it is said, the Choctaws and Chickasaws were one people, and it was *fabussa*, a sacred pole, who led us to our new home. *Fabussa* told the brothers, Chahta and Chikasa, to round up our people and journey east. Each night of our migration, before we camped we planted *fabussa* upright in the earth. For many mornings, we awoke to find her leaning to the east, telling us that our walk was not over. The journey was long and hard. We had insisted that our ancestors not be left behind, and the bundles we had made to carry the bones of our dead were very heavy. One night, weary from our travels, we planted *fabussa* atop a mound. When we awoke, we found her still upright, telling us that we had reached our new home. The mound was *Nanih Waiya* (stooping or sloping hill), a mound in present-day Mississippi that each year our tribe sends the elders to visit. Chahta set out one way from the top of the mound; Chikasa, another. This is how the Choctaw and Chickasaw tribes came to be.

This story is one of several Choctaw creation stories that have been handed down for generations.[1] Many Choctaws told and heard these stories in their many different versions until the turn of the twentieth century, when their popularity waned and appreciation of the art of Choctaw storytelling declined. Since the late twentieth century, Choctaws have renewed their interest in these stories, to which have been attached very few prohibitions on their performance. Choctaw storytelling has become one of the most popular activities at the tribe's most important annual

event, the Choctaw Labor Day Festival, and Choctaw community centers, built in all twelve districts of the Choctaw Nation and in Oklahoma
City, now actively encourage the telling of Choctaw creation stories and
other stories. In the 1980s the Choctaw tribal newspaper, *Bishinik*, published two Choctaw creation stories. In the 1990s tribal staff posted them
on the tribe's Web site.

It is increasingly with creation stories that we Choctaws begin the
larger story of the history of our tribe. Choctaws have always shown a
keen interest in the fascinating, complex, and sometimes startling set of
events that led us to the present. Our history is and always has been a significant part of what it means to be Choctaw. To understand what we do
today, how and why we do it, and who and why we are the way we are today, one must learn about and understand our history. More specifically,
our history—a history, as will be seen, that has been shaped by rupture,
rebirth, and discontinuity, as well as by continuity and persistence—provides the necessary background for understanding the nation building
of the late twentieth century. Toward these ends, this chapter provides
a broad overview of Choctaw history, culture, and society through 1970.
In many ways, this material is the bedrock of this book's later explorations of contemporary Choctaw experience and identity.

After briefly addressing the massive upheavals of the crumbling of the
Mississippian chiefdoms of the Southeast and the building of the modern
Choctaw tribe by descendants of these chiefdoms, I provide an extended
look at the structures and practices that organized daily life and experience for the Choctaws during the early colonial period, a period that began more than a century after the post-Mississippian event of tribal rebuilding. A focus of this part of the discussion is Choctaw sociocultural
distinctiveness. Because this distinctiveness so heavily shaped Choctaw
society at this time, and because Choctaws and others are keenly interested in the content and character of Choctaw social and ceremonial life
during the early colonial period, I try to provide a window into internal
tribal social organization and experience before I chronicle, later in this
chapter, the history of the tribe's external relations from the early colonial period to the 1970s.

Early Recorded Choctaw Society and Culture

The ancestors of the modern Choctaws were probably part of the great
Mississippian chiefdoms that dominated the interior of the present-day
southeastern United States between the tenth and sixteenth centuries.

The de Soto expedition (1539–43) characterized them as "complex" and "hierarchical." Archaeologists have revealed that these chiefdoms practiced maize agriculture, built political and ceremonial centers atop large flat-topped mounds, and maintained ranked forms of social organization, including at least in some places systems of higher- and lower-ranking chiefs (Steponaitis 1978, 1983; B. Smith 1978; Peebles 1983; Pauketat 2001; Wesson 2001c; Dye 2001). For reasons that are not yet known, these great societies collapsed before the first sustained contact with Europeans in the 1600s (Galloway 1995).

Scholars believe that, in the wake of this massive rupture, newly dislocated members of one or more of these chiefdoms came together to found the modern Choctaw tribe (Galloway 1995; Carson 1999; O'Brien 2002; Pauketat 2001). This event may be the basis of the Choctaw creation story with which this chapter begins. It is conceivable that two classificatory brothers and their families traveled east, past the crumbled foundations of their former polity, carrying their ancestors' bones and a ceremonial pole that had played a significant role in their now nonfunctioning society. When they reached an auspicious place for a new home, the two leaders decided to settle at a distance from one another, an act that may have been made possible by the group's absorption of remnants of Indian groups who had existed outside of the Mississippian social complex, as well as of descendants of, for example, the Moundville chiefdom, which collapsed shortly after 1500 AD (Galloway 1995; Carson 1999; O'Brien 2002; for additional information about the Moundville chiefdom, see Steponaitis 1983, and Knight and Steponaitis 1998). About two centuries later in the early 1700s, the Choctaw and Chickasaw tribes were still living near *Nanih Waiya*. The Choctaws lived in what is now south-central Mississippi and part of Alabama; the Chickasaws, in what is now northern Mississippi. Both tribes spoke languages classed as Muskogean by linguists (see, for example, Haag 2001). Their languages are so close as to be mutually intelligible.

By the time the modern Choctaw tribe experienced its first sustained contact with Europeans in 1699, Chahta and his descendants may have developed a very different society from the one built by their Mississippian forebears—an "essentially egalitarian" society "made up of independent communities knit together into loose confederacies" (Peebles 1983: 184–85; Galloway 1995; Champagne 1992). Adair's account in particular supports this view (1968 [1775]). Others argue that post-Mississippian Choctaw society was less hierarchical than that which probably preceded it, but that hierarchy and asymmetrical political relationships remained critical features of early historic Choctaw society (Foster 2001). White, for example, draws attention to what he calls a "system of dominant and dependent towns" among the Choctaws, with "many small towns" being "attached to larger towns as dependencies," and O'Brien, a specialist in eighteenth- and early-nineteenth-century Choctaw history, remarks that "Choctaw society was never egalitarian" (White 1983: 37, 82; O'Brien 2002: 110). Eighteenth-century French accounts, which catalogue relationships of dominance and subordination among coordinate Choctaw political units through the mid-1700s, support this view. Among those who emphasize social and cultural continuities between the Mississippian chiefdoms and the early historic Choctaws is Carson (1999). Carson argues that the Choctaws continued, among other things, the Mississippian practice of sun worship, the use of some Mississippian cosmological motifs, Mississippian concerns with purity and pollution, and the Mississippian "belief that humans could use metaphysical forces for their own ends" (1999: 19; see also Pesantubbee 2005).

At the beginning of the colonial period at the turn of the eighteenth century, the Choctaws numbered about 21,000 (Wood 1989). By the time this estimate was made, however, European disease and "crushing slave raids" by British slavers and their Indian allies between 1690 and 1710 may have drastically reduced the Choctaw population (Willis 1957: 128–29 n. 19; White 1983; Galloway 1995; Pesantubbee 2005). During the colonial period and no doubt earlier, the Choctaws produced corn and other items in surplus for trade with neighboring tribes. In addition to the Chickasaws to their north, the Muscogee Creeks lay to their east (in what is now eastern Alabama and central Georgia), and the Cherokees, to their northeast (in most of what is now Tennessee and parts of seven surrounding states). The Choctaws were heavily involved in intertribal trade at the time of the first European settlement in their area, so much so that the Choctaw language was "the Mobilian trade language known to all the Southern tribes" "from the Tennessee to Tampa" (Cotterill 1954: 6; Swanton 1931; Wesson 2001c; Gibson 1965). At this time and throughout the colonial period, the Choctaws were "a major power east of the Mississippi," a "powerful people, holding with the Creeks the balance of power in the interior Southeast" (Galloway 1995: 1; Wesson 2001b: 273). Until at least the late 1700s, the Choctaws and other tribes in the Southeast exercised a high degree of sovereignty and self-determination (Spicer 1969). Living

Choctaws often respond to this period of Choctaw history with pride and increased self-confidence, but also with anger at the fact that the American period (1776–present) has seriously limited our ability to exercise our sovereignty, significantly decreased our political power, and extensively transformed Choctaw culture.

From the early 1930s through the publication in 1992 of Champagne's impressive *Social Order and Political Change: Constitutional Governments among the Cherokee, the Choctaw, the Chickasaw, and the Creek*, most scholars of the Choctaws believed that, beginning in the 1700s and continuing through the late 1800s for at least one Choctaw group, the Choctaws maintained a form of social and political organization that at the broadest level was based on two moieties or sets of descent groups, the *Inholahta* and the *Eukatatlapé*. This conceptualization of eighteenth-century Choctaw society was based almost entirely on the work of John Swanton, an anthropologist who served as president of the American Anthropological Association in 1932 and who "almost single-handedly wrote the entire ethnography of the southeastern Indians between 1926 and 1946" (Galloway 1995: 3). Swanton argued that the Choctaws' *Inholahta* moiety had assumed responsibility for matters of war and had been associated with nobility and even superiority; the tribe's less numerous *Eukatatlapé* moiety, on the other hand, had assumed responsibility for matters of peace and had been associated with servitude and inferiority (Swanton 1931, 1932). Champagne's analysis of the evidence found that eighteenth-century Choctaws had not divided themselves into only two groupings of clans (i.e., moieties) (Champagne 1992). Instead, the Choctaws had divided themselves into at least a half-dozen clan groupings. In other words, the Choctaws' earliest-known social organization was based on phratries, not moieties. O'Brien (2002) also argues that the two social groupings identified by Swanton were not moieties. Instead, they were ethnic groups, and the *Eukatatlapé* group was termed *Imoklasha*. Beginning in 1750, these two major Choctaw ethnicities experienced what he describes as a "cultural melding" that eventually created the "transethnic category," "Chatas."

The largest structured groups of Choctaw kin, groups that are probably best described as phratries, were called *iksas* by the Choctaws and played an important role in structuring Choctaw social interaction. For example, Choctaws called members of their own *iksa*, "*imokla*" and others, "*imoksinla*." They were expected to sit with their *imokla* during certain types of public gatherings and extend hospitality to all strangers who

were *imokla* to them (Swanton 1931; see also Spoehr 1947). One of a Choctaw's most important obligations to those of a complementary large intra-
tribal group (probably to either another phratry or to one of the two groupings, *Inholahta* and *Imoklasha*) was to pile and bury their bones as part of
an elaborate double burial that the Choctaws practiced from at least the
1700s through the early 1800s. These funeral rituals were "developed so
strikingly," Swanton wrote, "that more attention is devoted to [them] by
writers on the tribe than to any other native custom" (1931: 170).[2] Kidwell
argues that they were not only "a major time of social and ceremonial
gathering," as are funerals in many societies, but also a "source of Choctaw identity" (1995: 17; Pesantubbee 2005).

The oldest of these funerary ceremonies placed the dead—often with
weapons, tools, ornaments, food, and water—on a scaffold outside the
home until the body was so decomposed that it was ready for the services of an *hattak fullih nipi foni* (bone picker), who scraped the bones
with his or her fingernails and completed the preparations for the feast
that followed the bone scraping and bone washing (Swanton 1931; Innes
2001; Debo 1934). For months after the death, relatives and others "cried"
(*yaiya*) regularly over the body, a practice that reached the height of its
intensity during the cry that preceded the feast. It is believed that, during the meal, Choctaws sat with members of their own phratry, and when
the bones were dry, they were placed in a small chest and deposited in the
extended family's or sometimes the village's *a-bo-ha fo-ni* (bonehouse).
When a bonehouse filled, members of another phratry reburied the chests
in a larger boneyard and covered them with mounded earth. A festival,
said to be called "the feast of the dead," marked the conclusion of this
double burial, for which Choctaws living as far as a two-day journey are
reputed to have traveled (Halbert 1985c [1900b]). During the first half of
the 1800s, these funerary practices were replaced with individual burials
that involved the "pulling" of poles erected around gravesites but which
continued the practice of doing a cry prior to a final feast (Swanton 1931;
Halbert 1985c [1900b]; Pesantubbee 2005; Innes 2001). Delayed final services, cries and/or concluding feasts were parts of the funerals of some
Choctaws until at least the mid-twentieth century (Edwards 1932; Gibson 1965; *Bishinik*, July 1979: 10–11; Pesantubbee 1994).

Choctaw phratries were exogamous throughout the 1700s. It is believed
that a child was assigned to the phratry of his or her mother, an individual
whom the child called *ishki*, and it was expected that the child's mother's

brothers, or *immoshi*, would assume a central role in their informal education (Swanton 1931; Wright 1828; McKee 1971; Innes 2001). Phratries
were subdivided into nontotemic clans and matrilineages that appear to
have been ranked and that were also called *iksas* by eighteenth- and early-
nineteenth-century Choctaws (Faiman-Silva 1997). Champagne (1992)
states that there were six major groups of Choctaw matrilineal clans and
that these groups were associated with particular regions of the Choctaw
homeland. He also points out that the groups were divided into a number
of smaller, more localized *iksa* groupings. Swanton also treats segmentation as central to the early historic Choctaw kinship system (Galloway
1995; Swanton 1931). The submoiety *iksas* (i.e., matrilineal clans) were "of
all sizes and grades of importance," he adds, and it was not always clear,
no doubt especially during the process of segmentation, "where the application of the term *iksa* beg[an] or end[ed]" (1931: 81–82; see also Galloway and Kidwell 2004).

The first of two important features of the *iksa* arrangement is that there
were recognized heads of *iksas*, whom missionaries and others termed
"captains" (Champagne 1992; White 1983). These individuals appear to
have held important positions in local and tribal politics. A second important feature of the arrangement is that many *iksa* groups crosscut
Choctaw communities.[3] Wright, for example, describes Choctaw communities as sites in which members of different moieties and submoiety
iksas "intermix[ed]" and "liv[ed] together" while all remained aware of
their own (and presumably others') moiety and submoiety (i.e., clan) affiliations (1828: 215). Foster (2001) argues that, at the local level, matrilineal clan groups were less important than were Choctaw "house groups"
or extended families (see also Wesson 2001a). House groups were "the
most important everyday preremoval social units," Foster contends, in
part because they were more flexible than the matrilineal clan groupings (2001: 251).

Phratry, subphratry, and house group categories were themselves defined and ordered by a system of reckoning kin that kinship theorists
identify as a Crow-type kinship system (Spier 1925; Morgan 1870; Eggan
1937; Tax 1955). Beginning with the recognition of a distinction between
ego's mother's relatives and his or her father's relatives, this system over-
rides some generational differences in ego's father's matrilineal lineage,
and compresses the kinship distance between ego and some of the relatives in his or her mother's matrilineal lineage. A Choctaw called his or

her father's sister and father's sister's daughter by the same term, *inhukni* (aunt), and called his or her father, father's sister's son, and father's sister's son's son by the same term, *inki* (father). The greater importance of relatives in a Choctaw's mother's matrilineal lineage was underscored by kinship terms such as those used to refer to mother's brother's son and mother's brother's daughter: a Choctaw called these relatives *iso* (son) and *iso tek* (daughter) respectively, the same terms that he or she used to refer to his or her own children. Among the Choctaws, the Crow-type kinship system, a system that was used by the Chickasaws, Cherokees, and many other tribes, expressed and reinforced the centrality of the matrilineage and matrilineal clans.

Especially during the eighteenth century, a Choctaw's placement in a structured network of kin defined his or her obligations and responsibilities in a wide range of political, economic, and social activities, including ceremony and ritual (the funerary ceremonies described above being one example), justice (which for years was controlled by clans), and agriculture, which will be addressed after the following discussion of Choctaw towns and political organization (Champagne 1992; Kidwell 1995; O'Brien 2002; Carson 1999; Spoehr 1947). For reasons that will be described later in this chapter, during the nineteenth century Choctaws began disinvesting kin groups of control over justice and agriculture in particular but also over other activities. At that time and later, the tribe also permitted their phratries, then their subphratry *iksas* to dissolve, and they progressively modified their Crow-type kinship system until it was almost wholly replaced by an "American" system resembling that described by Schneider (1968) (Eggan 1937; Spoehr 1947). These changes did not, however, eliminate the important role of kinship in Choctaw society. Later chapters focusing on late-twentieth- and early-twenty-first-century Choctaws attest to the continuing importance of kinship in contemporary Choctaw life and experience.

The Choctaw communities that were large enough to be called towns numbered between forty and fifty in the early 1800s and were clustered into four major groupings (White 1983; Swanton 1931; Galloway 1995). The humid subtropical Mississippi and Alabama territory that the Choctaws called home was soaked by fifty inches of rain per year, covered with short-leaf and long-leaf pine, and interspersed with open prairie. Choctaw settlements tended to be located along riverbeds or "stream terraces" throughout the 1700s (McKee 1971; Doran 1976; Hudson 2001; White 1983).[4] Settlements were ringed by "borderlands," which were areas that supported an important part of the Choctaw economy—large game hunting, especially deer hunting—until the tribe all but eliminated deer from these territories in the 1780s during the last decades of the heyday of the European fur trade (White 1983; Champagne 1992; Carson 1999; Mooney 1997).

Large communities or towns (*okla*), each of which "had an open place or square with cabins about it constructed like those in the Muscogee (Creek) towns," practiced a high degree of political autonomy, especially in the 1700s (Swanton 1931: 221).[5] Swanton goes so far as to describe them as "constituting small States" (1931: 95; see also Champagne 1992). An important activity of the village chief (*mingo* or *miko*), also called a subchief or a civil chief, was redistributing food and other resources to community members, an activity that was facilitated by the maintenance of public granaries and that was greatly affected by the introduction of scarce European goods such as guns in the early 1700s (White 1983; O'Brien 2002; Carson 1999).[6] It appears that at least some villages also had an assistant chief (*tichou-mingo*); a war chief (*mingo ouma*), who managed and led military campaigns, often with the help of two assistants (*tascamingoutchy*); a prophet chief (*hopaaii mingo*), who probably focused on war; and/or a "squirrel chief" (*fanimingo*), who probably helped manage extravillage relationships (Swanton 1931; White 1983; Mooney 1997).[7] At least through the early 1800s villages maintained two basic grades of warriors, *hatak holitopa*, leading warrior or "beloved man," a collection of which may have acted as a council of elders, and *tashka* or common warrior (Galloway 1995; Mooney 1997; Swanton 1931). In the 1760s and 1770s, then again in the early 1800s, the categories of war chief and even warrior reached a high level of power and prestige relative to other categories of persons, including even the category of civil chiefs (Champagne 1992; White 1983; O'Brien 2002; Carson 1999).

From at least the eighteenth century through about the early twentieth century, healers (*alikchi*), who are variously referred to as doctors, conjurers, prophets, or medicine men in the literature, were an important part of Choctaw society (Mould 2003; Champagne 1992; O'Brien 2002; Swanton 1931). Early accounts suggest that at least some *alikchi* were quite powerful, virtually assuming the power to decide who would die and who would live (Swanton 1931). Gibson characterizes them as a "tribal clergy" and argues that they were believed to have "special powers of controlling evil spirits, conjuring and healing" (1965: 25). Today a few *alikchi*, now called "Indian doctors," live among the Oklahoma Choctaws, but during my fieldwork I encountered only a few Choctaws who admitted to even being aware of their existence. One woman described her visit to such a doctor in the 1930s when she was a young child. This doctor had received information about plant medicines, the woman explained, from the *bohpoli*, or "little people," who are two-foot-tall forest-dwelling creatures who have been mentioned in the literature about the Choctaws (Swanton 1931; Mould 2003; Galloway and Kidwell 2004). In the period before removal, *alikchi* shared their clients with other religious specialists, especially rainmakers and prophets or *hopaii* (Champagne 1992; Debo 1934; Mould 2003). Healers and other religious specialists together were called *ishtahullos*, a category of persons who enforced certain moral standards and promoted supernatural definitions of power (O'Brien 2002). Rainmaking in particular became a "highly developed" and important "aspect of shamanism" in the late 1700s when Choctaw villages experienced a period of life-threatening droughts (White 1983: 29; O'Brien 2002).

Eighteenth- and nineteenth-century Choctaw villages were especially vulnerable to droughts because they tended to be farming towns, though there were many Choctaws who for centuries after contact are better described as hunters (Kidwell 1995; White 1983; Hudson 2001).[8] Until the 1860s, corn was the staple crop, a grain that is treated in one Choctaw story as the gift of a woman and in another as a treasure first found by a child (Fite 1949; Swanton 1931; Pesantubbee 2005; Wesson 2001a). Before removal, use rights in farming lands were probably controlled by matrilineages or house groups (Kidwell 1995; Galloway 1995; Foster 2001). As in other southeastern Indian societies, most notably in the Cherokee Nation, Choctaw women probably exercised a great deal of authority with respect to agriculture (Kidwell 1995; O'Brien 2002; Carson 1999; see also Perdue 1998). As Galloway and Kidwell (2004) point out, age was also an important basis for the Choctaw division of labor in the eighteenth century, with the elders of both sexes assuming household- and field maintenance duties. Some evidence suggests that, in addition to and in conjunction with female economic power (which was also derived from women's participation in the trade of pottery, pigs, and chickens [Carson 1999]), Choctaw women exercised a relatively high degree of social and political power. For example, Swanton provides evidence that "if the women wanted a certain chief he was almost certain of election" (1931: 101), and Carson (1999) provides evidence that Choctaw women formally participated in tribal negotiations with European and American nations and may have assumed authority over Choctaw tribal land. Finally, Michelene Pesantubbee (2005) places Choctaw women's participation in "international" affairs in the larger context of Choctaw women's roles in the 1700s, roles which she skillfully reconstructs. As Pesantubbee and others show, the basis for women's power was the matrilineage and matrilineal clans, the heart of Choctaw society. Among other things, this arrangement provided Choctaw women with "a guaranteed network of female relatives who lent support and companionship," as Choctaw scholar Devon Mihesuah points out (2003: 43). The central importance of the matrilineage and female authority was further expressed and reinforced by the tribe's matrilocal rule of residence, which encouraged men to live with their wife's matrilineage upon marriage.

In the 1730s extended families or house groups maintained small gardens where they grew corn, beans, and other plants using hoe and digging-stick cultivation (White 1983; Swanton 1931; Debo 1934; Foster 2001). They also contributed labor and other resources to communal "main fields" (White 1983; Champagne 1992). After planting in the late spring, women "took over," tending the fields and protecting them against pests, until the Green Corn Dance or busk, a five-day purification ceremony held in August, and the main harvest in the fall (White 1983; Wesson 2001c, 2001a; Champagne 1992; Debo 1934; for information about the contemporary Green Corn ceremony of the nearby Yuchis, see Jackson 2003). Carson (1999) argues that female authority over farming found its roots in the Choctaws' Mississippian past and helped constitute a gendered division of labor. Indeed, in the 1770s traveler Edward Mease claimed that he bartered exclusively with women for food, and in 1830 a field researcher wrote that maize farming was almost exclusively done by women (Swanton 1985 [1918]; Young 1985 [1830]). After the introduction of cotton in the early 1800s and the removal to what is now Oklahoma in the 1830s, farming, together with other agricultural activities such as the raising of cattle and hogs, was increasingly controlled by men (Spoehr 1947). In *Choctaw Women in a Chaotic World: The Clash of Cultures in the Colonial Southeast* (2005), Pesantubbee explores a range of events and processes that helped prepare the ground for such transformations, transformations that led to a decline in and devaluation of the power and importance of Choctaw women. Emblematic of these transformations, she shows, was the death by the mid-eighteenth century, due to a variety of factors, of the most important public form of recognition of Choctaw women's contributions: the tribe's Green Corn Ceremony.

Spicer argues that the eastern tribes' "major instrument" of adaptation to the European presence during the eighteenth and even the nineteenth centuries was the confederacy (1969: 15). The extent to which the Choctaw confederacy was politically integrated during much of this period has been the subject of some debate. As early as 1708, the French identified an individual, Chicacha Oulacta, as the Choctaws' "Great Chief," but scholars have raised many questions about Choctaw recognition of such a position during this period (Galloway and Kidwell 2004; Champagne 1992). Beginning in the 1700s, the Choctaws organized themselves into three principal districts: the western division, home of *Okla Falaya* (people who are widely dispersed); the eastern division, home of *Okla Tannap* (people from the other side); and the Sixtowns division, home of *Okla Hannali* (people of the six towns) (O'Brien 2002). Beginning in the 1750s, each district had a district chief and council comprised of *iksa* leaders, and a national council made up of district councils and chiefs met irregularly (Champagne 1992). Gibson describes the Choctaw arrangement during the period right before removal as "a sort of triumvirate similar to the classic Roman system" (1965: 26). Carson (1999) argues that until the early 1800s, each of the three Choctaw divisions exercised such a high degree of autonomy and even sovereignty that the Choctaw Nation is best described during this period as a confederacy of intermediate chiefdoms.

Choctaw district chiefs, it is often argued, were selected to their positions on the basis of merit and popularity (Swanton 1931; Foster 2001). Champagne (1992), however, provides evidence that in at least some cases Choctaw district chiefs inherited their positions from their *immoshi* or mother's brothers (see also O'Brien 2002; Carson 1999; Perdue 2003). Given the centrality of the matrilineal clan, the high status of *immoshi* relative to most other categories of kin defined in and by the tribe's Crow-type kinship system, and the presence of the structured set of responsibilities and obligations of *immoshi* to their nephews, it is likely that the specific instances of nephews inheriting district-chief positions from their *immoshi* is evidence of a more widespread eighteenth-century Choctaw practice, a practice that may even have been institutionalized. Even if this was not the case, it is a virtual certainty that *immoshi* were key promoters of the political careers of their nephews.

Regardless of the extent to which these leadership positions were hereditary, they may have conferred upon their holders comparatively little authority.[9] Champagne argues that the principal chief or *Mingo Chitto* in particular had very little authority; he also argues that Choctaws treated "national loyalties" as "secondary," viewing "political allegiances and loyalties" as primarily "owed to local villages, regions, or kinship groups" (1992: 47). Foster implicitly concurs. The "primary function" of the district chiefs, he contends, was simply to "negotiate issues of trade and land with Europeans," there being no "single polity" in his view that truly "united" the Choctaw people at this time (2001: 251–52; see also Champagne 1992; Carson 1999).

Eighteenth- and early-nineteenth-century Choctaws held meetings at the village, district and "national" levels. Council houses and square grounds were among the sites of these meetings during which leaders made speeches and decisions, and civilians observed the proceedings, danced and played games (Wesson 2001a; Claiborne 1880; Swanton 1931). Cushman (1999 [1899]) provides interesting details about what he terms the "ancient councils and great national assemblies" of the Choctaws, which may have drawn heavily on one particular Choctaw meeting in 1811. These meetings took place at night around a fire called "The Council Fire." Elders occupied the inner circle, "middle age warriors" formed a ring around the elders, and "young warriors" comprised the outer ring of discussions which tended to exclude women and children (see also Faiman-Silva 1997; Innes 2001; but see Carson 1999; O'Brien 2002; Pesantubbee 2005). Cushman contends that men around these council fires spoke in succession and expected not to be interrupted for any reason while they were speaking. "When a question had been discussed," he continued, "before putting it to a vote, a few minutes were always given for silent meditation, during which the most profound silence was observed" (1999 [1899]: 112). This account and others suggest that the Choctaws may have practiced a style of decision making common among the southeastern tribes, a style that placed a high value on rule by real or apparent "consensus or agreement" "rather than by command" or "absolute authority" (Spicer 1969: 21–22; Champagne 1992; Carson 1999; O'Brien 2002).

The events surrounding large meetings often included a game called *ishtaboli, toli* or stickball, a game that also had an "important role in mediating social relations and village conflicts," according to Kidwell (1995: 8–9; Swanton 1931; Howard and Levine 1990; Blanchard 1981; Edwards 1932; Debo 1934). It is impossible to overstate Choctaws' affection for stickball. Since at least the 1700s the game has involved two teams of varying numbers of body-painted players, each of whom carries an approximately three-foot-long hickory wood racket (*kapucha*) resembling a modern lacrosse stick.[10] The object is to strike a golf-ball-sized deerskin ball against (or sometimes through) the goal (*aiulbi*) of one's own team a certain number of times, generally not more than one hundred, using only the *kapucha* sticks. Goals are located at a distance from one another; each goal consists of a pole (*fabussa*), a tree, or less frequently, twin poles erected upright in the ground. In the eighteenth and nineteenth centuries, these games included high-stakes gambling. Women were heavily involved in the betting, allegedly whipping players whom they thought were not playing hard enough. Sometimes the stakes were very high: "In those ancient ball-plays," Cushman wrote, "I have known villages to lose all their earthly possessions upon the issue of a single play" (1999 [1899]): 130). Other old elements of the game that today have been all but eliminated include extremely violent play leading to the death or crippling of some players, and conjuring by *alikchi* for the entire night and morning preceding the game. *Alikchi* tried to "witch" the goal of their own people so as to attract the ball; they also tried to "scare the spirit of bad luck away" from that goal (Swanton 1931: 150).

The Europeans

The French, who established a colony that bordered the Choctaws to the south and west, initiated the first European relationship with the Choctaws in 1699. The French hoped that the Choctaws would provide them with deerskins and other items in exchange for European goods, thereby helping them exploit the commercial potential of their colony. They also hoped that a relationship with the Choctaws, who were both numerous and militarily potent at the time, would help them secure their colony from the designs of the British and to a lesser extent, the Spanish. "The French desperately needed various tribes as trade, political, and military allies in the economic wars—most notably the fur trade—against their primary competitors, the British," explain Wilkins and Lomawaima (2001: 31). In addition, until the failure of two missions the French established among the tribe in the early 1700s, some hoped to make Catholics of the Choctaws (Pesantubbee 2005; Spaulding 1967).

Until they were forced out of the region by the British in 1763, the French, called *Filinchi* in the Choctaw language, were the Choctaws' principal European relationship. It was an uneasy relationship, characterized by manipulation on both sides; a quiet kind of desperation, particularly on the French side; and mutual dependency (Champagne 1992; O'Brien 2002; Carson 1999; Pesantubbee 2005; White 1983; Kidwell 1995). The French kicked off the relationship by unloading presents on the holder of an office it appears that they created, an office that they called the Great Chief (or *Mingo Chitto* in the Choctaw language), with the hope that the officeholder would eventually head a hierarchy of dependent Choctaw chiefs and thereby unleash a flow of furs and military support to the French (White 1983; Kidwell 1995; Mooney 1997). The Choctaws, however, had their own ideas. By 1733 the French were giving presents not simply to a Great Chief but to as many as 111 "chiefs," including heads of *iksas*, town chiefs, and war chiefs; by 1763 the number had jumped to more than 600 (White 1983). Choctaw leaders used these presents, especially guns, to enhance their power and prestige among their people, especially among their warriors, as their tribe's demand for European-made metal tools, blankets, cloth, clothing, and war paint soared (O'Brien 2002; Carson 1999; White 1983; Kidwell 1995). Choctaws soon began overhunting deer to obtain more European goods (Carson 1999; White 1983). In this way they became embroiled in the fur trade, a trade that Champagne characterizes as "the primary economic relationship between Indians and the European colonists in the southeast throughout most of the eighteenth century" (1992: 52). The French strained to provide a quality and quantity of goods that met Choctaw approval. In so doing, they hoped to stem the periodic defection of Choctaw segments to the British, which helped give rise to a Choctaw civil war between 1747 and 1750 (O'Brien 2002; Champagne 1992; Kidwell 1995; White 1983).[11] They also hoped to more effectively persuade the Choctaws to take up arms against the enemies of the French.

Choctaw warfare against French enemies, especially the British-allied Chickasaws and Muscogee Creeks, raged almost unabated for the greater part of the 1700s (Pesantubbee 2005; Champagne 1992; White 1983). War-associated ceremonial activity flourished among the tribe. Choctaw warriors began regularly engaging in eight days of preparation for war by dancing, partially fasting, and trying to secure strength and courage by rubbing themselves with "the juice of herbs" provided by the *alikchi* (Swanton 1931: 162). One account contends that "every warrior had his totem; i.e. a little sack filled with various ingredients, the peculiarities of which were a profound secret to all but himself" (Cushman 1999 [1899]:

14; Debo 1934). These sacks, which are one of the clearest expressions of
what Kidwell (1995) refers to as the ancient Choctaw belief in "individual
power," purportedly contained "bone ash from ferocious beasts," "parti-
cles of red clay or colored sand," or "bones or feathers of brightly colored
birds" that had been boiled together (Gibson 1965: 25). War parties carried "the stuffed skin of an owl of a large kind" on expeditions, carefully
guarding this stuffed animal and "feeding" him meat. Women sometimes
accompanied the men to war, holding ammunition for them and offering
them encouragement. In at least one case, "armed [Choctaw] women" followed an "invading enemy" as they fled from an attack (Swanton 1931:
165). After victories, warriors received new or additional names in name-
giving ceremonies, each warrior danced and wore an otter-skin crown
with a broken white feather for each man he had killed, and war-party
members took sweat baths for rejuvenation and possibly purification. If
the chief of a party lost a skirmish, it is purported that "he [lost] all his
credit; no one [had] confidence in his leadership any longer," and he descended "to the rank of a common warrior" (Swanton 1931: 163). War chiefs
and war parties provided a vehicle through which Choctaws assimilated
remnants of tribes—and in at least two cases, entire tribes—during the
century that witnessed the ousting of the French by the British in 1763
(Halbert 1985b [1901a]; Bushnell 1985 [1909]; White 1983; Martini 1986;
Kidwell 1995; Watkins 1985 [1894]).

Quieted by an estimate that the Choctaws could mobilize as many as
six thousand warriors from their people alone, after 1763 the British (and by
century's end, the Spanish and the Americans) continued the French practice of providing presents to Choctaw leaders (Champagne 1992; O'Brien
2002; White 1983; Carson 1999). At the same time, the Choctaws began
suffering in full force the abuses of British traders and British-peddled
liquor, which by one account comprised an astounding 80 percent of all
goods sold to the Choctaws in 1770 (White 1983; Willis 1957; Mooney 1997).
The British mobilized many Choctaws, whom they provisioned for this
purpose, to fight the Muscogee Creeks in 1765; later, the British were able
to persuade certain populations of Choctaws to fight against the Americans in the American Revolution (O'Brien 2002; Carson 1999).

The intriguing among non-Indian powers for control over the region
did not end with the ousting of the British in 1783. In 1782 the Spanish
recaptured Florida and West Florida, whereupon they identified Choctaw

support as critical to their plans to cut off American trade in the Mississippi Valley and halt American settlement west of the Alleghenies (Champagne 1992; White 1983). Realizing their advantage, during the period between 1782 and the Spanish withdrawal in 1819, the Choctaws tried to play Spain and the United States off one another just as they had played the British and the French off one another in the mid-1700s (White 1983; Carson 1999; O'Brien 2002; Wesson 2001b). Their efforts were thwarted by several serious domestic problems.

By the 1780s, as a result of their participation in the fur trade, the Choctaws had largely eliminated deer, an important food source, from their territory. Season-long hunting journeys to areas west of the Mississippi helped address this problem; but in the 1790s a series of crop failures further threatened the tribe's food supply (Pesantubbee 2005; Champagne 1992; White 1983). Food shortages became so severe during this decade that Choctaws began stealing cattle, pigs, horses, and even crops from the fields of whites in the neighboring states, prompting the Governor of Mississippi to denounce them as "great pests" (White 1983: 98; see also Carson 1999). These raids also expressed Choctaw resentment at the growing encroachment of Americans into tribal territory (Carson 1999). American settlers, called *Miliki* in the Choctaw language, were numerous in the Choctaw region beginning in the 1770s and vocal about obtaining Choctaw land beginning in 1800 (Champagne 1992; White 1983; Willis 1957; Morrison 1987; DeRosier 1970). These and other factors led Choctaws to take advantage of the easy credit that the Spanish and later the Americans extended to them. By 1800 the Choctaws had racked up debt in the amount of forty-eight thousand dollars to the Spanish, and by 1822, they owed twelve thousand dollars to American trading houses (White 1983; Wesson 2001b; Plaisance 1954).[12]

Some Choctaws saw answers to the problems of food shortage, massive tribal debt, and American encroachment in the message that Tecumseh, a Shawnee political leader from Ohio who was then only in his early forties, brought to the Choctaw territory during a visit in 1811 (Edmunds 1984; Carson 1999). In the end, however, the opinion of Pushmataha ("Push"), one of the best-known chiefs in Choctaw history, prevailed. To join Tecumseh's great Indian Confederation and its British allies in a massive war against the United States, said Push to a gathering of his people, would be "but the beginning of the end that terminates in the total destruction of our race" (Spicer 1969: 272; Champagne 1992; Gibson

1965). By that point the Choctaws, like other Indians east of the Mississippi, were beginning "to be aware that the struggle to escape domination had become desperate and that not only their land, but also their ways of life, were threatened" (Spicer 1969: 12).

Institutional Change and Relocation

The first Protestant mission school, a boarding school, was established in the Choctaw territory in 1818 and was an expression of the belief introduced by the Americans that whites had a responsibility to transform Indian societies socially and economically (Kidwell 1995; Champagne 1992; DeRosier 1970). Able to accommodate eighty students at most, the school was besieged by more than three hundred applications when it opened (DeRosier 1959). Choctaws wanted to acquire skills that would help them resist the encroaching American society and remain on their lands (Kidwell 1995). They also wanted their "young men" to "be scholars and mechanics" (p. 43). Three years later, in 1821, two missionary schools were in operation, together serving 150 students per year, and Choctaw demands helped effect a shift from boarding to day schools (Kidwell 1995, 2001b; DeRosier 1959). Before decade's end, the outstanding graduates of these schools were being sent to pursue higher education at the Choctaw Academy in Kentucky (Baird 1972). Competition among chiefs over controlling schools and distributing them between political districts transformed schools and missionary-Choctaw relations while realigning and producing new uses of power among the tribe's leadership (Kidwell 1995).

Choctaw children began attending school in the context of a tribal economy and society undergoing rapid transformation. After the crop failures of the 1790s and the beginning of the decline in the fur trade at century's end, the Choctaws, following the Muscogee Creeks, initiated a shift to livestock raising and a pastoralist economy (White 1983; Kidwell 1995; Champagne 1992; Doran 1976). By 1830 livestock raising, particularly the raising of cattle (which had been introduced to the Choctaws by the Caddo Indians), had assumed a prominent place in the economies of all of the Five "Civilized" Tribes, each of which marketed their surplus cattle to citizens in the surrounding states (Doran 1976; Carson 1999). At the same time, interest increased in all aspects of cotton—cultivation, spinning, weaving, and even cotton harvesting for wages. In 1801 only about twelve Choctaws grew cotton (White 1983). By the 1820s, in response to the rapid rise in the price of cotton and the increased demand from the British textile industry, full-scale cotton cultivation was instituted; some farms cultivated as much as two hundred fifty acres and used black slave labor (Champagne 1992; White 1983).

With these changes in the Choctaw economy, relatively durable distinctions emerged that were based on wealth (but, as Carson [1999] insists, not on class).[13] Large-scale commercial cotton farmers, many of whom also were engaged in open-range commercial cattle herding, were a minority, totaling possibly as little as 10 percent of the Choctaw population (Champagne 1992). Overrepresented in this category were "mixed-bloods," the products of Choctaw-white sexual liaisons begun in the early 1700s (Morrison 1987; Foster 2001). For reasons related to their newfound economic success but also, more important, to their opposition to removal, this comparatively wealthy category of Choctaws began to exert significant political influence during a "series of [political] crises" that the Choctaws experienced in the mid-1820s, crises that replaced "full-blood" district leaders with "mixed-bloods" (Champagne 1992: 150–52, 2001; Baird 1990; Faiman-Silva 1997). Carson (1999) rightly points out that, especially for this period of Choctaw history but also for other periods, scholars have tended to explain Choctaw factionalism, as well as American Indian factionalism more generally, in terms of a division between "progressive mixed-bloods" and "conservative full-bloods." The use of this "racial paradigm" should be discontinued in American Indian studies, he argues, because it "connotes a false link between race and ideology," distorts tribal histories, and is "anachronistic" (1999: 87; see also O'Brien 2002; Perdue 2003; Sturm 2002). Carson notes, for example, that this "racial typology cannot explain the sizable number of biracial [Choctaw] men who supported the full-ancestry leaders [during the early 1800s], and full-ancestry men who supported the biracial leaders" (pp. 87–88). He also notes that the "progressive mixed blood"/"conservative full-blood" paradigm was a construction that U.S. federal policymakers and popular politicians such as Andrew Jackson used to distort tribal realities in an attempt to justify their treatment of tribes.

In the decades before removal, Choctaw leaders became convinced that the tribe's survival in the now vastly different political landscape rested not only on the education of their children but also on their adoption of Euro-American political instruments such as a police force, a constitution, and a code of written laws. In the early 1820s a tribal police

force, called the lighthorse, emerged.[14] Composed largely of recently unemployed warriors and "mixed-bloods," including lead officer and recent
University of Nashville graduate Peter Pitchlynn, lighthorse were controlled almost exclusively by each of the three district chiefs who personally selected all officers, coordinated the movements of each corps, and
deployed them on an ad hoc basis (Champagne 1992; Swanton 1931; Ferguson 1962; Baird 1972). Early Choctaw lighthorse generally "acted as
police, judge, and jury": after being dispatched to the scenes of local disputes, they were expected to hear the opposing views, issue verdicts, and
carry out punishments, including whipping or shooting offenders, on the
spot (Baird 1972: 21; Champagne 1992; C. Foreman 1956).

Several years later in 1826, the Choctaws adopted their first written
constitution and code of laws. The constitution institutionalized the division of the Choctaw polity into three districts headed by district chiefs.
The district chiefs were to comprise the executive, and they were to secure
their four-year terms by election, not simply by selection (Champagne
1992). Legislative powers were delegated to a bicameral body called the
council, to consist of the existing national council made up of *iksa* leaders, and a new "national committee" made up of eight men from each of
three districts (Champagne 1992; Gibson 1965). In the third coordinate
department of government, the judicial department, the Choctaws adopted the practice of trial by jury. The goal of these efforts "was not assimilation, but rather the retention of an independent national identity
by a group in control of its own destiny" (White 1983: 321).

The context of these efforts was the American movement for Indian
relocation. Even before Spain sold Florida to the United States in 1819,
Thomas Jefferson, Andrew Jackson, and others had begun talking about
relocating the Indian tribes of the American Southeast to a vast reserve
in the middle of the continent (DeRosier 1970; Champagne 1992, 2001;
Debo 1934). As the 1820s unfolded, proponents of this plan began arguing
that relocation, though born of the desire of non-Indians for Indian land,
would even serve the best interests of Indians, the logic being that geo-
graphically isolating Indians would protect them from exploitation while
providing them with the time and opportunity to become "civilized" so
that later they might "reenter" American society on equal footing with
and as U.S. citizens (Deloria and Lytle 1983; DeRosier 1970; Kidwell 1995;
Agnew 1980). Fueling these arguments were Euro-American ideologies
with "deeply religious roots," involving conflicts between the "savage

hunter" and the "settled farmer," and between the "disorder of the wilderness" and of land "overcome by God's law" (Kidwell 1995: 20).

By the late 1820s, questions about the legal relationship between tribes
and American state governments, and about the legal status of tribes—
both of which continue to be debated today—came to the fore as several
of the southern states, in an effort to induce tribes to relocate, claimed
at least partial legal jurisdiction over tribes. In 1832 Chief Justice John
Marshall invalidated these claims in his *Worcester v. Georgia* opinion,
pointing out that the U.S. constitution vested the federal government
with exclusive jurisdiction over intercourse with tribes. States do not enjoy priority over tribes, Marshall had implied a year earlier in *Cherokee
Nation v. Georgia*, as tribes are not parts of states but rather are separate
"domestic dependent nations." Among those who repudiated Marshall's
opinions and continued to maintain that states had the right to extend
their laws over Indian tribes was President Andrew Jackson.

Jackson was personally involved in removal negotiations with the Choctaws, the tribe that was selected as the first to be removed because John
Calhoun and others considered it to be the most "civilized" (Mooney
1997). In a series of treaties that began in 1801 with a cession of 2.6 million acres and that ended in 1830 with the Treaty of Dancing Rabbit Creek,
the Choctaws were dispossessed of the homeland to which *fabussa* had
led Chahta and his family more than two hundred years earlier. American leaders used bribery and military threats, among other tactics, during their treaty negotiations with the Choctaws (Champagne 1992, 2001;
DeRosier 1970; White 1983). Some Choctaw segments supported removal,
but it appears that the majority of the tribe opposed it (Champagne 1992;
Kidwell 1995; DeRosier 1970). Choctaws filibustered to raise the terms
of treaties until, just a few years before the Cherokee cases, the state of
Mississippi extended its laws over the Choctaws, and Congress passed the
Indian Removal Act in 1830. Choctaws then drafted their own removal
treaty, "agreeing to move but at a stiff price" (Kidwell 1995: 134; Champagne 1992; White 1983). In September of 1830, four months after the
U.S. Senate rejected the treaty the Choctaws had drafted, the Choctaws
signed their final removal agreement and prepared to relocate to their new
fifteen-million-acre homeland in Indian Territory, now Oklahoma. As
will be seen, the removal was a massive rupture, one of the most far-reaching in Choctaw history.

The tribe's new homeland was not "a wilderness," an "empty tract without human interest or history," as Osage writer Francis La Fleshe described the nineteenth-century view of "white people" toward the land in what is now the United States (qtd. in Spicer 1969: 279). During the seventeenth and eighteenth centuries, Caddoan tribes had lived in "substantial villages" in the Red River Valley, the southern part of the new Choctaw homeland, and during the eighteenth and early nineteenth centuries, the Osages had exercised hunting rights to the area (Gibson 1965). In 1800 near what is now the city of Idabel in the southeastern Choctaw Nation, the Shawnees built "Shawneetown," a large and prosperous farming and herding community, and in the 1820s small bands of Comanches, Kiowas, Kickapoo, and Pawnees regularly visited the area (Gibson 1965).

During the first year of removal, 15 percent of the then 20,000–member Choctaw tribe left for their new homeland (Thompson and Peterson 1975; Carson 2001; Gibson 1965). By 1833 as many as three-quarters had arrived, together with about 250 of the tribe's black slaves (Champagne 2001; Wesson 2001b; Wright 1951; Morrison 1987). By 1843 only 12,690 Choctaws lived in Indian Territory, a reflection of the high number who died on the perilous and poorly organized trek that was later termed the Trail of Tears (Carson 2001; DeRosier 1970; Gibson 1965; G. Foreman 1989b). By 1845 most members of the Five Tribes had been removed to Indian Territory (Champagne 1992). In 1855 there were 2,261 Choctaws in Mississippi (Kidwell 1995).[15]

The Choctaws endured unimaginable suffering and hardship on the Trail of Tears. By all accounts, the journey was long and hard. Some parties were forced to walk thirty miles in waist-deep swamp water, and some endured near-blizzard conditions. Nearly all experienced an inadequate supply of food, blankets, and horses with which to carry the sick, elders, and youth. Migrants were doubtless prohibited from taking with them their ancestors' bones, as Chahta and Chikasa had done, but many managed to squirrel away small rocks and other mementos of our former homeland that today are among our most cherished possessions. In *The Roads of My Relations* (2000), Choctaw Devon Mihesuah uses her family stories as the basis for a wrenching and vivid account of Choctaw experience on the Trail of Tears. This account thoroughly captures the ways by which current Choctaw Trail of Tears stories, now generations old, represent Choctaw affect, which for many non-Indians is the most elusive aspect of the Trail of Tears. In Mihesuah's story, as is characteristic of

Choctaw Trail of Tears stories, the strong feelings of sorrow and sadness that our ancestors experienced during this journey tend to be conveyed indirectly (but no less powerfully) through vivid images of our ancestors' nonverbal behavior, together with repeated representations of Choctaw stoicism. In Mihesuah's story, for example, Billie, then a young child on the Trail of Tears, sits motionless as her sister Survella sews up a gash in her chin that Billie received after a sprint to the wagon. Though the needle, which is used to sew leather, is big and "went in deep," Billie tells her sister that she feels no pain. In the background, Papa and Teague dig graves on the side of the road for family members who just died. Later, the family stands together on the edge of a bank to watch the sun set, "all blue and pink."

The importance that Choctaws place on Choctaw stories of the long, hard trek to Indian Territory is an expression of the fact that most living Choctaws treat the forced removal of our people in the 1830s and 1840s as the most significant event of pre-twentieth-century Choctaw history. Both individually and collectively, Choctaws have been struggling to come to terms with the Trail of Tears for generations, and the struggle appears far from over. Dinner-table discussions, cattle-pasture conversations, and the speeches of Choctaw politicians regularly explore the meanings and implications of the tribe's forced removal for the present and for Choctaw identity. In addition, Choctaws regularly experience deep feelings of loss and heartbreak when they reflect upon the tribe's removal. I have seen tears stream down the cheeks of more than a few of our elders when the subject comes up, as it often does, of this watershed event in Choctaw history.

Indian Territory

Upon entering their new homeland, the Choctaws encountered heavily forested mountain hills that gave way to vast rolling grasslands. Hopefully, the beauty of the landscape was of some comfort for the migrants and helped facilitate the physical and emotional healing process. Fortunately, the tribe's economic recovery from the tragedy, an important part of the project of rebuilding the tribe, was surprisingly quick. Some historians go so far as to say that "removal brought almost immediate prosperity" (e.g., Skaggs 1978: 34; DeRosier 1970). Mihesuah tells a story of a Choctaw family who worked "from dawn to dusk" after their arrival to build a house. "That was their way of forgetting what happened," she explains. As this family worked, a female child worked the family's garden, motivated not only by the family's need for food but also by the child's desire "to see life growing" again after the tribe's upheaval (Mihesuah 2000: 55).

During the decades leading up to the American Civil War, most Choctaws built small cabins at a distance from one another and took up diversified agriculture, raising a variety of grains, vegetables, fruit, and livestock, particularly cattle, primarily for subsistence (Lees and Atherton 2001; Fite 1949; N. Graebner 1945b; Debo 1934; Gibson 1965). The market for Choctaw cattle was practically nonexistent until the 1850s and limited in scope until after the turn of the century, discouraging commercial herding (G. Foreman 1989a; Morrison 1954). Nevertheless, before the American Civil War, Choctaws settling at a distance from the Red and Arkansas river waterways "tended to develop considerable ranches" with some Indian herds numbering in the thousands and the total cattle population exceeding 100,000 (Doran 1976: 68; N. Graebner 1945a; Morrison 1954; Doran 1976). Especially in the interior, western, and northern areas of the Choctaw Nation, which was characterized by only scattered human settlement, Choctaws produced their own pottery, and until the 1870s most made their own clothes (Doran 1975; Lees and Atherton 2001; Fite 1949; Edwards 1932).

In the fertile alluvial Red and Arkansas river valleys, by 1850 large-scale cotton cultivation began being widely practiced and "conditions" quickly began to approximate "those in the slave-owning, large scale cash crop production, Southern plantation regions" (Doran 1975: 507; Fite 1949; Doran 1975; N. Graebner 1945b). In these fertile valleys, where agricultural lands were more fertile than those of the old Choctaw homeland, Choctaws, including many "mixed-bloods," built "two-story dogtrot-style" log cabins and, less frequently, "mansion-style dwellings" on their plantations (Lees and Atherton 2001: 296–97; N. Graebner 1945a). Their actions fueled a process begun before removal, a process that Faiman-Silva describes as "a complex restructuring of Choctaw society and culture into a sometimes racially and increasingly class-stratified society, with the peripheralization of some segments and the transformation into bourgeoisie of others" (1997: xxvii).

At the head of the emerging Choctaw bourgeoisie of the new tribal order was Robert M. Jones, a Choctaw Academy graduate who had been born in Mississippi in 1808 (Gibson 1965). Described as one of the wealthiest men "in the entire Southwest" by Fite and in "the American West" by Gibson, Jones controlled six plantations on the Red River in the years prior to the American Civil War, including a five-thousand-acre plantation called Rose Hill (Fite 1949: 347; Gibson 1965: 26; Debo 1934). At one point he owned five hundred black slaves, a fleet of steamboats that traveled between Red River Landing and New Orleans, and several cattle ranches for which he likely imported stock from the West Indies (Gibson 1965; Debo 1934; Doran 1976; Lees and Atherton 2001; N. Graebner 1945b). In the 1830s Jones took a trip to the Southeast to purchase more slaves (Morrison 1987). In the 1840s he acquired a sugar plantation in Louisiana (Gibson 1965).

By steamboat, Jones and other river-valley Choctaws exported cotton, as well as grain, furs, hides, and meat products, to New Orleans and, during the American Civil War, to Mexico (Gibson 1965; J. Morgan 1979; Wright 1930). They imported, among other products, machinery, furniture, carpets, and slaves (Gibson 1965). By 1860 the Choctaws had increased the number of the slaves with which they had arrived in Indian Territory by more than two thousand (Littlefield 1980; N. Graebner 1945b). Black slaves totaled 2,349 in 1860, 14 percent of the Choctaw Nation population (Doran 1975). Of the Five "Civilized" Tribes, only the Cherokees had more slaves. In the whole of Indian Territory, now eastern Oklahoma, black slaves numbered 8,376 before the American Civil War; Five Tribes Indians, 47,927 (Doran 1975; Fite 1949).

The trading towns that began dotting the new Choctaw homeland shortly after removal and that were critical to Choctaw efforts to rebuild their tribe sported post offices, market centers, stores, blacksmith shops, and hotels (Gibson 1965; Morrison 1954). In Doaksville, David Folsom, a Choctaw Academy graduate, became editor of a newspaper, the *Choctaw Telegraph*, less than two decades after removal (Littlefield 2001; Imon 1977; Gibson 1965). The paper failed after only a few years but not for a lack of people who could read. Before 1855 the Choctaws had become a literate people due largely to tribally subsidized weekend camps held by missionaries near schools and churches (Gibson 1965; Edwards 1932; Baird 1990). "Whole families came and camped near the church or schoolhouse," Gibson explains, and for two days reading, writing, and arithmetic were taught in the Choctaw language to adults (1965: 26).

From the earliest postremoval years Choctaws made education a priority in the new tribal political order that they were building in Indian Territory. By 1838 Choctaw children, who at that time were educated almost entirely in the English language, were going to school in twelve neighborhood schools (Gibson 1965; Howard and Levine 1990; Spaulding 1967). Before long, the best male students were attending academies built at the tribal towns of Goodland, Fort Coffee, Spencer, and Armstrong; the best female students, seminaries that were built at Goodwater, Pine Ridge, Wheelock, and New Hope (Gibson 1965; Kidwell 2001b; Debo 1934). By 1847 the tribal government was providing scholarships for the outstanding graduates of these academies to attend colleges and universities, including Dartmouth and Yale, in what the tribe referred to as "the States" (Spaulding 1967; Gibson 1965). Twenty-two students received such scholarships in the 1868–69 school year; forty, in the 1892–93 school year. The neighborhood schools were one place of employment for returning graduates: by the 1870s Choctaws made up two-thirds of the teachers in eighty-four tribally controlled neighborhood schools (Debo 1934). With this development, bilingual and bicultural education in the Choctaw Nation, which dates to the 1820s, may have flourished (Noley 1979).

Building upon the work begun in 1826 with the writing of the first Choctaw constitution, the Choctaws wrote and passed six new constitutions during the period before the Civil War. These acts were some of the most critical to Choctaw efforts to erect a new political order in their new homeland. The first postremoval constitution, the Constitution of 1834, centralized the legitimate use of force (Champagne 1992). Controlling the tribe's police, who continued to be called lighthorse, was the executive branch, which consisted of three district chiefs before 1857 and only a principal chief, who headed national, district, and county levels of government, after 1857. The polity was divided into three districts, named in honor of preremoval chiefs Pushmataha, Apukshunnubbee, and Moshulatubbee. By 1850 these districts contained county and precinct subdivisions (Champagne 1992; Debo 1934). In 1842 the unicameral legislature that had been established in 1834 gave way to a bicameral legislative branch consisting of an upper house of delegates based on district representation and a lower house of delegates based on population (Debo 1934; Knight 1953). After 1850 a system of county, circuit, and supreme courts comprised the tribe's judicial branch (Clarkson 2002).

Two of the tribe's constitutions (1838 and 1857) addressed important changes in the tribe's relationship with Chikasa's people, the Chickasaw tribe. Under the terms of the Choctaw-Chickasaw Treaty of 1837, almost 5,000 Chickasaws, together with more than 1,150 black slaves, were assimilated into the Choctaw Nation as a fourth political district (Gibson 1971). In 1855, after years of campaigning for their independence, the Chickasaws regained their own government and control of their own finances (Champagne 1992; Kidwell 2004). Both tribes, however, shared a legal interest in the entire Choctaw and Chickasaw territory well into the twentieth century, and the Chickasaws did not fully regain their autonomy from the Choctaws until they initiated a period of rebuilding their tribe in the 1970s.[16]

The new, postremoval Choctaw tribal government affirmed Choctaw as its official language (Noley 2001). This government was controlled to a large extent by a relatively small number of individuals—perhaps less than two hundred families—and it barred women from voting or holding political office (Faiman-Silva 1997; Debo 1934; Choctaw Nation 1973 [1894]; Lambert 2001a). It conspired to undermine the authority of the lineage in two ways. Through laws—one of which, for example, gave men equal rights in custody matters, whereas formerly children were assigned to the lineage of the mother—the formal political structure supported the shift in family organization, first noted by Spoehr in the early twentieth century, from the consanguine type, which for the Choctaws was built around the matrilineal lineage, to the conjugal type, wherein "greater emphasis" was placed on the "elementary family" and "restricted bilateral extensions" "at the expense of the lineage" (1947: 213, 225). Christianity and Euro-American ideologies regarding the nuclear family also supported this shift (Foster 2001; Kidwell and Roberts 1980).

A second way the authority of the lineage was undermined was through the new, postremoval property-rights arrangement, affirmed in the 1838 Constitution. The new, postremoval arrangement contained a subtle—but from the perspective of the lineage, a significant—change from the preremoval property-rights arrangement. The new arrangement continued to construe the tribal domain as owned in common by all Choctaws, and as such it represented a strong restatement of Choctaw rejection of Euro-American concepts of private property. The change that affected the relative power of the lineage concerned the question of who was accorded control over assigning use rights in tribal lands. The preremoval arrangement gave control over the distribution of use rights to groups, specifically to lineages or house groups (Galloway 1995; Kidwell 1995; Foster 2001). The 1838 arrangement, in contrast, permitted any individual to claim use rights to any spot provided that the spot was either unclaimed or had been abandoned for two consecutive months. After this blow, the lineage never regained formal legal control of any significant aspect of tribal-property management in the Choctaw Nation.

In 1861 the Choctaws signed a treaty with the American Confederacy, which assumed the federal government's treaty obligations and offered the tribe a delegate in Congress (J. Morgan 1979; C. Smith 1975; Debo 1934). Siding with the Confederacy received the almost unanimous support of the Choctaw people (Gibson 1965; Debo 1934; but see Foster 2001). After the war, only 212 Choctaws were recognized as having been loyal to the Union, and Choctaw leaders explained their alliance in terms of their belief that the Confederacy had offered the tribe the best chance of maintaining its autonomy (Champagne 1992; Debo 1934). During the war, the strongly proslavery Choctaws required all able-bodied men to enroll in the militia, and the tribe issued its own currency (Williams 1981; C. Smith 1975; J. Morgan 1979). Choctaws experienced the destruction of substantial amounts of their personal property, a temporary but prolonged closure of their schools, and the loss of possibly as much as 24 percent of their population (Lees and Atherton 2001; Kidwell 2001b; C. Smith 1975; Debo 1934; Cohen 1982). All Choctaw forces were surrendered in 1865 at the town of Doaksville, where later Stand Watie, a Cherokee, became the last Confederate general to surrender (Debo 1934; Gibson 1965; Lees and Atherton 2001; Strickland 1980). In negotiating their reentry into the Union, the Choctaws lost one-third of the Choctaw-Chickasaw territory, agreed to provisions facilitating railroad development on their lands, and eventually granted limited citizenship to their freedmen over the objections of most Choctaws, who wanted the freedmen removed from their territory, and the majority of freedmen, who did not want to be under Choctaw jurisdiction (Debo 1934; Champagne 1992; Cohen 1982).

Emancipation and the advent in 1872 of railroads through the Choctaw Nation unleashed a wave of invited and uninvited whites into the tribe's homeland. Emancipation prompted Choctaws to fill the labor vacuum with white farm-laborers from neighboring states (Williams 1981; Fite 1949). After the mid-1870s, this population, which was forbidden by tribal law to raise crops and cattle for their own consumption and was sometimes housed in "crude shacks of logs or plain lumber," raised most of the cotton grown on Choctaw lands (Morrison 1987: 104–5; Knight 1953; Fite 1949; L. Graebner 1978). As late as 1890, they and their children were described as "illiterate, roving, ragged, and profligate," as well as "very nearly naked" (Morrison 1987: 104–5).

Other categories of invited whites did not fare as poorly. Among them were white ranchers who helped make cattle one of the two primary exports of the postrailroad Indian Territory economy (Champagne 1992; N. Graebner 1945a). Either by working for Indians as they expanded their herds or by leasing grazing land from Indians, white cattle ranchers sometimes profited handsomely from working in Indian Territory. The same was true for dozens of white professionals who partnered with Choctaws to exploit the tribe's natural resources, especially timber and coal. Together, Choctaw-white corporations began harvesting millions of feet of Choctaw timber and hundreds of thousands of tons of Choctaw coal each year (Faiman-Silva 1997; Morrison 1954; Debo 1934). Before statehood in 1907, six Choctaw towns became "sites of some of the heaviest coal production in the U.S." (Gibson 1965: 28; McKee 1971).[17] This brought tens of thousands of white miners to the Choctaw Nation. One partnership recruited miners from as far away as Europe (Hightower 1984). By 1889 there were 15,000 miners in the Choctaw Nation, and by 1907 there were 25,000, "most of them foreign-born and including Italians, Swedes, British, Welsh, Germans, Lithuanians, Slovaks, Poles, Magyars and Russian Jews" (Gibson 1965: 28; Debo 1934). The tribal government collected annual royalties, fees, and taxes from Choctaw-white partnerships, as well as from railroad companies and non-Indian individuals. By 1890 this amount exceeded ninety thousand dollars per year (Debo 1934).

Tens of thousands of whites illegally immigrated into the Choctaw Nation during the late nineteenth century. The Arkansas River, which traversed the Choctaw territory, comprised one of the "three important focuses" of what Doran describes as the "white invasion" into Indian Territory (1975: 511; see also Debo 1934; Champagne 1992; Cohen 1982). By 1890 Choctaws comprised only 25 percent of their own territory's population (Doran 1975). The tribe passed laws to control immigration and intermarriage, to increase the numbers of law enforcement and other regulatory personnel, and to heighten the degree of tribal control over the labor of noncitizens (Debo 1934; Morrison 1954; Knight 1953; N. Graebner 1945a). "Permits," which were immigration papers certifying where, when, and for how long individuals had the right to live or work in the Choctaw Nation, were administered by the lighthorse, which numbered six thousand in 1880 (Faiman-Silva 1997; Knight 1953; Debo 1934). The success of these initiatives was thwarted by a number of things: the high numbers of American citizens in the Choctaw Nation; the extent of the civil and criminal infractions of these outsiders; the fact that the U.S. government usurped Choctaw control over these citizens, then extended the American court system over Indian Territory in the 1880s; the failure of the U.S. government to adequately administer their old and new areas of jurisdiction; and Choctaw preoccupation with U.S. initiatives to allot tribal land and destroy tribal sovereignty (Champagne 1992; Debo 1934; Morrison 1954; Cohen 1982).

With the support of white cattle ranchers and the help of lobbyists that the tribe had maintained in Washington DC since the 1850s, the Choctaws helped secure the exemption of the Five "Civilized" Tribes from the General Allotment Act of 1887 (Brown 1931; Champagne 1992; Debo 1934; Baird 1990). Many Five Tribes Indians strongly opposed allotment, including the 1895 Choctaw Nation Senate, which passed a bill (with only one dissenting vote) making it a crime to hold land in severalty or "betray Choctaw lands into the hands of any foreign power."[18] Inspired by the anti-allotment Crazy Snake movement of the Muscogee (Creek) Nation to their north, anti-allotment Choctaw citizens organized a small Choctaw movement led by Stephen Roberts of Atoka (Brown 1944, 1931; Debo 1934; Faiman-Silva 1997). Other Choctaws were strongly pro-allotment, including the Indian editors of one of the territory's leading newspapers, the *Indian Citizen*, and Choctaw Greenwood "Green" McCurtain (Debo 1934). In 1895 McCurtain went on a pro-allotment speaking tour. The following year he was elected chief by the Choctaw people on "a pro-allotment, pro-assimilation platform" (Brown 1931; Samuels 1997). In 1898 and 1902 McCurtain was reelected Choctaw chief (Champagne 1992).

Recognizing the inevitability of allotment and under threat from the Dawes Commission, Indian Territory tribal leaders began negotiating with the United States in 1896 (Brown 1931). The following year, the Choctaws and Chickasaws signed the Atoka Agreement, consenting to allotment and the dissolution of most formal tribal structures (Debo 1934). This agreement was incorporated into a larger act to dissolve the Five "Civilized" Tribes, the Curtis Act of 1898.[19] The Choctaws ratified both the Atoka Agreement and the Curtis Act by popular vote (Brown 1931). With these acts, the process of dismantling the Choctaw tribe began, another massive rupture for the Choctaws.

For living Choctaws, this brutal attempt at the termination of our tribe, the implementation of which is outlined below, is another touchstone event in the history of our people. Talk about this event, which is a part of day-to-day Choctaw life and experience, centers on two things. The first is the devastating effects of allotment on our land base. Allotment dispossessed Choctaws of the vast majority of Choctaw land, as will be seen below. The second focus of Choctaw reflections on allotment is the razing by the United States of an elaborate set of formal Choctaw political and legal institutions. Many Choctaws treat these institutions, which were discussed above, as the clearest and most powerful expression to date of Choctaw creative and intellectual potential. As will be seen in chapter 3, our tribe has come far in the struggle to rebuild our formal institutions, our polity, and our land base in the aftermath of allotment upheaval. But we remain painfully aware of the fact that what we have accomplished thus far falls far short of what we created and what constituted our land base in the days of our glory in the nineteenth century. With respect to our nineteenth-century political and legal institutions, we fear that such potent expressions of our sovereignty may never again exist, and many of us respond with anger and bewilderment when we ask ourselves how the federal government—or anyone, for that matter—could destroy what for us were the priceless works of art of a great civilization.

In the fall of 1904, as the Dawes Commission was compiling tribal rolls in preparation for allotment (a process that ended two years later in 1906), Five Tribes leaders and tribal members launched a social movement with which most living Choctaws are familiar. At several points during the nineteenth century (especially during the 1830s), federal policymakers had considered the possibility of a future state governed by a confederacy of Indian tribes in the general area that is now eastern Oklahoma (Cohen 1982). From 1904 to 1906 (when it was clear that, in violation of the removal treaties of the Five "Civilized" Tribes, the Five Tribes would indeed be subsumed in an American state), Choctaw chief McCurtain, Cherokee chief Rogers, and other members of the Five "Civilized" Tribes lobbied hard for the creation of a separate Indian state. Indian leaders proposed that the state span the lands of the Five "Civilized" Tribes and be called "Sequoyah." This movement, called the "Sequoyah movement," was brought to an end logistically when the act for the admission of the state of Oklahoma became law on June 16, 1906. The Sequoyah movement continues to live on, however, in the hearts and minds of Choctaws and other Five Tribes Indians, who enjoy exploring the question of what our lives, experiences, and societies would look like if the movement had succeeded and we were now living in a separate Indian state.

Following the Sequoyah movement's failure in 1906, the Choctaws prepared for their inclusion in a new state that would be only 5 percent Indian (Debo 1940; Doran 1975). The tribal rolls, which enumerated 75,519 Five Tribes Indians "by blood," 2,582 intermarried whites ("I.W.s"), and 23,405 freedmen, were completed less than nine months later (Debo 1940). The Choctaw rolls included 19,036 Choctaws "by blood," 1,585 "I.W.s," and 5,994 freedmen (Wright 1951; Faiman-Silva 1997; McKee 1971).[20] Choctaws "by blood" and "I.W.s" were allotted 320 acres of average allottable land; freedmen, 40 acres (Morrison 1987; Debo 1940; Wright 1951).[21] Acreage for about ninety town sites was reserved from allotment, as were over 1.8 million acres of Choctaw and Chickasaw land that was rich in timber, coal, or asphalt (Debo 1934). The timber and mineral lands were set aside to be sold at a later date, after which the profits from such sales would be distributed per capita to the nonfreedmen citizens of the Choctaw and Chickasaw tribes.[22]

The Post-Allotment Era

The Curtis Act of 1898 and its companion legislation, the Supplemental Agreement of 1902 and the Five Tribes Act of 1906, radically transformed Choctaw political organization and constituted a massive rupture. The tribal government was eviscerated. It became "an empty shell" with only a few staff and very few powers (Gibson 1965: 29), an entity that Kidwell describes as a "shadow government" (2004: 528). The chief became an appointed position selected by the U.S. president (BIA to the Chickasaw, Creek & Choctaw, August 4, 1959). Tribal courts were abolished (Cohen 1982). The legal ties that bound Choctaws to one another were replaced by individual legal relationships with the Office of Indian Affairs (OIA), which was renamed the Bureau of Indian Affairs (BIA) in the 1940s (Quinten 1967; Prucha 1985; Cohen 1982; Jackson 2003). Further weakening the Choctaws was the loss of millions of acres of allotment lands, often as a result of unscrupulous speculators and grafters who targeted orphan or "full-blood" enrollees and conspired with corrupt state officials and judges to acquire Indian allotments (Debo 1940; Strickland 1980; Faiman-Silva 1997). Of the thirty million acres allotted to Indians of the Five "Civilized" Tribes, by mid-century twenty-seven million had been acquired by non-Indians (Wright 1951; Strickland 1980).

Initially, federal laws had placed restrictions on the sale of all eastern Oklahoma Indian allotments and in other ways limited Indian control

of allotments. Such laws were based on the racist assumption that Indians, like children, were both vulnerable to exploitation and incapable of
managing private property. Beginning in 1904, Choctaws and other eastern Oklahoma Indians were allowed to apply for the removal of their restrictions upon demonstrating "competence" to the OIA, and in 1908 Congress removed the restrictions from the lands of those of less than one-half
Indian blood, arguing that these Indians could be assumed "competent"
on the basis of their white "blood" (Debo 1940, 1934; Faiman-Silva 1997;
Baird 1990). The result of these laws was not only the eventual loss of
thousands of acres of allotment land but also the division of each of the
Five "Civilized" Tribes into two categories: "restricted" Indians, who remained legally segregated from non-Indians and endured continued federal
paternalism and supervision; and "unrestricted" or so-called competent
Indians, who were encouraged to assimilate into the larger, non-Indian
population (Quinten 1967; Cohen 1982).[23]

Between 1916 and 1928, Congress enabled hundreds of members of the
restricted category to move into the category of unrestricted by funding
"competency commissions" to travel through eastern Oklahoma inter-
viewing those of one-half or more "Indian blood" for "readiness" to control their own lands and finances (Debo 1940; Faiman-Silva 1997). Out
of a total population of the Five "Civilized" Tribes of 75,519 enrollees at
the turn of the century, only 11,386 remained under OIA jurisdiction in
1926 (Debo 1940). In 1950 the number of members of the Five "Civilized"
Tribes holding OIA-managed accounts totaled only four thousand (Minutes of the Inter-tribal Council of the Five Civilized Tribes, July 11, 1951).
As late as 1955, Congress was still referring to Indian members of the Five
"Civilized" Tribes who held restricted lands as "incompetent" (Minutes of
the Inter-tribal Council of the Five Civilized Tribes, February 19, 1955).

After allotment, one of the few duties of the Choctaw chief was to
facilitate the settling of the Choctaw-Chickasaw tribal estate, thereby
completing the process of the privatization of Choctaw lands. While the
estates of the Cherokee and Seminole were closed in 1920, the Choctaw-
Chickasaw estate remained unsettled until the mid-twentieth century
(Debo 1940; Morrison 1954). From the sale of most of the unallotted timber lands between 1913 and 1916, and the sale of some of the unallotted
mineral lands in 1919, Choctaws received twelve per capita payments by
1925, totaling $1,070 for each individual (Minutes of the Delegate Conven-
tion of Choctaws, June 5, 1934; Debo 1940; Quinten 1967).[24] In 1923 the

Choctaws and Chickasaws held in common assets totaling $25 million, or approximately $1,000 per person (Resolutions of the Choctaw-Chickasaw State Conference, June 7, 1923). To mobilize against tribal leaders they thought were failing to put the necessary pressure on federal officials, Choctaws and Chickasaws held at least four meetings between 1922 and 1926 (Resolutions of the Choctaw-Chickasaw State Conference, June 7, 1923; E. N. Wright to C. J. Anderson, June 19, 1926; Call for Choctaw Election, August 11, 1926; Protest against the Employment of J. Howell, n.d.; I. F. Wade and C. J. Anderson to Hubert Work, n.d.; *Kiamichi Valley News*, July 25, 1925). Fifteen years later, the two tribes held in common nearly 400,000 acres containing about two billion tons of coal and asphalt (Debo 1940; Morrison 1954; Wright 1951). In the late 1940s the U.S. government prepared an offer of $3.5 million for this land, but after listening to testimony from Choctaw Chief Harry J. W. Belvin, it offered as much as $8.5 million (Hunke 1986). After the terms of the sale were approved by popular vote of the two tribes, Choctaws and Chickasaws received a per capita payment at mid-century (Wright 1951).

As individuals, Choctaws began active participation in the larger, non-Indian society during the years that immediately preceded Oklahoma statehood in 1907. Between 1930 and 1960, this participation became so extensive that the Choctaw population of southeastern Oklahoma declined by 40 percent as Choctaws pursued economic opportunities outside their former homeland, and many became subject to classification by their non-Indian neighbors as either "white" or "black" (Faiman-Silva 1997). Many Choctaws seized opportunities to exercise leadership. Choctaw Allen Wright, a former Choctaw chief (1866–70), named the new state of Oklahoma, combining the Choctaw words *okla*, meaning "people," and *humma*, meaning "red" (Haag 2001; Kidwell 2001a; Debo 1934). Gabe E. Parker helped design the state's Great Seal and was one of three Choctaw members of the state's constitutional convention, one of whom was elected sergeant-at-arms of the convention (Wright 1951). Though Indians affiliated with the Five "Civilized" Tribes constituted only 5.3 percent of the Oklahoma population at statehood, during the first half of the twentieth century at least nine Choctaws were elected to the state legislature, including Choctaw William A. Durant, who served on the first state legislature and was selected Speaker of the House (Wright 1951; Debo 1940; Doran 1975).[25] As early as the 1910s, Choctaws were representing Oklahoma in the U.S. Congress. Choctaw William Stigler served four terms in the U.S. House of Representatives, and Choctaw W. B. Pine was elected to the U.S. Senate beginning in the mid-1920s, when he replaced Robert L. Owen, a Cherokee.[26] The following decade, Choctaw Victor Locke Jr. served as Oklahoma delegate to the Republican National Convention. During this period Choctaws also represented their new state through military service (see esp. Champagne 2001). In World War I and World War II, Choctaw language speakers made signal contributions to the war effort by serving as code talkers: Choctaw Joseph Oklahombi received the Congressional Medal of Honor, and Choctaw Otis W. Leader, the Croix de Guerre (Kidwell 2004; *Bishinik* March 2000; Baird 1990). In addition, from 1929 to 1933 Choctaw Pat Hurley served as U.S. secretary of war (Baird 1990).

As the boundaries between Choctaws and non-Choctaws were being blurred for many Choctaws, they were being institutionally maintained for some tribal members, many of them children. Per the Five Tribes Act of 1906, the tribal academies of the Five Tribes were placed under federal management, and beginning in 1907, 751 Choctaw children were placed in the old Choctaw academies, including the Jones Academy for Boys, named for Choctaw Chief Wilson N. Jones (1890–94), and Wheelock Academy for Girls (Debo 1940, 1934; Samuels 1997). Hundreds of other Choctaw children attended Indian boarding schools, including Chilocco Indian School in northeastern Oklahoma and church-run boarding schools for Indians such as Goodland Indian School in southeastern Oklahoma, the oldest Protestant children's home in the United States (Lomawaima 1994; Imon 1976; *Kiamichi Valley News*, September 11, 1925).[27] Choctaw leaders, including D. C. McCurtain, Benjamin Dwight, and Harry J. W. Belvin, protested federal policies of separate Choctaw (and Indian) education, insisting that Choctaw children attend public schools with whites (Resolutions of the Choctaw-Chickasaw State Conference, June 7, 1923; Minutes of the Delegate Convention of Choctaws, June 5, 1934; Minutes of the Inter-tribal Council of the Five Civilized Tribes, April 9, 1952, and April 2, 1955). By the mid-1930s, 85 percent of Choctaw children were attending the Oklahoma public schools (Minutes of the Delegate Convention of Choctaws, June 5, 1934). Separate Choctaw (and Indian) education, however, continued for some Choctaw children, particularly those who were from single-parent, guardian, or destitute families, who were of at least one-quarter "Indian blood," and who inhabited the category of restricted (Lomawaima 1994; Minutes of the Inter-tribal Council of the Five

Civilized Tribes 1951–55; Wright 1951).[28] Indian children also attended such schools "to continue a family tradition," when public schools were "unavailable or unfriendly," "for temporary relief in case of illness, invalidism, or unemployment," or "to escape excessive discipline or responsibilities at home" (Lomawaima 1994: 32–34). Wheelock Academy in the Choctaw Nation closed its doors in 1955, and Chilocco Indian School in the Cherokee Nation, in 1980; but Jones Academy in the Choctaw Nation, now tribally controlled, is still in operation, serving from 1952 to the present as a nonreservation boarding dormitory for disadvantaged Indian youth from a variety of tribes (Samuels 1997; Lomawaima 1994).[29] In 1952, when the academic program was discontinued at Jones Academy, academy youth began attending public school in the nearby town of Hartshorne (Samuels 1997; Minutes of the Inter-tribal Council of the Five Civilized Tribes, April 2, 1955). In 2002 Choctaw chief Gregory Pyle announced that this practice would soon change: Jones Academy would become a school once again, serving grades one through eight by 2008 (*Bishinik*, November 2002).

During the first half of the twentieth century, control over the affairs of "restricted" Choctaws by the OIA was often extensive. Regardless of their status as "restricted" or "unrestricted," Choctaws who had retained their allotments often leased part of their allotment to non-Indians for grazing or farming; or, if an allotment contained oil reserves, allottees often sought royalty income from companies contracted to extract this resource. For "restricted" Choctaws, the OIA managed all aspects of the leasing and oil-extraction process, including the deposit of rental and royalty income into OIA-controlled "IIM" (Individual Indian Money) accounts. The OIA closely managed disbursements to IIM accountholders (see Biolsi 1992 for vivid descriptions of OIA management of disbursements among the Sioux). Choctaw OIA accountholders were issued store orders rather than cash to obtain goods; OIA agents determined "when an Indian was ill" and thus whether a medical disbursement could occur; and accountholders regularly experienced difficulty securing cash loans from the OIA agents supervising their financial affairs (Quinten 1967: 36). Living Choctaws who were subjected to these constraints often describe their visits to their local OIA agency as humiliating, and the behavior of OIA agents as arbitrary and capricious. One Choctaw who worked as a secretary in a local OIA office during the 1930s said he was struck by how unnecessary these controls were. Almost all of the restricted Choctaws were "as competent as the rest of us" to manage their affairs, he said.

By the late twentieth century, it had become widely accepted by scholars that during the first half of the twentieth century many Choctaws had
pursued a strategy of cultural and social assimilation. "Nothing set the
Five Tribes people apart quite so much," Baird writes, "as their outspo-
ken advocacy of assimilation with the white majority" (1990: 11). Howard
and Levine characterize Choctaw "sentiment" during the early twentieth century as "ultra-assimilationist," with many Choctaws undergoing
"rapid white acculturation" and making "an all-out effort to remodel their
culture to approximate that of whites" (1990: 12–13; Baird 1990; Faiman-
Silva 1997). Hunke (1986) notes that in the 1930s leaders of the only Oklahoma Choctaw community still holding Choctaw dances and stickball
games decided to stop such performances, citing as their reason "opposition" from Choctaw tribal officials, among others (Howard and Levine
1990). In a PhD dissertation about the twentieth-century Choctaws, Michelene Pesantubbee, a Choctaw herself, asserts, "No one among the Choctaws had kept the traditional rituals or ceremonies going after the 1930s"
(1994: 283). In the late 1940s anthropologist Alexander Spoehr concluded
that, due in part to the Choctaw pursuit of social and cultural assimilation, Choctaw kinship had "lost its importance as a means of widely establishing and regulating social relations" and "of integrating the local
group" (1947: 208, 213). Finally, scholars point out that the Five "Civilized"
Tribes, including the Choctaws, provided much of the leadership for the
Society of American Indians (SAI), a pan-Indian organization founded in
1911 (Baird 1990; Hertzberg 1971).[30] The SAI, which Robert Warrior has
identified as part of the "first important movement of twentieth-century
American Indian intellectual history," embraced a "mainstreaming ideology" and promoted Indian "integration" into the larger, non-Indian society (Warrior 1995: 14; Hertzberg 1971; D. R. Miller 1978; Baird 1990).

In the last part of chapter 5, a chapter that explores community experience and identity in a small town in the Choctaw Nation, I present evidence from interviews and archival research that complicates current
scholarly understandings of Choctaw relations with non-Choctaws (and
with the larger non-Indian American society) during the first half of the
twentieth century. I argue that the Choctaws in this town were shoehorned into the categories of "white" or "black" by non-Indians seeking
to erase Choctaw distinctiveness, and that Choctaws resisted these efforts by maintaining boundaries between themselves and non-Choctaws
and by retaining core principles of Choctaw identity that derived from

their preallotment past. Because this resistance rarely occurred in public (interethnic) contexts and instead gained expression in the private, domestic sphere and in semiprivate Choctaw-only contexts, it probably has simply escaped the notice of those seeking to understand Choctaw behavior during this period.

For reasons that are not yet fully understood, none of the Five "Civilized" Tribes chose to "reorganize" for the purposes of limited self-governance under the Oklahoma Indian Welfare Act of 1936 (OIWA)—the Oklahoma version of the Wheeler-Howard or Indian Reorganization Act (IRA)—for decades after OIWA's passage (Philp 1977).[31] There were parts of the Five "Civilized" Tribes that organized almost immediately, including the United Keetowah band (Cherokee) and three Muscogee (Creek) tribal towns (Philp 1977). In addition, individual Five Tribes Indians took limited advantage of an OIWA provision that permitted groups of individuals to form credit associations for participation in a revolving credit fund, and several groups of Five Tribes Indians relocated to property obtained through the IRA's land purchase program (Wright 1951; Strickland 1980; Faiman-Silva 1997; Cohen 1982; Philp 1977).

Statements made by two of the most respected scholars on the Choctaws in the early to mid-twentieth century, historians Angie Debo and Muriel Wright, suggest that by the 1940s the structures that defined the Choctaws as a corporate group and the boundaries that divided Choctaws from non-Choctaws were probably the weakest they have ever been in this tribe's history. Debo traveled widely in southeastern Oklahoma in connection with the research that she conducted on the Choctaws and other Five Tribes Indians. After gaining a reputation as a scholar and defender of Five Tribes Indians, she was hired by BIA officials to conduct a house-to-house economic survey of the Five "Civilized" Tribes. Drawing upon this experience, in 1940 she opined to a general audience, "It is highly improbable that any of these five extinct Indian republics will ever collect its scattered members and regain its lost autonomy" (1972: 373).

Several years later, Choctaw Muriel Wright wrote a book about Oklahoma Indians. In trying to describe the social, economic, and political reality of this population in the early 1950s, she wrote: "The [Oklahoma] Indian population has been so thoroughly absorbed into the general population of the state that many 'Indians' themselves, if asked to answer the question of 'race,' would very likely reply 'white'" (1951: 3). It is unclear what Wright may have thought about this conclusion, particularly given that her personal history was so tied up in the political history of the Choctaw tribe: her grandfather, Allen Wright, had been Choctaw chief in the late nineteenth century and had named the state of Oklahoma; her father, Dr. E. N. Wright, had been active in tribal affairs during the first few decades of the twentieth century and had even been elected Choctaw chief in an "unofficial" Choctaw election later denounced by the OIA; and she herself, in addition to writing books about Oklahoma Indians, had attended and recorded some of the most important Choctaw meetings and events of the 1930s and 1940s (Wright 1951).

However weak the corporate structures of the tribe may have been as the Choctaws hit the mid-century mark, a Choctaw tribe did still exist, and, continuing a practice begun in 1906, a Choctaw chief was still being appointed by the U.S. president. In 1948 the seventh appointed Choctaw chief of the twentieth century took office, Harry J. W. Belvin.[32] Belvin served twenty-seven years as Choctaw chief. During the first half of his reign he seriously jeopardized the potential for rebuilding the Choctaw tribe and strengthening its corporateness. In his quest to sell and distribute to Choctaw individuals the proceeds from the sale of the remaining Choctaw tribal lands, he persuaded Representative Carl Albert of Oklahoma to introduce federal legislation, passed on August 25, 1959, that initiated a process of terminating the Choctaw tribe as a legal entity (see P.L. 86-192, 73 Stat. 420 [1959]; Kidwell 2004; Strickland 1980). His actions led historian Donald Fixico to conclude that "the Oklahoma Choctaws seized the initiative in abrogating their trust relationship with the government" (1986: 170). As will be seen in the following chapter, however, evidence that I collected raises questions about the extent to which the Choctaw citizenry supported Belvin's actions (see also Kidwell 2004). The evidence I collected, in fact, permits the reconstruction of a Choctaw youth movement during this period that sought the reaffirmation, not the abrogation, of the trust relationship between the Oklahoma Choctaws and the U.S. government.

With Belvin as their chief, the Oklahoma Choctaws became one of as many as 109 cases of termination initiated during the period between 1945 and 1960 (Fixico 1986; see also Wilkins and Lomawaima 2001).[33] Due in part to the efforts of the Choctaw youth movement, however, the Choctaws did not become part of the 3 percent of the total Indian population that was terminated (Prucha 1985). In the 1960s three successive

amendments to the 1959 law extended the deadline for Choctaw land liquidation and tribal termination, with the final deadline set for August 25,
1970 (P.L. 87-609, 76 Stat. 405 [1962]; P.L. 89-107, 79 Stat. 432 [1965]; P.L.
90-476, 82 Stat. 703 [1968]). It was in the year prior to this final deadline
that Choctaw youth launched a resistance movement, mobilizing against
Chief Belvin and the termination of their tribe. The history of this movement, which I uncovered through interviews and archival research, opens
the next chapter. In late August of 1970, the youth that spearheaded this
movement celebrated a major victory: the repeal of the 1959 law and the
end of eleven years of serious efforts to terminate our tribe (P.L. 91-386,
84 Stat. 828 [1970]; see Kidwell and Roberts 1980).

Choctaw youth celebrated another victory that fall. On October 22,
1970, an act was passed formally restoring elections for chiefs of the Five
"Civilized" Tribes (see 84 Stat. 1091 [1970]; Strickland 1980; Cohen 1982;
McKee and Schlenker 1980). Under leaders that they themselves, not the
U.S. president, selected, all of the Five "Civilized" Tribes began formally
rebuilding their tribes during the 1970s. In all five cases, the institution
building that has taken place has been extensive.

From the disintegration of the Mississippi chiefdoms in the 1500s to
the year 1970, when federal legislation to terminate the Choctaw tribe
was repealed and the Choctaws' right to elect their own leaders was restored, the journey of the Choctaw tribe has been long and hard. As has
been seen, the tribe's actions and responses to the challenges of the past
half millennium can be characterized by Choctaw flexibility, creative
problem solving, resourcefulness, resistance, accommodation, and endurance. After the crumbling of the Mississippi chiefdoms, Choctaw flexibility, resourcefulness, and creative problem solving made possible the creation of a new society, the modern Choctaw tribe. The tribe established
elaborate kinship structures and networks that structured nearly every
aspect of Choctaw existence, and for two centuries after *fabussa* led the
ancestors of the modern Choctaws to a new homeland, the tribe thrived
economically, politically, and socially. This was no small feat during the
colonial period, a brutal period for southeastern Indians. The colonial period eradicated whole tribes, irreparably fractured others, and burdened
nearly all southeastern Indian peoples with the insatiable demands of war-
ring Europeans who pressured Indians to do not only their fighting but
also their commercial exploitation of what is now the American Southeast. The Choctaws managed to exercise a high degree of sovereignty and
self-determination during this period, strongly and successfully resisting

attempts by the French, British, and Spanish to control and dominate them, and playing European colonial powers off one another.

Almost from the date of the creation of the United States in 1776, Choctaw experience in their "international" dealings with the Americans has been difficult, unsettling, and often demoralizing. As has been seen, the Choctaws have experienced betrayal, hypocrisy, disrespect, and dispossession at the hands of the Americans, especially at the hands of the U.S. government. The Choctaw-initiated period of tribal institution building and political restructuring that helped define Choctaw experience during the 1820s, together with the nation building of the early postremoval period, did little to curb repeated assaults on Choctaw tribal sovereignty and self-determination. The Choctaws were forcibly removed from their Mississippi homeland to what is now Oklahoma on the Trail of Tears; experienced extensive land dispossession and the razing of many of the tribe's most cherished political and legal institutions at the turn of the twentieth century; and were threatened by yet another attempt at federal termination of their tribe from 1959 to 1970. In surviving these assaults and massive ruptures, the Choctaws have shown great endurance, as well as flexibility, resourcefulness, accommodation, and resistance. In the legislation passed in 1970 that restored the right of the Five "Civilized" Tribes to elect their own leaders, the Choctaws, as well as the Chickasaws, Cherokees, Muscogee Creeks, and Seminoles, saw an opportunity to again rebuild.

In the wake of the political reconstitution and nation building that began in the 1970s, scholars have struggled with the question of how best to characterize the political history of the Five "Civilized" tribes between the extensive leveling of the past that was accomplished in 1906 and the creation of the new political orders in the 1970s. The most problematic assessment is that of anthropologist Sandra Faiman-Silva (1997). To explain Choctaw political history from contact to the present, Faiman-Silva invokes an extralegal notion of "tribe" that she fails to define and that overlooks the critical point that American Indian tribes are existing legal entities whose sovereign powers and political rights are legal facts. Faiman-Silva argues that the Choctaws began their history as a "nation," were transformed into a "tribe" during the 1800s by the United States, and since the early twentieth century have existed as only an "ethnic minority" (1997, 1984). The Choctaws may not match popular Euro-American stereotypes of a tribe, but they do occupy the specific politico-legal category of "American Indian tribe." Legally, politically, and economically, the Choctaws exist as a tribe. Even so, Faiman-Silva maintains that during the first half of the twentieth century the Choctaws ceased to exist as a tribe, and she implies that this identity cannot be restored.

Others disagree with this characterization of the contemporary Choctaw as only an ethnic minority, not a tribe, and, in so doing, they imply that tribal rebirth not only was possible but also was accomplished. For them, questions about Choctaw tribal identity are limited almost entirely to the period between 1906 and 1970. Strickland argues that, for each of the Five "Civilized" Tribes, this period should be understood as a "lapse" in "tribalism" (1980: 74–75). Noley argues that, at least among the Choctaws, it was a period of "dormancy" for our tribal government that lasted "for most of the twentieth century," and a period of "malaise" for the Choctaw people that lasted a half century (2001: x–xi). Citing the determinations of the U.S. courts on a narrower version of this question, Ross Swimmer notes that this period is legally defined as a period in which the governments of the Five "Civilized" Tribes were "suspended" (see *Harjo v. Kleppe* 420 F. Supp. 1110 [D.D.C. 1976] and *Morris v. Watt* 640 F.2d 404 [D.C. Cir. 1981]).

These assessments are rightly suggestive of the very high level of attenuation of Choctaw tribal relations and structures during the period that followed the rupture of allotment. They do, however, overlook the fact that some Choctaw corporate structures continued to exist through this period. For example, at no point did the Choctaws cease to hold at least some land and monies in common or lose formal recognition of the position of tribal chief. Moreover, Choctaw social and political boundaries became more permeable, but at no point did such boundaries entirely dissolve. In addition, the Choctaws continued to occupy the politico-legal category "American Indian tribe." The period from 1906 to 1970 is best characterized as a period during which the Choctaws experienced not a "suspension," "dormancy," or "lapse in tribalism" but rather a waning of their corporateness.

3. "Because We Were Proud to Be Choctaw"

Political Mobilization and the Reconstitution of the Tribe

"In 1969, I got a knock on the door," said seventy-five-year-old Choctaw Charles Brown about the beginning of the Choctaw youth movement that helped effect the repeal of the 1959 Choctaw termination legislation. Brown, a Choctaw full-blood, had been the youth movement's most important leader. At the suggestion of Choctaw elders, I had traveled to Oklahoma City to document his story. This story was a story not only of a battle to defeat federal efforts to dissolve the Choctaw tribe (for the second time in less than a century) but also of the grassroots movement that initiated the era of Choctaw tribal nation building in the late twentieth century. As will be seen, it is a story that began rather modestly with a simple knock on the door of a man named Charles Brown.

Continuing the discussion of Choctaw culture, society, and history begun in chapter 2, this chapter documents one of the most important eras of Choctaw history, the era during which the Choctaws rebuilt their tribe in the aftermath of one of the most pointed threats to Choctaw tribal survival in the tribe's history. The tribal nation building that followed the suppression of this threat has been literally life-altering, significantly impacting Choctaw experience and society. The political, economic, and social transformations that the tribe's reconstitution has wrought in the tribe's homeland have been far-reaching and profound. What it means to be Choctaw has been extensively reworked. Now a part of a vigorous, vibrant, and thriving tribe, not the declining, dejected, and enervated tribe that existed during the mid-twentieth century, Choctaws take great pride and find much self-respect in their new formal political structures and institutions, tribal programs and services, and successful tribal businesses. The many derogatory comments that I heard Choctaws make during my youth about us as a people are becoming markedly less common, and almost no one anymore expresses the doubts they had in earlier times about whether our tribe will be around for our grandchildren. By addressing the changes and change-makers that help define the era of Choctaw nation building, this chapter provides the essential context against which nearly all late-twentieth- and early-twenty-first-century Choctaw actions and responses must be understood. The story of Choctaw nation building told in this chapter will be followed by an exploration in chapters 4, 5, and 6 of the social, political, and economic consequences of the new political order.

I begin with the Choctaw youth movement of the 1960s and 1970s, a movement defined by the refusal of Choctaw youth to accept a vision of the tribe's destiny in which Choctaw pride derived only from the actions and achievements of the ancestors. Choctaw youth insisted that the tribe regain its political, economic, and social standing, recapture the glories of the past, and rise like a phoenix from the ashes of the past. They insisted that the Choctaw people overcome the many obstacles that threatened the realization of this vision, obstacles that included widespread and endemic poverty, entrenched feelings of hopelessness and resignation, and the desire of many tribal members for the per capita checks that would follow the liquidation of Choctaw tribal assets and the final settlement of the Choctaw tribal estate. The Choctaw youth movement of the 1960s and 1970s was a potent expression of a much larger Indian youth movement that emerged during this period, a nationwide movement called Red Power. More broadly, the Choctaw movement, like the larger Red Power movement, also resembles the late-twentieth-century "surge of heritage politics" among "Guatemala's Mayans, Bolivia's Aymara, and Ecuador's Quechua" that "recoded 'Indian' from a mark of subordination to an emblem of pride" (Starn 1999: 148).

The U.S. federal antipoverty legislation of the 1960s and the passage of the U.S. Indian "self-determination" legislation in the 1970s abetted and fueled Choctaw nation building, as will be seen. In implementing antipoverty programs, especially a Housing and Urban Development (HUD) program begun in 1964, the Choctaws successfully negotiated bureaucratic constraints in order to alleviate poverty and create new tribal corporate structures, structures that in the early 1970s became symbols of tribal nation building. In 1975 new federal legislation provided openings for tribes across the country to themselves implement federal programs and services then being run by the BIA, a significant change at the federal level that fueled rapid expansion at the local level of the then tiny Choctaw tribal bureaucracy. These developments, together with the widespread Choctaw interest in more fully expressing their sovereignty and the resurgence of Choctaw nationalism, prompted the Choctaws to write a new constitution in 1983, one of the most important events in late-twentieth-century Choctaw history. In addition to creating a tripartite tribal government, the constitution defined the geographic scope of the reconstituted polity and established requirements for tribal citizenship. These structural transformations, as will be seen, fueled further expansion of tribal programs and services, affirmed the importance of tribal economic development, and prompted tens of thousands of Choctaws to reestablish ties with their tribe. (In 1995, Choctaw citizens totaled 93,000.) In 2000 the Choctaws celebrated the millennium like few other Americans: against all odds, our tribe had survived the assaults of the twentieth century and earlier.

Documenting this era involved interviews and archival research in the Choctaw Nation and in Oklahoma City. As will be seen, urban Choctaws, specifically Oklahoma City Choctaws, played a major role in defining and perpetuating the historical trajectory that the Choctaws forged during this era. The significance of urban members in this history is, in fact, one of the most striking features of the story of how the tribe was rebuilt. Accordingly, for this part of this book I made three weeklong trips to Oklahoma City. There and in the Choctaw Nation, I experienced very strong support from Choctaws for my goal of documenting the rise of the tribe. Tribal leaders and bureaucrats, elders, and former youth-movement activists were remarkably generous with their time, experience, and knowledge of this era. I treated accounts of what consultants themselves had seen, done, or heard as my most reliable data. I also gave great weight to accounts that could be confirmed by written documentation.

Historians and social scientists are trained to analyze data in terms of the political context that informs its production. They are also trained to handle with great care data about highly politicized events. The era of Choctaw nation building is a highly politicized event; consultants' narratives were shaped to a very high degree by present-day Choctaw tribal politics and political concerns. Accordingly, each piece of interview and archival data was evaluated in terms of the political position, motives, and goals of the sources of those data. This was especially important given the timing of my research. I arrived in the field during the season prior to a tribal election in order to document a race for chief, which is the subject of the next chapter. The entire seventeen months of my field research therefore took place during a period of marked Choctaw politicization of the recent past. The election heightened, among other things, the political salience of a particular narrative of Choctaw nationhood created by Choctaw chief Hollis Roberts during the second half of his nineteen-year administration. This narrative of Choctaw nationhood, which will be addressed in greater detail in the following chapter, asserted that the Choctaw tribe had been rebuilt almost entirely by Roberts, and that the rebuilding had begun as late as 1978 when Roberts became chief. It also assigned a date on which the Choctaw tribe was said to have been reborn—July 9, 1983, the date of the ratification of the first Choctaw constitution in more than a century. Even Choctaw civilians, and some former youth-movement activists, tended to avoid disclosing information that challenged this narrative. In addition, when I posed what many respondents perceived to be too many questions about the period between the 1960s and 1978, I often encountered silence and other forms of resistance. As might be expected, Roberts's supporters tended to exaggerate his role in rebuilding the tribe. Opponents of the chief, on the other hand, tended to downplay or even dismiss his role. Unlike Roberts's supporters, however, they and many tribal elders freely shared their experiences in tribal affairs during the pre-Roberts era, including their participation in the Choctaw youth movement of the 1960s and 1970s.

The Choctaw Youth Movement

The Choctaw youth movement began in 1969 in Oklahoma City (see also Kidwell 2004), where thousands of Choctaws had migrated during the first half of the twentieth century and where many more were "transplanted" in the 1950s by the federal relocation program (Kidwell and Roberts 1980).[1] Like many Choctaws at the time, as now, Charles Brown left the Choctaw Nation during his early adulthood, seeking work.[2] In Tulsa he found employment first at Douglas Aircraft and later with the U.S. Postal Service. Believing that formal education would enhance his job prospects, Brown completed his high school degree and moved to Kansas City to attend watch repair school. In 1950 he moved to Oklahoma City, where he worked as a watch repair person for Tinker Air Force Base. In 1969, before launching a successful career as a small business owner in Oklahoma City, he launched the Choctaw youth movement. Within a decade, he had gained such a tremendous political following among Choctaws, who further developed and defined the ideas of Choctaw nationalism that he reintroduced, that he was able to challenge professional politician Hollis Roberts, a former state legislator, for the tribe's highest office. In 1978 Brown lost the race for Choctaw chief by only 339 votes (McKee and Schlenker 1980).[3]

The knock that Brown heard on his door in 1969 was made by another Choctaw who was then living in Oklahoma City, a man who had just returned from a visit to Talihina in the Choctaw Nation. "He told me," Brown said, "that he wanted to know what was going on." At the Indian hospital and the BIA office in Talihina, the man explained, staff members had said to him, "It's too bad what's happening." Brown was puzzled. As far as he was aware, there was not something momentous, even ominous, that was about to happen in the Choctaw Nation. He told his visitor that he would look into the matter.[4]

Brown learned that our tribe was scheduled for federal termination through a phone call to Choctaw Jim Wade, a member of one of Talihina's most prominent families. Wade's father was the town's chief of police; his brother, Malcolm, was later elected mayor. (Later, Malcolm also served on the Choctaw Tribal Council.) Wade told Brown that in less than a year—on August 25, 1970, in fact—the federal government planned to complete the dissolution of the Choctaw tribe. The federal government's obligation to provide the Choctaws with health, educational, and other benefits for Indians would end, and Choctaw tribal assets, including more than ten thousand acres of tribal land, would be liquidated. From the final settlement of the Choctaw tribal estate, each Choctaw would receive a per capita check.

Until that moment, Brown was unaware of the full meaning of the promises that longtime Choctaw chief Harry J. W. Belvin had been making to the Choctaw people since the late 1940s. For more than two decades Belvin had publicly upbraided the BIA for failing to expeditiously liquidate Choctaw tribal assets following the implementation of the federal allotment legislation. Belvin had repeatedly told the Choctaws that one of his principal goals as chief was to secure for them the per capita monies that would derive from what he described as the "final settlement." Belvin expected his experience as both a state representative and state senator to facilitate this process. In 1954, at a meeting of the Inter-tribal Council of the Five "Civilized" Tribes, he told the chiefs of the Cherokee, Muscogee (Creek), and Seminole tribes, as well as the governor of the Chickasaw tribe, that the vast majority of Choctaws were simply "not interested in tribal matters" and supported "the discontinuance of the tribal entity" (Minutes of the Inter-tribal Council of the Five Civilized Tribes, July 14, 1954).

Archival evidence reveals that Belvin was not the only Choctaw leader of his time who sought to complete the process begun in 1906 of liquidating the tribe's assets. Belvin was a presidential appointee, like all Choctaw chiefs who served during the first seventy years of the twentieth century, but in 1948 and 1952 the BIA permitted the Choctaws (not the rest of the Five "Civilized" Tribes) to vote on whom to recommend for federal appointment (Wright 1951). Belvin won both of these elections. The campaign literature of only some of the candidates in only one of these elections is available. The extent to which the BIA may have hand-selected these candidates or defined their positions is unclear, but the fact that two candidates promised to dissolve the BIA suggests that the BIA's role may have been limited to simply coordinating the event.[5] At least three of the candidates, including Belvin, pledged to seek per capita payments for Choctaws by liquidating Choctaw tribal assets. The flyer of candidate Marion Locke, which is worth quoting at length, is especially revealing of this political position:

> We all know our Tribal Affairs should have been settled many years ago. For 40 years we have paid our tribal officials thousands and thousands of dollars in hopes of them effecting such a settlement, so far nothing but the proposed sale of the coal and asphalt lands has been accomplished. Assuming the coal and asphalt lands are sold and the money from such sales be paid to the Choctaws immediately after Congress approves the contracts as per agreement, and that the $1,000,000 we now have in the U.S. Treasury is also paid to our people as we were promised, we will still be far from a final settlement. We have approximately $150,000 tied up in the Tuskahoma Project. We have over 7,000 acres of unallotted land, we have the Talihina timber reserve and we also have the land thrown to the Choctaw-Chickasaw nations by the Texas-Oklahoma boundary survey. There is perhaps 5,000 acres of these lands. Since the building of the Denison Dam the overflows on the Red River are under control and the lands have become very valuable. Most of it is held by Texas people who have no right to it whatever.

> *Suits should be filed to recover these lands. The lands so recovered and all other tribal property we have, including the Tuskahoma Project, should be sold, and all claims against the government should be settled. All funds derived from such sales, suits and settlements should be paid to the Choctaws in a per capita payment as soon as possible.*
>
> *. . . If I am elected Chief of the Choctaws I will strive to dispose of all problems that have been confronting the Choctaw people since termination of our tribal government, and to effect a final settlement. (Candidates for Principal Chief of the Choctaw Nation, June 21, 1948, I. A. Billy Collection, box 8, folder 5, OHS Research Division)*

The last paragraph of Locke's flyer suggests that, in the years leading up to 1969, Choctaws may have perceived of their tribe as already terminated, specifically by the turn-of-the-twentieth-century allotment legislation. If this was the case, Choctaws may have seen the legislation that Belvin supported in 1959, the termination legislation that was scheduled to take effect in 1970, as simply an affirmation of their existing status, not as a break from the past. Choctaw youth-movement activists claimed that Choctaw support for what they termed "Belvin's plan" had two bases: the proposed per capita checks, and the strong personal affection and loyalty that many Choctaws felt for Belvin. Choctaw support of per capita checks was an expression in part of severe problems of joblessness and poverty in the Choctaw Nation. In 1969 the BIA sounded an alarm about Choctaw unemployment in one Choctaw Nation county, identifying it as "critical"; in 1970 Choctaw unemployment throughout the Choctaw Nation was more than twice the state average. In 1981 southeastern Oklahoma had the lowest average per capita personal income of any region in Oklahoma (Faiman-Silva 1997). "Tribal members found individual advantage in the per capita payment," Kidwell explains, "and it seems that individualism had supplanted the notion of communal property" (2004: 529).

Youth-movement activists alleged that, until the year prior to the date the legislation was to take effect, Belvin failed to disclose to the Choctaw people that his plan involved tribal termination. If the word "termination" had been mentioned to the Choctaw people, it should be pointed out, they would have been fully aware of what this meant. By the late 1960s the Choctaws and most other tribes were well aware of the federal effort to terminate tribes. The Choctaws in particular were also aware of what, specifically, termination would mean for them individually and collectively. In the years leading up to 1969, the Choctaws had witnessed the termination of at least four tribes in their home state of Oklahoma: the Wyandots, Peorias, Ottawas, and Modocs (Strickland 1980; Deloria and Lytle 1983; Prucha 1985).[6]

Ross Swimmer, former principal chief of the Cherokee Nation (1975–85) and former assistant secretary of the Interior of Indian Affairs (1985–89), was well acquainted with Belvin and the Choctaw people during the years leading up to 1969. His account of Choctaw actions during this period—a rare account of a knowledgeable outsider, who was also an Indian, that I gained through an interview—affirmed the accounts given by Choctaws that during these years our people were preoccupied with per capita payments. In addition, Swimmer claimed that many Choctaws did indeed support the termination of their tribe. He explained that many Choctaws believed that American Indian tribes were a thing of the past and that the integration of Indians into the larger, non-Indian society was the future. "Belvin wanted it [termination of the tribe]. The Choctaws wanted it," said Swimmer. "What happened is that the settling of tribal affairs, particularly the coal and asphalt lands—of taking a big check, then distributing it *per capita*—was a huge enticement. Belvin got caught up in that. . . . They *really* thought that the point was to assimilate."

Given that the Choctaw termination legislation was public knowledge as early as 1959, it is likely that at least some Choctaws (and probably many) were aware of the plan to terminate our tribe. In addition, given the literature about the assimilationist position taken by a certain segment of the Choctaw population earlier in the century (see chapter 2), it is likely that at least some Choctaws other than Belvin supported the proposal, although no Choctaw whom I interviewed was willing to admit this. Swimmer's firsthand account of his interactions with Choctaws during this period does not preclude the possibility, which is also very likely, that a great number of other Choctaws, as youth-movement activists claimed, were unaware that the tribe was slated for termination. Elders in particular insisted that this was the case. One of those who remained unaware of the impending termination until as late as 1969 was Charles Brown. Another was the man who had knocked on Brown's door in 1969.

Upon hearing the news from Wade that tribal termination was imminent, Brown contacted every Choctaw he knew to tell them "what was happening." "The opposition to Belvin's actions came primarily from

urban Choctaws," specifically those in Oklahoma City, notes Kidwell
(2004: 530). In Oklahoma City, Brown went door-to-door informing Choctaws about Belvin's plan and asking for their help in preventing this plan
from being carried out. Brown worked through Choctaw kinship networks to disseminate the news of this threat and to urge Choctaws to
get involved. Almost every night, he and a secretary would meet, and before long a core group of eight to twelve "organizers" had emerged. Those
involved from "very early on," said Brown, were Darryl Brown, Alfeas
Bond, Ed Anderson, Vivian Postoak, Robert Anderson, Floyd Anderson,
Bobbi Curnutt, Dorothy D'Amato, Carrie Preston, Carol Gardner, and V.
W. "Buster" Jefferson. Also among these early activists were Jefferson's
wife, Jerry, a Ponca Indian, and Will T. Nelson, a non-Indian. These young,
grassroots leaders "wanted to save the tribe," said Brown, "because it was
our tribe" and "because we were proud to be Choctaw." They refused to
accept the belief popular at the time that American Indian tribes were
destined for extinction. They refused to accept a vision of complete Choctaw assimilation into the larger, non-Indian society. Their political mobilization was oriented toward (1) taking actions to secure the repeal of
the legislation and persuade outsiders that Choctaws opposed the termination of our tribe; and (2) mobilizing support among Choctaws for the
legislation's repeal. In the Choctaw Nation, Choctaw youth encountered
some resistance among their people to the pointed challenge they were
making to the judgment and wisdom of one of the Choctaws' most popular chiefs. But by presenting their people with an alternative vision of the
future, a vision in which the tribe would regain its strength, dignity, and
renowned singularity, they eroded this resistance and even managed to
persuade Chief Belvin that the reconstitution of the tribe, not its demise,
was the Choctaws' destiny. In pursuing their goals, Brown and his fellow
organizers created a Choctaw nationalism that foregrounded a construction of the tribe as timeless.

In an effort to secure the repeal of the legislation before the August 25,
1970, deadline, the youth activists made phone calls, sent telegrams, and
wrote letters protesting the termination of our tribe. They lobbied Congress, writing at least one letter to every member of the U.S. Congress and
speaking frequently with the senators and representatives from Oklahoma.
They telephoned, wrote, and visited staff at the BIA area office in Muscogee and at the central office in Washington DC. They contacted the head
of the BIA. Brown played a critical role in this part of the mobilization

effort, writing much of the correspondence and making most of the phone calls. This fact prompted fellow Choctaw youth-movement activist Buster Jefferson to claim that "Charles Brown almost single-handedly stopped Belvin's effort." Brown saved copies of much of the correspondence that he and other youth activists had written and received.

Continuing the effort to secure the repeal of the legislation and persuade outsiders that their tribe opposed termination, the organizers created a Choctaw anti-termination petition for distribution in Washington DC. Networks of Choctaw kin facilitated the circulation of this petition and the collection of signatures. In the course of this effort, youth leaders heard news that the secretary of the interior was scheduled to give a talk in Will Rogers Park in Oklahoma City. Again using networks of Choctaw kin, they mobilized several hundred Choctaws to attend the event, at which time they "let him [the secretary] know," as Brown put it, that contrary to popular belief, "we Choctaws were committed to keeping the tribe, not dissolving it."

By October of 1969 the youth had solicited and secured the support of an organization called Oklahomans for Indian Opportunity (OIO) (scrapbook, I. A. Billy Collection, box 1, OHS Research Division; Kidwell 2004). The OIO was an organization of Oklahoma Indian youth that had been founded five summers earlier at the University of Oklahoma by a U.S. senator's wife, LaDonna Harris (Comanche), who later became a nationally known Indian activist (Harris 2000). From OIO, youth-movement activists acquired ideas about the political potential of Indian tribes, received valuable leadership training and experience, and located young Choctaw recruits for their movement while OIO began pursuing federally funded economic development in Choctaw communities (Kidwell 2004). The OIO was a principal means through which leaders and members of the Choctaw youth movement became exposed to the ideas of a larger, nationwide Indian youth movement that was emerging during that decade, the Red Power movement. This larger movement spawned and was defined by national Indian organizations that included the National Indian Youth Council or NIYC, founded in 1963 by eastern Oklahoma Indian Clyde Warrior, and the American Indian Movement or AIM, founded in 1968 by, among others, Sioux activist Russell Means (Smith and Warrior 1996; Fixico 2000; Cornell 1988; Warrior 1995). Both NIYC and AIM offered "a pointed critique of the 'Uncle Tomahawk' native establishment," an establishment symbolized by such Indian leaders as Choctaw chief Belvin (Warrior 1995: 28–29).

To facilitate the launching of the anti-termination Choctaw youth movement, which ultimately itself helped define the Red Power movement, Choctaw youth established a formal group, OK Choctaws, Inc., initially only for Choctaws living in Oklahoma City. Early meetings of the group were held in the houses of youth-movement leaders. A newsletter, which organizers referred to as a "paper," was created primarily to educate Choctaws about the termination legislation but also to foster connections among Choctaws, promote the new urban group, and publicize meetings. The paper became a potent vehicle for disseminating the ideas of an emerging Choctaw nationalism. Distribution of these "papers" was extensive. "We handed those papers out everywhere!" Brown explained. "We handed those papers out at singings, revivals, Indian powwows, and especially churches.[7] . . . We asked people to send copies to relatives in California, Chicago, Dallas. We asked for the names and addresses of all the 'out-of-states' [by which he meant Choctaws who lived outside Oklahoma]. Then we began sending *them* the papers. We knew we had to fight all over the United States. . . . Choctaws were scattered everywhere!" After the publication of a few newsletters, organizers began finding it impossible to accommodate in their homes the large numbers of Choctaws who began showing up at meetings. Leaders then began regularly renting space owned by the Muscogee (Creek) Nation in a building on Southwest Thirty-fourth Street in Oklahoma City. During this period OK Choctaws meetings were also held at Southern Oaks in Oklahoma City.

With a core organizing group well-established, the tribal homeland became the principal site of youth-movement organizing and political mobilization. Choctaw youth used networks of kin that extended throughout southeastern Oklahoma to help organize talks in the Choctaw Nation and encourage Choctaws in the tribal homeland to attend these talks. The movement's principal spokesperson was Brown, who gave speeches in Hugo, Atoka, McAlester, Talihina, Antlers, Spiro, Broken Bow, Bethel, Idabel, and other towns in the Choctaw Nation.[8] Brown and the organizers also traveled to Dallas, home of a large Choctaw community, where Brown spoke, and the growing numbers of youth leaders helped answer questions. The youth urged Choctaws to support the repeal of the Choctaw termination legislation, an event that they promised would bring about the tribe's rebirth. In explaining this prophecy, they developed and disseminated a set of ideas that later became the basis of a new Choctaw nationalism. The youth promised that the Choctaw tribe would become a major power once again. They promised that the tribe would regain its strength and self-respect, and that the tribe would elevate the Choctaw people to levels heretofore unknown. It was not the time, they said, to write the tribe's obituary. The tribe's destiny was not death. It was greatness. The youth activists made the Choctaw Nation not only "loom out of an immemorial past" but also "glide into a limitless future" (Hobsbawm and Ranger 1991: 11–12), a proposal that pro-termination Choctaws such as Chief Belvin probably assumed to be impossible given the then recent efforts to end the separate political histories of U.S. Indian tribes.

Support for this alternative vision of the Choctaw future and for the emergent Choctaw nationalism was tremendous. So many wanted to be a part of this vision and the group that was promoting it that the youth-movement activists helped Choctaw Nation residents establish chapters of the OK Choctaws group in different parts of the tribal homeland. The largest and most active of these chapters was located near Spiro in the northeastern corner of the Choctaw Nation. Another strong chapter, led by Hazel and Marvin Webb, was built near Smithville in the east-central part of the Choctaw Nation. Choctaws living in the tribal homeland "did a lot," said Brown, explaining that during those years it was not unusual for him to hear of a Choctaw or a group of Choctaws who had been "doing things for months," such as "stuffing anti-termination materials in mailboxes" along southeastern Oklahoma's rural routes. People in the Choctaw Nation "deserve a lot of credit for having made things happen," Brown declared.

The emergence during the late 1960s of a potent, urban-based Choctaw organization, an organization that, as will be seen, Chief Belvin believed was attempting to wrest control over tribal affairs from him and from the rest of the tribal government, may not have been unusual among American Indian tribes at the time. During this period, the BIA central office in Washington DC expressed "concern over the strength of organizations of off-reservation members relative to the tribal governments" across Indian country (Roth 1997: 10).[9] The Choctaw youth movement did indeed begin as an "off-reservation" initiative, but within two years of its founding, Choctaws within the tribal homeland were joining the movement in such large numbers and were so rapidly assuming positions of leadership in the movement that by 1971, as will be seen, the movement's center had shifted from Oklahoma City to the Choctaw Nation. It is worth noting that Oklahoma City, as the next chapter shows, is still an important site of tribal political power and influence. In the early 1990s, for example, after talks between Buster and Jerry Jefferson, on the one hand, and then director of tribal economic development Wilma Robinson, on the other, elected Choctaw leaders bought several office buildings for OK Choctaws, now OK Choctaw Tribal Alliance. According to Mrs. Jefferson, for these buildings the tribe paid $35,000. The status of this urban Choctaw group is, however, considerably diminished from the two points of its greatest power: the beginning of the Choctaw youth movement (1969–71) and, as will be seen, the years during which David Gardner was chief (1975–78). Tribal political power and leadership is now overwhelmingly concentrated in the Choctaw Nation.

The extent to which Choctaws resisted the Choctaw youth movement is unclear. Interview evidence suggests that there was at least some resistance in all parts of the Choctaw Nation, especially in the area near Boswell where Harry J. W. Belvin was born in 1901 to a white mother and a Choctaw/Cherokee father, who was a lawyer, on a 1,280–acre ranch that grew corn and cotton and supported three hundred head of cattle and fifty horses (Hunke 1986). The extensive network of kin of which Belvin was a part, a network that had helped him win the position of chief in 1948 and 1952, was critical to the development of a countermovement to the Choctaw youth movement. This countermovement defined the youth movement as a personal attack against Belvin and urged Choctaws to remain loyal to their chief.

Youth organizers were well aware of what they themselves described as the "fierce loyalty" that many Choctaws had for Belvin. Elders described Belvin's popularity in the Choctaw Nation as enormous. Known for being unusually "in touch" with "the Indian people," a reputation in which he took great pride, throughout the twenty-seven-year period during which he served as Choctaw chief Belvin devoted significant amounts of time going door-to-door visiting Choctaws, a practice that, Choctaws said, endeared him to our people.

An archival source corroborated this oral-history data. In a letter dated November 16, 1958, prominent Choctaw Muriel Wright wrote, "Belvin is liked, it is said, because he visits around among the Choctaws, and tries to keep them informed and interested in all that is going on in Indian matters" (letter to "Uncle Brookes and Aunt Besse" from Muriel Wright, Peter J. Hudson Collection, OHS Research Division).

One Choctaw whom I interviewed described Belvin as having been quite powerful at the time that Brown "took him on;" Belvin was a man, this stout elderly woman told me quietly as we pulled weeds from her front yard, who "really called the shots" in southeastern Oklahoma during the 1960s and 1970s. As an expression of his power and popularity, during the decade prior to the emergence of the Choctaw youth movement, Belvin was selected Outstanding American Indian of the year (Hunke 1960). Also as an expression of his power and popularity, at nearly all of the talks that youth-movement activists gave in the Choctaw Nation, they said that they encountered hostile defenses of Belvin from at least some Choctaws.

Archival sources reveal that Belvin responded to the Choctaw youth movement by, among other things, scheduling public meetings for Choctaws throughout the Choctaw Nation. In a written announcement of one such meeting that was scheduled for October 3, 1969, in the courthouse of the town of Atoka in the west-central part of southeastern Oklahoma, the chief wrote that "every Indian in the area is strongly urged to attend this most important meeting," which "will answer charges of oio workers and the okc [Oklahoma City] Council of Choctaws" that "things have been mishandled" during his administration as chief. He continued: "When the Choctaws know the truth about this gad-fly organization that is trying so hard to get control of the Choctaw Tribe, I know that they will fight the move as true Americans. . . . I trust that the Choctaws throughout the Choctaw Nation will make it their business to know what the oio and the Oklahoma [City] Council of Choctaws are trying to do to the Choctaws" (scrapbook, I. A. Billy Collection, box 1, ohs Research Division).

In a flyer announcing a talk that the chief was to give on September 1, 1969, in Tushka Homma, Belvin declared, "Many false rumors and much misinformation are, at present, being circulated regarding the [termination law and its amendments], and this meeting will provide opportunities for the Choctaws to get the full meaning of the Act and its consequences to the Tribe including the 'Final Settlement' that has been talked about by the older Choctaws for the past 63 years. It is time that the Choctaws woke up" (scrapbook, I. A. Billy Collection, box 1, ohs Research Division).

It is unclear what Belvin said to the Choctaw people during these and other talks that he delivered in the Choctaw Nation during the fall of 1969. By the summer of 1970, however, he had reversed his position. Then keenly aware of the fact that the Choctaw people did not support his effort to terminate the tribe, he, together with the commissioner of Indian affairs, supported the repeal of the legislation (Kidwell 2004). This repeal occurred on August 24, 1970, one day before the Choctaws were to be terminated (see 84 Stat. 828). Two months later on October 22, 1970, a law was passed formally restoring the right of the Five "Civilized" Tribes to select their own chiefs (84 Stat. 1091 [1970]; Strickland 1980; Noley 2001).[10] Immediately, Belvin began preparing for what he must have thought would be the fight of his life, the fight to keep his job after having supported legislation that had generated so much opposition from his people. The Choctaws' election was scheduled for August 14, 1971.

"Vote for Harry J. W. Belvin and Keep the Choctaw Nation on the Map": The 1971 Race for Choctaw Chief

For the next ten months, Belvin campaigned hard for the position of chief. He gave speeches. He visited hundreds of Choctaw homes. He made scores of phone calls. He sponsored dinners. He attended dozens of public events. "Belvin was everywhere," said one Choctaw about the period leading up to the 1971 race for chief. Belvin told his people that the termination legislation was a federal initiative, not his initiative, and he pointed to the Trail of Tears and allotment as evidence of the long-standing federal desire to dissolve the Choctaw tribe. He promised "to fight to prevent any [future] move to terminate the Choctaw tribe" and declared that his goal was to restore the Choctaw tribe to its former glory ("Vote for Harry J. W. Belvin" leaflet, 1971, I. A. Billy Collection, box 1, OHS Research Division). He pledged to "continue all Choctaw programs," "expand programs," and "establish a Choctaw Constitution and a legal Choctaw Council." "Vote for Harry J. W. Belvin," his slogan read, "and Keep the Choctaw Nation on the Map." His principal opponent was not Charles Brown, whose renowned battle for the tribe's highest office came in 1978, but rather a two-term mayor of McAlester and a successful Choctaw businessman, Fritz Neill. Like Belvin, Neill pledged to rebuild the tribe and expand tribal programs ("Fact Sheet about the Election for Choctaw Chief, Campaign Flyer of Fritz Neill," Section X—Choctaw Elections, OHS Research Division).

Belvin reminded the Choctaws that the first year he had served as chief, he had started the three-day Choctaw Labor Day Festival, an enormously popular tribal event then as now. As will be seen below, he also recast the meaning of at least two specific actions he had taken as chief to alleviate poverty and improve the quality of life for Choctaws: a HUD housing program he had started, and the Choctaw councils he had established in various parts of the Choctaw Nation and in Oklahoma City.

Ten years earlier, tribes had been made eligible for federal programs that together were known as the Great Society programs.[11] For example, beginning in 1961, tribes were included in the list of entities eligible for the programs of the Area Development Administration (ADA), and beginning in 1963, in the list of entities eligible for programs under the Manpower Development Training Act (MDTA). By the end of the decade, tribes were participating in the poverty programs of the Office of Economic Opportunity (OEO) and the housing programs of HUD. These changes gave federal sanction to the idea that the responsibility of tribal leaders was not simply to settle the tribal estate, as U.S. leaders had told the Choctaws at the turn of the twentieth century, but also to improve the social welfare of their tribes.

Well aware of the fact that poverty in the Choctaw Nation was widespread and endemic, in the early 1960s Belvin submitted an application to HUD to establish a tribal housing authority. According to Gary Batton, a Choctaw who was assistant director of the Choctaw Nation Housing Authority at the time of my research, HUD denied the Choctaws' application. For reasons that included the fact that, at that time, the Choctaws were not exercising police powers over tribal land, HUD said that the tribe did not meet the bureaucratic requirements for a tribal housing authority. Undaunted, Belvin decided to organize the Choctaw Nation Housing Authority as a state agency. Following HUD guidelines for state agencies rather than those for tribal housing authorities, Belvin learned that HUD expected a mayor to undertake certain duties and responsibilities in connection with the housing project, duties that included selecting a board of commissioners to oversee the project. Belvin assigned himself the role of mayor for the purpose of the project. He then created the required board of commissioners, to which he appointed prominent Choctaws.[12] By the month prior to the 1971 race for chief, 364 mutual-help homes and 116 units of low-rent housing had been completed, and 274 mutual-help homes were under construction, accomplishments to which Belvin proudly pointed during his 1971 campaign. Housing program records suggest that, when Belvin's housing program was initiated, it was viewed as simply an effort to improve the standard of living for poor Choctaws (Choctaw Nation 1971). By 1971, however, the program had been recast as more than simply a poverty program: it was a symbol of Belvin's desire and determination to rebuild the tribe.

Also recast was the meaning of Belvin's act of creating Choctaw councils in some southeastern Oklahoma counties and in Oklahoma City. Prior to the termination crisis of 1969 and 1970, Belvin had promoted the creation of councils of Choctaws at the county level in the Choctaw Nation and at the city level in Oklahoma City. (In 1969, the Oklahoma City council, on which Charles Brown sat, endorsed the Choctaw youth movement's actions and position, and council members other than Brown participated in the youth movement.) Belvin invited the leaders of each of these councils to meet with him on a quarterly basis as an informal tribal council, a body that was often called the general council. These councils had no legal power. According to McKee and Schlenker (1980), their purpose was to provide Belvin with advice about how best to improve the social welfare of Choctaw individuals and families. In other words, the councils were a data-gathering and planning network oriented toward facilitating the process of applying for and establishing in the Choctaw Nation the poverty programs classified as Great Society programs. In 1971, however, Belvin's act of creating a two-tiered system of councils looked a lot like the act of a chief who had been trying for some time to rebuild formal tribal political structures.

A significant issue in the 1971 election, the first election in more than sixty years that expressed the Choctaws' legal right to select their own chief, was the question of who would be permitted to vote. The BIA charged an election committee made up of eight Choctaws to decide this and other questions related to election procedures and regulations. The committee consisted of Eric Bohanon (chair), Bentley Beams, Joe Spring, Robert Anderson, Ben Dancy, Vincent Going, Opal Harkey, and Irene Heard ("Choctaw Election," August 14, 1971, I. A. Billy Collection, box 1, OHS Research Division). For the 1948 and 1952 elections, held at the BIA's discretion to produce a nominee for federal appointment, the BIA had limited eligible voters to those who had been enrolled nearly a half-century earlier on the Dawes (Allotment) Rolls as Choctaws "by blood." Because this rule would permit only elders to vote in the 1971 election, and, at least from a Choctaw perspective, would do little to promote the goal of reconstituting the Choctaw tribe, it was dismissed as inappropriate for the 1971 election.

An alternative was to limit voting rights to those of one-fourth or more Choctaw "blood." At the time, as earlier in the century, the Indian Health

Service (IHS) was using a minimum "blood quantum" requirement of one-fourth to limit health services to Choctaws at the Talihina Indian hospital (and to other Indians at Indian hospitals and clinics elsewhere), a practice that prompted some Choctaws whom I interviewed, as well as anthropologist Faiman-Silva (1997), to claim that in the mid-twentieth century the Choctaws had a minimum "blood quantum" requirement for tribal membership, which is not the case. Unlike many other Indian tribes, at no point in the history of our tribe have we ever instituted a minimum blood quantum requirement for tribal membership.

In 1971 the BIA had been urging tribes to institute a one-fourth minimum blood quantum requirement for tribal membership for at least thirty years, generally in connection with the process of "organizing" tribes under the Indian Reorganization Act of 1934. In 1971, however, the BIA recommended that the Choctaw election committee accord the right to vote to all lineal descendants of those enrolled on the Dawes Rolls ("Choctaw Election," August 14, 1971, I. A. Billy Collection, box 1, OHS Research Division). In fact, it is not clear that the BIA or the Choctaws even entertained the idea of limiting Choctaw enfranchisement based on blood quantum. The BIA could not have assumed that few Choctaws were less than one-fourth Choctaw "by blood;" some of those listed on the Dawes Rolls in 1906, after all, were recorded as one-sixty-fourth Choctaw by blood, and two decades after the BIA made its recommendation, as much as 75 percent of the Choctaw tribal membership had a blood quantum of under one-quarter (Faiman-Silva 1997; Noley 2001).

The committee decided to permit all lineal descendants of Choctaw-by-blood Dawes enrollees to vote. Accordingly, committee chair Eric Bohanon arranged for registrars in about thirty different polling places to have copies of the Dawes Rolls with which to confirm the eligibility of the 1,882 Choctaws who presented themselves at the polling places (scrapbook, I. A. Billy Collection, box 1, OHS Research Division; *Talihina American*, August 18, 1971; "Fact Sheet about the Election for Choctaw Chief," Section X—Choctaw Elections, OHS Research Division). An additional 605 Choctaws voted by mail, a large number of whom were probably from Oklahoma City. (Nine hundred absentee ballots were sent out.) Absentee voters made up as much as 25 percent of all of those who voted (*Talihina American*, August 18, 1971; scrapbook, I. A. Billy Collection, box 1, OHS Research Division).

Belvin won the election. The fact that he had endorsed Choctaw tribal termination from at least 1959 to the end of the 1960s was either widely excused or not widely believed. The chief managed to avoid being widely labeled as a traitor. He managed to avoid widespread characterization of his acts as acts of treason. Finally, he managed to recreate himself as a chief who would lead the Choctaw people on a path to magnificence, a path that he himself had not envisioned—and perhaps not even imagined—for his people. It was a path and a destination that had been defined by the tribe's youth.

Belvin's 1971–75 Term as Choctaw Chief

Unlike his leading opponent in the 1971 race for chief, Belvin had promised to create a Choctaw constitution that vested power in a tribal council, a promise that may have been an important factor in winning him the election. The youth had popularized a vision of a Choctaw constitutional democracy in which power was distributed among at least two tribalgovernmental entities—the executive and a tribal council. This formal political arrangement represented a continuity of the tribe's nineteenth-century past and a radical break from that which had existed since 1906. In 1906 the U.S. government had not only diminished the power that had been distributed among three Choctaw governmental branches but also consolidated it into a single office and office-holder, whom they prohibited Choctaws from selecting by popular vote. In other words, the U.S. government had replaced the Choctaws' constitutional democracy with a dictatorship. The work of rebuilding the tribe had begun with the creation of new corporate structures in the 1960s to implement federal poverty programs and had continued with the formal restoration of tribal elections in 1970. A redistribution of formal political power was the critical next step.

During the first three years of his four-year term, Belvin did little to rebuild the tribe's formal political structures and even failed to appreciably expand the skeletal executive branch. Choctaws who worked for Belvin often commented on how tiny the tribal bureaucracy was and how limited the tribal programs were in the early 1970s. One of Belvin's former personal assistants, exaggerating to make her point, said, "All the business of the tribe that Belvin dealt with could fit in a cigar box. He used a Chief [brand] writing tablet and that's all he needed. The business of the tribe fit into his top desk drawer. It was just nothing like it is now." Another said, "Belvin worked hard. . . . Belvin was a friend of mine. [But] back then, the Choctaw Nation had no money, nothing. No grants, no money. Back then, no one paid attention to the Choctaw Nation." In the mid-1980s, Belvin's brother Frank defended Belvin's act of simply running any kind of bureaucracy at all, asserting that at mid-century the Choctaw "tribal government was only a long-forgotten shadow" (Hunke 1986: 197). Another Choctaw, scholar Grayson Noley, describes this period as one in which the Choctaw tribal government was in "ruins" and had "no real structure" (2001: x).

Across the country, tribal governments were in especially poor shape during the period from the mid-1950s to the late 1970s. On many reservations and tribal trust lands, "tribal chairman and council members were part[-]time or completely unpaid," "tribal resources were very limited, tribal budgets generally tiny, and tribal bureaucracies limited or nonexistent" (Roth 1997: 4).[13] Reflecting upon the state of the Rosebud Sioux tribal government when he became chairman of the tribe in 1954, Cato Valandra remarked: "There was only one tribal employee, paid directly by the tribal council," and "the activities of the tribe were not well-known," even to the Rosebud Sioux tribal council (Cash and Hoover 1971: 186). Before the mid-1960s the Fort Yuma–Quechan tribal government "was mostly the low-paying, part-time preoccupation of [only] seven men and women who met once a month in a hot, ramshackle building," and there were no tribal jobs other than council treasurer (Bee 1982: 38). It was not until 1967 that the office of Fort Yuma–Quechan tribal president became a full-time salaried position and a decade later that the tribal office staff reached even twelve persons, "including the tribal president, vice president and secretary, along with bookkeepers and assistant bookkeepers to keep tabs on funds for the tribal programs" (p. 39).

In 1973, two years into Belvin's term, the BIA reminded the chief that he had done little to address the problem of Choctaw tribal membership. In a study of the tribe's "development potential," an aspect of tribal affairs in which Belvin was very interested, the BIA took the chief to task for in many cases failing to maintain any records or even the scantiest amount of information about the Choctaws who were born after 1906, the population whom they referred to as "the unenrolled" (Planning Support Group, BIA 1973). Simply stated, the problem they identified was that Belvin was not opening the tribal rolls to Choctaws who were under sixty-seven years of age. Many of "the unenrolled" were participating in formal tribal affairs, but they were doing so as descendants of enrolled members. For many acts of their formal political participation, "the unenrolled" were required to present either documentation of their descent from someone who was enrolled in the tribe, or a BIA-issued CDIB (Certificate of Degree of Indian Blood). Belvin was aware that the incorporation of this category of Choctaws on the Choctaw tribal roll would create formal ties between these individuals and the Choctaw tribal government and encourage their political participation. This would not serve his interests: his base was elders and a segment of the forty- to sixty-five-year-old population; his greatest threat was the youth.

By not drawing up a comprehensive list of all tribal members (and perhaps even resisting such an action), Belvin failed to aggressively pursue the vision of the tribe popularized by the Choctaw youth, a vision that drew much of its inspiration from the tribe's nineteenth-century polity. Throughout the nineteenth century, Choctaw leaders had maintained lists of tribal citizens, vesting Choctaw lighthorse with the responsibility of traveling the tribal homeland at regular intervals to conduct the tribal census (Debo 1934). Nineteenth-century Choctaws were well aware that a well-defined membership is vital to expressing the status of our tribe as a nation; social theorist M. G. Smith (1974) points out that it is critical in determining even whether a collectivity exists as a corporate group.

In the 1960s and 1970s, the Choctaws were not unusual among American Indian tribes in failing to clearly define their membership, a consequence in part of the devastating effects of federal policies to destroy tribal sovereignty that were implemented at several different points in the twentieth century. At the time that the BIA chided Belvin for his failure in this regard, the BIA was urging tribes all over the country to adopt "a more precise definition of membership, and concurrently, of voter lists" (Roth 1997: 8). This was termed "clarifying membership," and often it "meant deciding who was in and who was out, and who had voting rights" (p. 8). A federal task force expressed surprise and concern at the poor condition of tribal rolls during this period. It found, for example, that only one tribe in the states of Washington and Oregon, which today contain thirty-nine federally recognized tribes, had a "satisfactory tribal roll" and that "these tribes urgently need a means of defining their membership" (p. 8).

In 1974, the last year of his term, Belvin managed to secure much-needed capital for the tribe during a trip he took to Washington DC with

Principal Chief of the Cherokee Nation W. W. "Bill" Keeler and several of their assistants. Keeler's assistant was Ross Swimmer, who provided me with a firsthand account of the trip. "Pat Nixon gave us a tour of the White House," Swimmer began. The entourage then met with the secretary of the interior. When asked, the chiefs told the secretary that, as regards tribal programs and government, they "just weren't quite sure what they wanted to do." They were there just to "talk" with him. At the end of the trip, the secretary presented the tribes with $400,000, saying, "Here—this is for planning." The tribes received this amount in "planning grants" each year for the following five years. Belvin had little time to decide what to do with his share. By the end of 1974, he had begun preparing for the August 1975 race for chief.

The Ousting of Belvin: The 1975 Choctaw Election

In 1975 the Choctaw people, frustrated by the apparent lack of progress in rebuilding the tribe, decided that it was time for a change. In 1971 they had given Belvin a second chance. Four years later, many concluded that the chief, then seventy-four years old, had not been sufficiently "aggressive," as it was often put. The sincerity of Belvin's newfound commitment to tribal rebuilding was also questioned, particularly by Choctaws living in Oklahoma City. As the Choctaw people prepared for the upcoming election, Oklahoma City, still a stronghold of anti-Belvin Choctaw sentiment, again became a critical site of Choctaw grassroots leadership.

Interviews, together with postelection historical evidence discussed below, strongly suggest that Oklahoma City Choctaws played a major role in organizing the challenger's campaign. They claimed that their involvement exceeded even this: the Oklahoma City Choctaws were the ones, they said, who selected a challenger for Belvin, introduced the idea of running for chief to that individual, and convinced him to run. Whatever may have been the process by which he entered the race, the man who emerged in early 1975 as Belvin's leading challenger was David Gardner, a Choctaw from Belvin's hometown of Boswell. Oklahoma City Choctaws knew Gardner from, among other things, the years he had spent in nearby Norman while pursuing graduate studies and teaching classes at the University of Oklahoma.

Gardner strongly supported the goal of reinstating a constitutional democracy for the tribe. One Choctaw woman who had campaigned for Gardner and who lived in a small town just outside Oklahoma City told me that she and many others found Gardner's "vision," especially of future tribal corporate structures, to be one of his greatest strengths. In addition, Gardner was young—just thirty-five years old. Choctaw youth had established themselves as a significant political asset for the tribe just six years earlier when they had launched the movement to stop the tribe's termination. Seeking to capitalize on this, Gardner aligned himself with the youth movement during the campaign, and his young age helped focus attention on one of Belvin's greatest weaknesses: his advanced age.

Some Choctaws described the 1975 election as even more bitter than the 1995 election, the election that is the focus of the next chapter. Although, as was mentioned earlier, Choctaws criticized Belvin for not being aggressive enough in rebuilding the tribe, Belvin was known to be an aggressive campaigner, and his 1975 fight for another four-year term reinforced this reputation. By all accounts Gardner, too, showed great tenacity during the protracted struggle to oust Belvin, despite the fact that Gardner's personality was not well suited for fiery political contests. One of Gardner's close male friends described him as "shy, a good speaker but not a great speaker, educated, and a man with great grace and dignity."

During the months leading up to the election, Gardner and his campaign staff feared that it would be very difficult to unseat the old chief. They seem to have seriously overestimated Belvin's power and popularity, which they perceived to be very high, especially in the Choctaw Nation. Though they spent considerable time campaigning in the Choctaw Nation, many of them believed that those most likely to cast a vote for their candidate would be Choctaws living outside of the Choctaw Nation. Accordingly, they focused on mobilizing and capturing votes from this segment of the Choctaw population. They were well aware that, in the 1971 election, 25 percent of all those who had voted lived outside Choctaw tribal boundaries, a population that later came to be known as "absentees," as will be seen in the next chapter.

Accordingly, Gardner invested much time mobilizing Choctaws in Oklahoma City and, to a lesser extent, in Dallas. One Choctaw pastor of a church in Dallas that had many Choctaw members, the Reverend Bertram Bobb, remembered well the talk that Gardner gave to his congregation. At the time of our interview, Bobb had long since migrated to the Choctaw Nation and had been elected to multiple terms on the Choctaw tribal council. Reverend Bobb said that the central themes of Gardner's talk were "instilling a sense of pride in being Choctaw" and "improving the image of the Choctaws." Bobb said that Gardner's remarks greatly stirred both him and his congregation, and later he urged his congregation not only to vote but also to vote for Gardner. He also promoted Gardner on his local radio show, a show that focused on Bible readings and discussions of Christian Scripture.

Gardner won the election. In addition to his vision and youth, there were a number of other factors that together help explain his success. First, he was the son of a reverend, Critten A. Gardner. At that time churches were one of the strongest extant Choctaw corporate structures, providing important arenas for local "extrafamilial social encounters" among Choctaws and acting as "the physical and social focal points of rural Choctaw life" (Foster 2001: 253; Faiman-Silva 1997: 125; Pesantubbee 1994). Between allotment and the early 1980s, many Choctaw efforts to maintain a sense of community were organized through Christian church congregations (Foster 2001). Gardner's status as the son of a reverend probably significantly weakened the strong support that Belvin had long enjoyed among Choctaw preachers and many churchgoers, support that was based in part on the fact that Belvin's brother was one of the most well-known Choctaw preachers of the mid-twentieth century. In the 1940s Belvin's brother Frank had organized dozens of Indian churches in eastern Oklahoma, and in the 1950s he had served as superintendent of Indian work for the Southern Baptist Home Mission Board (Hunke 1986).

Another factor that may have helped swing the election in Gardner's favor was the fact that Gardner was one of Belvin's relatives. Gardner's inclusion in Belvin's network of kin may have seriously impaired this network's effectiveness in mobilizing support for Belvin's reelection. The weakening of Belvin's kin network may have significantly impacted, even crippled, Belvin's campaign.

Two of Gardner's minor policy objectives appealed to certain segments of the Choctaw electorate and thus may also have helped make the difference in the race. Gardner and his family had moved to the Chickasaw Nation when Gardner was just thirteen. Reflecting the deep impact that his experiences in Chickasaw Nation had on him personally, Gardner strongly promoted the development of a more formal partnership between the Choctaw and Chickasaw nations and the strengthening of informal ties between the two tribes. This political goal was and is strongly supported by a significant minority of Choctaws who, like myself, are of both Choctaw and Chickasaw ancestry. Members of this minority group are products of a pattern of extensive intermarriage between Choctaws and Chickasaws that developed in 1837 when the Chickasaws were politically assimilated into the Choctaw Nation for an eighteen-year period (see chapter 2). The kinship ties that link the Choctaw and Chickasaw nations through this minority group are infused with great symbolic importance, as the modern Choctaw and Chickasaw tribes are said to have been founded by two brothers, Chata and Chikasa, who together play a leading role in a Choctaw creation story (see chapter 2). Territorial ties strengthen these family- and creation-story-based ties. For example, in 2000 as many as six thousand Choctaws lived in the Chickasaw Nation (Levine 2004).

Three years before his 1975 election, Gardner had created a nongovernmental organization, the Choctaw-Chickasaw Alliance. By the electoral season, chapters of the Choctaw-Chickasaw Alliance existed in Durant, Spiro, McAlester, Hugo, and Antlers in the Choctaw Nation, and Ardmore and Tishomingo in the Chickasaw Nation (Pesantubbee 1994). Gardner's commitment to strengthening formal and informal ties between the Choctaw and Chickasaw nations no doubt won him votes from Choctaws who joined this organization, a large percentage of whom were probably of both Choctaw and Chickasaw ancestry, and some of whom were active in his campaign.

During the race, Gardner also promoted the "preservation" of the Choctaw language, as he put it. Gardner strongly believed that the Choctaw language was valuable and deserved greater appreciation and respect. Later, he would take great pride in his accomplishment of securing permission to reprint a Choctaw dictionary. In 1975 the strong promotion of the Choctaw language by a candidate for Choctaw chief was somewhat unexpected. A substantial segment of the Choctaw electorate, which included Belvin himself, had been reared to value and pursue cultural assimilation (Pesantubbee 1994). Belvin, for example, had been reared by a Choctaw language speaker who had actively discouraged his children from speaking Choctaw (Hunke 1986). Gardner's strong promotion of the Choctaw language was born from his deep fear that the language was "dying out," as he put it. By the end of the century, according to one observer, only about 730 of the tribe's then 130,000 members were able to speak Choctaw with any fluency (Faiman-Silva 1997); another observer, however, argued that at this time there existed as many as 5,000 Choctaw language speakers among the Oklahoma Choctaws (Kidwell 2004).

At the time, as now, some Choctaw churches were and are important sites for Choctaw language retention and acquisition, especially thirty-seven Choctaw Methodist churches and fourteen Choctaw Presbyterian churches, the combined membership of which totals about 1,000 (Pesantubbee 1994). In these churches, it is not uncommon for some preaching to be done in the Choctaw language, for services to include the singing of Choctaw-language hymns, and for some church members to speak Choctaw to one another. In addition, these churches use what Choctaw scholar Michelene Pesantubbee describes as "some Choctaw cultural forms." She explains that in the 1990s, as in the 1970s, members of these churches used arbors, held feasts, encouraged certain child-rearing techniques such as not requiring children to sit still during services, and promoted "values such as sharing and respect for elders" (p. 264). She also points out that until the 1970s members of these churches continued the nineteenth-century Choctaw tradition of using camp houses for extended meetings.

Gardner pledged to revitalize the Choctaw language at a time when Choctaws in the southern part of the Choctaw Nation—Choctaws that included members of some of these Choctaw churches—were launching a movement to foster a greater appreciation and respect for Choctaw culture and history. Choctaws involved in this movement no doubt considered Gardner a likelier supporter of Choctaw cultural revitalization than was his opponent, an assessment that may have won Gardner some votes. The small but important Choctaw cultural revitalization movement of the late 1970s and early 1980s appears to have begun in 1974 when Reverend Donald Eugene Wilson of Idabel, a Choctaw pastor who was then serving all fourteen of the Choctaw Presbyterian churches, began promoting Choctaw dance, then considered nearly moribund among the Oklahoma Choctaw, as a youth activity that "would provide wholesome recreation and at the same time emphasize the distinct cultural heritage of the Choctaws" (qtd. in Howard and Levine 1990: 15; Pesantubbee 1994). According to Pesantubbee, the idea for such activities came from the youth of the Choctaw churches. Pesantubbee explains that in the 1970s these youth "wanted to know why Choctaws did not practice many of the traditions found among other native groups," they wanted an identity that was not "based solely on a contemporary westernized culture," and they wanted a Christianity that was expressed "not only in Western forms" (pp. 253, 283, 282). From the 1970s through the 1990s, these youth encountered significant resistance—mostly from older Choctaw church members—to the goal of "relearning Choctaw ways" (p. 285). Older members of Choctaw churches often constructed (and still construct) efforts to "return to the old ways" as "a step backward," and many denounced Choctaw dances, in particular, as "sinful" (pp. 101, 244). Nevertheless, in order to keep young people from leaving the Choctaw church and to increase Choctaw church membership, church members agreed to make some, very limited, changes. While Pesantubbee explains that most remained opposed to Choctaw dancing, "Indian" music, and other "Indian" cultural expressions that they claimed suggested that another religion—a religion other than Christianity—was being practiced, they permitted, among other things, the occasional wearing of traditional Choctaw dress, the continuance of gospel singing in the Choctaw language, and the performance of the Lord's Prayer in "Indian" sign language. In the 1970s, despite continued church-based opposition, Choctaws Shirley Loman and Buster Ned followed Wilson by organizing Choctaw dance groups in the southeastern and southwestern parts of the Choctaw Nation respectively, and Choctaws in Talihina founded a nongovernmental organization, the Choctaw Nation Historical Society (*Bishinik*, August 1978; Howard and Levine 1990). In addition, in the late 1970s an organization called the Choctaw Nation Homemakers Association began teaching beadwork, and other Choctaw women began marketing baskets and "Indian" jewelry for an arts-and-crafts cooperative in Antlers, a mid-sized Choctaw Nation town (Faiman-Silva 1997). Based on fieldwork conducted in the early 1980s, anthropologist Sandra Faiman-Silva reported that in the southeastern Choctaw Nation "Choctaws voiced strong enthusiasm for continuing to revive their traditional arts and crafts, and many were eager to learn basketry and beadwork" (1997: 140; Pesantubbee 1994).

Gardner's victory party was held at a small motel in the geographic center of the Choctaw Nation. Among the invited were five or six carloads of Oklahoma City Choctaws who had helped organize his campaign. Once in office, Gardner rewarded these Choctaws for their major role in getting him elected by appointing some of them to key positions in the Choctaw Nation government. One such appointee was Robert Loyce Walker, who became business manager for the tribe (Oklahoma City Council of Choctaws 1981). In addition, Gardner began paying the fees on two booths that, beginning in the mid-1970s, Oklahoma City Choctaws began maintaining each year at the Oklahoma State Fair. These booths are a major fund-raising vehicle. From the mid-1970s through the 1980s, food sales at these booths generated twenty thousand dollars a year for the Oklahoma City Choctaws.[14]

The Gardner Administration: 1975–78

The acquisition of a new headquarters for the tribal government was one of Gardner's most significant accomplishments as chief. In 1976, he and his staff secured for the tribe the former campus of Presbyterian College in Durant (Pesantubbee 1994). Upon its acquisition, this property became a powerful symbol of Choctaw aspirations to rebuild a large and powerful tribal government. The property's primary structure, a large, red stately building, houses a large auditorium, and the college's numerous former classrooms, converted into offices by the tribe, sport very high ceilings and beautiful wood trim. Gardner's staff, of course, occupied only a small portion of the building, but their day-to-day experience of passing so many spaces for future offices no doubt fueled their dreams of expanding the tribal bureaucracy and adding legislative and judicial branches to complete the tribal government.

The dreams and aspirations of the Gardner administration were dashed by a devastating event: Gardner developed cancer, specifically lymphoma. This illness racked his young body rapidly, making it impossible for him to fulfill his ambitious goals for the tribe. Gardner managed to build a community health representative training center, an extended health care facility, and a community building (McKee and Shlenker 1980). He also managed to establish a formal alliance between the Choctaw and Chickasaw nations. But, only two and a half years into his four-year term, he died, leaving his family, staff, and the Choctaw people stunned and devastated.

The Beginning of the Hollis Roberts Era and
the Establishment of a New Choctaw Constitution

Gardner died on January 13, 1978. Soon after, it was decided that an election would be held to determine his replacement. By this point, a consensus had emerged that Choctaw youth were best suited to undertake the formidable task of rebuilding the tribe. The 1978 election thus pitted two representatives of the Choctaw youth against one another: Charles Brown—who, though aging, remained the clearest and most potent symbol of the vision, competency, and spirit of Choctaw youth—and a man from the generation after Brown's, thirty-five-year-old Hollis Roberts.

Roberts was born in Hochatown in the southeastern corner of the Choctaw Nation. He was a formidable opponent, even for Brown, who had won the hearts and minds of the Choctaw people by leading the movement to stop tribal termination and by developing a new Choctaw nationalism. There were three primary things that made Roberts electable in 1978. He was a professional politician, he had extraordinary charisma, and he was Gardner's assistant chief. Before serving in that position, Roberts had served six years as a member of the Oklahoma House of Representatives and fourteen years as a city councilperson of Hugo in the south-central part of the Choctaw Nation (Park 1987). Roy Lyles, a non-Indian who was chairman of the Democratic Party for Choctaw County when Roberts ran for state representative, told me that the party was thrilled to support such a competent and charismatic young man for election as Hollis Roberts. "In the run-off election for the position [state representative]," he said, "Hollis pulled in more votes than any candidate has ever got." Roberts's appeal extended far beyond the Choctaw population: in 1970 Indians comprised only 6 percent of the population of Roberts's home county, Choctaw County (Strickland 1980). One of Roberts's close male friends described him as "aggressive, self-educated, a born politician, a common fellow who was raised the hard way, a man who is very skilled at remembering people's names, and a man who sure knows the political process and is just a natural politician." In addition to his wealth of experience in politics and the natural talent he brought to this profession, Roberts's status as Gardner's assistant chief was a tremendous asset in the 1978 race for chief. Gardner was well loved by the Choctaw people, and his tragic death no doubt encouraged Choctaws to support the man whom Gardner had chosen as his second-in-command.

The election was remarkably close, a testament to Brown's popularity, his reputation, and the place of honor that Choctaws have assigned him in Choctaw history. Brown lost to rising-star professional politician Hollis Roberts by only 339 votes (McKee and Schlenker 1980; see also Faiman-Silva 1997). Roberts took the oath of office in Montgomery Auditorium on the campus of Southeastern Oklahoma State University in Durant (Park 1987). Like his predecessor's, Roberts's service as chief ended abruptly. On June 6, 1997, during his twentieth year as chief, Roberts was convicted in federal court in Muskogee, Oklahoma, of three of seven counts of aggravated sexual abuse and sexual assault.[15] He was sentenced to eleven years in prison. This event and others have made early-twenty-first century Choctaws circumspect about Roberts's reign as Choctaw chief.

A key event of the early Roberts administration was the passage of a new constitution in 1983, the first since 1860. This historic event began to unfold during the Gardner administration. In 1977 several members of the Choctaw tribal council and grassroots Choctaw leaders filed a lawsuit to defend the validity of the 1860 Choctaw Constitution, the constitution under which the tribe was operating when the U.S. government dismantled the tribe at the turn of the twentieth century (*Bishinik*, August 1978).[16] In 1977 the Choctaw council, which had no legal authority or power, consisted of forty-eight persons, four from each of twelve local council organizations, including the council in Oklahoma City (*Bishinik*, August 1978). The idea for such a suit was born from a 1976 Muscogee (Creek) legal decision in which a U.S. court found that the Creek tribal government established under the 1867 Creek Constitution had never been dissolved by statute but instead had been explicitly extended (see *Harjo v. Kleppe*, 420 F. Supp. 1110 [D.D.C. 1976]; Strickland 1980: 75).

On the same grounds, in 1981 the court found that the 1860 Choctaw Constitution was still valid (see *Morris v. Watt*, 640 F. 2d 404 [D.C. Cir. 1981]). This nineteenth-century constitution provided for a tripartite tribal government. It also prohibited women from voting in tribal elections or holding tribal office, and it granted tribal citizenship to whites who had married Choctaw citizens and, following the Act of May 21, 1883, to blacks who had been slaves (or who were descended from slaves) of Choctaw citizens (Choctaw Nation 1973 [1894]). To determine whether the Choctaws wished to keep this old constitution or devise a new instrument of self-governance, the court remanded the secretary of the interior to hold an election in the summer of 1983. Larry Mings, a Choctaw who was superintendent of the BIA's Talihina Agency at the time of my research and who, as a BIA employee in 1983, had helped organize the election, provided me with one of several firsthand accounts of the election. "1983 was a big year," Mings began. "It was real hectic for a while." Before any action could be taken, he said, a list of all those permitted to participate in making this historic decision needed to be compiled. "There were fifty something different lists," he exclaimed, raising his eyebrows and rocking back and forth in his office chair. "We had to try to determine who was a lineal descendant [of those listed on the Dawes Rolls at the turn of the century]."

For the most part, BIA agents, including Mings, did not hunt down eligible voters. They simply advertised that such an election was to occur and asked Choctaws to present themselves for "registration." In the end, 6,970 of those who registered were determined to be entitled to cast ballots, and 3,000 voted (Choctaw Nation 1983). When asked about the role of descendants of freedmen and descendants of intermarried whites in this event, Mings said, "No, freedmen didn't organize. Neither did intermarried whites." Fewer than ten descendants of Choctaw freedmen even tried to register to vote in the election, Mings recalled.

On the scheduled election days, the BIA deployed 120 of their agents to staff the polling places and hired dozens of local Choctaws to assist. There were three stages to the election. In the late spring of 1983, there was a referendum. Voters responded to approximately a dozen questions pertaining to the 1860 constitution and to a proposed new constitution written by Roberts and his staff. Among other things, Choctaws were asked to determine rules for tribal membership (or citizenship). According to several Choctaws whom I interviewed, the BIA refrained from commenting on these rules, a reflection perhaps of the fact that five years earlier in 1978 the U.S. Supreme Court had affirmed that tribes have exclusive jurisdiction over determining their own memberships (see *Santa Clara Pueblo v. Martinez*, 436 U.S. 49 [1978]).

Election results revealed that tribal membership would be limited to lineal descendants of at least one Dawes enrollee who was Choctaw "by blood," and no minimum Choctaw "blood quantum" would be required for membership. Many Choctaws claimed that in the early 1980s there was little to no talk about establishing a minimum blood quantum requirement for tribal membership. "It simply wasn't an issue," explained one Choctaw. By the end of the century, this had changed, as will be seen in the next chapter. Some Choctaws now promote the institution of a one-fourth minimum blood quantum requirement for Choctaw citizenship.

Interviews also revealed that the referendum contained several other questions that inspired little comment or discussion among Choctaws. There was widespread popular support, for example, for making women eligible to vote in tribal elections and hold tribal office. A proposal to establish a new, tripartite tribal government also won easily. It was decided that an executive department, headed by a chief, would manage, administer, and direct the operation of tribal programs, activities, and services; the chief would be responsible for preparing an annual tribal budget; and he or she would have the power to veto any legislative act, rule, or regulation of a tribal council. A legislative department would consist of a tribal council and would assume responsibility for, among other things, enacting legislation "for the general good of the Choctaw Nation and for the administration and regulation of the affairs of the Choctaw Nation." A judicial department would consist of a three-member tribal court appointed by the chief. This court would have exclusive jurisdiction over deciding disputes arising under any provision of the new constitution or any rule or regulation enacted by the tribal council (Choctaw Nation 1983).

Several Choctaws whom I interviewed identified two referenda decisions as "controversial." The first was the decision to make only Choctaws with a Choctaw blood quantum of at least one-quarter eligible for chief, assistant chief, and tribal council. One elderly woman, who had a one-eighth Choctaw blood quantum, told me that prior to the vote some Choctaws mobilized against this proposed requirement, arguing that it was "unfair," "discriminatory," and "at odds" with the tribe's preference for requiring no minimum blood quantum requirement for tribal membership. Another consultant, a full-blood man who was then serving on the tribal council, told me that at the time, as now, he could not understand why some of his fellow Choctaws were objecting to the idea of instituting a minimum blood quantum requirement for chief. "We're talking about the chief!" he exclaimed. "The chief has just gotta be pretty close to the old Choctaws, the Choctaws of long ago." He constructed such closeness as solely "biological" (rather than, for example, cultural) and as an important component of a Choctaw leader's legitimacy. At the same time, he emphasized his very strong belief that our tribe should have no minimum blood quantum requirement for tribal membership. Such a requirement "would make a lot of Choctaws non-Choctaw," he explained, perhaps even his own two great-grandchildren, who have a Choctaw blood quantum of one-eighth. The idea that his own great-grandchildren could ever be considered non-Choctaw struck him as absurd.

The second controversial referenda decision was the decision that Choctaws in each of twelve districts of the Choctaw Nation would elect one council member to represent their district.[17] This decision eliminated the four seats on the existing tribal council that were reserved for Oklahoma City Choctaws (*Bishinik*, August 1978). Because all twelve districts lay within tribal boundaries, the decision also prevented Choctaws who lived outside the Choctaw Nation from gaining additional seats on the council, an outcome that would have been possible had Choctaws voted for the option of basing tribal council representation on residence. "If Choctaws had voted in 1983 to base tribal council representation on residence," explained one council member, "at least nine of the twelve positions on the council would now [the mid-1990s] be held by absentees."

In the second stage of the election, Choctaws voted on whether to adopt a proposed new constitution incorporating the referenda decisions. In the third stage, a chief and tribal council were elected.[18] Choctaws ratified the new constitution by a vote of 2,253 to 780 on July 9, 1983 (Choctaw Nation 1983). Twelve members were elected to the new tribal council, and Hollis Roberts was reelected chief. Before the year's end, Roberts had appointed three tribal judges, including the first woman in Choctaw history to serve as a judge in a Choctaw tribal court, Juanita Jefferson.

Referring to the first two stages of the historic 1983 election, one Choctaw, a grassroots tribal leader at the time of our interview, suggested that many Choctaws were not fully aware of the historic importance of the event. "When the constitution was sent out to be voted on," he explained, "we didn't know what was going on. We didn't know what this was all about. A lot of people just didn't send it in." Ross Swimmer described the experience of the Oklahoma Cherokees in similar terms: "We didn't know exactly what we were doing then, in the holding of elections and the writing up of the new constitution. We just did it. We didn't know what the Bureau would do—if they'd sign it [the new constitution]. We just did it. I didn't really know what to think of the 1970 Act [which permitted the Five "Civilized" Tribes to popularly select their own chiefs]. [At the time,] I didn't know if I supported elections and a new constitution and everything that was happening."

These statements bring to the fore an important feature of the on-the-ground experience of tribal nation building during the period that immediately preceded the rebuilding of formal political structures among the Five "Civilized" Tribes. At that historical moment, it was unclear to both leaders and nonleaders whether any of the key actions being taken, such as resuming tribal elections and creating new constitutions, would instigate anything at all, much less major social, political, and economic transformation. The means by which to achieve fuller expressions of tribal sovereignty were unclear; the historical outcome of their nation-building projects, uncertain; and the question of how the U.S. government would respond, a major unknown.

Land, New Demographic Realities, Tribal Ties, and the Reopening of the Tribal Rolls: The Immediate Aftermath of the Passage of the New Constitution

Despite the uncertainty surrounding the political upheavals of the early 1980s, the Choctaws pressed on. The ratification of the constitution proved to be a significant turning point, instigating intensive nation building. The Choctaw tribal government was radically restructured and expanded. Formal political power was redistributed, amplified, and legitimized. With these new formal political structures in place, tribal leaders assessed and began to address other core issues. Among them were the condition of the tribal land base and three core issues that pertained to people. As will be seen shortly, the Choctaws found their land base inadequate, adopted a policy of expanding it, and initiated processes of land acquisition. One of three core issues that pertained to people concerned the tribe's new demographic realities, which did not become fully known until about twelve years after the rolls had reopened. Though this was too late for leaders to tailor most new political structures to best accommodate these realities, the demographic portrait of the reconstituted citizenry, summarized below, was valuable in helping both leaders and citizens come to terms with several key ways that the tribe had changed during the twentieth century. Work on two other core issues having to do with the Choctaw citizenry began almost immediately after the installation of new tribal leaders, as will be seen. To strengthen tribal ties, which had been stretched and weakened during the twentieth century, tribal leaders built up the then five-year-old tribal newspaper and constructed additional community centers. At the same time, they developed procedures for managing the enormity of the process of tribal enrollment, a third core issue involving people. Tribal leaders found a way to manage the high volume of applications from those who did not meet the tribe's citizenship requirements, ensured that the enrollment process went smoothly, and at times quashed resistance among their people to the bureaucratization of tribal citizenship.

When the Choctaws decided, through the new constitution, to reinstate their nineteenth-century geographic boundaries, the contrast between the size of the land base during the late nineteenth century and the size of the land base in the late twentieth century was striking. From the late 1860s to allotment, all 7.5 million acres of land within these

boundaries had been tribally owned and controlled. Though the trust relationship holds that the United States "has both a legal and moral duty
to assist tribes by protecting their lands, resources, sovereignty and cultural heritage," by the 1970s the Choctaws' tribal trust land had been reduced to only 10,746 acres (Wilkins and Lomawaima 2001: 145; McKee
and Schlenker 1980). Choctaw individuals owned an additional 132,677
acres of the land within tribal boundaries (McKee and Schlenker 1980).[19]
By 1988, however, Choctaw individuals had experienced only nominal
success in increasing their holdings, acquiring less than 30,000 additional
acres (Faiman-Silva 1997). Tribal leaders were more effective in expanding the land base under tribal (not individual) control: between 1973 and
1997, tribal leaders managed to increase the tribal land base nearly sev-
enfold (Faiman-Silva 1997).[20] Even so, as late as 1997 Choctaw tribal trust
land totaled only 75,000 acres (Faiman-Silva 1997).

The 1983 constitution defined rules for tribal citizenship and opened
the tribal rolls for the first time since allotment in 1906. The reopening
of the rolls focused attention on the dramatic demographic changes that
have occurred in the Choctaw Nation. When the last Choctaw constitution was passed in 1860, the vast majority of Choctaw Nation residents
were Choctaws. Non-Choctaws living in the tribe's homeland included
thousands of the Choctaws' black slaves and a limited number of whites
(see chapter 2). Events of the nineteenth and twentieth centuries, however,
reduced the Choctaws to a tiny minority in their tribal homeland.

This demographic fact was patent long before an accurate picture
of Choctaw demographics began to emerge in 1995, twelve years after
the reopening of the rolls. Between 1960 and 1980, Charles Brown, David Gardner, and other Choctaws who called for Choctaws to take pride
in being Choctaw managed to effect a doubling of the number of self-
identified Choctaws in one Choctaw Nation county—reflecting a national
pattern in which, as Fixico describes it, "many mixed-bloods were reluctant to admit that they were part Indian"—but even after this movement,
leaders were well aware that the percentage of Choctaw Nation residents
who were Choctaw was much smaller than the percentage of Choctaw
Nation residents who were non-Choctaw (Fixico 1986: 11; Faiman-Silva
1997). Several years later in the mid-1990s, it was revealed that Choctaw
tribal members make up only about 10 percent of the population of our
tribal homeland. Whites make up about 80 percent; non-Choctaw blacks,
about 5 percent; and non-Choctaw Indians, Asian Americans and others,
about 5 percent (Faiman-Silva 1997).

Twelve years after the reopening of the rolls, tribal leaders received confirmation of another significant demographic change that had occurred as a result of the transformations of the twentieth century. Tribal leaders were well aware in 1983, as earlier, that allotment had initiated a massive out-migration of Choctaws from the Choctaw Nation and that the flow of Choctaw people across tribal boundaries had not stopped. They were also aware that these population movements had wrought significant changes in tribal demographics. By the mid-1990s, the tribal rolls provided a perspective of the scope of this migration and its impact on residence patterns. In 1995 it was revealed that 83 percent of the then 93,000 enrolled tribal members lived outside the Choctaw Nation (Faiman-Silva 1997; *Bishinik* January 1995). The impact of these two demographic facts—the fact that Choctaws are a tiny minority in their tribal homeland, and the fact that most tribal members live outside the tribal homeland—on present-day Choctaw life and society will be seen in the following chapters.

Especially in the immediate aftermath of the passage of the 1983 constitution, tribal leaders strengthened and actively promoted the development of ties between Choctaw individuals and the tribal government. They also fostered ties among Choctaws. The year that Roberts became chief, a tribal newspaper, *Bishinik*, was created.[21] *Bishinik* is a Choctaw word for a little bird that delivers news. The *Bishinik* tribal newspaper, which is sent free of charge to all tribal members, is published by the tribal government and provides Choctaws with news about tribal matters and about Choctaw births, deaths, and birthdays.

The construction of additional tribal community centers, a high priority of tribal leaders in the early 1980s, also strengthened ties among Choctaws and ties between Choctaws and the tribal government. One Choctaw struggled to describe the social impact of the building of one such center in his community. Prior to the building of the center, "We used to meet in courtrooms," he told anthropologist Sandra Faiman-Silva in the early 1980s. "I don't like courtrooms. To me that wasn't a good fellowship meeting at all, sitting in a courtroom. . . . That was not the place you could feel fellowship" (1997: 207). One sixty-five-year-old Choctaw grandmother beamed when she described to me the strong feelings of fellowship that she experienced in the early 1980s after a Choctaw community center was built near her home. She was particularly proud of the new community events for Choctaws that she and other Choctaws who lived nearby were able to organize through their own fund-raising efforts. These events included Choctaw ball games and Christmas parties. At that time, interaction among Choctaws "revolved around Christian churches and basketball and softball games" (Kidwell 2004: 530). By early 2003 the tribal government had built fourteen community centers; it had also drawn up plans to construct three more (Chief Gregory E. Pyle to enrolled Choctaws, February 5, 2002).

One of the most significant ways that the tribal government strengthened tribal ties was by formalizing the relationship of many Choctaws to one another and to the reconstituted tribal government, specifically by expanding the tribal rolls to include all generations of Choctaws, not just Choctaws born in 1906 or earlier. A two-step process for tribal membership was instituted. First, individuals were required to apply for and receive from the BIA a CDIB card affirming their identity as lineal descendants of one of more people listed as "Choctaw by blood" on the Dawes Rolls. Only after receiving a CDIB was an individual permitted to apply to the Choctaw tribal government for inclusion on the tribal rolls and for a tribal membership card. Choctaw tribal bureaucrats explained to me that there were so many people seeking tribal membership cards who did not meet the tribe's membership requirements that tribal leaders decided to continue to rely on the BIA to issue CDIBs. (CDIB holders almost always meet Choctaw tribal membership requirements.) Tribal bureaucrats also explained that the tribal government wished to avoid alienating or offending individuals by rejecting their applications; the BIA, rather than the tribe, would send rejection letters to the thousands who applied for but who did not meet the eligibility requirements for a CDIB.

Tribal membership cards listed not only the name, address, age, and tribal voting precinct of a member but also his or her Choctaw blood quantum. "When everyone started getting tribal membership cards [in the 1980s]," said one individual who received a tribal membership card with a one-sixteenth designation, "well, that's when people started getting all concerned about blood quantum." Choctaws regularly compared their blood quantum designations with one another, he said, and more than a few started "using it [blood quantum] to divide people." While Choctaw concerns with blood quantum, as chapter 2 shows, long predate the large-scale issuance of CDIBs in the early 1980s, the large-scale distribution and dissemination of CDIBs played an important role in maintaining and reinforcing the salience of blood quantum among Choctaws. Some of the ways blood quantum has maintained its salience beyond the late-twentieth-century period of tribal rebuilding are explored in chapter 4.

In the 1980s the tribal government began strictly requiring individuals to present either a CDIB or a tribal membership card to take advantage of tribal programs and services. During my field research, Choctaws told me dozens of stories about the widespread introduction of CDIBs and tribal membership cards in the early 1980s. Several council members spoke briefly about Choctaw resistance to the bureaucratization of Choctaw citizenship. One of them said that, when he was elected to the tribal council in the 1980s, many of the old people complained to him about having to get a CDIB to show to the clinic. The people who complained "were so loud," he said, that he approached a high-level tribal administrator about it. "*They* know they're Indian. *Everyone* knows they're Indian. They don't like having to get and show this card," he said that he told the administrator. According to the council member, the administrator turned to him, put his hand on the council member's shoulder, and said, "Tough!"

The bureaucratization of Choctaw citizenship was part of the process by which tribal leaders institutionalized the new structures and processes of nation building in the immediate aftermath of the passage of the new constitution. Hardening the boundaries around the tribal citizenry—boundaries that had been made permeable by events of the twentieth century—reinforced Choctaw distinctiveness and reinstated the tribe as a citizenship-conferring nation. The strengthening of ties among Choctaws and the reestablishment of formal ties linking each citizen to the tribal government were assertions of sovereignty that both helped constitute and promote Choctaw corporateness. Like land, these structures were foundational, providing frameworks upon which other structures could be built.

As this work on foundational structures was being carried out, attention was paid to expanding tribally controlled programs and services, an expansion described later in this chapter. The rapid institutional growth that accompanied these initiatives emboldened the Choctaws, who, for reasons I will explain, had waited nearly a decade before taking full advantage of the opportunities created during the mid-1970s for tribes to resume control over tribal social-welfare policy and implementation.

In the immediate aftermath of the Choctaw political upheavals of the early 1980s, Choctaw success in running federal Indian programs and ex-

panding the tribal "state" strengthened the ability of the tribal state to undertake tribal economic development. From the mid-1980s to the present,
as will be seen in the concluding section of this chapter, Choctaws, like
many other tribes, have placed a high priority on tribal economic development. Choctaw success in this area has heavily impacted programs and
services, permitting a dramatic expansion of tribal programs and significantly decreasing Choctaw dependence on federal funding.

Tribal Programs

One of the most important functions of any government is to improve the
social welfare of the nation by providing programs and services. Historically, American Indian tribal governments have tended to take very seriously this responsibility. Their ability to carry out this important mandate, however, has been crippled to varying extents at different points in
time by the U.S. government. Some tribes, such as the Fort Sill Apache
Tribe and the Navajo Nation, were literally imprisoned during parts of the
nineteenth and twentieth centuries and thus experienced almost no opportunity to pursue actions oriented toward improving the lives of their
people. In contrast, for three hundred years following their first sustained
contact with Europeans in the early 1700s, the Five "Civilized" Tribes
experienced comparatively few exogenously imposed constraints on their
ability to pursue social-welfare initiatives. This ended at the turn of the
twentieth century when the evisceration of the governments of the Five
"Civilized" Tribes ended their tribally controlled social-welfare programs
and initiated a seventy-year period during which they, like all tribes, experienced few opportunities to devise and implement tribal programs and
services. Indeed, from the turn of the twentieth century through the mid-
1970s, the Office of Indian Affairs, renamed the Bureau of Indian Affairs
in the 1940s, controlled the development and implementation of social-
welfare policies for Indians, policies that tended to define Indian social-
welfare "problems" and "solutions" in terms of the goal of social and cultural assimilation.

In 1975 there was a loosening of the BIA stranglehold on directing the
course of planned social change when the Indian Self-Determination and
Education Assistance Act (ISDEAA) was passed, an act that represented a
"fundamental philosophical change," according to Getches, Rosenfelt, and
Wilkinson (1979: 110). The crux of this change was simply the idea that

"tribal programs should be funded by the federal government, but the programs should be planned and administered by the tribes themselves" (pp. 110–11). Upon request, tribes received the funds for federal programs for Indians and administered these programs—which included health-care, education, and job-training programs—themselves. To help make this administratively possible, ISDEAA provided funds for tribes to build and expand their governments (Cohen 1982). Later, tribes were offered an alternative to contracting called compacting. Unlike contracting, which earmarks funds for specific purposes, compacting permits tribes to apportion their share of BIA and IHS program funds in ways that Indians themselves believe will best meet the needs and priorities of their societies.

Many Indians were suspicious of ISDEAA and other federal laws passed during the early years of what is now termed the "era of self-determination" of federal Indian policy (1961 to the present). For example, some Indians initially believed that ISDEAA was a veiled federal effort to terminate tribes. Others continue to question whether the devolution of control over tribal programs and services reflects U.S. recognition of tribal sovereignty and self-determination, as U.S. leaders claim; or whether the shift from federal control to contracting/compacting was simply a shift from one common government funding arrangement to another. Indian scholar Russell Barsh argues, "Peeling layers of misleading rhetoric from 'self-governance,' what emerges is simply a block-grant arrangement. Participating tribes have entered into contracts for annual lump-sum payments of their 'Indian' funding with the objective, in principle, of setting their own priorities for program spending" (1994: 58).

The Choctaws took only limited advantage of the opportunity to contract BIA and IHS programs during ISDEAA's first eight years (1975–83). This can be explained in part by the preoccupation of the Gardner administration with the chief's terminal illness (1975–78), followed by the preoccupation of the early Roberts administration with the passage of a new constitution (1978–83). In addition, the Choctaws, like many other tribes, were probably wary of participating in a federal initiative rumored to be a termination initiative. The Choctaws had defeated the effort to terminate their tribe only five years prior to the passage of ISDEAA, and interviews revealed that many Choctaws were suspicious of the first Choctaw-controlled programs of the twentieth century. Choctaw Housing Authority employee Gary Batton described the housing program's earliest years as plagued by the problem of locating willing participants, especially for mutual-help homes, which require individuals to allow home construction on at least one acre of land that they themselves own.

Choctaw Perry Thompson, who happens to be my councilperson and who, at the time of my research, had served many terms on the council, was one of several Choctaws who provided insight into initial Choctaw responses to the first major tribally controlled program of the twentieth century, the housing program. Thompson explained that when he was twenty-two, an "agent" arrived in the south-central part of the Choctaw Nation and "said that they were going to give the Choctaws 'Indian homes.'" Everyone in the area, Perry said, was "real scared. . . . . They were afraid their land was going to be taken. No one would get an Indian home. They said they didn't want 'em. . . . I was the only one who said, 'OK' . . . and I've been livin' in that home ever since!"

Eight years after the passage of ISDEAA, when it was clear that ISDEAA was not a veiled federal effort at tribal termination, and when it was clear that the Choctaws would realize their goal of rebuilding their tribal nation, the Choctaws began taking full advantage of their rights under ISDEAA to contract programs and expand the executive branch of their tribal government. For the Choctaws and many other tribes, contracting often meant not simply taking over programs but starting them, and funding for new programs was sought from a number of federal agencies, not simply from the BIA and IHS. Among the most important programs created by Chief Roberts and Assistant Chief Pyle during the mid-1980s were a vocational development program, which served one thousand Choctaws during its first decade, and a food distribution program, which by the mid-1990s was providing six thousand Choctaws with eighty pounds of food per month. Another early tribal program, the Head Start program, enjoyed great success under Choctaw tribal control: by the mid-1990s, eleven Head Start centers had been built, up from zero in 1978, and one thousand poor Choctaw children, many of whom attended these centers, had received car seats from the tribal government. In 1985 Choctaw participation in contracting federal Indian programs made the front page of tribal newspapers throughout Indian country. The Choctaws became the first tribe to contract full hospital administration from IHS when they took over the Indian hospital in Talihina (Faiman-Silva 1997). That year, the tribe also assumed control over IHS clinics at Hugo, Broken Bow, and McAlester. After 1983 Choctaw leaders made a priority of another program that predated the ratification of the new Choctaw constitution, the Choctaw housing program. Over the next twelve years, the tribal government built 825 new homes and provided rental assistance to hundreds of others.

The Choctaws' experience during the 1980s with creating new programs and contracting existing BIA and IHS programs was so positive that Chief Roberts, Assistant Chief Pyle, and other Choctaw tribal leaders soon began forging agreements with the federal government to compact their Indian funding. By 1991 the Choctaws were themselves administering twenty-one million dollars of federal program funding, and when I conducted my research, the tribe had compacted all BIA and IHS programs and services except one: the CDIB program (Roberts 1991). For reasons described earlier, tribal leaders still choose to use the BIA to verify the claims of CDIB applicants that they descend from individuals listed on the Dawes Rolls as Choctaw by Blood.

Contracting and compacting were critical in enabling the Choctaws, under the leadership of Chief Hollis Roberts, to expand their executive branch. With virtually each new program, new staff was added. New offices, new departments, and new divisions of the tribal bureaucracy emerged. By the early 1990s it had become clear that a second major source of tribal bureaucratic growth had emerged: tribal economic development, which will be addressed below, began generating comparatively large amounts of capital, capital that Chief Roberts, Assistant Chief Pyle, and other tribal leaders began using to further expand tribal programs and the tribal "state." By the mid-1990s when I was conducting my research, the tribal government was running between forty and fifty tribal programs, and the number of tribal employees had grown to 1,500. At that time, revenues from tribal businesses were providing 35 percent of the tribal government's operating funds (Faiman-Silva 1997).

In 1997 an event occurred that threatened to derail Choctaw nation building. On June 6, 1997, a federal court found Chief Roberts guilty of sexually abusing female tribal employees and sentenced him to eleven years in jail. As Choctaw chief since 1978, Roberts had been a primary architect of the new order. He had seized the opportunity to rebuild the tribal government, was primarily responsible for establishing the plethora of new tribal programs, and had designed and implemented the ambitious program of tribal economic development that will be outlined below. Chapter 4, which describes and analyzes the Choctaw tribal election of 1995, provides a detailed look at this man, one of the most important figures of twentieth-century Choctaw history, at the eve of his political career. Though Roberts was reelected in 1995 to a fourth term as

chief, when he was imprisoned two years later the future of Choctaw nation building seemed uncertain.

Roberts's imprisonment conferred the office of chief to forty-seven-
year-old Gregory E. Pyle. Pyle brought to the job fourteen years of experience as assistant chief; a combination of personal characteristics that
include integrity, intelligence, and forthrightness; and the experience of
having been born outside the Choctaw Nation (in California) and participating during his childhood in a pattern of circular migration between
California and the Choctaw Nation, an experience that helped him bridge
the divide, discussed at length in chapter 4, between absentees, that is,
Choctaws who live outside tribal boundaries, and Choctaws who reside
in the tribal homeland.

Chief Pyle accelerated the growth of social-welfare programs and initiatives by reorganizing the tribe's executive branch, investing millions
of dollars in profits from tribal businesses to build new institutions and
programs, and fighting to retain existing levels of federal program funding.
Pyle made health care a top priority. He built a new hospital, a residen-
tial rehabilitation center for female substance abusers, a diabetes clinic
and wellness center, and other health care facilities. He headed a comprehensive alcohol-and-drug-abuse recovery program and a program that
provided more than five thousand elders and disabled Choctaws with eye-
glasses, dentures, hearing aids, wheelchairs, walkers, crutches, and canes.
He greatly expanded the number of health care professionals employed by
the tribe. In the early 2000s he developed a program that provided med-
ications at a reduced price to Choctaws living anywhere in the United
States. In 2005 a recently retired Choctaw doctor who had practiced medicine in Oklahoma City spoke at length to me about his recent visit to
the new Choctaw hospital for medical care. "In all my years of medicine,
I have never seen a more efficient, more professional, and more outstanding health-care delivery system as the one that Chief Pyle and Gary Batton have built for our tribe," he said. "The whites need to learn a thing or
two from the Choctaws. The whites' health-care system is a mess!"

In a number of other areas, Pyle expanded existing programs and created new ones. For example, he extended housing benefits to Choctaws
living in all fifty states and increased tribal scholarship funds for Choctaw college students. In 2001 he opened the first of six independent living
communities, an innovative tribal social-welfare initiative that brings
together Choctaw elders who are able to live independently to reside in

planned communities. By 2006 Pyle and his government were offering as many as eighty tribal programs for the Choctaw people.

Pyle also continued the ambitious program of tribal economic development started by Roberts and summarized below. By the early 2000s, revenues from tribal businesses were funding 80 percent of the costs of tribal programs, and the number of tribal employees had grown to almost six thousand (Chief Gregory E. Pyle to enrolled Choctaws, April 3, 2003). Pyle's accomplishments, together with his tremendous popularity, helped him win the election for chief in 1999, the first election following Roberts's imprisonment. Pyle's accomplishments also contributed to the fact that in 2003 he ran unopposed for chief.

Tribal Economic Development

American Indian tribal governments are unique among American governments in that their self-defined responsibilities include not simply governing and improving the welfare of their people but also developing and managing their nations' resources for the benefit of their citizenries (Lopach, Brown, and Clow 1998). During the mid- to late nineteenth century when most reservations were created, the federal government seriously constrained the ability of most tribes to engage in tribal economic development. Tribal economic development creates more formal structures linking tribal governments to larger regional, national, and international economic structures and relations. This ran counter to the mid- to late-nineteenth-century federal goal of socially and economically isolating tribes, relocating them to and containing them on reservations, so as to promote white settlement and development in various parts of the United States, most notably in the American Southeast (through the removal of the Five "Civilized" Tribes) and the American West. Later, the political consequences of tribal economic development—which include the strengthening of tribal corporate structures and the promotion of tribal sovereignty—threatened federal efforts to weaken and control tribal governments. Weakening tribal governments was a federal priority during the era of allotment and assimilation (1887–1928) and the termination era (1945–61); controlling tribal governments was a prominent feature of federal efforts to reorganize tribes during the 1930s. From the turn of the twentieth century to the beginning of the era of self-determination, under conditions that were unfavorable to tribal economic development, only a handful of tribal governments owned and operated economic development enterprises.

The emergence of the era of self-determination of federal Indian policy in the early 1960s created more favorable conditions for tribal economic development. As part of the new federal policy of strengthening and expanding tribal governments, the BIA heavily promoted its role of providing technical assistance to tribal governments to build or expand tribally owned and operated businesses. The BIA began advising the Choctaws on tribal economic development at least as early as 1973 when Belvin was chief, but by 1978 when Roberts became chief, the Choctaws still had no income-producing tribal government businesses (Planning and Support Group, BIA 1973; Roberts 1991). Between the late 1970s and 1983, the Choctaws launched two major projects recommended by the BIA. Both were located in the Choctaw homeland, and both performed poorly. Until Chief Greg Pyle sold one of these businesses, the small resort of Arrowhead Lodge, the tribal government struggled to minimize the financial losses of this initiative, and after having invested $183,000 in the second project, a fiberglass boat factory, the tribe abandoned the business in 1983 (Faiman-Silva 1997).

The Choctaws experienced much more success with tribal economic development after they reestablished their tripartite tribal government in 1983 and greatly expanded other formal political structures. After 1983 Roberts established dozens of tribal businesses. Chief Pyle continued this work. Choctaw tribal businesses, which are summarized below, together generate several hundred million dollars a year. The value of the tribe's assets has increased from $14.5 million in 1981 to $144 million in 2002 (Faiman-Silva 1997; Choctaw Nation, May 18, 2002). At the end of the twentieth century, Faiman-Silva described Choctaw economic development as "stunningly successful" (1997: 211).

Roberts made tribal gaming an important part of the portfolio of Choctaw tribal businesses, despite the fact that, from the passage of the Indian Gaming Regulatory Act (IGRA) in 1988 to the enactment of the Oklahoma State-Tribal Gaming Act (OSTGA) in 2004, the highest level of gaming in which the Choctaws were lawfully permitted to engage was not full casino gambling (termed Class III gaming) but rather high-stakes bingo, pull tabs, and some electronic games (Class II gaming) as well as parimutuel betting. The first Choctaw high-stakes bingo palace, built the same year that IGRA was passed (1988), was a 28,000–square-foot facility that provided 140 jobs. It was the first tribal bingo facility to have a million-dollar winner, and it made a profit of one million dollars the year after it opened (Faiman-Silva 1997). By the mid-1990s, Roberts had built three other high-stakes bingo palaces and was providing free round-trip bus service between Dallas and the bingo palace in the tribe's capital in Durant. He and his staff had also begun using the advertising media of radio, billboards, television, and newspapers to promote Choctaw gaming.

At the turn of the twenty-first century, Chief Pyle expanded the tribe's gaming enterprises by purchasing a horse racing facility and by renaming the tribe's bingo palaces "casinos." In addition, in the mid-1990s Pyle helped transform the tribal gaming landscape in Oklahoma, bringing about a change that sharply and significantly increased gaming revenues for not simply the Choctaw Nation but also for Indian nations throughout Oklahoma. Together with the leaders of several other tribes, Chief Pyle helped lead the charge to pass Oklahoma State Question 712 (SQ 712) by a 59.5 percent vote in November of 2004. SQ 712 was a legislative referendum that enacted the OSTGA, an act that restored to Oklahoma's tribes some of the gaming rights of which they had been stripped by the passage of IGRA. OSTGA permitted Oklahoma tribes to upgrade their electronic machines to Vegas-style slot machines and to offer some Class III games, including blackjack and poker. The restoration of these rights to tribes—rights that resulted in what some observers term "Class II plus" tribal gaming in Oklahoma—was made contingent upon tribes negotiating compacts with Oklahoma, compacts that authorize Oklahoma to receive some of the proceeds from tribal gaming. Within a year of OSTGA's passage, twenty-four Oklahoma tribes had entered into gaming compacts with the state, and Oklahoma had announced that it expected to receive from tribal gaming approximately seventy million dollars each year. By October of 2005 the Choctaws were operating as many as seven tribal casinos, and tribal gaming had secured a place as the most lucrative type of Choctaw tribal business.[22]

After gaming, the most visible Choctaw tribal businesses are travel plazas. Most of the tribe's thirteen travel plazas offer gasoline, convenience stores, small restaurants, spaces for pull-tab gaming, and discount cigarettes. Roberts built travel plazas in more than a half-dozen Choctaw Nation communities. During the late 1990s and early 2000s, Pyle expanded this important source of tribal income and jobs. Choctaw travel plazas are discussed in depth in chapter 5, which explores, among other things, community experience and identity in a small town in which the Choctaw tribal government built a travel plaza during my research.

During the 1980s and 1990s, Roberts diversified the tribe's commercial enterprises and led the tribe into manufacturing. Shopping centers were acquired, and a large manufacturing plant built. Tribal shopping centers, which are located in the tribal homeland, had more than fifty tenants in the mid-1990s, including a Piggly Wiggly grocery store; five restaurants, including Dairy Queen and Subway; and two major department stores, JCPenney and Anthony's. In the south-central part of the Choctaw Nation, Roberts built a large manufacturing plant, which he named Choctaw Nation Finishing Company. Under a contract with Raytheon, a contractor for the U.S. Department of Defense, the Choctaws began making airfoil assemblies of the Paveway missile, the guidance section and the airfoil container for the Paveway, the 373 container as part of the Paveway project, and the Joint Stand Off Weapon (JSOW) containers.

With the creation of the Choctaw Manufacturing and Development Corporation (CMDC), Chief Pyle increased Choctaw tribal involvement in manufacturing. He also gave priority to Choctaw tribal participation in the service economy. For example, by the late 1990s the tribe was running a personnel consulting firm. This firm has done business in Guam, Turkey, Japan, Korea, Singapore, England, Italy, Germany, and Portugal.

As mentioned above, Chief Pyle has funneled a significant portion of the funds generated through tribal economic development into programs that improve the welfare of the Choctaw people. Improvements in the Choctaw Nation infrastructure have been an important part of this larger goal. In comparing the Choctaw Nation of the early 1980s (when she conducted her fieldwork) to the Choctaw Nation of the late 1990s, Faiman-Silva mentions infrastructural improvements as one of the most striking differences between the two eras. "Little more than a decade ago, the Choctaw timber region seemed more remote," she writes. "Many Choctaws were without automobiles and telephones. Nation towns such as Bethel, Smithville and Honobia appear more spiffy: dirt roads have been paved, bridges widened and rebuilt; modern Choctaw community centers stand proudly in every Choctaw county; post offices and gas stations have been modernized" (1997: 116).

A less visible difference between the early 1980s and the turn of the twenty-first century are the increased opportunities for Choctaw cultural expression, opportunities created in part by funds from tribal economic development. Under Chief Pyle, these opportunities have increased dramatically. Pyle invested a comparatively large amount of funds and staff in initiatives to teach and preserve the Choctaw language, for example. Due in large part to these efforts, by 2003 the Choctaw language had become an accredited course in as many as twenty-seven public schools, and Choctaws living anywhere in the world are able to receive instruction in the Choctaw language through tribally run Internet courses (Chief Gregory E. Pyle to enrolled Choctaws, April 3, 2003; see also Noley 2001: xii; Kidwell 2004). The University of Oklahoma, which offers courses in the Choctaw language at three different levels, has emerged as an important partner in helping the Choctaws increase the number of Choctaw language speakers and enhance Choctaw appreciation of the tribe's language, culture, and history. Choctaw language initiatives provide one of many examples of the ways tribal empowerment has continued beyond the period of tribal rebuilding.

Conclusion

Several things are striking about this story of how the Choctaw tribe was rebuilt. First, Choctaw nation building was a large-scale social movement that began as an act of resistance against the efforts of a more powerful nation to complete the process of absorbing a dependent tribal society. Exogenous threats to a society's continued existence, especially to societies that are less powerful than those that are threatening their survival, provide fertile conditions for political mobilization by members of the imperiled societies. In the Choctaw case, as in other cases, the threats being made to the survival of their relatively disempowered society also provided fertile conditions for the emergence of nationalism (see esp. Alfred 1995). As was seen, Choctaw nationalism served as a powerful tool of resistance for the youth organizers, structuring the way they defended their society against the threat of tribal termination and facilitating their efforts to mobilize support for tribal rebuilding among members of their society.

A second thing that is striking about this story is the production site for this nationalism. The Choctaw nationalism that fueled tribal rebuilding emerged not within the Choctaw tribal homeland but rather in an urban area almost ninety miles away. Urban migrants are only sometimes characterized as maintaining close ties with the rural areas from which they hail and are only rarely found to exercise political leadership in the communities they have left, especially during the period when they are away. Moreover, the urbanites who initiated the movement to rebuild the Choctaw tribe were neither powerful nor wealthy. Their resources—financially, educationally, and politically—were few. Ironically, the geographic distance of these activists from the tribal homeland may have helped make possible the leadership role they assumed in the Choctaw Nation during 1969–71 and again in 1974–75. As was seen, in the late 1960s the adoption of the goal of tribal rebuilding meant challenging the tribe's formal political leadership and alienating, in particular, Chief Harry Belvin, the man who, as one consultant put it, "really called the shots in southeastern Oklahoma." Because the urban activists were positioned outside Belvin's political turf, the risks they incurred in spearheading the movement to stop tribal termination—and especially the two movements in the 1970s to depose Belvin—were likely far fewer than those that their southeastern Oklahoma counterparts would have incurred. In other circumstances, the location of such grassroots leaders outside of the tribal homeland may have created problems of acquiring legitimacy. But in this story, the urban activists were thoroughly integrated into networks of kin that extended into and encompassed the rural homeland; they offered a vision of the future that their rural counterparts found powerful and compelling; their movement was well organized; and they were assisted by Indian organizations that promoted American Indian pride and tribal empowerment, such as LaDonna Harris's Oklahomans for Indian Opportunity. In addition, as the geographic boundaries of the Choctaw Nation had not yet been reestablished, it is possible that during the periods when Oklahoma City Choctaws provided the most leadership for our tribe—the late 1960s and parts of the 1970s—they were not considered by their rural counterparts as even positioned outside the Choctaw Nation.

A third striking feature of this story is the piecemeal fashion in which tribal structures were rebuilt. The Choctaw Nation reemerged part by part over a period of several decades. Year after year, work continued on the building of different parts, parts that were the work of Belvin, Gardner, Roberts, Pyle, tribal council members, and others. In form and function, the parts that Choctaws built and used to reconstruct our nation were diverse, and in number, the parts that they considered essential were many. They included, for example, the creation of tribal programs, the expansion of the tribe's land base, the reinstitution of the legislative and judicial branches of the tribal government, the reinstitution of criteria for tribal citizenship, the expansion of the tribal bureaucracy, the building of tribal community centers, the refashioning of the tribal newspaper, and the building of dozens of tribal businesses. For the Choctaws, nation building unfolded through a series of two-step processes—the building of parts, then the cobbling together of these parts. The product of these processes belies the piecemeal nature of the reconstruction. The product was and is a complex and well-integrated institutional arrangement.

The following chapters explore the social, political, and economic consequences of these transformations and what it means to be Choctaw in the context of the new political order. The next chapter begins this exploration with an ethnographic look at two sets of relations that are helping structure the new order: the relations of citizenship that bind together enrolled Choctaws, and the relations of citizenship that link enrolled Choctaws to the Choctaw tribal government. By describing and analyzing a tribal election, I provide a view of how Choctaws are negotiating and experiencing these reinstituted relations of citizenship and how these relations are helping define what it means to be Choctaw at the turn of the twenty-first century.

4. "Tomorrow Is the Day YOU Are Chief"

Leaders, Citizens, and Political Groups in the 1995 Election

"Tomorrow is the day YOU are chief!" roared Hollis Roberts to a crowd of about four hundred on the eve of the 1995 Choctaw tribal election. "YOU call the shots! Do you want your friends and neighbors lifted up? Or, do you want to slip back and go by the wayside? . . . Do you want to continue to advance? Or do you want to slide back to the last seventy years?"

The audience, packed tightly into a newly refurbished auditorium in Talihina in the geographic center of the Choctaw Nation, sat quietly and nearly motionless during the election-eve speech of the graying fifty-two-year-old who had served as Choctaw chief for the past seventeen years. Under the lights, he looked visibly weary, perhaps even a bit discouraged, as he addressed the Choctaw people for what his opponents hoped would be the last time. Roberts was said to have confessed to one of his employees earlier that week that it had been a difficult campaign, one of the hardest of his political career. During the past several months, "the trash tellers," as he called them, had helped his opponents wage what a coalition of 131 female tribal employees had collectively described in a letter to the Choctaw people as a "mean-spirited," "slanderous," and "spiteful" campaign to "destroy" their "decent and honorable employer" who was "a dedicated family man" (Robinson, Ketchum, Easterwood et al. to enrolled Choctaws 1995). Yet it was not this "mudslinging," as Roberts and his employees had called it in a different letter to the Choctaw people, that had made this campaign Roberts's most difficult (Hollis E. Roberts to enrolled Choctaws, June 1995). It was the fact that less than a month before the election a federal grand jury had indicted the chief

on two counts of aggravated sexual abuse, five counts of abusive sexual contact, and one count of sexual abuse.[1] Almost two years after he
went on to win the 1995 election, Roberts was convicted on four of these
counts, forcing his resignation and beginning his eleven-year imprisonment.[2] Two years before his conviction, in the confines of an auditorium
packed with many of his most ardent supporters, Roberts could almost
maintain the illusion that these charges were not looming large over his
campaign as well as his person. Before he rose to speak that night in Talihina, eight leaders had addressed the crowd, one after another, to support his reelection. Among those selected for these talks were Assistant
Chief Greg Pyle, two members of the tribal council, the mayor of Talihina (who happened to be a former tribal council member), and a former
lieutenant governor of Oklahoma. Through these endorsements, Roberts
hoped to persuade Choctaw voters that there was a consensus of support
for his reelection not only among the rest of the elected Choctaw tribal
leadership but also among the leaders of Oklahoma state and town governments. Roberts knew that many of his constituents believed that the
support of both Indian and non-Indian leaders is critical to the ability of
a Choctaw chief to get things done.

Events such as the Talihina campaign rally provide opportunities to examine who and what the Choctaws are in the late twentieth and early
twenty-first centuries. The political rhetoric deployed by the chief and
others during this event invokes Choctaw ideas as to what constitutes a
"strong" tribe, by what measures we feel that the state of our tribal nation
should be evaluated, the character of our leaders' relationships with our
people, and Choctaw models of the tribe's citizenry. In addition, events
such as the Talihina rally provide forums for the Choctaw citizenry to respond informally to the rhetoric of tribal politicians. Citizens have conversations in parking lots before or after such events, make quips during
leaders' speeches, and issue invitations to friends of friends—or even to
strangers—to attend, for example, the next meeting of a group of Choctaws of one-quarter or more Choctaw "blood quantum."

At the base of the structures through which Choctaws are expressing and negotiating their ideas about the past, present, and future of our
tribe and the meanings of being Choctaw are the reinstituted relations of
citizenship that bind together enrolled Choctaws and that formally link
them to the Choctaw tribal government. Like many other polities that

are undergoing or have recently undergone political centralization, the Choctaws have been attempting to forge a sense of national unity from a diverse assemblage of people, relationships, and social arrangements, the bases of which are briefly addressed below. The reinstituted relations of tribal citizenship are a critical part of this process. Through events such as a tribal election, one of the most important events through which Choctaws practice their citizenship, Choctaws have created certain expectations about, for example, how candidates for tribal office should present themselves to the Choctaw electorate. At the same time, the new regularities that are being produced by the new order are also producing new divisions and articulations of difference. Both types of processes are evident in the material presented in this chapter, which places the spotlight on the ways by which Choctaws are negotiating and experiencing their citizenship. The durability of the products of these processes of homogenization and pluralization, however, cannot be assumed. When commonalities and differences are created, as they are during a tribal election, they may or may not have staying power. Choctaw diversity, in particular, appears to be remarkably resistant to the processes of ordering and categorization that shape Choctaw society during an election.

Two aspects of the 1995 Choctaw tribal election are critically examined in this chapter. The first, which I address in the course of the second, explores the content and character of the campaigns of the two frontrunners in the race for chief, Hollis Roberts and Doug Dry. What arguments did each leader make as to why he and not his opponent should be chief? What messages did they deliver; what campaign promises did they make? What internal tribal problems did they identify? As regards their campaign strategies, how did they categorize the Choctaw electorate, and what categories of voters did each target for votes? Leaders often show a deep knowledge of the political bodies they head, particularly if the process by which they attain their position requires that they mobilize and gain the support of a significant portion of the membership of their group. Describing and analyzing the actions and rhetoric of the leading candidates in a fight for our tribe's highest office thus brings to the fore much about what it means to be Choctaw at the turn of the twenty-first century. Among other things, the campaigns of these politicians help expose some of the current issues in our tribe, how we Choctaws see ourselves, what critiques we have of our tribe, what we see as our strengths, and what ideas we have about the kind of tribe we want to be in the twenty-first century.

Analysts of any political contest often find the actions and rhetoric of the candidates for a leadership position to be far less elusive than the second major part of any such contest: the responses of the people. Especially during democratic elections, the biggest questions for analysts often center on how voters are responding to the political campaigns of hopeful leaders. Which candidate is generating the most support? Have voters been mobilizing in large numbers? If so, who is mobilizing, and why are they mobilizing? Where on the political landscape are the areas of most intense political activity? Citizen responses to Roberts and Dry, as well as to the election itself, are this chapter's primary focus. It is in the context of this discussion that I address the actions and rhetoric of Roberts and Dry.

Choctaw responses to the tribal elections of the new order help expose something about the nature of our tribe that becomes clear only after spending time among Choctaws before, during, and after tribal elections. Before and after elections, Choctaw experience often defies attempts at meaningful generalization. Few regularities or patterns characterize our citizenry, and our diversity stands out as one of our tribe's most striking features. The bases for this diversity are many. For example, the skin color of Choctaws ranges from deep black to a very light white. In *The Roads of My Relations*, a collection of stories by Choctaw scholar Devon Mihesuah, Reggie, a white anthropologist among the late-twentieth-century Oklahoma Choctaws, expresses surprise "at how different the [Choctaw] people looked from each other" in skin color (2000: 166). In addition, great differences in wealth and lifestyle separate our tribe. Some of us are most often found in Italian suits, wearing expensive jewelry and sporting freshly manicured nails. Others of us spend most of our waking hours in T-shirts, with baseball caps or cowboy hats atop our heads. A third basis of our diversity is the diversity of the ways we make a living, a diversity I also encountered every day of my fieldwork (see also Howe's [2001] treatment of Choctaw occupational diversity). Choctaws are ranchers, bankers, police officers, preachers, post office workers, nurses, theater owners, doctors, farmers, and electricians. They run general stores, work in factories, build fences for a living, and own bait-and-tackle shops. Some tribal members are schoolteachers; others are office workers, beauticians, Wal-Mart managers, or bouncers at bars and nightclubs. One

Choctaw family owns an outdoor furniture shop. Many early-twenty-first-century American Indian tribes are similarly diverse. "Perhaps at no other time in our collective histories," notes legal scholar and former attorney general of the Seneca Nation Robert Porter, "are our [tribal] nations comprised of so many different kinds of people, different cultural foundations, and different political philosophies" (1998: 88).

During the Choctaw electoral season, the regularities and patterns that, prior to the electoral season, were so striking for their absence began to emerge. Constructions that divided the Choctaw citizenry into three sets of binary categories began increasingly to color public discourse, especially when the challenger in the race for chief, Doug Dry, began to deploy these constructions strategically in his rhetoric. These categories were tribal employee/non–tribal employee; resident/absentee; and quarter-or-more/under-a-quarter. The first opposition, tribal employee/non–tribal employee, divided the citizenry into those who were employed by the tribe (approximately 1,500 at the time) and their nuclear families, on the one hand, and all other Choctaws, on the other. As will be seen, this division became politically salient only after the challenger and his supporters publicly identified tribal employees as a coalition that was playing a critical role in the election. The second opposition divided the tribal citizenry into residents, who are Choctaws who live inside tribal boundaries (about 17 percent of the citizenry), and absentees, who are Choctaws who live outside the Choctaw Nation.[3] Though Choctaws have used residence, whether defined by the *okla* (town) or district, as a basis for political division since at least the 1700s, it was not until the massive urban migrations of the early twentieth century and the emergence of relatively powerful coalitions of urban Choctaws in the 1960s that residence with respect to the tribal "national" boundary accrued salience as a means of making and remaking Choctaw social and political categories.

The third binary opposition that became salient during the 1995 electoral season was a divide between "quarter-or-mores," who are Choctaws with at least one-quarter Choctaw blood quantum (about 25 percent of the citizenry), and "under-a-quarters," who are Choctaws with under one-quarter Choctaw blood quantum. Like residence, blood quantum has received near constant use among the Choctaws for almost two centuries as a means of expressing and constructing internal differences and commonalities. Despite the durability of blood quantum and residence as tools for building alliances, mobilizing large portions of the citizenry, and constructing Choctaw identity, the meanings assigned to the social categories they generate, the contexts in which these categories become the most salient, the specific placement of the boundaries that create such categories, and indeed the categories themselves historically have not been durable. The materials I present in this chapter about these divisions are thus expressions of a particular historical moment.

During the electoral season, these three sets of binary oppositions informed the meanings of and/or themselves helped create organized groups of Choctaw citizens. Some of these groups played an active role in the election. I discuss three at length in this chapter: (1) the coalition of tribal employees mentioned above; (2) an organized group of absentees who called themselves OK Choctaw Tribal Alliance; and (3) two sister organizations comprised of quarter-or-mores, Choctaws for Democracy and Native Women for Justice. These and other groups who were politically active during the electoral season tended to be contingent alliances. Politically integrated and in some cases centralized, they were critical in helping recast the Choctaw citizenry from a mass of voters that in the months prior to the electoral season were not well differentiated to an entity that during the electoral season appeared to be well ordered by crosscutting divisions.

My status as a Choctaw probably did not significantly affect my inquiry into the actions and rhetoric of Roberts and Dry, both of whom were eager to speak with non-Choctaws about their message, campaign promises, and, especially in the case of Dry, their critique of the Choctaw tribal government. Both politicians, for example, welcomed the attention of non-Choctaw reporters, especially reporters from local television stations and newspapers. My status as a Choctaw greatly facilitated my examination of the responses of the Choctaw electorate to the candidates and to the election as a whole. Many Choctaws perceive the presence of non-Choctaws at election-related events, even public ones, as intrusive. Anthropologist Sandra Faiman-Silva (1984), for example, reported that during her fieldwork Choctaws instructed her to stay out of tribal politics. My status as a Choctaw also complicated my efforts. There were only about 35,000 Choctaws who registered to vote in the 1995 tribal election (Roberts 1995; *Oklahoman*, June 3, 1995). Only about 16,000 actually voted (Choctaw Nation, July 8, 1995). Given these small numbers, organizers tended to treat each vote, including my vote, as critical. Daily

I was encouraged to vote for one or the other candidate, and daily I was pressured to disclose my choice for chief. Each day I refrained from stating my position on the issues and the candidates. This was made possible by the fact that my family did not support a single candidate for chief. Some of my relatives were staunch Roberts supporters; others thought his opponent should be our next chief. Although my fence-sitting took a personal toll, it enabled me to interact with members of several different Choctaw political groups and thus to better examine the nature and existence of these groups.[4]

I begin by identifying and describing three social facts about tribal politics in Indian country in order to help situate my material in the larger context of the political realities that characterize American Indian tribes in the early twenty-first century. The first is that tribal politics are something about which tribal citizenries tend to care deeply. The second is that tribal politics often involves the heavy use of non-Indian forms by Indian citizenries. Indians have imported from the larger American society particular campaign practices, for example. They have also imported some formal governmental structures whose origins are primarily Euro-American. In most cases, Indians have transformed and in other ways made these practices and structures their own. A third social fact is that internal tribal divisions tend to be critical to an understanding of American Indian political life. Whether based on age, blood quantum, kinship, religion, or other characteristics, the groups that form within tribal citizenries are principal sites for the development and elaboration of, among other things, critiques of the past, prescriptions for the future, arguments about identity, and ideas about the meaning of nationhood.

After this discussion, I identify some general features of contemporary Choctaw political groups and informal tribal political organization in the new order. I then use my ethnographic data to illustrate these features and provide detailed descriptions of the actions, perspectives, and rhetoric of the members of different groups. I discuss the tribal-employee group first. I then turn to the absentee group. I close with the quarter-or-more group. Broadly traversing the Choctaw political landscape during my discussion of different Choctaw political groups, one of my primary goals is to provide an on-the-ground view of the assemblage of different perspectives, political views, and personal backgrounds that characterize the contemporary Choctaw tribe.

My choice to broadly cover the Choctaw political landscape required that I address some features of Choctaw elections and Choctaw politics less fully than I would have liked. One such feature involves kinship; another, blood quantum. For example, I discuss the ways kinship informed the political mobilization of each group. In so doing, I shed some light on the role of kinship in Choctaw politics and political mobilization. There is much more about this role, however, that can and should be explored in future studies. The same is true of issues of blood quantum. Such issues are a part of my descriptions of each of the three groups and are heavily emphasized in my descriptions of the quarter-or-more group. My descriptions, however, expose only the first few layers of meaning that different categories of living Choctaws have been attaching to blood quantum at the turn of the twenty-first century.

Tribal Politics in Indian Country: Framing the Choctaw Case

American Indians tend to be keenly interested in tribal politics, a social fact that from the outset informed my decision to explore a tribal election in this book. Among Choctaws, as among other Indians, conversations often revolve around tribal politics, especially during elections, "the focal events in the democratic process" for most tribes (Meredith 1993: 68). "Whites call [successful elections] 'political victories,'" notes Choctaw Le-Anne Howe in her novel *Shell Shaker*, "but it is so much more in Indian politics" (2001: 21). Recently the U.S. Senate Committee on Indian Affairs estimated the rate of voter turnout in tribal elections, a key indicator of Indian interest in tribal politics, to be as high as 85 percent (Wilkins 2002a). In 1994, 86 percent of the eligible voters of the Chippewa-Cree tribe of Rocky Boy's Indian reservation voted (Lopach et al. 1998), and, in 2001, 87 percent of Florida Seminoles voted (Cattelino 2004). Lopach et al. (1998) reported a 70 percent turnout for an election of the Fort Peck Assiniboine and Sioux Tribes, and Navajos, Lumbee political scientist David Wilkins (2002b) points out, historically have voted at a higher rate in tribal elections than have non-Indians in non-Indian American elections. Choctaw voter turnout in tribal elections tends to be lower than that of many other tribes. In the tribal elections of 1995, 46 percent of eligible Choctaws voted (Roberts 1995; *Oklahoman*, June 3, 1995; Choctaw Nation, July 8, 1995). It is not clear why more Choctaws do not vote in tribal elections, especially given that many Choctaws describe our people as having a very high interest in tribal politics.

American Indians vote at a much lower rate in non-Indian American elections than they do in tribal elections, which probably reflects not simply anti-Indian sentiment at many polling places but also greater Indian interest in tribal elections relative to non-Indian American ones. While 86 percent of Chippewa-Cree tribal members voted in the 1994 election on Rocky Boy's reservation, for example, only 20 percent voted in non-Indian elections in 1992 (Lopach et al. 1998). Similarly, while 64 percent of Indians in Nevada told the Inter-tribal Council of Nevada that they voted in tribal elections, less than 40 percent of the same respondents said that they voted in non-Indian national, state, and local elections (Rusco 1973). Nationwide, Indian voter participation in federal elections is said to be about 20 percent (Wilkins 2002a). How that compares to Choctaw voting rates in federal elections is unclear. Anecdotal evidence that I collected during my fieldwork suggested that Choctaws were at least as interested in the elections of the larger, non-Indian society as were non-Indian Oklahomans. It also suggested that Choctaw political expression in non-Indian political contests reflects an important social fact that comprises part of the background for understanding Choctaw political perspectives: the Choctaw homeland is a Democratic stronghold in a state that has voted Republican in nine out of ten presidential elections between 1960 and 1996 (Hardt 1998a, 1998b).[5]

Throughout Indian country, tribal politicking and the tribal political process take place in political (and often social) arenas that almost without exception are sharply differentiated from those of the larger, non-Indian society. Within these tribal political spheres, it is important to note that for various reasons tribal political practices and processes often closely resemble those of the larger, non-Indian society. "I campaign the same way as any other [American] politician does that's in a political battle," chairman of the Rosebud Sioux tribe Cato Valandra stated in the late 1960s (Cash and Hoover 1971: 171). He explained, "We form our committees, we have our people in the various districts who make periodic reports to us. We'll have a lot of people in this afternoon who see how things are [in the different communities]. You've got to have your people who are sympathetic to your administration working for you. And talking and the whole bit" (p. 71).

Multiple-term tribal chairman Norman Hollow of the Fort Peck Assiniboine and Sioux Tribes described campaign practices on his reservation in similar terms (Lopach et al. 1998). He organized campaign rallies, potluck dinners, and occasions for speeches during tribal electoral seasons, he said. He also purchased radio spots for himself. Among the Seminole tribe of Florida, politicking for tribal elections is "done more by background talk than big campaigning," but "huge all-reservation, candidate-hosted cookouts," a campaign practice in which most non-Indian American politicians also engage, are virtually required for those making serious bids for tribal office (Kersey 1996: 119). In an ethnography about an Athabaskan village in Alaska, Phyllis Fast (2002) mentions a runoff election for chief. The winner utilized a common non-Indian American campaign practice in his successful bid for tribal office: he made door-to-door campaign stops. On the Wind River reservation in Montana, the Northern Arapahos, Fowler notes, "have readily accepted the electoral process." Among other things, the elected tribal business council is "fully institutionalized" and accepted (Fowler 1982: 1).

It should not be assumed that these newer forms always exist alongside older, pre-Columbian forms. Instead, as Porter (1998) and Wilkins (2002b) suggest, in many parts of Indian country political practices and forms that have been imported from the larger non-Indian society have become so entrenched that prior practices and forms, if they continue to exist at all, are sometimes virtually unrecognizable as such. This political reality is patent in my descriptions of the 1995 Choctaw tribal election. Here the observations that Porter and Wilkins make about selected tribes resonate with my observations about and knowledge of my own tribe. "In too many indigenous nations [in the United States]," Porter writes, "the most obvious and well-known governing tradition is not the tribal one, but the American one" (1998: 94). "We have too many members," he continues, "who can only conceive of life as it is portrayed by American society" (pp. 98–99). Focusing his comments on the Navajo, Wilkins points to similar developments and phenomena. "The Navajo people," he observes, "have witnessed the executive and legislative branches of their government, and the judicial to a lesser extent, assume the functions, the institutions, the technologies, the politics and in some respects, even the goals of the larger society" (2002b: 94).

The most striking non-Indian artifact in tribal political arenas is the formal institutional structure of tribal governments, the structure within which tribal politicking and informal tribal political action take place. Most tribal governments, including that of the Choctaws, are divided into executive, legislative, and judicial branches (File of Tribal Constitutions,

Office of Tribal Government Services, Bureau of Indian Affairs, Washington DC; O'Brien 1989; Cornell and Kalt 1991, 1992). Within this tripartite structure, tribes have exercised some institutional choice during the past three decades, with the result that patterned similarities and differences now characterize the governments of many tribes. Most tribes, for example, have chosen to emphasize the legislative branch "with the tribal council as the dominant element" (O'Brien 1989: 174) that in some cases even selects the executive (Wilkins 2002a).[6] The Choctaws, like the Pueblo of Isleta and the Northern Cheyenne Tribe, are among those tribes who emphasize the executive branch instead, a choice that has had important consequences (O'Brien 1989; Lopach et al. 1998).[7] To stress the executive, as Lopach et al. (1998) point out, is to place a higher value on strong leadership. The only tribal officer who is selected by the entire electorate, the Choctaw chief is granted a four-year term as opposed to tribal council members whose terms run two years.[8] These rules—which the Northern Cheyenne Tribe, among other tribes, have adopted—further strengthen the executive and centralize power among tribes privileging the executive branch (see Lopach et al. 1998). Some such tribes, including the Seminole Tribe of Florida, recently have been debating the advantages and disadvantages of concentrating power in the executive (Kersey 1996). The heavy emphasis that Choctaws place on strong leadership can be seen in the political actions and processes described in this chapter.

Internal divisions are an important feature of political landscapes throughout Indian country. There is much about American Indian subtribal groups, however, that is not well understood. In my examination of these groups among my own tribe, one imperative was to identify the bases for these internal divisions. As is reflected in my material, such bases helped define the identities and political positions of these groups. Important throughout Indian country, the bases for internal divisions among tribes vary widely, reflecting the histories and often the cultures of different tribes. Historically, class or rank has divided tribes such as the Kiowas (Richardson 1940), the Kwakiutl (Codere 1966), the Natchez (Swanton 1911), and the Tlingit (Lowie 1920), while it has been conspicuously absent among the "classless" or so-called "egalitarian" tribes (O'Brien 1989: xvi), many of whom are Plains tribes (see Lowie 1920). Among modern tribal nations who are composed of two or more contact-era tribes that were placed on the same reservation and rendered a single tribe legally, such as the Confederated Tribes of the Warm Springs Reservation and the

Cheyenne-Arapaho Tribes of Oklahoma, old tribal affiliations often inform contemporary divisions (R. White 1990; Berthrong 1992).

Tribes such as the Northern Arapaho make age a critical basis for sociopolitical division, reflecting the prior existence among this tribe of an age-grade system (Fowler 1982). The Crow Tribe's most salient political groups—which, like the political groups of many tribes, are fluid and flexible rather than fixed—are based to some extent on clans. During political campaigns, Crow politicians often bring clan "bosses" gifts of cigarettes, buckskin, wool blankets, or money, and they make promises of jobs to Crow voters on the basis of clan membership (Lopach et al. 1998). Political groups that are "as tightly defined as single families" periodically have controlled the tribal governments of the Blackfeet Tribe (p. 226) and Alaska Native villages (Dombrowski 2001). On the Fort Peck reservation, Sioux politicians have solicited votes from a politically salient group that is based on the common descent of its members from widows and orphans of men killed at the Battle of Little Big Horn (Lopach et al. 1998).

The Cherokee Nation of Oklahoma experiences a divide between two very durable politico-religious groups, the "Cherokee Baptists" and the Keetoowahs (Sturm 2002). Religion is also a basis for division at the Oglala Sioux tribe's Pine Ridge reservation, where peyotists and Christians have often squared off (Biolsi 1992; Crow Dog and Erdoes 1990). Finally, the best treatment to date of divisions based on religion in contemporary Native America—divisions that also implicate and involve conflicts over the meanings and relevance of "culture" and the basis for Native identity—is Kirk Dombrowski's *Against Culture: Development, Politics and Religion in Indian Alaska* (2001). In southeast Alaska Native villages, some of the most interesting and passionate intragroup conflicts revolve around divisions between Native members and Native nonmembers of Pentecostal churches.

Divisions based on residence, meaning community affiliation, have long histories in many parts of Indian country. Increasingly, such divisions are being made to include (or are being redefined entirely in terms of) "new" divisions between those who live "on" and those who live "off" reservations or tribal trust lands (see, for example, Miller 2001: 48–49; Dombrowski 2001). This political reality can be seen in the Choctaw material I present. Other schisms that in many but not all places have emerged only during the past half century are those that are based on opposing views of tribal economic development (see, for example, Bordewich 1996 and

Knack 2001). Porter explains, "In any given indigenous community, some individuals, if not most of the tribe, have decided that pursuing casino gambling and related forms of grand scale economic development is the most important priority of tribal government. . . . Fighting over money—how to make it and how to spend it—appears to have become the greatest direct source of tribal infighting" (1998: 78). Such fights are often about conflicting visions of the kind of space that tribal members want for their reservations or tribal homelands. It is not uncommon, for example, for some subtribal groups to oppose development because they prize the rural character of their reservation and the relative scarcity within its borders of non-Indian residents and tourists. Other subtribal groups promote development for the promise it offers to end the perceived social and economic isolation of their tribe and tribal homeland.

Some tribes experience what has been described as a "cultural gap" between "traditional" and "nontraditional" people (Porter 1998: 79), a "gap" that often forms the basis for social and political division (see esp. Alfred 1995 but also Neely 1991, and more generally Garroutte 2003). Divisions based on blood quantum, an important feature of Choctaw society, also appear to be relatively common (see, for example, Finger 1991). Perdue (2003) has rightly pointed out that our understanding of the nature, existence, and meanings of "bloodedness" and "blood" divisions in tribal nations has been obscured by non-Indian American ethnocentrism. For example, she points out that non-Indians have often assumed that Indians who are the product of intermarriage with whites have a weaker affiliation with their tribes than do full-bloods. Other critical perspectives on blood-quantum-based internal tribal divisions are beginning to emerge. Anthropologist Circe Sturm (2002), for example, explores the meanings, local definitions, and political significance of the categories of "mixed-blood" and "fuller blood" among the Oklahoma Cherokees, emphasizing among other things the constructedness of these and other categories among the second largest tribe in the United States.[9] Finally, mention should be made of a whole class of internal tribal divisions whose bases are far less ordered and rational than are those types of divisions outlined above. Choctaw Devon Mihesuah identifies divisions that are born from feelings of insecurity, "the desire to have what others possess," and perhaps even feelings of self-hatred as divisions that sometimes acquire great social and political import (2003: 58).

Choctaw Political Groups

As mentioned earlier, the primary bases of three Choctaw political groups that were among the most active during the 1995 electoral season were tribal employment (i.e., working for the tribal government), residence (specifically, residence outside the Choctaw homeland), and blood quantum (specifically, a blood quantum of at least one-quarter). These bases defined interests in particular electoral outcomes. The interest of tribal employees qua tribal employees, for example, was to keep the incumbent in office, an electoral position that political scientists characterize as a position that is oriented toward maintaining the status quo. The bases of Choctaw political groups also, as will be seen, provided platforms for group members to realize their commonalities, undertake collective action, and express the distinctive culture of their political group. The tribal-employee group, for example, placed a very high value on maintaining strong boundaries around their group. Members of the absentee group, who did not maintain such rigid boundaries, regularly swapped stories about their own migration from the Choctaw Nation or the migrations of their ancestors. Finally, about a half-dozen members of the quarter-or-more group told me they relished the opportunity that their group provided for them to spend time with other Choctaws who were phenotypically "Indian."

Interviews and participant-observation research with members of each group, together with my experiences and background as a Choctaw, revealed some general features of Choctaw political groups and informal tribal political organization, features that help define the character of the relations of citizenship that bind together enrolled Choctaws. First and most important, among the Choctaws, such groups tend to be fluid and flexible. Although there exist requirements for political-group membership, the memberships of these groups tend not to be fixed. Members experience few obligations to these groups, and the general pattern is that most members drift in and out of participation and even inclusion in these groups. Leadership tends to be based on charisma and other criteria that support a high degree of flexibility of leadership rather than on criteria that support the institutionalization of leadership as do, for example, the criteria of heredity or specialized knowledge. In Choctaw terms, charisma is based primarily on friendliness, wit, openness, and grit (or what Choctaws often describe as "being aggressive"). Generosity, or being "the greatest giver," as Howe describes it, is also important (2001: 22). Leaders of informal political groups tend to serve only for as long or as short as they and the membership of their group desires.

Some Choctaw political groups are centralized. Others have organizational structures that decentralize power and authority. The political groups that centralize power tend to be relatively durable; those in which power is more diffuse sometimes represent more temporary configurations of people. The quarter-or-more group described in this chapter, for example, did not exist as such until the 1995 electoral season. (The use of blood quantum as a basis for political groups, however, has a long history among the Choctaws.)

However durable may be the most durable of Choctaw political groups, a fundamental aspect of these groups is that they are contingent. They mobilize in response to certain events. When such events occur, Choctaw groups appear to rise up from the political landscape, morphing quickly into fairly well-organized groups from specific population bases that tend not to maintain well-defined separate social or political structures. At other times, depending upon the group, the group appears either to fully dismantle or to lose all but a core of its membership. It is not uncommon for Choctaw political groups simply to abandon hard-won claims that they have made on the political territory shortly after the conclusion of the event that prompted their mobilization.

The contingent nature of Choctaw political groups is part of the reason I chose to do fieldwork during a period that included a tribal election. Elections are events that frequently "awaken" dormant political groups, precipitate the emergence of new groups, and incite older sets of alliances to combine or recombine. In these political processes, Choctaw politicians play a critical role. In the election examined here, incumbent chief Hollis Roberts prompted the mobilization of a political group based on employment with the tribe. His challenger, Doug Dry, later exposed its existence, rendering it politically visible. At the same time, Dry promoted the mobilization of two overlapping political groups: one based on residence, and one based on blood quantum. Both were autonomous of the politician. That is, neither was structurally dependent upon the politician its members chose to support. This was not the case with the tribal-employee group, as will be seen in the following section; the ties that tribal employees maintained with their politician were constitutive of their group.

The Group Headed by Roberts

During the electoral season, incumbent chief Roberts mobilized a political group that was based on tribal employment, a group that then controlled the tribal government. Politically centralized and quite durable relative to other Choctaw political groups, this group had a history that spanned nearly two decades. Originating in Roberts's earliest campaigns for chief in the late 1970s, the group had experienced changes in the membership criteria on which it was based. Initially it had been based on family reputation or affiliation with several key communities in the south-central part of the Choctaw Nation, communities with which Roberts, its leader, had personal connections or kin ties. By the early 1990s, employment, specifically employment with the tribe, had become its primary basis. This had occurred as Roberts gradually had incorporated members of the group into the tribal government until the boundaries that defined tribal employees and their nuclear families had become the boundaries of the political group. Unlike the Wind River reservation where about 75 percent of the jobs held by Indians were tribally funded (Fowler 1982), only about 10 percent of Choctaws who were Choctaw Nation residents were tribal employees in the late 1990s. It is worth noting that at the time of the rapid expansion of the tribal bureaucracy, Roberts had privileged the hiring of light-skinned Choctaws, particularly those with blonde hair and blue eyes, with the result that appearance or phenotype had become an associated additional basis of the political group. In contrast, in the Cherokee Nation during the same period, candidates with stereotypically "Indian" phenotypes were preferred for tribal positions that involved extensive public interaction (Sturm 2002).[10]

The members of the Choctaw group that was based on tribal employment maintained very strong boundaries between themselves and most other Choctaws. Because of this, I expected to experience problems of access to this group. Fortunately, this was not the case. I had several relatives who worked for the tribe, including one who held a fairly powerful position. This opened many doors for me, as did the fact that one of my closest friends and primary consultants, Randy Bailey, was a tribal employee. Randy was very well liked by his colleagues, held a director's position within the tribal bureaucracy, and enjoyed social and political benefits—from which I, too, benefited—that derived from the fact that his brother was slated to become assistant chief if Roberts were to win the election but fail to escape conviction of the sex crimes for which he was charged. Most tribal employees were eager to answer my questions, maintain and develop friendships with me, and share information about their jobs, their workplace, their families, and their life experiences. I interacted with them in their offices, at break rooms, in the halls of tribal buildings, and at Roberts's all-staff meetings, which took place in the auditorium of the tribal headquarters in Durant. I also interacted with them in their homes, on the campaign trail, and at parties. One weekend I accompanied about a half-dozen of them on a wild boar hunt on tribal land in the south-central part of the Choctaw Nation.

On a day when three tribal employees independently had told me that the pressure of the upcoming election was taking a toll on them and their families, I had a long conversation with a man named Rich who had emerged as a popular secondary leader of Roberts's political group. A thirty-two-year-old father of three when I met him, Rich had accepted a position as one of the tribe's vocational counselors, he said, upon his return to the Choctaw Nation from Oklahoma City. In "the city," as he called it, he had spent four years managing several restaurants and bakeries. I later learned that his past experience as an urban resident set him apart from most tribal employees, comparatively few of whom had lived anywhere but in the Choctaw Nation. The fact that he had lived elsewhere appeared to have little impact on how Rich was regarded by his co-workers. Rich was glad to be back "home" in the Choctaw Nation, he told me, and he was especially grateful that he had gotten a job with the tribe.

A week earlier, I had watched Rich make an impromptu speech at an informal gathering of tribal employees in a sparsely decorated room at the rear of the tribal complex in Hugo. "Chief is innocent of the charges made against him!" he declared, raising his arms toward the ceiling. Referring to Roberts's indictments for sex crimes allegedly committed at the tribal complex in Durant, he articulated a view that later became the "official" tribal-employee response to this weakness in his employer's campaign. "The [sex crime] charges are politically motivated! The Choctaw people are smart enough to see this. The coincidences are too compelling: first, there's the timing of the charges, and second, there's the fact that the ladies [who accused the chief] hooked themselves up with the opposition!" Rich was aware that, to most effectively support Roberts—or, indeed, to support him at all—tribal employees needed to adopt some explanation of the charges against Roberts, preferably an explanation that was palatable to the women of the political group. More than 60 percent of all tribal employees, after all, were women. This was not the first action that I observed Rich taking to incite the mobilization of the political group to which he belonged. Following the lead of the group's leader, Roberts, several weeks earlier Rich had begun telling group members that all current tribal employees would be fired if Roberts did not win. He also began urging his colleagues to "prove their dedication to their chief and their tribe" by helping reelect Roberts.

Once mobilized, the political group that was based on tribal employment played an active role in the election. Reflecting the primary basis of the group, group members pursued actions oriented toward, in political science terms, maintaining the status quo, which was maintaining the existing leadership. Many worked tirelessly for Roberts's campaign, spending their evenings and weekends on the campaign trail. Together, they tacked hundreds of neon-yellow "Reelect Roberts" campaign signs on trees and telephone poles throughout the Choctaw Nation, acted as ushers and audience members for Roberts's campaign rallies, and canvassed shops, parks, and small-town neighborhoods for votes, frequently with spouses and children trailing behind. Informing the collective action they undertook was the fact that interactions between members of this political group historically were quite high and their relations, remarkably intimate. Tribal employees did not simply spend their work time together. They dated one another, partied together, attended their kids' basketball games, and went to "the lake" together. Gossip traveled very quickly among them. Tacit rules governed their interaction. Their knowledge of one another ran deep: they knew the likes and dislikes, the family histories, the friends and enemies, and even the size of the bank accounts of a surprisingly large number of their fellow group members. Sometimes, tribal employees mentioned that they were kin to another tribal employee (or to several of their fellow tribal employees), which suggested that kin ties played a role in shaping the content and character of their group. In addition, tribal employees often used the metaphor of a family to describe their group. One woman struggled to describe the experience of being a member of this group. Finally, she simply said: "All of us live, eat, sleep and breathe Choctaw Nation!" By "Choctaw Nation" she meant the tribal bureaucracy.

During the electoral season, one of Roberts's many challenges was to try to disguise the fact that this political group had been mobilized, that

it was indeed a political group, and that the people working on his campaign were an interest group. The Choctaws who were cheering at his
words during campaign rallies, campaigning door-to-door for him, writing letters of support for him, and in other ways making public expressions of support for him needed to be perceived not as representative of
a political group he headed but rather as "representative of the Choctaw
people as a whole," as Roberts himself put it. Additionally, his campaign
would best be served by rhetoric that attempted to stem the mobilization
of other political groups, especially a group that was based on "high Choctaw blood quantum." Several of Roberts's campaign advisors seemed to
think that a rhetoric that instead defined the citizenry as a tribal "mass,"
glossing over divisions between and among the Choctaw people, had the
best chance of offering Roberts success.

The rhetoric that Roberts delivered to crowds at the Talihina campaign rally and at other events reflected these decisions. Roberts decided
to base his campaign not on a set of issues, which might have divided the
membership, but rather on "his record as chief," a strategy that is common among non-Indian American incumbent politicians as well as Indian ones. This record demonstrated Roberts's "proven leadership and
reliability," one leader at the Talihina event argued. It showed that Roberts had built the tribe from "nothing," several others insisted at similar events. All over the tribal territory, as well as in cities that included
Oklahoma City and Dallas, Choctaw voters were reminded that Roberts
had taken office at a time when there were only eighty tribal employees,
no income-producing businesses, and a tribal net worth of $2.6 million
(Roberts 1995). In scarcely more than a decade and a half, Roberts had
built a Choctaw government of over 1,500 employees, established businesses that generated over 150 million dollars a year, and increased the
tribe's net worth to over $68 million (Roberts 1995; see chapter 3). In
type and tenor, Roberts's story, as well as his person, closely resembled
that of several other powerful, long-term American Indian chiefs of the
late twentieth and early twenty-first centuries. These include Peter Mc-
Donald of the Navajo Nation and Philip Martin of the Mississippi Band
of Choctaw Indians.

Roberts's story, distilled by his employees and campaign staff into a
few powerful sentences and punctuated by symbols of "progress" in the
manner of Arapahoe politicians (Fowler 1982), was the centerpiece of his
campaign, as it had been in several of his earlier campaigns for chief. To

many of Roberts's campaign workers and constituents, it was a story that bespoke such greatness in a leader that it virtually required that the Choctaw people reelect him. The story was delivered at each whistle stop on the campaign trail; outlined in the pamphlets that were handed out at rallies, county fairs, and other events; and detailed in the form letters that were mailed to all registered Choctaw voters. A vote for Roberts, the electorate was told, was a vote for a great statesman who was more than simply the architect of the Choctaw Nation. It was a vote for a man who, many argued, *was* the Choctaw Nation. Roberts was said to symbolize the potential of the Choctaw people. He was also said to embody the spirit of the Choctaw Nation.

With these actions and rhetoric, Roberts further developed and reinforced a radically different narrative of Choctaw nationalism than that which Charles Brown had developed. Brown had promoted a construction of the Choctaw Nation as timeless. To gain and regain election, Roberts, in contrast, promoted a narrative of Choctaw nationhood that foregrounded the event of a Choctaw rebirth and a leveling of the past, that defined the date of the nation's rebirth as the date a new constitution was ratified (1983), and that fashioned himself as virtually the sole creator of the new order. By the time I conducted my fieldwork, this narrative was remarkably well developed and had been disseminated widely among the tribal citizenry. Some Choctaw citizens called into question the extent to which the narrative, particularly with respect to Roberts's role in creating the new order, accurately represented recent Choctaw history; almost no one, however, did so publicly.

The argument that Choctaws should use tribal economic development as the principal measure by which to evaluate the state of their tribal nation was an argument that permitted Roberts to capitalize on his greatest strength. It was also an argument that made sense in a broader context. Indian tribal governments have "the explicit responsibility of developing and managing the tribe's resources for the benefit of the membership," a critical responsibility that, as Lopach et al. point out, other American governments simply do not have (1998: 9; see also chapter 3). When paired with economic realities that often include high levels of poverty in Indian nations, this political reality has given rise to what has been called a "politics of scarcity" in Indian country, a phenomenon in which overcoming scarcity is construed as the principal task of tribal leaders (Lopach et al. 1998; see also Wilkins 2002a). The tribal chairmanship of Florida Seminole Howard Tommie, for example, was termed "a great success" in part because "[Tommie] exploited every facet of the Indian self-determination movement and delivered the Seminoles to the brink of economic and political independence while guaranteeing their sovereignty" (Kersey 1993: 133). Hoping for a similar result, Southern Paiutes in the American Southwest recently have been breaking with tribal tradition by selecting leaders for the "youthful energy" and "skill at dealing with bureaucrats" (Knack 2001: 307). In the 1995 Choctaw tribal election, Roberts emphasized replacing symbols of poverty and deprivation (such as dilapidated homes and high rates of substance abuse) with symbols of prosperity and—in his words— "progress" (such as new roads, homes, jobs, and tribal businesses). In so doing, he refracted a larger rhetoric being used by tribal politicians across Indian country.

Given the popular appeal of this rhetoric in the Choctaw Nation, Roberts's primary opponent, Doug Dry, faced a formidable challenge. A forty-two-year-old lawyer, Doug Dry had served as a staff attorney for Oklahoma Indian Legal Services in Oklahoma City, a prosecutor for the Court of Indian Offenses for the Seminole Nation, and a prosecutor for the Muscogee Creek Nation (*Muscogee Daily Phoenix*, June 15, 1995). He was a major in the U.S. Marine Corps Reserve who had served in Desert Storm (Doug Dry to enrolled Choctaws, May 22, 1995). He was also a former football coach and a husband to a full-blood Cherokee (*Muscogee Daily Phoenix*, June 15, 1995; Dry 1995). Early in the electoral season Dry decided to focus public attention on Roberts's political group. He urged Choctaws who attended Roberts's campaign events not to conclude that the hundreds of campaign workers who surrounded the chief were his "true" supporters or even, as Dry put it, "your rank-and-file Choctaws." Most of these campaign workers, he correctly pointed out, were Roberts's employees, and they supported Roberts, Dry contended, only because the chief's re-election offered them the best chance of retaining their positions in the tribal government. To strengthen his argument, Dry distributed copies of the transcripts of the preliminary testimony of tribal employees who had brought charges of sexual abuse against Roberts. Roberts's employees, Dry and others alleged, were being sexually abused and assaulted by the man for whom they were now campaigning. "How could they be true Roberts supporters?" Dry asked voters. In this and other ways, Dry exposed tribal employees and their nuclear families as a political group. As a result, tribal employees were made politically visible, a transformation

to which the tribal citizenry responded by expressing greater mistrust of
those who worked for the tribe. This was significant, for in the 1990s the
Choctaw tribal government, like the Oklahoma Cherokee tribal government, was a "powerful ideological center," shaping tribal public opinion
to a very high degree (Sturm 2002: 106). Members of the tribal-employee
group responded to this distrust by expressing a stronger commitment
to Roberts and his campaign, trying to convince their fellow Choctaws
that their support for Roberts was "sincere" and "true," as one of them
put it. Through these moves and countermoves, the political group that
was based on tribal employment eventually emerged as one of the most
politically salient of the electoral season.

The day after a major fund-raiser had been held for the chief, I ambled
down the halls of the tribal complex in Durant looking for a program director with whom I was scheduled to meet. As she was not in her office,
I poked my head in office after office inquiring about her whereabouts.
Beneath my feet I noticed that the floors were slick. They were probably
polished last night, I thought. In each office I dispensed greetings or engaged in some friendly conversation with those whom I knew, and I introduced myself to those whom I had not yet met. Almost immediately
I was struck by the tidiness of the workers' desks. Paperwork was neatly
stacked. Framed pictures of friends and family had been dusted and arranged more neatly. Files had been put away. Astrid, a high-level tribal bureaucrat, must have demanded that the offices be cleaned up, I thought as
I made a mental note to ask one of my primary consultants, a tribal program director, if that had indeed been the case. Earlier that week it had
been pointed out during one of Roberts's all-staff meetings that I had attended that it was critical for tribal employees to "project an image of efficiency to the Choctaw people." In the Choctaw Nation, as on the Flathead reservation and elsewhere in Indian country, "accountability" and
"efficiency" have become important political values (see Lopach et al. 1998;
Bordewich 1996; Howe 2001). Perhaps Astrid thought that organizing
the principal spaces where tribal civil servants interacted with civilians
would help address this aspect of what was being described as an "image
problem." Interrupting my thoughts was a twenty-three-year-old secretary who engaged me in conversation as she slowly packed her belong-
ings in a white box emblazoned with the words "Program Expenditures."
This young woman, I remembered, had recently been told by a high-level
tribal bureaucrat to move to the basement offices of the complex, a place

that tribal employees referred to as "the dungeon." Because of this, many had said that they thought she was the next to be fired. I provided room for her to talk about the anxiety she must have felt at this informal demotion, but she declined my overtures. Instead, she launched into a monologue affirming her commitment to her political group in its key role in reelecting Roberts, a monologue practiced by many tribal employees during the preelection period. She had put in sixteen-hour days during the past several weeks working and campaigning for the chief, she said. Then, she explained: "I do it because the chief goes one step beyond for his employees in *every* way. We are loyal to the man because he is loyal to us . . . And, [because] he has made Choctaw Nation!"

From an adjoining office, a head poked around the corner. "You see, Chief's the best chief of all time," stated a woman with an unusually raspy voice. As she looked me straight in the eye, almost motionless, I wondered whether she was simply interested in the topic of conversation, eager to take a break from her work, or hungry to secure (from me) another vote for Roberts. Regardless, I encouraged her to continue, as my major objectives included exploring the perspectives of tribal employees toward their leader and inspecting expressions of the distinctive culture of this political group, especially its "moral imperatives" (Fowler 1982). Referring to the annual Choctaw Nation Labor Day Festival, this woman tried to convey the magnitude of Roberts's impact. "It's Labor Days," she began.[11] "That's how I can tell [Roberts] has changed things here. Twenty years ago, you'd see beat-up pickups and dirty kids. Now, everyone has nice cars, nice clothes. People come in $150,000 to $160,000 RVs [recreational vehicles] and camp. . . . And they don't even care if they take those $160,000 vehicles and run 'em through the mud."

Members of Roberts's political group daily deployed expressions of support, affection, respect, and admiration for their leader. I quickly learned that such expressions were part of the culture of their subtribal group and, more specifically, a moral imperative of their group. One evening as I was buying a Diet Coke at one of the tribal travel plazas, I began a conversation with a middle-aged woman named Pat behind the counter. Though I did not know this woman or her family, I was delighted to find that she was quite uninhibited in describing her experience as a tribal employee. At several points she even flouted the rules governing proper behavior of members of her political group. After providing several examples of her co-workers' words and deeds, she described the political group as a cult ruled by a system of intimidation, a system of intimidation that resembled that of the Nomee administration of the Crow Tribe, who had fired Crow civil servants who had not supported Nomee within a few days of the 1994 tribal elections (Lopach et al. 1998). "I just can't believe it!" Pat exclaimed about the way her co-workers related to Roberts. "He is just a man! But you would think he was Jesus Christ himself by how everyone here [within the political group] is about him!"

Older male members of this political group were much less strident in their expressions of devotion to Roberts than were the members of the group about whom Pat generalized. For example, on a hot day in June I found myself in the lobby of the Durant tribal complex sitting in a taupe-colored fold-up chair listening to William "Hoppy" Dennison, lead officer of the tribal police, tell stories about the race riots that had taken place in 1980 in his home town of Idabel.[12] Before long, talk turned to Roberts. "Hollis has done more for Choctaw Nation than all of the other chiefs put together," he began. "He's a strong politician and a smart—no, a brilliant—man." Hoppy's blue eyes sparkled as he spoke about a man who had become legendary in southeastern Oklahoma, a man for whom he had served as a tribal employee and as the lead tribal police officer for the past four years. Roberts was a man whom Hoppy had watched grow to adulthood. "Choctaw Nation had no money before Roberts. There was nothing. The people wanted a man in there who would *fight* for them." By "fight" he meant fight against non-Indians. This is similar to what Fowler identifies as an important Arapahoe criterion for evaluating elected tribal leaders, the ability "to resist intimidation and behave aggressively toward non-Indians" (1982: 241–42). Additionally, the Choctaws, like the Arapahoes, construct the leaders of their tribe as protectors. Roberts, for example, framed himself as a protector often during his campaign, many times pledging "to continue to fight for your rights and your sovereignty" (Hollis E. Roberts to Choctaw voters, June 7, 1995).

Defining the tribal police as the protectors of the protector, Hoppy continued the discussion about Roberts. "This is the first election he's had protection," he noted as he glanced at his Glock 19, nine-millimeter weapon and straightened up in his tribal police uniform. According to Howard Meredith, relations between tribal police and tribal members tend to be "relatively amicable," "except in cases where tribal police have become too closely identified with tribal politics" (1993: 85).[13] Hoppy, I noted to myself, seemed to be skating quite close to that line of identifying too closely with tribal politics. "Some of us [tribal police officers] go with him wherever he goes," he continued. Justifying his role as a member of what Kim Marlow Reed, the director of the Choctaw Nation Law Enforcement, termed "Roberts's secret service," Hoppy exclaimed rather solemnly and dramatically, "You know, anyone could kill and assassinate [the chief]! Hollis is a very powerful man, and lots would like to have his power." Foremost among those seeking Roberts's power, of course, was the man whose rhetoric is described in some detail in the following section, Roberts's principal challenger in the 1995 race for chief, Doug Dry.

The Group Based on Residence

From the comfort of a dark easy chair in his modest home in Oklahoma City, Choctaw elder Charles Brown, a longtime Roberts opponent and an important grassroots political leader during the late 1960s and 1970s (see chapter 3), described life in southeastern Oklahoma late in the electoral season. "Lots of people are scared [down there]," he said quietly and even rather ominously. "Threats are common. People are afraid they might be killed. One girl claims to have had her goats poisoned." Brown's words referenced the power and pervasiveness of rumor during Choctaw electoral seasons, the outlandishness of which is legendary in the Choctaw Nation and is an important theme in LeAnne Howe's novel *Shell Shaker* (2001). As Brown's wife busied herself by straightening the kitchen cabinets, Brown spoke at length about the 1995 election, the recent history of the Choctaw Nation, and the Roberts administration. Earlier, several of Doug Dry's campaign workers had solicited Brown's advice, as well as his help, in ousting Roberts. This year, however, Brown had resisted the urge to thoroughly disrupt his life for a tribal election, an urge to which he had given in many times before. His Oklahoma City restaurant, he explained, remained open throughout the electoral season.[14] Brown was one of several Choctaw leaders who, after having acquired leadership positions in different Choctaw political groups primarily on the basis of his charisma, had drifted in and out of such positions over the years.

Other Oklahoma City Choctaws did respond to the call for action that the event of the tribal election brought to the city in March of 1995, just one month before the bombing of the Alfred P. Murrah Federal Building on April 19. Given that absentees make up such a large percentage of the Choctaw citizenry (83 percent), and given that Choctaws living in Oklahoma City have a history of heavy political participation in tribal affairs, it probably came as no surprise to Roberts, Dry, or Choctaw tribal council members that Oklahoma City Choctaws mobilized for the election, and they mobilized early. This mobilization began with the efforts of at least several dozen Oklahoma City Choctaws. One such organizer was Leona, a fifty-eight-year-old full-blood woman who lived in a neighborhood on the edge of Oklahoma City. In addition to campaigning for the challenger, Doug Dry, a man whom she described as "our last hope," she began making frequent trips to the Choctaw Nation in order to attend the meetings of two groups that were comprised of Choctaws of one-quarter or more Choctaw blood quantum, groups that together formed a single political group that will be addressed later in this chapter.

At the same time, Leona became more active in a group called OK Choctaw Tribal Alliance (hereafter referred to as "the Alliance"), a group defined by the status of its members as Choctaws who live in Oklahoma City and, more broadly, who live outside the tribal territory. Since the early 1990s, the Alliance has maintained a membership of about two hundred, almost all of whom live in Oklahoma City. Membership in the group is fluid. Participation waxes and wanes in response to certain events. Such events include, for example, anti-Indian comments made by area public officials, a national drive to address problems in urban Indian health care, inaccurate depictions of the Five "Civilized" Tribes in the city's public schools, and Choctaw tribal elections. Just as kin ties played an important role in the mobilization of Oklahoma City Choctaws against efforts to terminate our tribe in the late 1960s (see chapter 3), kin ties play an important role in constituting the current membership of the Alliance, the most politically visible urban Choctaw group.

The Alliance is part of a larger network of organized groups of non-resident Choctaws. There are "significant populations" of Choctaws in Oklahoma City, Tulsa, San Francisco, Los Angeles, Dallas, and other cities (Noley 2001). In the late 1990s the number of enrolled Choctaws who lived outside the tribal territory numbered about 77,000. To the extent that these Choctaws even affiliate themselves with organized groups of nonresidents, the structures that connect these organized groups are structures in which power is decentralized and diffuse. In *Longing for Exile: Migration and the Making of a Translocal Community in Senegal, West Africa*, anthropologist Michael Lambert found that the structures and linkages that connect Jola residents in Senegal's capitol city of Dakar to the rural Jola homeland in the Casamance region several hundred miles to the south were so extensive that the Jola had become a translo-cal community. This theoretical model better describes the present-day Choctaw tribe, the other Five "Civilized" Tribes, and many other Amer-ican Indian tribes than do conventional models of Indian tribes as sedi-mented in tribal homelands. Lambert's ability to generate this model is no doubt connected to his experiences and identity as an enrolled mem-ber of the Eastern Band of Cherokee Indians of North Carolina.

During the 1995 electoral season, the downtown Oklahoma City head-quarters of the Alliance became an informal campaign base, and the Alli-ance membership became a pool from which organizers emerged. As the Alliance started to become a salient political group in the 1995 elections, I began investigating the political perspectives of its members and expres-sions of the distinctive culture of the group. Despite the fact that I had been reared in Oklahoma City, I experienced some difficulty researching the group. At several points when I spent time at Alliance headquarters, I felt that some members regarded me with suspicion, felt unable or un-willing to speak freely in my presence, and preferred that attention not be focused on their group. At other points, I felt that I enjoyed an accep-tance by virtue of my Oklahoma City upbringing that the group of tribal employees and the group that was based on a high Choctaw blood quan-tum could not give me simply because I am neither a tribal employee nor a high-blood-quantum Choctaw. I attended a few events that brought Al-liance members together, including meetings, dinners, and workshops the group sponsored. I also spent time with individual Alliance members, sometimes in Oklahoma City and frequently in the Choctaw Nation.

The Alliance draws members from two of four different categories of Choctaw urban migrants. Not included in the Alliance membership are Choctaws who have been reared in the city but have moved to the tribal homeland. Such migrants have been increasing in number among tribal citizenries throughout the United States (Porter 1998). Also missing from the Alliance are those who pursue a circular pattern of migration charac-terized by moving away from, then moving back to, the Choctaw Nation, and illustrated by Rich, the tribal employee whom I mentioned earlier in this chapter. Alliance members are Choctaws who either have migrated to the city themselves or are descended from one or more migrants. Jack-son (2002) found similar categories of migrants in an urban Indian orga-nization in a city in the American upper Midwest. Often, kin ties bind Choctaw migrants and descendants of migrants. Migrants often induce their descendants to join the Alliance. Less commonly, descendants of migrants induce their migrant ancestor to join the group.

Choctaws who had migrated to the city themselves were well represented in the Alliance at the time of my research. Almost all said that they did not see themselves ever returning to the Choctaw Nation, citing the lack of jobs in the Choctaw Nation, the lure of the city, and, for some, their elderly status, as reasons for remaining in the city. Several of the older Choctaws had attended institutions such as Goodland Indian School or Chilocco Indian School, and some spoke Choctaw. It was, in fact, not unusual to hear Choctaw spoken in the lobby, the large meeting room, or the back rooms of the Alliance headquarters.[15] It was, however, rare to hear Choctaw spoken during formal Alliance meetings, for almost all of the descendants of migrants, like the overwhelming majority of Oklahoma Choctaws, could not speak it (see chapter 3).[16] I cannot recall ever hearing a member of the tribal-employee group speaking Choctaw. I heard some members of the quarter-or-more group converse in the language, but, like the absentee group, during formal meetings the quarter-or-more group used only English.

Those in the absentee group who are descendants of migrants are diverse, especially in terms of their level of formal education, their degree of informal connection to the Choctaw Nation, and their depth of knowledge about the Choctaw people. In general, they were less consistent in their participation in Alliance activities and events than were migrants. Members of both categories, however, drifted in and out of participation in the group. Members of both categories were group leaders. Descendants of migrants tended to gain leadership positions on the basis of charisma. In contrast, migrants tended to acquire power and influence on the basis of a perception supported by many of the nonmigrant members of the group. This perception was that migrants were somehow more culturally authentic as Choctaws and as Indians because they had closer ties with the Choctaw homeland.[17] Throughout Indian country, the proximity of physical ties (especially residence) to (or on) the tribal homeland is important in constructions of cultural authenticity.

The mobilization of Alliance members was precipitated in large part by the rhetoric of the challenger in the race for chief, Doug Dry. Dry's decision to woo voters who lived outside the tribal boundaries, as will be seen, was the decisive event in this transformation. The core of Dry's message, however, was also well received by many Alliance members.

Dry claimed that Roberts had created nothing less than a dictatorship. Dry said that Roberts controlled every decision, defined every tribal policy, and punished with impunity all those who disagreed with him.[18] In a Doug Dry administration, the challenger continued, the Choctaw Nation would become "a democracy." Such a critique of the incumbent administration has been part of tribal politics and political campaigns on other U.S. reservations and tribal trust lands. On the Blackfeet reservation in the 1990s, for example, opponents responded to the public remarks of the tribal vice chairman by shouting, "This is a dictatorship!" (Lopach et al. 1998: 223), and on the Oneida reservation, one of the tribe's political groups has been seeking to, as they put it, "restore democracy" by ousting longtime tribal leader Ray Halbritter.[19] Such expressions may, however, be comparatively rare in Indian country. Indian leaders, it appears, tend to be criticized more often by their constituents for being "weak," "ineffective," and "incompetent" than for being dictatorial or overly powerful (see, for example, Porter 1998; Wilkins 2002a). The emphasis Choctaws have placed on the executive branch helps explain Dry's choice of rhetoric, an emphasis that has helped create conditions for the kind of concentration of power that characterizes tribal governance in the Choctaw Nation in the 1990s and 2000s.

As part of an effort to "restore democracy," as Dry put it, Dry proposed measures to increase citizen participation in the tribal government. He promised to link each of the then twelve tribal community centers electronically to the tribal council house in Tuskahoma, to the tribal headquarters in Durant, and to the secondary tribal complex in Hugo, bringing the tribal government, as he put it, "closer to the people" and encouraging citizen involvement and even local governance. Dry also promised to establish a Choctaw national library where any tribal member could inspect any nonconfidential tribal record and research tribal policy issues and initiatives. Such ideas of creating or in some cases reforming participatory processes within present tribal governmental structures are not uncommon in Indian country and, in fact, are part of a grassroots movement among Indians to create more openings for citizen involvement in tribal governing structures. Toward this end, some are focusing on reforms at the local or community level (Meredith 1993); others, such as the Comanche Nation and the Fort Peck Assiniboine and Sioux Tribes, have effected greater citizen participation by overhauling their constitutional schemes (Porter 1997; Lopach et al. 1998).

Many Alliance members focused on another promise Dry made. Dry promised to bring an end to what was described as "institutionalized discrimination" against two different categories of Choctaws: quarter-or-mores and absentees. By arguing that absentees, or Choctaws living outside the tribal territory, and quarter-or-mores had serious grievances against the current administration, Dry hoped to exploit vague but growing feelings of anger and resentment that some members of these two categories of Choctaws had begun feeling toward the incumbent chief and his administration. Toward this end, Dry validated many of their fears about the prejudices of tribal government leaders, fed their suspicions about Roberts's motives, and heightened their feelings of mistrust for the man who had enjoyed the kind of power, prestige, and access to tribal coffers that Roberts had during the past two decades. Dry did not try to convince these two categories of voters—the voters on which he concentrated his efforts—that Roberts's record as chief was unimpressive. Nor did he try to convince them that they or the Choctaw people as a whole should not feel gratitude toward or respect for Roberts and his many accomplishments. After all, even among these voters, Roberts often was described as a hero for, as some described it, "single-handedly building the tribe." Instead, Dry simply tried to convince them that the incumbent had targeted them for unequal treatment. These charges of discrimination were carefully listened to by many Choctaws, particularly, as will be seen, by quarter-or-mores. The charges that our tribe discriminates against quarter-or-mores are particularly interesting given the fact that our tribal constitution, passed in 1983, gives quarter-or-mores more political rights than it does under-a-quarters: our tribal constitution permits only quarter-or-mores to run for tribal chief or tribal council representative (see chapter 3).

While campaigning in Oklahoma City, Dallas, and other areas outside the Choctaw Nation, Dry provided two examples of discrimination against absentees. The first was the tribe's redistributive policies, policies that made only those who lived in the tribal territory eligible for most tribal programs and services. The second was absentees' lack of representation on the tribal council. Roberts had eliminated the two tribal council positions for absentees in the early 1980s, Dry told voters, and had since blocked all efforts to restore these positions. Dry announced that in a Doug Dry administration, residence would no longer govern the distribution of tribal resources, three positions for absentees would be added to the existing council, and in all other ways absentees would receive "equal treatment" at the hands of the Choctaw government (see also Dry 1995).

Many members of the absentee group that was based in Oklahoma City quickly lined up behind Dry when he began publicly airing his "pro-absentee" views. At least a half dozen began campaigning for Dry, and the Alliance headquarters became an informal center for Dry campaign activity. Unlike the membership of the political group that was based on tribal employment, however, Alliance members did not back a single candidate. Divided in their choice for chief and on other issues, the Alliance membership informally organized and reorganized several times during my research, producing a pattern of shifting political divisions and subdivisions. Sometimes new divisions experienced crises of leadership and further fragmentation; at other times, clarity, focus, and durability were found in new organizational forms. These structural changes were largely a consequence of interactions that took place at the Alliance headquarters.

One point of conflict was the group's headquarters itself, which was made up of two office buildings in downtown Oklahoma City. Roberts and the tribal council had purchased these buildings for the group the year prior to the election. During the electoral season, some group members expressed a fear that Roberts might "take away these buildings" if most of the group voted for Dry. One Alliance member raised this possibility at one of the group's monthly meetings. "We finally got this [the headquarters]," a man named Hoss exclaimed. As he shifted his legs up under the long fold-up table at which he was sitting, he gestured first at the walls of the room, then out toward the street. "And we [absentees] are trying to get more [services, benefits, etc.]. We just can't do it, and you know that, if we come out against Hollis!"

For a moment, the room fell silent. Then several people sighed in exasperation. Others signaled their disapproval with nonverbal gestures. I expected one of the many supporters of absentee rights (and of Dry) to counter Hoss's statement. Instead, Dan, a Roberts supporter, slowly rose up from his chair. Objecting to the specific vision of the future that Hoss had invoked, he said softly but decisively that he thought the tribal government should be giving priority to those living in the Choctaw Nation. After all, he explained, the Choctaw Nation is a sovereign nation. To leave the nation is to defect to a foreign country. If you really want tribal benefits and services, as well as a council member, he told the Dry supporters in the room, go ahead and move to the Choctaw Nation. Suddenly, a young woman named Evie jumped in to support Dan: "Choctaw Nation *can't* extend programs to Oklahoma City," she told the group. "Choctaw Nation is bound by program requirements that won't *let* them extend services to absentees!" Evie must have been quite surprised when several years later she learned that Roberts's successor, Chief Greg Pyle, had extended to absentees a number of tribal programs (see chapter 3).

The Dry supporters in the Alliance rejected these and all other arguments that were made in support of the then current tribal policy. Tribal program requirements, they insisted, can and should be changed to accommodate an absentee population that comprises more than 80 percent of the Choctaw citizenry. "Roberts is *using* us," several also exclaimed as they argued that the tribal administration receives federal dollars for each member it enrolls. "We shouldn't be punished for moving away," one group member cried, this time to the eight tribal council members who had journeyed by van to Oklahoma City on an unusually cool summer evening to meet with the group. "We shouldn't be punished for moving away," she continued, "because we *had* to do it: there aren't jobs in Choctaw Nation." "I moved away, too," responded Randle Durant, the speaker of the tribal council, as he glanced nervously around the room in the Alliance headquarters that, as was mentioned above, the tribal council had helped purchase for the group. "But then I got up enough money together to come back. Our policy from a long, long time back is that if you leave the Choctaw Nation, you're going out on your own."

Indians living within their tribal homelands frequently support a policy toward absentees such as that which Durant articulated during the electoral season (see, for example, Sturm 2002).[20] Those living "off" the tribal homeland increasingly have been criticizing such policies. The successes absentees have had in extracting from their tribal governments revisions of such policies references the growing political power of absentees, a power that is derived largely from the power of their vote. After all, as early as 1983, absentees determined the results of the election for principal chief of the Cherokee Nation of Oklahoma (Sturm 2002); twenty years later in 2003, they were the swing vote that determined the choice for chief of the Eastern Band of Cherokee Indians of North Carolina, a tribe that in the late twentieth and early twenty-first centuries has several times affirmed its commitment to greatly restricting absentee voting. Oklahoma City, Dallas, Los Angeles, and often other cities are now part of the "required" list of campaign stops for politicians of the Five "Civilized" Tribes of Oklahoma; the high number of absentee voters in each of these tribes simply requires it (Meredith 1993).

Since 1998 the Oklahoma Choctaws have significantly revised tribal policies toward absentees and have created a political atmosphere in which the rhetoric articulated by Durant is no longer viable. We have also elected a new chief (Greg Pyle 1997–present) who was born outside the tribal homeland (see chapter 3). Other tribes are integrating absentees into tribal governing structures, a growing trend in Indian country. Crow tribal members elect to their executive committee two representatives from the off-reservation population, and two from each of six reservation districts (Lopach et al. 1998). The Caddo Tribe of Oklahoma elects representatives from each of four districts, with Oklahoma City as one of these districts (Meredith 1993). Last, Fort Belknap absentees, though not yet formally integrated qua absentees into tribal governing structures, have been "competitive candidates" in council races, holding out the promise that absentee voices will soon be a part of tribal governance on this Montana reservation (Lopach et al. 1998).[21]

Quarter-or-Mores

A third Choctaw political group that mobilized during the 1995 election was a group that was composed of two sister organizations, Choctaws for Democracy and Native Women for Justice. Both of these groups organized around the identity of quarter-or-more, meaning a Choctaw with one-quarter or more Choctaw blood quantum, and both recruited and won many of the same individuals. Late in the electoral season, their overlapping memberships exceeded two hundred. This was about 1 percent of the total Choctaw quarter-or-more population. In the late 1990s, quarter-or-mores comprised approximately 23,250 individuals, or 25 percent of the tribal citizenry (Faiman-Silva 1997; see also Noley 2001).[22] As mentioned earlier, by tribal law only quarter-or-mores are eligible for elected tribal positions, including the position of tribal chief.

Though I am not a quarter-or-more, I experienced few problems collecting information from members of this political group. Initial acceptance was aided enormously by three things. First, I was well acquainted with several members of this group prior to the electoral season. Second, I shared with the members of this group a political position that was central to the identity of their group: I strongly believed that quarter-or-mores should not experience discrimination at the hands of our tribal government. My willingness as an under-a-quarter—or a Choctaw who is recognized as having less than one-quarter Choctaw blood quantum—to embrace such a position, I was told, might be part of a "domino effect," as they termed it, through which eventually most under-a-quarters would come to believe that quarter-or-mores should have "equal rights" in our tribe.

The third reason that I experienced little difficulty collecting information from members of this political group derived from the fact that all members of this group lined up against Roberts. Though a strong favorite in the race, Roberts, according to group members, had refused to publish in the tribal newspaper "pro-Dry" political advertisements or letters to the editor, making it very difficult, group members said, for them to share their views with the Choctaw electorate.[23] Roberts did this, they claimed, to increase his chances of reelection. This group therefore welcomed the attention I gave to their perspectives and positions. They also sought my vote. I regularly attended their meetings, most of which took place in the southeastern corner of the Choctaw Nation; accompanied them on the campaign trail, often with Dry in tow; attended informal events and gatherings with them, including cookouts, fairs, and shopping expeditions; and spent time in their homes. I felt uncomfortable in my dealings with members of this group only once: when I was investigating a radical faction of the group. I found some of the faction's arguments—particularly the argument that Choctaws of less than one-quarter Choctaw blood quantum should be disenrolled—threatening and offensive, though interesting and politically significant.[24] (Both they and I were well aware, it should be pointed out, that such a proposal would likely not ever make it to the point of being put to a vote, as is required to change our membership requirements. Under-a-quarters make up 75 percent of our tribe, and no under-a-quarter could be expected to vote for his or her own disenrollment.)

The political group that was based on blood quantum began mobilizing when Dry began calling for an "end to discrimination against quarter-or-mores" and identifying what he called "quarter-or-more rights" during his campaign. Dry argued that the tribal government gave preferential treatment to under-a-quarters. It is well known, he contended, that Roberts hires only under-a-quarters. It is also well known, he claimed, that under-a-quarters are given priority when scholarships, housing, and other benefits are distributed to the Choctaw people by the Roberts administration and tribal council. In a Doug Dry administration, Dry claimed, quarter-or-mores, and particularly full-bloods, would no longer be treated as second-class citizens.

Dry buttressed these arguments with the claim that any negative experiences that quarter-or-mores may have had with their tribal government—such as unreturned phone calls, "lost" paperwork, and brusque treatment by tribal bureaucrats—were not the result of the tribal government's recent reconstitution and rapid expansion. According to Dry, quarter-or-mores were not falling victim to bureaucratic irregularity; they were falling victim to institutionalized discrimination. This argument was important, for, as Lopach et al. (1998) point out, a result of "official" unfairness—that is, unfairness that is constructed as such by the people—is frequently a loss of governmental legitimacy. By trying to get the Choctaw people to revoke the legitimacy they had conferred upon Roberts's tribal government, Dry hoped to upend the strong feelings of loyalty that many Choctaw people felt toward Roberts during the mid-1990s.

The key mobilizers of the political group that was based on blood quantum were quarter-or-mores who had begun a circular pattern of migration in young adulthood and had completed their return to the Choctaw Nation after at least two decades of absence and within the decade prior to the 1995 race for chief. Two of these leaders had spent many years in California; another, in the upper Midwest, among other places. Each had at least one non-Indian grandparent. Probably as a consequence of time spent among certain populations of non-Indians, each held romanticized views of full-bloods. At best, these romanticized views were expressed in terms of the idea that full-bloods were people who deserved respect. At worst, they were expressed in ways that constructed full-bloods as living embodiments of an idealized tribal past. Full-bloods themselves experienced some difficulty dealing with such views and to varying degrees resisted return migrants' attempts to sanctify them. Even so, they expressed an eagerness to partner with these leaders and confer legitimacy upon them as leaders. In general, members of this political group strongly valued the willingness of the return migrants to express outrage over how the Choctaw Nation of the 1990s was treating quarter-or-mores and especially full-bloods.

This treatment was not limited to alleged instances of institutionalized discrimination. Under Roberts's leadership, the tribal government explicitly opposed itself, its citizens, the tribe's policies, and the future of the group itself to a negative, even offensive, image of the full-blood. An image of the full-blood as "backward," unsophisticated, nonaggressive, and dull was being explicitly contrasted to and used to define and legitimize an image of a modern Choctaw Nation as "forward-thinking," sophisticated, aggressive, and clever. It is difficult to overstate the lack of subtlety with which such images were deployed in the 1990s. Shortly before the electoral season, for example, I observed high-level tribal officials lobbying at various levels of the tribal government for the adoption of a tribal policy that would prohibit tribal employees from offering services to citizens unless and until the citizen took the initiative to ask for help. The strength of this policy, its Choctaw promoters told full-bloods and others, was that it would help "destroy the full-blood mentality." Several other times I observed the tribe's employment practices, which gave preference to light-skinned Choctaws, being rationalized, even justified, in terms of stereotypes of full-bloods. For example, in Roberts's 1995 State of the Nation address to the Choctaw people, the chief explained, "If you put two full-bloods in the same room, they'll sit there and watch each other's backs like chicken hawks. 'That one there's not doing his share,' one will say. 'That one there's not pulling his weight.' Now I can put a white boy [i.e., a light-skinned Choctaw male] in there in between them, and he'll do three times the work of those full-bloods!"

Another time, at a party for Roberts that was held at the tribal community center in Hugo I heard one tribal council member express a preference for filling educational programs with "mixed-bloods," as he put it. "Mixed-bloods [simply] learn better than full-bloods," he explained to me and to others. I winced at this remark then, as now, not only because I strongly disagree with this statement but also because I was aware that this man was a full-blood himself. This was not the first or the last time I heard a Choctaw full-blood make a derogatory remark about full-bloods. I can recall at least a half-dozen times that this occurred during my research. The prevalence of such behavior in the Choctaw Nation of the 1990s helps explain, I believe, the passion with which many quarter-or-mores and especially full-bloods responded to Dry's rhetoric. Dry treated a high degree of Choctaw "blood" as a strength, not a weakness. In so doing, he challenged key stereotypes about Indians that were being promoted by some Choctaws and had become entrenched in the Choctaw Nation, stereotypes that at that time (and to a lesser extent today) were limiting the ability of our tribe to fully exercise our sovereignty. Members of the quarter-or-more group often talked about these stereotypes and their use by their fellow tribal members as appalling, inexcusable, and demoralizing. Two of them responded by creating a log that documented the dates and times when elected tribal officials denigrated full-bloods or, more broadly, quarter-or-mores. Their anger included feelings of betrayal and disbelief, as all of the individuals making such statements were quarter-or-mores (since only quarter-or-mores are eligible for elected leadership positions), and some were full-bloods. Other tribes have also been documented as holding the same or similar stereotypes about full-bloods (e.g., Hittman 1973).

Despite the obvious appeal that Dry's message held out for quarter-or-mores (as well as for absentees), by all accounts the political mobilization of quarter-or-mores was not easy. This is reflected in the election results. Dry captured only 2,768 votes, which was 18 percent of the vote (Choctaw Nation, July 8, 1995; *Oklahoman*, July 9, 1995). Though a breakdown of votes by blood quantum has not been released (and may not have been compiled), voting results do reveal that 1,185 of Dry's votes (which equals less than half of his total votes) came from Choctaws who were living in the Choctaw Nation, many of whom probably were quarter-or-mores (Choctaw Nation, July 8, 1995).

Locating quarter-or-mores proved to be something of a problem for leaders of the political group that was based on blood quantum. Circe Sturm (2002) points out that the Cherokee Nation contains approximately seventy "traditional Cherokee communities" that are home to many individuals who inhabit the category of "over one-quarter" Cherokee blood quantum and that have other features that would make these communities fertile ground for political mobilization on the basis of high blood quantum.[25] The Choctaw Nation has no such communities. While the southeastern quadrant of the Choctaw Nation is said to have the highest concentration of quarter-or-mores, quarter-or-mores have chosen to spread themselves fairly widely over this region, as well as over the Choctaw Nation as a whole, instead of living in predominantly Indian settlements as have some of their fellow members of the Five "Civilized" Tribes.

Choctaw Nation residents who are quarter-or-mores tend to live in towns that are made up mostly of non-Indians but also of other Choctaws and other Indians, towns that range in size from very rural to mid-sized urban. One such town is the focus of the following chapter, which explores the meanings of being Choctaw at the local level, that is, at the level of a small, southeastern Oklahoma town.

In addition to having to seek out quarter-or-mores over a tribal territory that spans hundreds of square miles, leaders of the political group that was based on blood quantum experienced some success exploiting networks that linked quarter-or-mores with one another. Most such networks were networks of kin. It was not uncommon for a quarter-or-more who chose to join the group to be part of a set of Choctaw families with a relatively high number of members who historically had reproduced with only Choctaws. When this was the case, it was not uncommon for that individual to attend a first meeting of the quarter-or-more group by him- or herself, then attend subsequent meetings with kin. Alternatively, recruits showed a pattern of bringing kin to the first meeting they attended. In addition to these networks of kin, there existed additional (and sometimes overlapping) networks of quarter-or-mores who had met through work or church or through common participation in some type of activity. For example, in the quarter-or-more group there existed about a half-dozen women who had forged close relationships with one another through their joint participation in an annual activity of helping make and deliver Christmas baskets each year to poor families, both Indian and non-Indian.

Group members frequently said that they defined "quarter-or-more" as those whose blood quantum was at least one-quarter. Virtually the only quarter-or-mores who were willing to join the group, however, were those with stereotypically "Indian" phenotypes. Several quarter-or-mores who were able to "pass" as white told me that they wanted nothing to do with what they inaccurately termed "Dry's full-blood group." For the most part, this had to do with fact that those making these charges constructed themselves, on the one hand, and the members of the quarter-or-more group, on the other, as existing on opposite sides of a racial divide (though most definitely not on opposite sides of the boundaries that define Choctaw nationality). Referenced here is a decoupling of "race" and Indian national identity that is mentioned in Sturm (2002) in relation to the Oklahoma Cherokees and that I will address in relation to the Choctaws in chapter 5. Such a decoupling is not uncommon throughout eastern Oklahoma and is perhaps the most pronounced among the Muscogee Creeks, in whose homeland my grandmother was reared. The Creeks forged a national identity that was explicitly multiethnic in the eighteenth century and have continued to resist Euro-American constructions such as that articulated by Gellner (1983) which link "race" and "nation" and argue that racial homogeneity is a critical characteristic of a nation.

When it became clear that racialization was seriously inhibiting the mobilization of quarter-or-mores who could pass as white, group leaders increasingly based their recruitment efforts on phenotype. Those who were phenotypically Indian were approached at gas stations, schools, and grocery stores. They were also approached at Roberts's campaign rallies, where the chances were high that these individuals were Choctaws (rather than, for example, Indians of other tribes or Mexican Americans). Once located, quarter-or-mores who expressed an interest in this subtribal group were brought together for fellowship, "consciousness-raising," food, and entertainment. Each of these many meetings involved the articulation and rearticulation of the refrain that quarter-or-mores "deserved respect" and "should be given equal rights" in our tribe. At the same time, group leaders suggested, sometimes quite explicitly, that full-bloods were the most "authentic" category of Choctaws, a construction that is common among many tribes in the United States (Garroutte 2003). Discussions at these meetings often centered around the practical and logistical issues involved in defeating Roberts. For example, it was often discussed how the Choctaw people felt about Roberts, how they felt about quarter-or-mores, how not only quarter-or-mores but also under-a-quarters could best be mobilized, and how to deal with the fact that Roberts's power was so entrenched, especially in the Choctaw Nation.

Several times members of this group told me they expected to experience the most success mobilizing outside the Choctaw Nation, an assumption that I am not sure is accurate. As a result of this assumption, Oklahoma City, Dallas, and western Arkansas, as well as the Choctaw Nation, became places of recruitment. One such effort took place in the Chickasaw Nation, the Choctaw Nation's immediate neighbor to the west. When I met the organizers about twenty miles west of the Choctaw Nation border, I was introduced to one of the group's newest members, a grandmother of eight who was a quarter-or-more and an absentee. This woman lived about ten miles east of the eastern border of the

Choctaw Nation (which is the Oklahoma-Arkansas state border) in western Arkansas where she had spent the past seventeen years working in a chicken processing plant. As she plopped herself down in a cracked fold-up chair, she wiped sweat from her forehead. She and a half-dozen other members of Native Women for Justice had been sitting in the sun all afternoon at the annual Chickasaw Nation Festival in Tishomingo, Oklahoma. Among the tables where food, jewelry, and arts and crafts were being sold, about a half-dozen group members had set up a table. While selling Native Women for Justice T-shirts, these mobilizers had spoken to dozens of Chickasaws, Choctaws who lived in the Chickasaw Nation, and Chickasaws with both Chickasaw and Choctaw ancestry about what they described as the need to oust Roberts. In so doing, they had tried to mobilize Choctaw quarter-or-mores and/or absentees, make money for Dry's campaign, and raise public awareness about Roberts's regime among Indians of other tribes.

Whether they were "on the road" campaigning or "back home" having meetings, members of this political group experienced very few conflicts between themselves. One conflict, which lasted for several weeks and elicited very strong emotions from a number of members, centered on the question of whether to continue to begin the group's meetings with a Christian prayer. Some group members lobbied against such prayers; many more strongly supported them. A second, more serious, conflict revolved around the issue of "Choctaw traditions" and Dry's public statement that Choctaws should "return" to their "traditions." Such statements are not unheard of and may not even be unusual for tribal politicians. Phyllis Fast (2002) notes that, in the context of an incipient "movement" in some Alaska Native villages to identify what is "traditional" and "indigenous," existing and would-be Gwich'in leaders advocate a "return to 'traditions.'" In southeast Alaska, Dombrowski (2001) found something similar; he also, however, found considerable opposition to this "goal" or policy initiative among Native members of Pentecostal churches. In 1999 Oklahoma Cherokee chief Chad Smith ran on a platform of "return to Cherokee culture" (Sturm 2002: 103), and Wilkins (2002b: 93) identifies as a critical policy issue in the Navajo Nation "cultural retention," as well as the call "to revive traditional values and beliefs" that was issued in a vision (see also Meredith 1993).

Some members of the Choctaw quarter-or-more group opposed Dry's idea of "returning to traditions," claiming first that the Oklahoma Choc-

taws no longer practice any cultural expressions that derive from the precontact past. This argument is more easily supported than the argument
that such continuities do exist; any consideration of such a question, however, must address the questions of what constitutes cultural continuity with the precontact past and how such continuities might be identified. In the course of arguing that Choctaw traditions were "already gone"
(see also Pesantubbee 1994), many members of this group argued that
such practices should not be reinstated or, as some put it, "brought back."
Several explained that Choctaw traditions were pagan and thus threatened to undermine Christianity in the Choctaw Nation (see Dombrowski
2001 for an excellent discussion of Alaska Native perspectives that reject
and even denounce Native "culture"). Other Choctaws explained that if
Choctaws were "to return to traditions," some ground might be lost in
the battle against stereotypes of Indians as "savage," "uncivilized," and
"wild," stereotypes from which full-bloods especially may have been eager to distance themselves. Still others explained that Choctaws needed
to continue "to move forward, not back in time." Dozens of those who
articulated this rhetoric were members of Choctaw churches, especially
the fourteen Choctaw Presbyterian churches that are concentrated in the
southeastern corner of the Choctaw Nation. These churches tend to have
very high numbers of members who are quarter-or-more.

In a field-based study of these Choctaw churches in the late twentieth
century, Choctaw scholar Michelene Pesantubbee (1994) provides greater
insight into these views about Choctaw "traditions," views that are probably produced and reproduced the most by Choctaws affiliated with these
churches. In trying to explain what she describes as "the stigma associated with Choctaw traditional beliefs and ceremonies" among the Choctaws during the 1990s, she identifies "internalized devaluations of Choctaw culture," "unfamiliarity with Choctaw traditions," and widespread
stereotyping by Choctaws of certain religio-cultural expressions as expressions of ignorance, heathenism, paganism, and even devil worship
(pp. 204, 280, 272). Pesantubbee describes a wide range of expressions as
being stereotyped by Choctaws in this way, including Choctaw dance;
"Indian" music that uses drums, flutes, or claves; sweat lodges; smudging;
and even ideas such as "the interrelationship of all of creation." Moreover, she points out that Choctaws often regard efforts to "relearn Choctaw ways" as "a step backward." Last, she notes that such ideas are very

much entrenched in the Choctaw Nation, arguing that "change seems a long way off" (p. 191).

Another Choctaw scholar, Devon Mihesuah, also draws upon her experiences among our tribe to describe and help explain the rejection of Native culture by some Natives. "They believe that 'white is best,'" she explains, "because they either learned that ideology in boarding schools or that idea was passed down through the generations to modern Natives from an ancestor who attended a boarding school" (2005: 14). Natives who reject Native culture do not want their children to become white, she continues. Instead, "they want them to have equal access to the socioeconomic privileges that whites have" (2003: 90). Adding that Christianity and popular stereotypes also often play a role in the construction of such views, Mihesuah describes an interview that she conducted with a Cherokee full-blood woman who was descended from a prominent Cherokee leader. When this woman was asked whether she spoke Cherokee and went to stomp dances, she said to Mihesuah, "Hell no, I'm no heathen" (2003: xvi).

The arguments that Choctaws presented as to why Choctaw "traditions" should not be relearned were some of the same arguments that Chief Roberts had been using for years to promote images of Choctaws in business suits and discourage the efforts that a small number of Choctaws in the Choctaw Nation had been making since the 1970s to learn about and express "Choctaw culture" (see chapter 3). "Roberts views traditional Native American culture as 'regressive,'" explains Faiman-Silva (1997: 213). Members of the political group that was based on blood quantum presented arguments to one another using many of the same words and some of the same examples used by Roberts. I interpret this as evidence of the strength of Roberts's influence in the 1990s. I also interpret it as evidence that in the modern Choctaw Nation the executive tends to shape (Choctaw) public opinion to a significant extent—probably to a much greater degree than does the executive in most other tribal nations—and reflects the emphasis the Choctaws have placed on strong leadership.[26] Prior to Roberts, these tendencies toward constructing a strong executive gained expression and started developing during the Belvin era (1948–75), when an enormously popular Choctaw leader, Harry J. W. Belvin, served twenty-seven years as chief (see chapter 3). It is possible that such tendencies predate the Belvin era and perhaps even the relocation of the Choctaws from the Southeast in the 1830s. Of the more than 560 tribes in the United States, the tribe that has vested the executive with the most power, both formally and informally, is probably the Mississippi Band of Choctaw Indians. This tribe is composed of the descendants of Choctaws who did not relocate to what is now Oklahoma (see chapter 2), and Galloway and Kidwell argue that its contemporary leadership "harken[s] back to [an eighteenth-century Choctaw] tradition of powerful district leaders" (2004: 517).

The high degree to which the executive tends to shape public opinion in the modern Choctaw Nation was further driven home to me after Roberts's successor, Greg Pyle, took office. Pyle, who was promoted to chief when Roberts was sent to prison on June 6, 1997, began openly supporting expressions of "Choctaw culture" and "Indian culture" shortly after he became chief. He also began using the bully pulpit to express his belief that a high Choctaw blood quantum is a strength, not a weakness. By the early 2000s I began seeing evidence of less resistance among members of my tribe to the idea of bringing back traditions and less prejudice against full-bloods. Particularly with respect to the view toward "traditions," Greg Pyle has been steering our tribe closer to a position to which, it seems, much of Indian country has been moving since the 1970s. This is a position in which Indian cultural expressions are no longer being seen as antithetical to strong, efficient, and effective tribal governance and modern tribal nation building.

Conclusion

The 1995 Choctaw tribal electoral season—which brought into relief the ways by which Choctaws are negotiating and experiencing the relations of citizenship that bind together enrolled Choctaws and link them to the tribal government—created pockets of intense political activity both within and outside of the Choctaw Nation. One such pocket developed within the tribal bureaucracy. Another emerged in Oklahoma City. A third drew together high-blood-quantum Choctaws living in all parts of the Choctaw Nation and the surrounding regions. As Choctaws began mobilizing during the race for the tribe's highest office, Choctaw informal political structures proliferated, increasing the extent to which many of us perceived of our society as ordered rather than resistant to such ordering. Increasingly during the electoral season, Choctaws sorted themselves (and were sorted by others) into three sets of binary categories, each of which became the basis for an organized political group. These oppositions were tribal employee/non–tribal employee, resident/absentee, and quarter-or-more/under-a-quarter. While identifying and exploring this phenomenon of the contingent nature of Choctaw subtribal groups, a key characteristic of which is their malleability or flexibility over time, I considered the varied ways by which Choctaws experience tribal elections and construct their Choctaw identity and citizenship. In order to provide a portrait of sorts of the Choctaw people, I addressed not only some commonalities of experience that unite certain categories of Choctaws but also some differences that divide us, differences in our socioeconomic, educational, and racial backgrounds as well as in our perspectives and political views. Refracted in these perspectives are the primary issues, valuations, grievances, and goals that defined the 1995 electoral season.

Two sets of issues that assumed cardinal importance during the historical moment explored in this chapter were issues of tribal economic development and issues of the unequal treatment of certain categories of Choctaw citizens. The electoral rhetoric, the responses of political groups, and the election outcome strongly endorsed the course of tribal economic development spearheaded by Roberts. The next chapter looks more closely at Choctaw economic development, exploring the specific ways by which tribally owned and operated development projects are impacting Choctaws at the local level. Also foregrounded during the 1995 electoral season were charges of unequal treatment on the basis of residence outside the tribal territory and on the basis of high blood quantum, charges that were not uncommon during the later part of the Hollis Roberts administration. The day after the 1995 election, some quarter-or-mores interpreted the 83 percent vote for Roberts as a vote for the continuation of practices and rhetoric that dishonored and disrespected high-blood-quantum citizens. Absentees, in contrast, were well aware that the vast majority of them had voted for Roberts and thus tended not to view Roberts's re-election as a statement about residence-based discrimination. It is likely that issues of unequal treatment, though critical in the mobilization of the political groups discussed in this chapter, did not significantly influence the 1995 election outcome. The attention that was given to these issues during the electoral season did, however, have enduring social, economic, and political consequences. Roberts's assistant chief, Greg Pyle,

listened carefully to these grievances, and when he became chief following Roberts's imprisonment, he made absentees eligible for many more
tribal programs and services, and he began vigorously fighting discrimination on the basis of (high) blood quantum.

This chapter placed the spotlight on the two leading candidates for
chief and the citizens who joined one or more of three organized political
groups. These individuals, however, together make up only a small fraction of the Choctaw citizenry. From the beginning of the electoral season
to the early-July election day, most of the space on the Choctaw political
landscape was occupied by a silent majority. Members of this majority undertook little to no political action in connection with the election. Some
voted; many more did not. Significant differences characterized the members of this majority who were absentees, and those who were residents.
Absentees often knew little more about the election than that which appeared in the monthly tribal newspaper, which is sent free of charge to all
tribal members and which each month articulated the narrative of how
Roberts rebuilt the tribe. Roberts was able to bank on the absentee vote
during the 1995 election, as he had done during several prior elections.[27]
In 1995 Roberts captured nearly 87 percent of the absentee vote.

The rest of the silent majority lived in the Choctaw Nation. As such,
they were often privy to the actions taken and the rhetoric practiced by
Roberts, by Dry, and by all three political groups, including the group that
was based in Oklahoma City but had strong ties to the Choctaw homeland. In addition, these individuals were often both implicated by and
subjected to categorization in terms of the three sets of binary categories
that were brought to the fore during the electoral season. After the election, I reflected on the wallflower behavior of those who helped make up
the silent majority and who lived in the Choctaw Nation. How were these
Choctaws, who participated only minimally, if at all, in the tribal election, experiencing the relations of citizenship that bind together enrolled
Choctaws and link them to the Choctaw tribal government? And how
were the relations of Choctaw citizenship affecting experience and identity at the local level? To pursue these and other questions, I conducted
research in a small Choctaw Nation town in which the tribal government
was finishing construction of a tribal economic-development project. An
examination of the social, political, and economic consequences of the

building of this project provided a focus for my explorations of the consequences of the new order. It especially helped foreground the ways by which the tribal government was negotiating its relationships with non-Choctaws, as well as with Choctaws, living in the Choctaw Nation, and the ways by which the Choctaws of a small Choctaw Nation town were negotiating their relationships with local non-Choctaws in a historical context defined by marked non-Indian denial of the continued existence of Choctaw identity.

5. "The First of Many Good Things to Come from the Tribe"

Identity, Race and Economic Development in Kalichito Town

Much fanfare accompanied the completion in the mid-1990s of a tribal travel plaza in the three-hundred-member community of Kalichito in the south-central part of the Choctaw Nation. The day of the Kalichito project's "Grand Opening," dozens of residents of the town—mostly Choctaws—huddled together in clumps in the wide black parking lot of the new tribal business. It was cold, overcast, and unusually windy. Swaddled in their warmest winter coats, Kalichitoans and tribal bureaucrats listened quietly to tribal leaders as they expounded upon the historic importance of the Kalichito project, its importance, it was exclaimed, "not only to the Choctaw people but to all southeastern Oklahomans!" After a dramatic severing by tribal council representatives of a ribbon that encircled part of the complex, Kalichitoans joined tribal bureaucrats and others in a series of whoops and cheers. Weaving in and out of the crowd was a photographer for *Bishinik*, the Choctaw tribal newspaper. As pictures were hastily snapped of tribal leaders against the background of the project, several local Choctaws, all of them women, shuffled politely out of the way. Kalichito's Choctaw women knew that the ceremony had been designed to permit their tribal leaders, especially their chief, to maximize the political gain that derived from building such a business.

The new tribal business had been built on a tract of scrubby ranchland—an abandoned farm, really—that the tribal government had purchased many months earlier. Located very close to a major highway in the Choctaw Nation, the travel plaza, open twenty-four hours a day and most holidays, houses a small room at the front of the building where customers can engage in pull-tab gaming. It also houses a sizable cigarette store, a well-stocked convenience store, and a grill, where Choctaws serve up hamburgers, hot dogs, fries, and other American delicacies to customers. Outside the complex, a number of pumps feed gasoline to cars, pickups, tractors, and eighteen-wheelers. About five months after the project opened, several customers told me that, for reasons that will be explained later, they had traveled up to one hundred miles from Texas for Choctaw Nation cigarettes and gasoline.

The community in which this project was built is a community to which I have given the pseudonym "Kalichito."[1] It is a town of 104 households. The new tribal travel plaza occupies a site at the crossroads of a highway exit and the most traveled of the country roads that lead to the town's center, a country road that formerly was neither paved nor easily located for those unfamiliar with the town. This country road continues east from the travel plaza for about a quarter mile. At that point it winds to the right, then sharply to the left and under a canopy of trees before it opens up into the town center. There, on Main Street, a gas station, small grocery store, church, and eatery define the town's primary gathering places. A few blocks to the north are other downtown spots, such as the fire station. At the base of a hill on the other side of town, a tire-and-muffler store sits comfortably under a very large pecan tree. The town's eastern edge is marked by a long tan building, clothed in aluminum siding and emblazoned with the name of an agricultural products business. In and around Kalichito's downtown of peeling paint, wide windows, and old streetlights, small houses trimmed in green, navy, or black dot dozens of acres of former (and current) farmland and fenced pasture. All day long, cows stand at attention in the town's many fields, watching pickups blow dust down the road. In the background, one or two of the town's hunting dogs can often be heard harassing a squirrel or some other small animal in one of the town's many creek beds.

From the fall of 1995 through the late spring of 1996, I spent part of nearly every week in this town, which I selected for participant-observation research because it was the site of a tribal project that would begin operation during my research. The event of the building of the project provided a focus for my exploration of the social, political, and economic consequences of the new order. In the months that followed the project's grand opening, I explored the specific ways by which this project was

affecting this community. Because this was a tribal-government project, because Choctaw citizens lived in this community, and because the
project provided jobs for local Choctaws, the event of the building of the
project brought into relief the relations of citizenship that bind together
enrolled Choctaws and link them to the tribal government. At the same
time, it foregrounded relations between the tribal government and the
many non-Choctaws who live in the Choctaw Nation, as well as relations
between local Choctaws, whites, and blacks in Choctaw Nation communities. As was mentioned in chapter 3, whites make up about 80 percent of
southeastern Oklahoma residents, an artifact first of nineteenth-century
tribal policies that permitted white immigration, and later of the Curtis
Act of 1898, an act that paved the way for the large-scale appropriation
of Choctaw lands by non-Indians in the early twentieth century. Blacks,
who make up about 5 percent of southeastern Oklahomans, first entered
the Choctaw Nation as slaves of the Choctaws when the tribe was relocated to what is now Oklahoma in the 1830s. In the late 1800s, comparatively large numbers of blacks from places east of Indian Territory began
relocating to the area. Between 1890 and 1910, for example, approximately
60,000 blacks migrated to what is now Oklahoma (Aldrich 1973). By the
mid-1990s, Choctaws were a tiny minority in their tribal homeland, com-
prising as little as 10 percent of the southeastern Oklahoma population.
In Kalichito, Choctaws comprise approximately 20 percent of Kalichito's population, double the average percentage of Choctaws in Choctaw
Nation communities. The fact that Kalichito was more highly marked
as Choctaw than most Choctaw Nation communities aided my efforts,
as it amplified the tensions in which I was interested.

I begin by addressing local resistance to the project. I then explore
tribal government perspectives on the building of the project, using data
from research I conducted not only in Kalichito but also in the tribal capital in Durant. Among other things, this provides the background for my
explorations of the local economic impact of the project. The project created dozens of locally rare and highly valued nonagricultural and nonfactory jobs in the area, jobs that also required from Kalichitoans a min-
imal commute. For the many Choctaw (and non-Choctaw) families of
Kalichito who have been struggling for decades to climb out of poverty
and deprivation, the material impact of this tribal job creation trumps
in importance all other ways the building of this project has affected
this community. My respect for and appreciation of the fact that many

Kalichitoans treat economic concerns as paramount is expressed in this chapter through an extended discussion of the material consequences of the project's job creation. This discussion includes stories of how, specifically, the project is financially affecting the project's new jobholders and their kin, and it precedes my core discussion of the local social and political consequences of the new tribal development project and Choctaw nation building.

In the second half of the chapter, I explore the more subtle ways the project has affected Kalichito life and experience. Together with other public expressions of the tribe's presence in the town, the building of the tribal travel plaza has helped Kalichito's Choctaws resist the multigenerational efforts of whites to deny the Choctaw identity of most Choctaw residents. The increased public visibility and public recognition of Choctaws as Choctaws has helped define the local social and political significance of the building of the Kalichito project. To illuminate this, I trace the history of experience and identity in this community in some detail, probing the ways by which the local meanings of being Choctaw have been several times reconfigured since Choctaws began settling and founding Kalichito in the 1830s. Local social constructions of the categories of Choctaw, white, and black have varied over time, as have the ways by which these categories have been bounded, experienced, and defined.

As will be seen, before Oklahoma statehood in 1907, Choctaw and non-Choctaw experience in this town was structured by Choctaw tribal law and sociopolitical structures. After Oklahoma statehood, new structures—both at the local level and at the larger regional and national levels—developed and took hold, dramatically transforming experience in this community. Racial boundaries were redrawn not only through new local social classifications of farms, which helped give rise to patterns of racially marked agricultural work experience, but also through local white acceptance and implementation of Oklahoma laws mandating the segregation of "whites" and "blacks." Attendance at segregated schools, as will be seen, played a signal role in organizing experience in Kalichito during the early poststatehood period, as did other boundary-drawing institutions and structures, such as community sports. My discussions of contemporary experience in Kalichito help expose, among other things, the ways by which these early poststatehood constructions of identity, as well as those that predate statehood and even removal, inform present-day Kalichito identity and experience. These discussions also help expose the ways by which prestatehood and early-poststatehood structural legacies are intersecting with other structural reconfigurations that find their origins in the tribal rebuilding of the late twentieth century.

Local Resistance to the Building of the Project

The building of a tribal project in Kalichito was an expression of the vertical entrenchment of a tribal government engaged in the larger project of welding together a nation (see Kurtz 2001). By building a tribal-government institution in a local community within its boundaries, the Choctaw government increased the extent of the political incorporation of this community into the new political order and thus extended its reach vertically. Theories of nation building suggest that local communities often resist such efforts. They struggle to avoid ceding power and control to a centralizing order and in other ways fight to maintain their autonomy.

Many Kalichitoans did indeed resist the building of the tribal travel plaza in their community. Others, however, did not. I observed local resistance to the project only among non-Choctaws. To my knowledge, no Choctaws resisted the project, and, in fact, all of those who shared their views with me said that they strongly supported it. In *Nightwatch: The Politics of Protest in the Andes* (1999), Orin Starn shows how Andean peasants linked the development of new, order-producing institutions in their rural villages to a politics of peasant emancipation. Instead of denouncing certain locally developed and implemented technologies of control, discipline, and order—especially patrols and justice-making institutions—as instruments of domination, peasants treated these order-making efforts as keys to the betterment of rural life. Choctaws in Kalichito responded similarly to the possibility that tribal nation building might not simply replace some local structures but also expand the number of local order-making institutions. Their non-Choctaw neighbors appeared not to find this response incomprehensible or even puzzling. Indeed, locally, the question of who supported and who resisted the project was not a subject of much debate. Instead, it was taken for granted that support for and opposition to the project was structured along Choctaw/non-Choctaw lines.

Before, during, and after the building of the project, many non-Choctaws resisted the project by publicly expressing fear and resentment of the tribe. Many complaints centered on the consequences—both real and imagined, and both existing and expected—of their nonmembership in the tribal nation that was transforming southeastern Oklahoma.

For example, non-Choctaws often argued that "it was not fair" that the Choctaw tribal government "helped only Choctaws" when "everyone around here is hard up," and often they expressed fears that "the tribe" was "taking over" southeastern Oklahoma. Pointing to the new travel plaza, and pointing out that tribal leaders had purchased ten thousand acres of southeastern Oklahoma in the tribe's name during fiscal year 1995–96, some said that they thought that "before long" non-Choctaws "would lose [their] farms to the tribe" and within a generation the tribe would "no longer let [non-Choctaws] live in Choctaw Nation." (Though the emotions behind such fears were real, the fears themselves were not realistic. It is extremely unlikely that the tribal government will do anything but continue to tolerate the presence of large numbers of non-Choctaws in the Choctaw tribal homeland.)

About a half-dozen times, non-Choctaws in Kalichito responded to the building of the tribal travel plaza in particular and to tribal nation building more generally by declaring that the federal government should dissolve Indian tribes. I found this statement offensive but important to help me better understand local forms of resistance to the rearrangements of the new order. The same can be said of my encounters with negative stereotypes of Choctaws, the deployment of which constituted another form of local non-Choctaw resistance to the new order. In conversations in local stores, on the street, or on the steps of churches after Sunday morning services, it was not uncommon for non-Choctaws in this town to refer to Choctaws as lazy, as savages, as drunks, or as people with little intelligence. It was also not unheard of for Kalichito's non-Choctaws to characterize Choctaws as people who "don't want to work," who "can't control their emotions," or who "aren't to be trusted." Several non-Choctaws claimed that such attributes "ran in the blood," a common local and regional construction. The more "Choctaw blood" one had, it was sometimes claimed, the stronger the expression of the above set of putative racially defined behavioral characteristics tended to be. Several times, however, I also heard Choctaws who supported the travel plaza and tribal nation building invoke some of these stereotypes, sharing with non-Choctaws the mistaken belief that such behavioral characteristics were blood based and that they accurately described Choctaws. I later learned that these stereotypes had been part of a larger set of techniques used in this town to control Choctaws in the years that followed the dismantling of most formal tribal structures at the turn of the twentieth century. In other words, these stereotypes refracted a larger history of race relations in this town, a history that was central to an understanding of the full meaning of the local social impact of the building of the project and will be explored in some depth later in this chapter.

Evidence from elsewhere in Indian country suggests that the responses of Kalichito's non-Choctaws to the tribal travel plaza and to Choctaw tribal nation building are part of a larger, patterned set of non-Indian responses to the acts of tribal nation building that have taken place on many reservations and tribal trust lands during the late twentieth and early twenty-first centuries. In the early 1970s, for example, after Rosebud Sioux tribal leaders attempted to reclaim jurisdiction over lands in two counties (and parts of two other counties) encompassed by reservation boundaries, non-Indian residents of the reservation decried what they described as the tribe's efforts to "take over" the area (Biolsi 2001). More recently, white residents of several predominantly white towns on the Cheyenne River Sioux reservation launched a coordinated attempt to protest the efforts of the tribal government to exercise jurisdiction over these towns (Bordewich 1996), and 1,500 non-Indians living on or near the Flathead reservation formed the group Montanans Opposing Discrimination to pursue the goal of limiting tribal governing power (Lopach et al. 1998). Importantly, Biolsi (2001) places the social production of tensions between Indians and non-Indians living within tribal boundaries in a broader, national context, identifying the discourse of Indian law as a critical producer of such local-level tensions. Indians and local non-Indians living on or near reservations are made into the "deadliest enemies" of one another, Biolsi argues, by the local, zero-sum games that federal Indian law creates and by other means. He explains that federal Indian law helps structure local political interests along Indian/non-Indian lines, fueling conflicting rights-claims at the local level, exacerbating racial tensions on or near reservations, and obscuring the federal role in the production of such conflicts and tensions.

Tribal Government Strategies and Perspectives

Because the tribal travel plaza created an interface between the tribal government and a local community, it provided an opportunity to explore the specific ways by which the tribal government was negotiating its relations with local communities. Through research in the tribal capital in Durant, as well as in Kalichito, I pursued questions about the strategies and perspectives of the tribal government. How, specifically, were tribal officials negotiating their presence in this community, and what did they see as the purposes and meanings of the institution building that was the Kalichito project?

I found that, from the outset, tribal officials expressed concern about local resistance to the building of the project in Kalichito, a resistance that they assumed—correctly—would be limited to non-Choctaws. I also found that, before ground was even broken on the project, tribal officials began taking actions to stem this resistance. The tribal government included non-Choctaws in the planning process of the project, kept them informed about its progress, and gave gifts to the town. In an ethnography about the Florida Seminoles, Jessica Cattelino (2004) describes similar overtures on the part of the Seminole tribal government, especially acts of tribal gift giving to non-Indian communities located in close proximity to Seminole economic development projects. In the immediate aftermath of one act of tribal gift giving to Kalichito, I observed an act in which a local Choctaw even conspired with the tribal government to use one of these gifts to stem local, non-Choctaw resistance to the building of the travel plaza.

This act took place in Kalichito at a community meeting in a large, cream-colored aluminum building that housed Kalichito's Volunteer Fire Department. Parked carefully in the gravel outside the building was a new fire truck, a truck that Fire Chief Bucky Amandine and other locals termed a "pumper truck." Choctaw tribal leaders had given this vehicle, which was worth tens of thousands of dollars, to the town just before the travel plaza's grand opening. During the community meeting, a Choctaw who happened to be a budding local leader stood up before the crowd, which was mostly white but included some Choctaws and blacks, to speak about the new truck. "I wanted y'all to know that last week [on behalf of Kalichito] Bucky and I made pumper truck [Christmas] ornaments for the tribe," he began. "We presented these at the tribal council dinner [a dinner follows each of the council's monthly meetings]. That pumper truck outside—that shiny new pumper truck—is *the first of many good things to come from the tribe.* Many of y'all know—y'all already know— that when Choctaw Nation gets behind somethin' and gets behind people as it has got behind our community, things really take off. . . . And I should add that Hollis is real pleased with Bucky [the fire chief], real, real pleased."

Pointing to the fire truck, this Choctaw argued that it was in the interests of non-Choctaws, as well as Choctaws, to support, not resist, tribal nation building and the new political order. The fire truck, he declared, was the first of many good things to come from the tribe. During my field research, I observed many expressions of this rhetoric, a rhetoric that asserted that one of the tribe's central goals was to improve the lives of all southeastern Oklahomans, not just Choctaws. In chapter 6, evidence is presented that suggests that this tribal strategy has been having limited but important political payoffs. Capitalizing on the fact that many non-Choctaws, as well as Choctaws, living in the Choctaw Nation have negative views of the Oklahoma state government, through an extensive public-relations campaign the tribal government managed to generate significant support among non-Choctaw residents of southeastern Oklahoma for Choctaw tribal control, not Oklahoma state control, of all of the water in southeastern Oklahoma.

While tribal leaders stressed the benefits for the local communities within its boundaries of tribal nation building in general and the building of the Kalichito project in particular, they also publicly defined a goal of interfering as little as possible, as they put it, with existing local social and political structures and arrangements, including the local structures and arrangements that were entrenched in Kalichito. This "hands-off" policy, which could be viewed as a policy of indirect rule, made sense in terms of the tribal government's stated goals for Kalichito's travel plaza. These goals were cardinally informed by a corporate business model that provided little room for talk of anything other than expected and actual profits, and numbers of new jobs. Tribal officials said quite pointedly that they built the project in order to generate revenues for tribal programs and services and create jobs for Choctaw citizens. Among other things, I found that they pursued these goals with an almost single-minded focus.

I also found that when tribal officials talked about the Kalichito project, they spent little time addressing the project individually. Instead, they talked about the project almost entirely in terms of its relationship to and with other Choctaw tribal economic development initiatives. For tribal officials the Kalichito Project was simply one of about a half-dozen other businesses of its type: Choctaw travel plazas. (By 2005, the tribe was operating as many as thirteen tribal travel plazas.) Several Choctaw officials described these enterprises to me as a "safe" economic investment for the Choctaw tribe. One of the tribe's economic development specialists described travel plazas as "low risk"; another, as "sure money-makers." One Choctaw tribal council representative declared: "When a travel plaza opens, we all sleep well because we know the outcome will be positive." The framing of the Kalichito project and other tribal economic development projects as investments—investments, moreover, that can be and are typed and rated—can be explained in part by the strong desire of the tribal government to continue to lessen its dependence on federal funding. A significant portion of the Choctaw tribal government budget is now funded by revenues from the tribe's businesses. By 2003 tribal businesses were funding as much as 80 percent of tribal programs and services (*Bishinik*, November 2003).

As predicted by tribal corporate and financial models, in tribal government terms the Kalichito project was indeed successful. Within only a few dozen months of its opening, it began setting a new standard for Choctaw Nation travel plazas. Tribal officials reported that the gross revenues of the project exceeded $1.2 million, and its net profits, almost $126,000 during the first two months of 1998, creating the expectation that the project would make more than three-quarters of a million dollars that year. Excluding its smokeshop, the Kalichito project, according to tribal officials, ranked first among the tribe's travel plazas in terms of profitability, bringing in more than twice the revenues of four of these projects and more than ten times as much as the plaza that was located about sixty miles southeast of Kalichito.[2]

Despite the success of the new tribal business in Kalichito, field research in the tribal capital in Durant revealed that the tribal government paid comparatively little attention to the Kalichito project. This is largely because the revenues it generates are relatively small when considered in the context of the larger portfolio of Choctaw Nation projects and businesses. In 1998, for example, the Kalichito project contributed a mere 6 percent of the total revenues generated by Choctaw tribal businesses. The Seminole tribe of Florida, in contrast, made smokeshops a cornerstone of their tribal economy in the 1970s (Kersey 1996). Though tribal officials readily acknowledged that the Kalichito project made only a tiny contribution to total tribal revenues, they insisted that it and other low-risk enterprises occupy an important place in the expanding Choctaw tribal economy. Tribal officials explained that travel plazas help make possible the tribe's investment in "higher-risk" enterprises, one of which was the tribe's purchase in 2003 of Blue Ribbon Downs, a then failing horse-racing track located in the Cherokee Nation.

The definition of economic development enterprises in Indian country as "low risk," it should be pointed out, often means something quite different than it does in the rest of corporate America. The Choctaw tribal government categorizes travel plazas as low risk, but by American corporate standards these businesses can hardly be termed "safe." Tribal travel plazas sell cigarettes and motor fuels, which carry high state excise taxes, taxes to which tribes, as sovereign Indian nations, are not subject. The exemption of tribes from these excise taxes increases profit margins and permits tribes to offer cigarettes and motor fuels at prices below retail, sometimes well below retail. Indeed, low prices on cigarettes and gasoline is the reason some customers of the Kalichito travel plaza drive up to one hundred miles to Kalichito. Oklahoma and other states have responded to the success of tribal travel plazas (and free-standing tribal cigarette outlets), however, by attempting to capture a portion of the profits that tribes derive from cigarette and motor-fuel sales. While states are indeed prohibited from taxing tribes, tribal businesses, and tribal lands, Oklahoma and South Dakota, among other states, have argued that states have the right to impose state sales taxes on purchases of these products by non-Indians at tribal businesses (Johnson and Turner 1998; O'Brien 1989). For example, with this argument, by 2003 Oklahoma had successfully persuaded twelve tribes in the state, including the Choctaws, to negotiate tribal-state "compacts" specifying how, specifically, tribes will collect and remit to the state state-tax revenues on tribal motor-fuel sales to non-Indians (Johnson and Turner 1998; *McAlester News Capital & Democrat*, September 30, 2003; Lambert, in press). Compacts are written, intergovernmental agreements that state that some action will be performed. Partly because compacts often involve heated discussions between parties, some legal wrangling, and unpredictable results, to varying extents they often make some so-called low-risk tribal enterprises, such as Choctaw travel plazas, risky for tribes.

Finally, as mentioned above, tribal officials also defined job creation as a central goal of the Kalichito project. At any given time, the Kalichito project provides between thirty and fifty jobs, helping tribal leaders affirm their assertion that job creation is a high priority in the new order and helping them address the criticisms of their primary constituents (Choctaw citizens) that the tribal government is not creating enough jobs.[3] Some of the full- and part-time positions at the Kalichito travel plaza are permanent; others, periodic. Running and maintaining this business that is

open twenty-four hours a day and nearly every day of the year requires
managers, clerks, cooks, drivers, construction workers, plumbers, technical experts, grounds crews, electricians, and others. In salaries and other
operating costs, at the time of my research the Kalichito project was operating on budget of almost one million dollars a month.

The Critical Importance of Job Creation

It is difficult to overstate the importance that many southeastern Oklahomans attach to job creation. In 1997 the county in which Kalichito is
located had the highest rate of unemployment in the state—12.6 percent.[4]
That year, approximately 25 percent of residents lived below the poverty
level; more than 90 percent did not have a college degree.[5] The dearth of
jobs is a primary reason that the population of many counties in the Choctaw Nation has plummeted during the last eight decades. Between 1920
and 1990, while the population of the state of Oklahoma increased by 50
percent, the population of eleven of the thirteen counties that comprise the
Choctaw Nation declined, in some areas quite dramatically. The population of Coal County fell from 18,406 to just 5,780; the population of Atoka
County, from 20,862 to 12,778; and the population of Choctaw County, by
half: from just over 32,000 to just over 15,000.[6] Whites and blacks, as well
as Choctaws, have been affected. Focusing on Choctaws, Faiman-Silva
documented the economic strategies that poor, unskilled Choctaw laborers in southeastern Oklahoma used in the 1980s to supplement substan-
dard household incomes. Among these were "household resource pooling"
(1997: 149) and "mobilizing family and household members in complex,
predominantly kin-based sharing networks" (p. 146). Petty commodity
production, unwaged labor, informal sharing networks, and subsistence
production also helped boost the meager incomes of the twelve Choctaw
families that Faiman-Silva studied. Randall Erwin, a politician who was
then serving as one of southeastern Oklahoma's representatives to the
state House of Representatives and whom some Choctaws identified as
a Choctaw, also identified new jobs and "growing" southeastern Oklahoma as a high priority.

   Long before the tribe broke ground for the project, Kalichito's non-
Choctaw residents were aware that their chances of procuring a job at
the project were slim. The Choctaw tribe gives employment preference
to enrolled Choctaws, a policy that is part of a larger class of "Indian
preference" hiring and promotion policies used by the BIA, IHS, and most

tribes.[7] In *Morton v. Mancari* (417 U.S. 535 [1974]), a case brought by non-Indians to protest what they described as this policy of "racial discrimination," the U.S. Supreme Court upheld the legality of such policies, arguing that Indian preference does not constitute "racial discrimination" or "racial" preference. The court explained that, because the preference "is not directed towards a 'racial' group consisting of 'Indians'" and "instead . . . applies only to members of 'federally recognized' tribes," the preference "is political rather than racial in nature." Despite the prevalence of Indian preference policies in early-twentieth-century Indian country, some tribes have chosen to fill many tribal government jobs with non-Indians, but not without facing criticism from tribal citizens (see, for example, Bordewich 1996). In the Choctaw Nation, Indian preference has provided legal grounds for the tribe's leadership to fill the vast majority of tribal jobs with Choctaws.[8]

Several times I heard local non-Choctaws complain about Choctaw Nation hiring practices.[9] Each time, Choctaw phenotypes were used to delegitimize the tribe's employment preference law. Most Choctaws do not have phenotypes that are stereotypically Indian, a social fact that has shaped Choctaw experience, as will be seen later in this chapter. Many times local non-Choctaws shared with me their belief that, because many Choctaws *look* white, the tribe is not, as they sometimes put it, "really Indian." Globally, of course, skin color is only sometimes used by human societies as a marker of difference. One need only point to most of Africa, where ethnic differences exist in the absence of differences in skin color. In Kalichito, my research into local history revealed that, for several generations, the town's non-Choctaws have experienced difficulties acknowledging the Choctaw identity of Choctaws in their town who can pass as white. Here it is worth pointing out that, as is the case elsewhere in the Choctaw Nation, under-a-quarters are the largest category of Choctaws in Kalichito, but quarter-or-mores, including full-bloods, are present and are even overrepresented in Kalichito as compared to the Choctaw Nation as a whole. It should be noted that in southeastern Oklahoma, Choctaws with a blood quantum that is as high as one-quarter often pass as white. The same is sometimes the case with Choctaws with a Choctaw blood quantum of one-half.

At every opportunity (except for tribal council meetings), tribal leaders avoided telling stories of specific families who had benefited directly from tribally created jobs, a behavior that can be explained in terms of these politicians' desire to eschew charges of favoritism from their constituents. In the absence of such stories—stories that have become an expected element of the rhetoric of other U.S. politicians—many Choctaws, especially those at a distance from a development project, publicly expressed doubts that these jobs were making a difference.[10] My research confirmed that the jobs created by the Kalichito project were a boon to local families. Below, I briefly describe three of these families. I then explore some of the less apparent ways that the project has affected Kalichito, an exploration that requires an extended foray into the history of Kalichito and probes shifts in community experience and identity.

After the Kalichito project's grand opening, I observed evidence of a marked improvement in the financial condition and economic status of two categories of Choctaw families at Kalichito. The first were families that were classed in the poorest one-third of the town's residents. As a result of the new jobs created in Kalichito by the travel plaza, more than a dozen of these residents moved out of this category and into the upper half of the town's population in terms of wealth. For example, the Anderson family was among the poorest in the community before the project opened. In the weeks prior to the opening of the project, Ray Anderson, a Choctaw, secured a job at the project. Ray had earned a certificate in accounting from a community college in the Chickasaw Nation but had been unemployed for the past five years. Four and a half years earlier, he had moved back to Kalichito and back into the home of his parents, Ella and Bobo. Ella and Bobo, both of whom were Choctaws, lived in the eastern part of Kalichito, a part of town that is located on the other side of the highway from Main Street and the town center. To attend community events and gatherings, the family would pile into their pickup and travel east on the county road that passes about one hundred yards south of the project. They would then turn left, past the project, before taking the sharp right that puts them on the road that leads to the town center.

The first time I traveled the other way on this route, away from town, in order to meet this family, I was unaware that this part of the community even existed, cut off as it is from the rest of the community. After having rounded the second bend of a remote road, I stopped at the entrance to the dirt road to their house. A metal gate hung lopsided on its hinges. Rust and the fact that the gate's left corner hung too low to the ground made the gate difficult to open. As I made my way up the dirt road to the small white farmhouse, I counted about a dozen cows in the pasture. I later learned that eight of these cows were owned by Ella's sister, Barbara, and her family, who lived in a nearby town. All twelve cows regularly were rotated between Ella and Bobo's small pasture, and the three small pastures owned by Barbara's family, an arrangement that provides examples of both "household resource pooling" and "mobilizing family and household members in complex, predominantly kin-based sharing networks" (Faiman-Silva 1997: 149, 146). As I noted that Ella and Bobo's farmhouse was in very poor condition—nearly dilapidated, in fact—I prepared myself for an interview with what I imagined would be one of the poorest families that I would meet during my research. Eight months later, I watched Ella and Bobo's family income more than triple, bringing the family out from under the poverty line and placing them in about the middle of Kalichito residents in terms of wealth. It should be pointed out that a family in this area need not obtain a very high income to make such a jump: in the county in which Kalichito is located, the median household income in 2000 was only about $22,000.[11]

I also watched the Kalichito project improve the financial condition and economic status of some of the more prosperous families in Kalichito. Within six months of the project's opening, for example, one Choctaw, a man named Hal, added more than a dozen acres to his family's lands. He also expanded his family's cattle holdings. An imposing Indian like his older brother Walt, Hal was a highly respected member of the community. In the winter he obtained one of the project's better jobs. With the income from this job, he purchased twenty acres near land that had been part of his family's allotment at the turn of the century. One hundred acres of this land had been sold in the early 1930s, Hal said, to another Choctaw family for fifty dollars an acre. Not two months after Hal had purchased the twenty acres, he bought about a dozen moderate-to-high- priced cattle from a vendor twenty miles east of Kalichito. Cattle are a form of wealth that the residents of Kalichito (and the southern half of southeastern Oklahoma) often refer to as "our college fund for our grandchildren," "our fund for our trip to Disneyland," or "our retirement account." Hal placed these new animals, together with these local and regional meanings, on his new acreage. Then, he bought more land. This time he invested in ranchland outside Kalichito. Some of this land was in a mid-sized town located across the border in northeast Texas; the rest lay several hundred miles to the west in a state that was not even contiguous to Oklahoma.

Three months later and less than two weeks before I left the region, Hal told me that he was looking for more land. He wanted to try his hand at growing soybeans, he explained with a twinkle in his eye, "on some good farmland in or around town."

In addition to improving the quality of life for new jobholders, whether poor or relatively prosperous, the Kalichito project has had a direct positive financial impact on at least some local households with no travel-plaza employee. At least some new jobholders regularly share part of their paychecks with relatives outside their household. Hal, for example, told me that he often "helped out" relatives. I found confirmation of his claims in a family to whom he was related. As it turned out, Hal was regularly providing Tina, the only child in this family who was still living at home, with clothing and spending money.

One evening, I began climbing the hill to Tina's home, a 1,100-square-foot dark red bungalow. Tina was a Choctaw, like her father. Her mother was white. As I completed the climb, I smiled as I remembered that about three months earlier Tina's dad, Billy, had excavated the family stepladder from a garage at the back of the house, a garage that housed a small, half-rotted boat as well as Tina's mother's sizeable craft collection. He had then wrestled with three or four strings of Christmas lights—a garage-sale find—from about 2:00 p.m. until well after dusk, when from inside the house I and the whole family heard him let out a few curses. Within about ten minutes, all of us were out on the lawn, coatless in thirty-degree weather, trying to convince Billy that "no one was gonna notice" the unevenness of the lights that he had just strung across the front of the family's house.

With the money for clothing and incidentals that Hal was providing, Billy's teenage daughter said that she felt more comfortable with her peers. Giddy from her newfound social acceptance, she vividly described to me the world of local youth. Among other things it was from her that I first learned that Choctaw teenagers and white teenagers shared a youth-defined and -enforced social world that was separate from that of black teens. Friendships and dating relationships crossed the Choctaw-white ethnic boundary; rarely did they cross Choctaw-black or white-black boundaries. The patterned mesh of interrelationships that bound together Choctaws and whites was so entrenched, in fact, that Choctaw teens claimed only occasionally to "run around with only Choctaws." Tina and other Choctaw teens said that the only occasions in which they interacted exclusively with Choctaw teens were the Labor Day Festival in Tushka Homma and Choctaw community center events. The Choctaw community center to which they referred is the center in Tali, a pseudonym for a mid-sized town that is located thirteen miles to the north. Tina sat curled up in a denim beanbag chair during our interview. She glowed as she described the ways local Choctaw and white teens spent Friday and Saturday nights. "[On weekend nights], we drag Main [Street]," she said, smiling. "Everyone has to drag Main. You just drive up and down the street and see if anyone new happens to be in town, and waste gas. It gets kind of boring after a while. Then, the [Choctaw and white teenagers] in Pitchlynn or Hotema [pseudonyms for nearby small towns] might decide, 'well, it's boring here, so let's go see what the Kalichito group is doing.' They come over here [Kalichito], you meet up with them and talk with them. The next night, you go over to their town, and you drag Main over there."

Choctaw and white teen social interaction in Kalichito, as Tina's account shows, is part of a larger, multitown network of teen social relationships that is structured by race and town affiliation. Choctaw and white teens in the area see themselves as occupying a common social category, a category that is defined in part by its opposition to the category, "black," and they express belonging in this category in part through reciprocal visiting. At the same time, the centrality of town affiliation to the practice of "dragging Main" helps create, reinforce, and reproduce constructions of commonality between Kalichito's Choctaw and white teens. Tina's account introduced me to some of the ways Choctaws experience and negotiate the multiethnic, multiracial small town of Kalichito. As will be seen, the Kalichito project, together with other relatively recent public expressions of the tribe's presence in the town, has been recasting that experience. Tina and most other Choctaw and white teens still occupy a common social category, but it is increasingly less possible for whites in this multitown network to deny Choctaw distinctiveness and identity.

In sum, the project's most apparent—and for some Choctaws in Kalichito, its most important—consequence was its creation of dozens of jobs. These jobs improved the standard of living for both the poor and better-off Choctaws who landed these new jobs. The nonhousehold kin, as well as the household kin, of these new jobholders also benefited materially, as nonhousehold kin are part of patron-client networks that connect kin in and beyond the community. An interview with a teenager who was part of this network focused attention on an aspect of community experience and identity—specifically, the content and form of local social boundaries—that facilitated my exploration into other, less apparent ways that the Kalichito project has affected this community. This exploration involved an extended look at the history of shifts in the ways identity has been constructed in this community.

The Foregrounding of Choctaw Identity and Other Key Features of Community Life in Kalichito

Though local social boundaries placed whites and Choctaws in one category, and blacks in another, the Choctaw identity of many of the Choctaw residents of Kalichito was public and foregrounded. Local non-Choctaws—whether they were white or black—readily identified the Choctaws in Kalichito to me, and in conversations with one another they frequently referred to certain individuals as Choctaws. Sometimes I observed non-Choctaws in the community discussing Choctaw-related matters. Such topics included the tribal election, the tribe's plans to build a new hospital, and, as will be the focus of the next chapter, the claims of the tribal leadership that the tribe owns all of the water in southeastern Oklahoma. Choctaws themselves often publicly referenced their Choctaw identity. In local non-Choctaw as well as in Choctaw-only contexts, they talked about, for example, their support for the continued renovation of the old Choctaw boarding school of Wheelock Academy (which ceased operation in 1955), renovations, they said, "that would help preserve our history." They also brought up, for example, the topics of who in the community would get an "Indian home" that year, or whether for whatever reason they or another Choctaw in the community needed to make a trip that month to the tribal capitol in Durant. During community gatherings in the town, which included, for example, a pie supper and an Easter egg hunt, several times I overheard non-Choctaws in the community asking Choctaws whether "they could get Chief Roberts" to "pave the road that runs out past Otis's place," contribute a little money to help relocate a town well, or "let Grady use a backhoe for a few days."

A number of physical expressions of the tribe's presence today express and help reinforce local public recognition of the Choctaw past, present, and future in this community. These include, in addition to the Kalichito project, "Indian homes," food, and holiday gifts. One need not travel very far in Kalichito to encounter what people throughout Indian country refer to as an "Indian home." Indian homes, first built in the Choctaw Nation by

Chief Harry Belvin in the early 1970s, are homes that tribal governments build for tribal members and their families.[12] Such homes are physically distinctive. When I was conducting my fieldwork, I visited the Bohannon family three days after they had moved into a modest single-wide trailer on the easternmost edge of Kalichito. Tommy was seventy years old and an enrolled Choctaw. His wife, Bobbi, was sixty-six, of Cherokee ancestry, and told me that she was trying "to get on the [Cherokee] rolls."[13] The couple was rearing two of their grandsons, ages eleven and seven. All of the couple's seven children had moved away from the Choctaw Nation to get work, Bobbi told me. One was a butcher; another, a child psychologist. A third was working at a minimum-wage job in Texas while he competed on the rodeo circuit.

Their old house, they explained as they pointed toward the pecan trees on the other side of the pasture, was going to be "tore down and burnt." "The electric bill ran $200 a month in the summer to keep the place cool," Bobbi explained, and in the winter, heating was a problem as "Tommy got so old he could hardly chop wood." On the spot where their old house sat, their new home—an Indian home—would be built. "It's going to take three months to build. They're running ahead of schedule now," Bobbi beamed. The previous Friday, two of Bobbi's husband's kinfolks, two young Choctaws from a neighboring town, had helped the elderly couple move into the trailer. "I don't know what we would have done if they hadn't helped us," she sighed as she also explained that the young woman helps Bobbi with her housework and the young man helps chop and carry wood for the couple.

Tribally supplied food and holiday gifts are other concrete expressions of the penetration of the tribal government into the most remote corners of the Choctaw Nation and the efforts of the tribal government to more fully incorporate local Choctaw Nation communities into the new political order. Since the mid-1980s, poor families in Kalichito such as the Bohannons have been served by the Choctaw Nation Food Distribution Program. Each month, Choctaw families drive from Kalichito to a large Choctaw Nation food warehouse in a nearby town. They return with approximately eighty pounds of food for each member of their household.[14] In addition, at Christmas time, many of Kalichito's Choctaw children receive gifts from the tribe. When I was conducting my fieldwork, four of the tribe's bingo centers held toy drives (see also *Oklahoman*, December 22, 1995).

Together with fruit baskets and clothes, these toys were distributed to Choctaw children by tribal representatives.[15]

It took me many months to identify and confirm the fact that Choctaw identity in Kalichito was not only marked but foregrounded. This was due to an inescapable and central feature of present-day life in this community: Kalichitoans interacted very little with one another. Kalichitoans interacted at some community events, examples of which were mentioned above. In addition, teens socialized often, as did household kin. Finally, it was common for nonhousehold kin who lived nearby to visit one another, eat together, and maintain informal exchanges of goods and services with one another. In general, however, the lives of the vast majority of Kalichitoans were defined by a pronounced social isolation from other families in the community.

Kalichitoans tend to view their homes as a refuge from what many see as the difficult outside world. For reasons that will be discussed shortly, many endure long commutes to grueling jobs in factories in faraway midsized towns. Many regularly accept overtime work or second jobs, and more than a few spend many hours tending cattle in the fields outside their homes, homes which tend to be located at a distance from other homes in the community. Among other things, I was struck by how little current information community members had about others in their community. For example, I found that many Kalichitoans were unaware of where some of their neighbors worked, when and where a family in the community had gone on vacation, or when a community member had purchased a new truck. In addition, in this town, as in others in the Choctaw Nation, there are a fair number of what tribal lawmakers refer to as "shut-ins," that is, individuals who venture outside their homes only once or twice a week to buy essentials. Many Kalichitoans simply "keep to themselves," as several of them put it.

This reality heightened the difficulties of conducting field research. Once I had let go of my preconceptions about rural community life, which were idealized and romantic, and recommitted myself to writing an ethnography about my tribe that addressed not only tribal-level activity and interaction (the focus of chapters 4 and 6) but also community-level experience, I embarked on research that, by necessity, revolved around scheduled visits to people's homes.

Most of my visits were with elders, a population to whom anthropologists tend to gravitate because elders tend to be able to provide broad perspectives on changing social landscapes. In addition, unlike most of Kalichito's working adults, most elders in Kalichito have lots of time. As a population, they are also overrepresented in Kalichito, as they are throughout the Choctaw Nation. Many of the Choctaw Nation's young people have migrated to Oklahoma City, Tulsa, Dallas, or other cities (see also Faiman-Silva 1997).

The Past and the Present: The "Falling Apart" of "Community"

Elders often contrasted the present, which they saw as being marked by a virtual absence of "community," with the past. They claimed that, during their youth and young adulthood, there was extensive interaction between Kalichitoans. Virtually all described their community as having "fallen apart" since the 1950s. My field research supported their view that Kalichito currently is defined by a relatively high level of social disintegration, as are some other American Indian communities (see, for example, Shkilnyk 1985).

Interviews revealed that the primary source of this disintegration has been the decline of small-scale farming in this community. From the time of first settlement in Kalichito to the 1950s, almost all of the community's residents earned a living from farming. In the 1950s, "the bottom fell out of farming," one elder explained. "That was when the machines came in." By this she was referring to the investment by three or four of Kalichito's wealthier farming families in several pieces of large farm equipment as part of an attempt to save their farms and the farming way of life. For at least a few years before this event, farming had been losing much of its ground in this community and the region. Long hours, the increased expense of products required to grow a crop, the high level of risk, and other factors had come together during the 1950s to help drive the farmers of the community out of farming and, in many cases, into a type of poverty, characterized by too little food and by homelessness, that Kalichito's elders claimed was virtually unheard of in their community before the 1950s.[16] At the same time, the consequences of decades of what would later be called "poor farming practices" starting making themselves felt at this time. In the early 1950s the town's farmland began showing signs of serious erosion. Nearly gone was the rich topsoil that had once been very good farmland due to its history as old river-bottom land. As a result, crops were inferior, and the amount of labor and land required to produce a decent crop increased sharply.

Large-scale emigration from Kalichito was the result. Many Choctaws, whites, and blacks permanently relocated. Some blacks moved to nearby Tali, where they joined other blacks in a community that they called "blacktown" and that Choctaws and whites called "niggertown" (see also Sturm 2002 for similar constructions among the Oklahoma Cherokees). Since at least 1912, Tali has had what has also been called a "Negro section" (Imon 1977). Some whites and Choctaws who remained in the community turned to ranching; many more, to factory and other nonfarm jobs in nearby towns. A city to which I will give the pseudonym Lister, located twenty miles to the south across the border into north Texas, and Tali, thirteen miles to the north, became primary recipients of displaced Choctaw and white labor. Many of these former farmers became factory workers. During the late twentieth and early twenty-first centuries, Kalichito residents have been among the hundreds who have streamed in each day to the Campbell Soup, Philips Lighting, and Kimberly-Clark factories that decorate the outskirts of Lister. Lister's small bread factory and rubber factory have also been targets of job searches by Kalichitoans. One Choctaw told me that, beginning in the early 1960s when she was in her late teens, she started working for a glove factory in Tali, sewing gloves. "I worked in that factory through three changes in ownership," she said. At one point, she had to sew baby clothes, putting the little ruffle of lace across the shoulders and front of dresses. "They were so little," she said. "It was hard work." She worked in that factory for seventeen years before getting a job as a clerk at the Kalichito project. "The only place there were windows in the factory was in the lobby." Where she worked, she said, there were no windows. "It was hard not being able to look out. And there weren't even windows in the cafeteria there!"

By all accounts, the decline of small-scale farming in the 1950s was a seminal event in Kalichito's economic history and was thus a critical part of the larger context into which the Kalichito project inserted itself. The decline of small-scale farming in the 1950s atomized a community that most elders—white, black, and Choctaw—remembered as close-knit and characterized by a deep care and concern for others. The first half of the twentieth century, many said, was a time when parents, children, grandchildren, and grandparents spent time together as a family and when the families of the community spent time with one another. A good deal of information that elders, both Choctaw and non-Choctaw, provided about community experience and identity in Kalichito during the first half of the twentieth century seemed to support their own argument of a romantic past. Much more, however, did not. When the story of early-poststatehood experience in this town began to emerge through interviews, and when I placed this story in the larger context of the history of Kalichito during the period prior to the experience of my informants (e.g., the second half of the nineteenth century), I gained a much fuller understanding of and appreciation for what the rebuilding of our tribe in the 1970s and the building of the Kalichito project in the mid-1990s have really meant for this community. The public expressions of the tribe's presence in this town, of which the Kalichito project is the most potent, have been helping Choctaws reclaim the Choctaw identity of their town. This is one of the most important local consequences of tribal nation building, and it is a central argument of this chapter.

Elders, particularly Choctaws and blacks, wanted me to tell the story of their town's history. They wanted their experiences to be remembered, to be passed down to future generations. I eagerly complied with these requests in part because the story of the history of this town is a fascinating story that brings into sharp relief shifts in the ways identity has been constructed in small-town Choctaw Nation and the identity processes that are part of these shifts. In addition, as will be seen, past identity constructions inform contemporary constructions of identity, particularly Choctaw constructions of identity. Indeed, after tracing the history of this town, I explore the implications of past Choctaw identity constructions in the present. Finally, the history told below provides the context in which the Kalichito project must be placed, a context that informs local social understandings and meanings of the project, and of the past.

One thing that is brought to the fore by the below history of shifts in community experience and identity in Kalichito, as compared to community experience and identity in the present, is that during the nineteenth century the Choctaw tribal government shaped community life and experience in myriad ways. Today, the tribal government is once again a presence at the local level. As compared to the nineteenth century, however, the power and influence of the tribal government have eroded significantly in all areas but one: the reckoning of who is and is not a citizen of the tribe. The shift in this area of Choctaw life and experience is critical to understanding past and present Choctaw identity formations in Kalichito and the present-day role of the tribal government in shaping local and tribal identity-claims. Because of this, let me briefly address the ways by which this shift is negotiated and experienced in Kalichito.

On the question of who is a Choctaw, the modern Choctaw tribal government has increased its authority vis-à-vis local communities to the point that now the Choctaw tribal government has assumed near total control—within the tribe—over the public Choctaw identity assertions of individuals. Since the early 1980s, formal, bureaucratic definitions of who is a Choctaw—devised, implemented, and enforced by the tribal government—have take precedence over informal, community-based definitions that were so prominent after the attempted dissolution of the tribe in 1906. Prior to 1906, Choctaw national leaders, like the leaders of the other Five "Civilized" Tribes, appear not only to have consulted with but also even deferred to community leaders on the question of who was a tribal citizen (Debo 1940; Stremlau 2005). The new formal definition of Choctaw citizenship as limited to those listed on the Dawes Rolls under "Choctaws by Blood" and to their descendants, a definition that is enshrined in the Choctaw Constitution of 1983, has excluded many Choctaws, including several elderly Choctaws in Kalichito who have been recognized as Choctaws for as long as any of the Choctaws in the community can remember (see Carter 1999 for a perspective on the process of enrollment on the Dawes Rolls, which excluded some Choctaws). Local Choctaws sometimes referred to the individuals whom the tribal government (and through the tribal government, the federal government) places in the category "non-Indian" as "Choctaw but not enrolled." That is, unlike their tribal government, Kalichito's Choctaws do not deny the Choctaw identity of these individuals. The experience of those classed as "Choctaw but not enrolled" is often difficult. The transformations that have taken place in the public experience and identity of Choctaws locally—transformations that are detailed below—have made the visibility of these Choctaws qua Choctaws only partial and incomplete. These Choctaws continue to be recognized as Choctaws by the Choctaws in Kalichito. Local non-Choctaws, however, continue to deny their Indian identity, as do the Choctaw tribal government, the federal government, the U.S. courts, and other entities and organizations who use the criterion "enrolled member of a federally recognized tribe" to determine who is and is not an Indian.[17]

It is worth pointing out that such shifts in the locus of control of tribal membership from the local to the tribal level have occurred in many parts of Indian country during the twentieth century. In the early twentieth century, for example, southern Paiutes gave priority to local systems of tribal membership which often utilized not only the criterion of Paiute descent but also such criteria as "in-marriage, residence, a record of hard work, known character, and general ethics" (Knack 2001: 193). By the late twentieth century, a centralized Paiute tribal government had assumed total control over tribal citizenship and established formal legal criteria based on blood quantum (Knack 2001). Among the Choctaws, there has been surprisingly little community resistance in Kalichito, as elsewhere in the Choctaw Nation, to tribal governmental control over who is a Choctaw citizen. Jason Jackson's ethnography of the Yuchis (2003) suggests that, in contrast, community resistance to tribal governmental control over citizenship in the Muscogee (Creek) Nation is high, perhaps even the highest in Indian country. Many Yuchis contest the legitimacy of Creek-government control over Yuchi affairs and the legal designation of Yuchis as Muscogee (Creek) citizens by the Creek national government.

Like those in Kalichito whom local Choctaws term "Choctaw but not enrolled," another category of local Choctaws occupies an ambiguous position with respect to issues of boundaries and belonging in the Choctaw Nation: those whom tribal bureaucrats informally term "black Choctaws." "Black Choctaws" are enrolled Choctaws whose phenotypes are stereotypically African American.[18] Black Choctaws appear to be comparatively rare, at least in the Choctaw Nation and in Oklahoma City. Before conducting my research, to my knowledge I had never met a black Choctaw, and during my research I encountered only a few of which I was aware. This makes it difficult (and somewhat problematic) to generalize about how they are perceived by non-black Choctaws. Two things, however, are clear. First, many non-black Choctaws living in the Choctaw Nation hold racist views toward blacks, and this racism prompts them to draw and maintain boundaries between themselves and all blacks, including black Choctaws. Second, Choctaws do not appear to have widely incorporated the image of the Choctaw with a stereotypically black phenotype into their conceptions of Choctaw diversity and nationhood. Images of Choctaws with stereotypically white and stereotypically Indian phenotypes, in contrast, are central to Choctaw imaginings of their citizenry and of Choctaw identity. Drawing upon her own experiences as a Choctaw, Devon Mihesuah asserts that "the people [with Native and black ancestry] who look black will most likely be viewed as black" (2003: 91).

Interviews with two black Choctaws who lived near Kalichito provided a perspective, though limited, of black Choctaw experience in negotiating their Choctaw citizenship. One of them, a fifty-five-year-old man named Alvin, spent a significant part of the interview telling me that Chief Roberts, whom he claimed was a personal friend, was an excellent Choctaw leader in part because Roberts considered Alvin fully a Choctaw, despite (as Alvin put it) his black skin. During this monologue, Alvin implied that other non-black Choctaws, specifically those in his town, were reluctant to do the same, but he provided no specific examples of this and avoided directly addressing the issue. When asked to describe his participation in tribal affairs, Alvin spoke about his experiences "voting in every election," going to a Choctaw Nation clinic for health care, and receiving tribally supplied food. At no point did he imply that tribal officials had discouraged him or in other ways made it difficult for him to exercise his Choctaw citizenship. A second black Choctaw, Bernice, socialized with Alvin as part of their shared membership and participation in their town's black community. I was struck by the sharp contrast between Bernice's participation and interest in Choctaw tribal affairs—that is, her experience of her Choctaw citizenship—and that of Alvin. For example, Bernice told me that she "couldn't be bothered voting" in tribal elections, and she claimed not even to know the name of her representative on the tribal council, which is virtually unthinkable for a Choctaw living in the Choctaw Nation. I suspect that Bernice's relationship to the tribe may be typical of black Choctaws living in the Choctaw Nation. This would help explain their marked lack of visibility on the Choctaw political landscape. The following discussion addresses issues of Choctaw visibility—not just of black Choctaws but of white and even of phenotypically Indian Choctaws—from the first half of the nineteenth century to the present. This history, which is based on archival research and interviews with Kalichitoans, helps bring to the fore the fact that the tribal travel plaza, together with other public expressions of the tribe, have been helping Choctaws reclaim the Choctaw identity of their town.

Choctaws and Non-Choctaws: An Introduction
to the History of Kalichito Town

Choctaw settlement at Kalichito began shortly after the Choctaws were forcibly relocated on the Trail of Tears to their present-day tribal homeland during the 1830s and early 1840s. Imon describes the town as "dating far back into the early days of the Territory" (1977: 81). Archival sources note the birth of a black baby (probably a slave) as early as 1839 on a small Choctaw plantation in what is now Kalichito, and records from one of the town's several cemeteries reveal burials of Choctaws that date to 1864.[19] During the nineteenth century, the area in and around this community was among the most prosperous in the Choctaw Nation. Kalichito residents farmed rich river-bottom lands that produced comparatively large yields of corn, and later of cotton. Choctaw homes in this part of what was then Kiamitia County in the Choctaw Nation were located no closer than one-quarter mile to one another, and the fact that the entire population of the county totaled only about 1,250 in 1885 indicates that Kalichito must have been quite small (WPA Indian-Pioneer History Collection [interview with Julius P. Ward]; 1885 Choctaw Nation Census). Kalichito's Choctaws observed at least some preremoval Choctaw ceremonies and customs, as is indicated in a brief description of a Choctaw wedding ceremony that occurred in the community shortly after removal (WPA Indian-Pioneer History Collection [interview with Annie Maude Usray Self]).

One of the most important events in Kalichito's postremoval history was the completion in 1887 of the Monette, Missouri, to Paris, Texas, line of the St. Louis–San Francisco or "Frisco" railroad, which not only passed through Kalichito but also stopped there. Two years later, the community acquired a U.S. post office, the first postmaster of which was Choctaw (Foreman 1928). This ended the long treks that members of the community were said to have taken to the nearest post office in a town to the north (WPA Indian-Pioneer History Collection [interview with Paul Garnett Roebuck]). In 1896 two Choctaw citizens in the community established a store that became what Judge C. E. Dudley recalled as "the largest merchantile [sic] business in all this part of the Indian Territory" (Dudley n.d.: 49; see also Imon 1977).[20]

From the time of the first Choctaw settlement in Kalichito in the 1830s to the end of the nineteenth century, local experience and identity in this town, as in other Choctaw Nation towns, was shaped by public recognition of the Choctaw identity of many town residents and of the community itself. Everyday life, for example, was marked by public expressions of and encounters with the Choctaw tribal state. The tribal government operated a school system, regulated property rights, controlled immigration, levied taxes, and enforced tribal law. Non-Choctaws lived in Kalichito, as they did elsewhere in the Choctaw Nation in large numbers during the late nineteenth century. With exceptions, however, profound legal and social marginality defined the everyday life and experience of non-Choctaws. The political rights of those who were not Choctaw national citizens, for example, were severely limited and in some cases nonexistent. During the years prior to Oklahoma statehood, the everyday presence of the Choctaw tribal state helped define Choctaw identity as primarily a national, rather than a racial or ethnic, identity. Community leaders played a role in determining who was and was not a tribal citizen.

As the nineteenth century came to a close, non-Choctaws in the Kalichito area, bolstered by the apparent imminence of Oklahoma statehood and by the fact that they now outnumbered Choctaws, increasingly resisted what they saw as the "intrusion" of the Choctaw tribal government into their affairs. One such non-Choctaw who lived near Kalichito was Joe Brown. Remarking on Brown's efforts to flout Choctaw national authority was Brown's contemporary C. E. Dudley: "At that time [before Oklahoma statehood], people were supposed to get a permit from the Choctaw Nation to have cattle in this country. Joe Brown refused to pay for a permit and he was served with notice if he did not procure the permit his cattle would be moved across the river out into Texas. He still refused to pay and his cattle were gathered and they had them down around Grant, I think, when the Antlers Bank and Trust Company which had a mortgage on the cattle, prevailed upon Joe Brown to pay for the permit and advanced him the money and in that way the permit was secured and the cattle were not moved out" (Dudley n.d.: 38).

When Congress passed the Curtis Act of 1898 and related laws that were oriented toward dissolving the tribe, in Kalichito, as elsewhere in the Choctaw Nation, noncitizens of the Choctaw tribe, specifically white noncitizens, began experiencing both a dramatic expansion of their political rights and more secure property rights in the Choctaw Nation (see chapter 2). The creation of the new state of Oklahoma in 1907 helped institutionalize these new legal and political rearrangements. Together, these changes provided a basis for whites in Kalichito to claim legal and symbolic ownership of the community, despite its history as a Choctaw Nation community. These transformations also provided a basis for whites to deny that Choctaws had remained Choctaws through the turn-of-the-century upheavals. The status of Choctaw as a national identity, together with the nature of the upheavals as acts of legal, social, and political assimilation, raised questions about the continued public import of a Choctaw identity, even for Choctaws themselves (see Debo 1940). In

Kalichito these changes initiated a period of local public denial of Choctaw survival, a period that lasted until at least the 1970s when a sharp rise in expressions of and encounters with the Choctaw tribal government began making it difficult for whites in Kalichito to sustain claims that the tribe had been dismantled at statehood.

In the years following statehood, one of the most potent expressions in Kalichito of local public denial of Choctaw survival and of local efforts to legitimize white control over Choctaw land was the implementation of a black-white binary racial classificatory system. By whites, as well as by blacks and some Choctaws, most Choctaws in Kalichito were shoehorned into the categories of white or black. By at least the 1920s, a black-white divide had become entrenched in Kalichito and was playing a significant role in defining community experience and identity in this town. The backdrop for this transformation was the rapid diminishment after the turn of the twentieth century of Kalichito's importance, a consequence of the birth in 1901 and subsequent explosive growth of Tali thirteen miles to the north. Tali was home to six thousand people by the late 1920s (Imon 1976, 1977). By that time, it had become clear that if Kalichito would survive at all through the twentieth century, it would exist in the shadows of Tali. In 1926 a journalist for a major, statewide newspaper described Kalichito as "now a village of only a few hundred souls, its ancient glories departed" (Oklahoman, November 27, 1926).[21]

Local classifications of farms helped construct the black-white divide in this small farming community. Interviews with whites and blacks revealed that, during the period between statehood and the 1940s, Kalichito's farms were divided into two primary categories: "white farms" (which, as will be seen, included most Choctaw farms) and "black farms" (which included the farms of phenotypically black Kalichitoans, some of whom were descended from both Choctaws and blacks). "White farms," which were farms that were owned by Kalichitoans who were publicly classified (by whites) as white, were subdivided into large and small farms. Kalichito had more than a half-dozen large farms, which produced corn, cotton, soybeans, and other crops for profit and which employed almost one hundred blacks, more than three times as many blacks as lived in the community in the late 1990s. Nestled among these large farm businesses were smaller subsistence farms owned by other "whites." Chickens, milk cows, and small fish ponds rounded out these smaller enterprises, on many of which one or two blacks worked.

Black experience in Kalichito was shaped by backbreaking work in the fields, together with poverty and segregation.[22] Toward the end of better understanding the ways social categories were reconfigured during the early poststatehood period, I collected six accounts from African Americans about black life in Kalichito during the first half of the twentieth century. One of these accounts was that of Sally Crenshaw. In 1930 Mrs. Crenshaw, then twenty-three, had migrated from Arkansas to Kalichito. Only a short time after her migration, she married a second-generation black migrant. In 1972 she moved to Tali, where I interviewed her in 1996. About black experience in Kalichito during the 1930s and 1940s, this stately, eighty-eight-year-old woman said:

> We [blacks] worked for all the white peoples in [Kalichito]. We picked cotton, chopped corn, set out potatoes. Honey we just worked hours! . . . There was me, my husband, his sister, two brothers, and [my husband] and his daddy and some of my childrens 'cause they was old enough: I had Florence, and Retha, Hazel, Daisy and Dub . . . I had all o' them . . .
>
> [And even though my daddy-in-law] had two wagons and two teams, we had to walk [to the fields in the morning]! Yes sir, baby, sure did—carryin' my kids! And I didn't know they had the whoopin' cough! . . . [Then, at the end of the day] we had to walk a mile, mile-an-a-half home. I had to cook, wash baby diapers, hang 'em out. I had all dat to do, honey, 'fore I went to bed. I was tired, baby, I sure was!

Long working hours, grueling agricultural and domestic labor, and poverty were persistent themes in Mrs. Crenshaw's account and in the accounts of other local blacks, providing insight into the content and character of early-poststatehood black experience in Kalichito.

Aldrich (1973) notes that blacks in Oklahoma who depended upon employment as day laborers, as did Sally, tended to work on cotton fields as hoers and pickers. Generally, the whole family worked in the cotton fields, he points out, as a child could earn several dollars a day as a picker.[23] As Mrs. Crenshaw's account indicates, blacks in Kalichito lived at a distance from the white farms. This geographic divide helped bound (and define) the two categories of black and white in the community. Blacks told me that, alongside the small wooden houses in which they and their families lived, most of them maintained gardens. Some had a few chickens; at least one had a milk cow. For supplies and some food, they patronized stores run by their employers, several of which were on Kalichito's present-day Main Street. The largest such store sold dry goods, clothing, shoes, farm tools, and hardware (Imon 1977).[24] Kalichito's stores probably also sold "patent medicines," such as Bell's Pine Tar Honey, Dr. Mike's Heart Remedy, and Swamp Root, as did a store in a nearby small town (*Tuskahoma Item*, March 30, 1911). It is likely that blacks in Kalichito, like blacks in nearby towns, held their own events, such as picnics and dances (see, for example, *Albion Advocate*, July 5, 1918). Blacks in Kalichito may also have attended events in nearby towns. Such events were identified by local newspapers as events "for the colored."

Choctaw elders who talked with me about the community's poststatehood farming past confirmed the social importance of the black-white divide in Kalichito and the categorization of Kalichito's farms into "white farms" and "black farms." Older Choctaws in Kalichito, like older Yuchis in the Muscogee (Creek) Nation just north of the Choctaw Nation, "vividly described the agricultural work of their youth" (Jackson 2003: 41). From Choctaw elders, I learned that approximately one-third of the large "white farms" in Kalichito and at least a half-dozen of the smaller "white farms" were actually owned by Choctaws. As will be seen, at statehood whites initiated what Aihwa Ong describes as a process of conferring "honorary whiteness" upon nonwhites in their community who were not black, attempting to impose a schema through which local determinations of status and dignity were made in terms of "a national [U.S.] ideology that projects worthy citizens as inherently 'white'" (2004: 62). From Choctaw elders, I also learned that in the 1930s the head of household of at least one of Kalichito's "black farms" was a Choctaw, a man with both Choctaw and black ancestry. Third, I learned that, although most Choctaws in Kalichito were publicly recognized as either white or black, in several different contexts many continued to recognize their and others' Choctaw identity. The most common such context was the private, domestic sphere. Other contexts in which this occurred were semiprivate and exclusively Choctaw, as will be seen later in this chapter.

During this period of local public denial of Choctaw identity in this town, a period that extended well beyond the mid-twentieth century, a few Choctaws in the community existed publicly outside of the black-white "bipolar racial order" that then, as now, so strongly shaped social experience in the United States (Ong 2004). Interviews revealed that several community members who were described as "full-blood or nearly so" were classed as Indians not only by Choctaws but also by whites and blacks. I was unable to determine whether, or the extent to which, the high-blood-quantum Choctaws' public classification as Indian during this period indicated a shift from constructions of Choctaw as a national identity to constructions of Choctaw as part of a larger racial category, "Indian." Interviews with Choctaw elders strongly suggested, as will be seen, that many Choctaws continued to construct the category, Choctaw, as a national category while non-Choctaws treated high-blood-quantum Choctaws as part of a racial category. It is possible, however, that, in the context of a decline in supralocal expressions of Choctaw national identity, Choctaws increasingly racialized the Indian identity of high-blood-quantum Choctaws while maintaining their historic emphasis on constructions of Choctaw as a nationality.

The Intersection of Larger, Regional Structures and Local Structures during the Early Poststatehood Period

The strength of a binary racial classificatory scheme in a territory that only decades earlier had been owned and controlled exclusively by Indians both reflected and was reinforced by laws mandating the segregation of blacks and whites in the new state of Oklahoma. Article 13, section 3, of the Oklahoma Constitution (1907), for example, stated that there were to be "separate schools for white and colored children." "Colored children" were defined in this article as "children of African descent," and "white children," as "all other children" (Aldrich 1973: 36).[25] In other words, except for the relatively small number of Indian children who attended BIA boarding schools or church-run schools for Indians, Indian children in Oklahoma with no apparent black ancestry attended "white" schools after statehood. Elsewhere in America during this period, many Indian children were denied access to the public schools. School districts throughout Utah, Nevada, Arizona, and California, for example, refused to educate, among others, Paiute Indian children. In Nevada, "mixed-blood," as well as full-blood Paiute children, were barred from the public schools until the 1930s (Knack 2001).

The first Oklahoma legislature also passed laws outlawing miscegenation wherein "white people" were defined as "all people except the Negro race" (Aldrich 1973: 54). By not outlawing sexual liaisons between whites and Indians, Oklahoma matched the behavior of most other U.S. states during this period (Biolsi 2004). Aldrich cites five cases of marriage between

blacks and Indians that were prosecuted during the first half of the twentieth century and are revealing of state-level constructions of whiteness.
One of these Indians was a full-blood; another was three-quarters Indian
"blood quantum." The prosecution of these Indians under Oklahoma's
black-white antimiscegenation laws underlines the fact that, at least at
the regional level, at least some formal definitions of the category, white,
included all Indians, even full-bloods.

At the local level, these larger, regional structures of oppression that
were targeted at controlling blacks were used in Kalichito not only to control blacks but also to legitimize legal and symbolic control by whites over
Choctaws and Choctaw land. Local non-Choctaw elders saw the label-
ing of Choctaws as whites or blacks as negating Choctaw identity. Most
Choctaw elders understood that non-Choctaws saw it this way. They made
a point of stating, however, that during this period they and most other
Choctaws did not. For early-twentieth-century Choctaws, it was not their
racial classification as white or black that had the potential of negating
their continued identity as Choctaws: it was their new classification beginning in 1901 as U.S. citizens. These Choctaw elders had received notions
of Choctaw identity from parents and grandparents who had been born
before statehood. Such notions defined Choctaw identity as a nationality,
not a race (see also Baird 1990). I was reassured that these elders were not
simply imposing present-day constructions upon the past when I listened
to their grandchildren. Nearly a century has passed since local whites and
blacks in Kalichito began attempting to erase Choctaws by treating Choctaw identity as a racial identity (specifically, as an identity defined by stereotypically Indian physical characteristics), a process that has refracted
and continues to refract larger-scale efforts in the U.S. to racialize American Indian identities.[26] Influenced by these local and supralocal constructions, the grandchildren of Choctaw oldtimers in Kalichito tended to be
less insistent that race and Choctaw identity be decoupled, and in some
contexts they themselves even racialized their Choctaw identity (but in
a different way). Later, I will return to this phenomenon.

Interviews with whites and Choctaws provided insight into what whites
described as Kalichito's "white community," a label that Choctaws rarely
used but of which most of them were nevertheless a part. Community
events in the 1910s and 1920s, attended by whites and Choctaws, included
barbeques. "A beef would be killed," explained a ninety-one-year-old full-
blood Choctaw, "and a big hole would be dug and the beef would be put

in there." At one point during my research, I attended an elk roast at the home of a man whom community members recognized as a Choctaw but whom the tribal government did not. Guests clustered in a spacious living room under the watchful eyes of Oklahoma deer and Colorado elk that had been stuffed and mounted on the brown paneling. My enjoyment of this feast was considerably enhanced by two Choctaw elders reclining in twin La-Z-boys nearby, reminiscing about the past. I was the only one at the gathering, it seemed, who was interested in such matters, and, in fact, I was kidded about this interest throughout my research. Among the things that these elders told me and one another at the elk roast is that, during the late 1910s and early 1920s, they could remember "seein' eighty kids hangin' out at [a local store]." The store, one of them continued, "was run by J. D. Lightman, a Choctaw." "There was white kids and Indian kids living in the neighborhood 'round here," the other said pointedly, "and they were all mixed-up. White kids and Indian kids played together and went to school together." Blacks "ran around with each another."

Field Labor, Informal Social Interaction, Sports, Schooling, and Jim Crow Laws: Structures That Further Defined and Reinforced Local Racial Categories during the Early Poststatehood Period

Choctaws, whites, and blacks experienced the black-white divide in Kalichito during the early poststatehood period in terms of inequalities that structured the experience of labor in the fields, and in terms of structures that bounded informal social interaction, produced racially exclusive sports play, assigned local children to segregated schools, and implemented Jim Crow laws. Except for segregated schooling and Jim Crow laws, each of these structures was locally produced, defined and enforced, indicating strong local "white" support for and endorsement of regional- and national-level racist ideologies. Kalichito's local structures of oppression intersected neatly with structures of oppression that were being produced by the Oklahoma state and U.S. federal governments. In so doing, "white" Kalichitoans not only supported but also promoted the efforts of Oklahoma state and U.S. leaders to maintain and further develop racist policies and practices.

The accounts of the childhood work experiences of Choctaws, whites, and blacks in Kalichito exposed a critical, structured way that agricultural work telescoped identity and belonging into two primary racial categories. Choctaw and white children labored almost entirely on farms that their families either owned or rented, while most of Kalichito's black children labored on "white farms," as well as on their own farms. This reality was introduced earlier. I return to it now to elaborate on how it expressed and reinforced divisions between the experience of "whites" and "blacks" engaged in the same activity.

Black agricultural work, as represented by blacks themselves, was experienced in terms of its rootedness in relations of asymmetrical power (i.e., employee-employer), as well as in terms of its bodily effects (for an example, see the quote from Mrs. Crenshaw, which appears earlier in this chapter). In contrast, even in cases in which whites, and to a lesser extent Choctaws, noted that their families had used black field labor, the descriptions that whites and Choctaws gave of the many hours they spent in the fields showed a marked (perceived) disengagement from the relations of inequality that were mentioned so often by blacks. Choctaws and whites—many of whom, it should be remembered, were recalling their childhood—remembered the blacks who had worked in their fields as only a shadowy presence working at a distance from them, their siblings, and their parents. As a result, their recollections of their agricultural work experiences centered on the physical aspects of farming. When the social aspects of that work were brought up, as they often were, agricultural work was remembered as an activity shared by and with kin. The following account of a white lady, Georgia Smith, about the 1920s and 1930s was typical of white and Choctaw remembrances of agricultural work:

> The cotton, well a good year the cotton got real tall and a good year—plenty of rain and all that. And if it wasn't very good [the cotton stalks] was kinda low. And you put on a cotton sack which had a strap on it. It was straps over like this, and one part of it's shorter than the other. You dragged it on the ground. You picked your cotton. We did not pull bolls. We picked the cotton. This was the twenties and the thirties, and anyhow your shoulders got sore, your back hurt, and daddy always said, 'Anytime something made you sore go back the next day and work it out.' Same way with hoeing. When you hoed, it made your hands sore, blisters in your hands. And we did not have gloves! Picking corn—do you know how rough the shucks were? Well you took that ear of corn and broke it like that. I have picked corn and picked corn 'til my hands bled. It just takes the hide off 'em [your hands] because of how rough that corn was.

Mrs. Smith's account reflects the emphasis that Choctaws and whites were able to place on the bodily experience of farming because so few of them worked for families other than their own, and her reference to her father's advice on how best to endure this work reflects the numerous references that Choctaws and whites made to the kin who worked alongside them in the fields.

White and Choctaw accounts about pre-1960s Kalichito also matched one another in their inclusion of many of the same stories about informal social interaction. I heard stories about the same feuds, predicaments, social gatherings, and noteworthy events from both Choctaws and whites. Blacks had their own stories about community life during the first half of the twentieth century, stories that overlapped little with those of whites and Choctaws. One of the common stories told by whites and Choctaws, for example, centered on the day that Eddy Eyachubbee, a Choctaw, brought home a Model-T Ford. "The kids were all scared of it because the put-put-put noise was so loud," laughed Baxter Green, a white man. "One day [in the ensuing weeks]," he continued, "Eddy's son and I were playing near a bluff about a mile from the road, lookin' for squirrel [which was regularly eaten by the families of this community]. And here come Eddy—out of nowhere—bouncing over the scrub in that Model-T!" From many whites and Choctaws I heard accounts of near loss of life as a result of Eddy's driving. Eddy frequently drove into bushes, through fences, and "off into the scrub." Not long after these misadventures, Eddy migrated to California with dozens of others from Kalichito and nearby towns. I could find no one in Oklahoma who could tell me what had become of Eddy, but one person imagined that "he was probably raisin' hell on the LA freeways." These and other stories told by whites and Choctaws were revealing of the high level of social enmeshment of whites and Choctaws during the first half of the twentieth century and the fact that "whites" bounded informal social interaction in a way that excluded blacks.

In the Choctaw-and-white community of Kalichito, the set of local structures that maintained and enforced racial divisions included patterns of racially exclusive sports play. Choctaws remembered the community's organized sports teams as "mixed," but by this they meant that the teams included Choctaws and whites. Blacks were barred from participating, as they and others pointed out. The life histories of Choctaws and whites frequently included at least one story about playing sports. In contrast, at no point did I ever hear a black even mention sports. Kalichito's blacks may not have participated in organized sports. They may have chosen nonsports forms of recreational activity, or their heavy work demands may have effectively prohibited them from playing sports.

The importance of sports to the definition of Choctaw and white experience during the first half of the twentieth century was reflected in local newspapers from this period. It was also reflected in the account of one of the most well-known Choctaw elders from the communities that hug the southern border of the Choctaw Nation, Randle Durant. Durant had been reared in a nearby small town. During the late twentieth century, he was selected speaker of the Choctaw tribal council. About the 1920s, Durant remarked that, among other sports, "we played baseball, and only the catcher had a glove. Our bats were home-made and our balls were home-made. We would unravel our socks to make the baseballs" (1979: 50). He also noted, "As a young boy [in the 1920s], I rolled a hoop. The hoop was a metal hoop off of a wagon wheel hub. We would get a stick about 3 ft. long and nail a bucket lid to one and, and then bend the lid in a U shape. We would start the steel hoop rolling, using the U lid on the stick to push and guide the hoop. We would run races with each other, pushing these hoops. Sometimes we ran obstacle courses to see who could keep their hoop rolling without it falling over" (p. 50). The sports and games described by Durant—activities that heavily shaped his racially marked childhood experience—occurred primarily on family farms or on the lands surrounding his community. Of course, play also took place, as was reflected in many of the accounts that I collected, in the schoolyard and, less often, in the classroom.

Segregated public schools were critical structures that defined Choctaws and whites as constitutive of a single social and racial category during the years that followed statehood. Older Kalichitoans talked often of their experiences in "white schools," mentioning, for example, as one white man put it, that "it was all in one book, the Bluebook speller. In that one book were lessons in geography, reading, 'rithmetic, and penmanship." Sixty-seven-year-old Jessie Ann Lomax provided me with one of several accounts of Choctaw experience in "white schools." Her account included two features that I found to be quite common in Choctaw accounts of all periods of Kalichito history. First, despite the public identification of most local Choctaws as whites during the early poststatehood period, Choctaws remained aware of who in their community was a Choctaw. This critical feature of Choctaw experience historically has helped constitute Choctaw resistance to the local public denial of Choctaw identity. Related, Mrs. Lomax's account also exposed a specific way by which many Choctaws experienced the blurring of boundaries between whites and Choctaws even as they resisted the blurring of such boundaries by continuing to recognize the Choctaw identity of their neighbors. From her home, Mrs. Lomax, who was a quarter-or-more, described to me her experience as a high school student in the 1940s:

> I didn't see any difference [between] white kids and Indian kids. I played on the softball teams. I played on the basketball teams. We [Choctaws] blended right in. I had close friends that were white. . . . A lot of us [Choctaws] jus' went right on [through school].
>
> We didn't know we wasn't white. They [whites] accepted us just like everything because a lot of your folks' cousins was teachers. Or somethin' like that. Even now. I went to school with [a man who has represented our district on the tribal council]. I [also] went to school with [Pete, the second son of another prominent Choctaw family].
>
> We [Choctaws] participated. Pete was a good football player. There was no difference between us and the white kids. We sat right in there and made the grades . . . just like everybody else.

Mrs. Lomax's remembrances of her school experiences, which reveal a keen attention on her part to which of her schoolmates were Choctaw, suggests that she conspired with other local Choctaws to maintain knowledge of the Choctaw identities of various town residents. In so doing, she helped maintain the salience of the category of Choctaw and resisted white attempts to deny and erase the Choctaw past of her community and of southeastern Oklahoma. At the same time, her statement "We didn't know that we wasn't white" is revealing of the extent to which local public classifications of most Choctaws as white during this period affected the private, domestic identity-constructions of Choctaws.

The accounts that whites gave of this period of Kalichito's history differed sharply from those of Choctaws in the extent to which whites glossed over the Choctaw identities of prior generations of Kalichito's children. Whites saw most of these children as white, not Choctaw, despite the known Choctaw ancestry of these individuals. Choctaws, in contrast, consistently foregrounded the Choctaw identities of prior generations of Kalichito's children.

Like white oldtimers, elderly blacks also frequently referred to Choctaw individuals who had lived in Kalichito decades earlier as white. Clearly, what mattered to whites and blacks during the first decades of the twentieth century was not whether the larger category, "white," had a subcategory, "Choctaw" (the identity and boundaries of which Choctaws maintained privately and semiprivately), but rather on which side of the

black-white divide an individual fell. This was most vividly illustrated by
the account of an elderly black man, a longtime Kalichito resident named
Sam T. Stakes. Mr. Stakes's account of black experience in Kalichito during the period when Jim Crow laws were in effect matched those provided
by others, including one Choctaw from a neighboring town who recalled
seeing during his youth several white men "put a rope around a black
man's neck, and pull him around town on election day" (Durant 1979: 54).
Sam's description of life in Kalichito provides a perspective on why blacks
formed between twenty-three and twenty-seven "Negro towns" during
the first several decades of the century (Aldrich 1973). Blacks wanted not
only "to manage their own affairs" but also "to escape the discrimination suffered in the predominantly white towns" (p. 29). About Kalichito,
Mr. Stakes told me:

> Two busses ran through here in them days. Blacks sat at the back. If
> you need a drink of water, you had to go out where the horses drank.
> The water fountains said "white only."
>
> In [Earl's] restaurant, [too], they fed you in the back. One black guy
> some white guys would always pick on. An' he never did do nothin'.
> They throwed him in jail. Seems like they was always throwin' him
> in jail. Blacks [in this town] . . . well, they had taken a lots they
> didn't do.
>
> You didn't say "no" to a white man and you didn't go against what
> he said. You couldn't say nothin' to a white man. My grandaddy
> would tip his hat whenever he pass a white woman. If he didn't,
> they'd take him out an' whoop him and beat him. They always said,
> "Someone's gettin' out o' his place, gotta put him back in his place."
> They always said you was gettin' uppity. . . .
>
> The Klan—you never knew who they was. They didn't make it
> known really. You didn't know who they was. They had hoods on.
> You couldn't see who they was. You jus' hope and pray that they
> wouldn't pay you a visit.

In such a climate of violence against and dehumanization of blacks, blacks
as well as whites focused almost entirely on black-white racial categories
and boundaries. The extent to which Choctaws who were publicly classified as white supported local and regional violence against blacks by,
for example, becoming victimizers themselves is unclear. Choctaws living in all parts of the Choctaw Nation shared with me their belief that at
least some Choctaws were members of the Klan during the first half of
the twentieth century, but I was unable to confirm any single example of
this. One white man whom six Kalichitoans independently identified as

a former Klan member was married to a Choctaw woman and sired several Choctaw children. His children, as well as his wife, have phenotypes that are stereotypically Indian. The death of this man in the early 1960s made it impossible for me to determine whether (or the extent to which) his active Klan participation was shaped by his desire to protect his family from victimization by the Klan; or whether his hatred was an expression of local hatred of only those with black ancestry.

Indeed, no one whom I interviewed could recall any Choctaw who was classed as black under the Jim Crow laws, excepting those Choctaws who had black ancestry. I did, however, find an account of a Choctaw from a nearby town who claimed that, for one sixty-mile trip to the north, he and his mother and father, who did not have black ancestry, boarded the back of the railroad car with blacks. His father was a full-blood; his mother, a Choctaw of one-quarter blood quantum; and he himself, a Choctaw of three-quarters blood quantum who, as he put it, had "very light" skin. When he waved out the window of the train at a little girl on the platform, he said that the little girl turned to her father and said, "Look, Dad, look at the white kid with the niggers" (Durant 1979: 54). This event suggests that the black-white divide shaped the experience and identity of Choctaws to a significant extent. In this family with a high degree of "Choctaw blood," both parents were misrecognized as black. Their child was misrecognized as white. This would have been unthinkable as little as two decades before this event occurred.

Some Choctaws conspired in the social misrecognition or public reclassification of many Choctaws as whites during this period. One Choctaw Kalichitoan, Marshall, attended school two decades later than did Mrs. Lomax. Like Mrs. Lomax, he was a quarter-or-more. Marshall said that he was in the first or second grade in Kalichito Elementary in the early 1960s when the town was ordered to integrate its school. "Classes were all white," he explained. "The day it [integration] was supposed to happen, us white kids rounded the corner [to the school], and what did we see? Well, there was the whole school board settin' up on top o' the steps. All o' them—and one of 'em was my daddy—was settin' up there with shotguns. I don't know whether they was a gonna shoot them nigger kids or what. But in any case didn't none of them nigger kids try to find out. It wasn't 'til the fourth or fifth grade," Marshall continued, "that them [black] kids showed up. They put 'em right in there with all o' us *white* kids" (emphasis mine). Marshall's account includes an act of racial self-identification as white on the part of a Choctaw (who is also a quarter-or-more). Such acts are not uncommon in present-day Kalichito. Following this historical section, I will explain the meanings of such acts in the course of exploring contemporary constructions of Choctaw identity.

Choctaw Identity Assertions during the First Half of the Twentieth Century

As was described earlier, during the period of local public denial of Choctaw identity in Kalichito that began at statehood, Choctaws continued to keep track of which individuals and families were Choctaws and which were not. Interviews with Choctaws suggested that this knowledge was retained, produced, and circulated primarily in the private, domestic sphere, the sphere that Chatterjee has identified as "the domain of sovereignty," which, he argues, is impervious to colonization (1993). Kin networks served as conduits for the dissemination of this knowledge and for continued assertions of Choctaw identity. Such networks connected Choctaw households in Kalichito with one another, and often with Choctaw households in other parts of the Choctaw Nation and in cities such as Oklahoma City and Dallas. Debo described such networks as they existed among the Muscogee Creeks in the mid-twentieth century as constituting "hidden ties" (1951: 17). She also explained that the formal and informal "organizations" that connected fellow tribal members in the nineteenth century "continued to function underground" through the first half of the twentieth century (p. 32).

Debo's descriptions, born from field research in 1949 among the Choctaws (and other of the Five "Civilized" Tribes), is suggestive of the fact that, between statehood and the mid-1970s, virtually the only nondomestic contexts in which many Choctaws were socially acknowledged to have continued to exist as Choctaws were semiprivate spaces that were occupied almost entirely by Choctaws and/or by other Indians. The most important such spaces were Indian boarding schools (see esp. Lomawaima 1994). During the first half of the twentieth century, at least two of Kalichito's Choctaw children, both of them full-bloods (but from different families), were sent to such schools. A boy was sent to Goodland Indian School; a girl, to Wheelock Academy.[27] Later, both of these individuals were sent to Chilocco Indian School in northeastern Oklahoma. In the context of local non-Choctaw constructions of Indian identity that placed high-blood-quantum Choctaws in the Indian category and lower-blood-quantum Choctaws in the white category, the removal of some phenotypically Indian individuals from Kalichito was probably perceived by non-Choctaws as acts that helped cleanse the community of Choctaws. Such acts were no doubt perceived as acts that helped legitimize white ownership and control of the town.

Interviews revealed that the Choctaws of Kalichito also made Choctaw identity assertions by participating in all-Choctaw meetings and some all-Choctaw church services. I uncovered no such events that took place within the geographic limits of Kalichito. One all-Choctaw meeting was held in 1934 at Goodland Indian School, which is not far from Kalichito. There Choctaws discussed whether they should organize under the Oklahoma Indian Welfare Act. Several others were held during the 1920s to discuss the final settling of the tribal estate. In addition, irregularly during the first half of the twentieth century, federal agents or representatives from private agencies offered Choctaw women workshops in canning and other domestic arts (see also Debo 1951). By so doing, they recognized and promoted the efforts of Choctaws to maintain the salience of the category "Choctaw." Interviews suggested that information about these events was passed through networks of Choctaw kin that extended into and encompassed Kalichito.

Even in contexts marked by an overrepresentation of Choctaws relative to whites, some Choctaw identity assertions were denied. In one such context, the Talihina Indian Hospital, the critical factor was that it was whites, not Choctaws, who were deciding who was Choctaw and thus who could occupy a semipublic space that was set aside for Choctaws. The U.S. government built this hospital in the Choctaw Nation in 1916 (Peck 1963).[28] According to former hospital employees, for decades the hospital maintained a policy of treating only those Choctaws of one-quarter or more Indian "blood."[29] This restrictive policy was replaced in the late twentieth century by a policy that provided Indian health benefits to, at a minimum, all enrolled Choctaws and other members of federally recognized tribes.[30] Now, "the tribes as sovereign entities," explains Meredith (1993: 129), "have determined who their members are. This in turn determines who is eligible for Indian Health Service assistance."

The "old hospital policy" is often regarded by present-day Choctaws as an example of prior federal attempts to deny the Indian identity of all but a small segment—now 25 percent—of the Choctaw tribe. Other Choctaws, many of them quarter-or-mores, treat the old policy as an example of a rule that the tribe should adopt not only to determine entitlement for health benefits but also to determine tribal membership.

Interviews uncovered only one public context in which Choctaw identity assertions regularly were recognized in Kalichito during the first half of the twentieth century: in the schoolyard of the local "white" elementary school. Classes were in English, but several whites told me that during recess it was not unusual for Choctaw children to speak Choctaw. At least some whites learned some Choctaw in the schoolyard. "We [whites] had to," one of them explained. "We wanted to play, too. We didn't have no choice, really." It is worth pointing out that the Choctaws who were sent from Kalichito to Indian boarding schools during this period were either prohibited (in the case of Wheelock) or strongly discouraged (in the case of Goodland) from speaking Choctaw.

During the first half of the twentieth century, Choctaws did not maintain their Choctaw identity because they were waiting for their tribe to reclaim its status as an important social, political and economic power in the region. Indeed, few Choctaws claimed that during this period they foresaw the late-twentieth-century rebuilding of their tribal government and the creation of tribal economic projects such as the Kalichito project. Choctaws resisted the attempted erasure of Choctaw identity that occurred at the local, state, and national levels during the first half of the twentieth century because they were proud of their Choctaw ancestry and because denying their Choctaw identity would dishonor their ancestors, particularly those who had endured such profound suffering on the long trek to what is now Oklahoma on the Trail of Tears. White reconfigurations of Choctaw identity and the brutal way in which whites controlled nonwhites provided little room for Choctaws publicly to challenge new social categories and identity-constructions. Choctaws resisted by refusing to see themselves as whites wanted to see them—as non-Choctaws and non-Indians—and by refusing to accept ideologies that constructed the categories of white and Choctaw as mutually exclusive. In the private, domestic sphere and in semiprivate, Choctaw-only contexts, they continued to assert their Choctaw identity.

Contemporary Constructions of Choctaw Identity

There are many ways that the above history of Kalichito shapes contemporary life and experience. Let me focus on one: contemporary Choctaw constructions of identity. One of the most striking and, for whites, one of the most puzzling aspects of present-day Choctaw identity-constructions revolves around the fact that many Choctaws in Kalichito, as elsewhere in the Choctaw Nation, periodically refer to themselves as white. For example, the above history included a quote from a quarter-or-more referring to himself as one of the "white kids." Most Choctaws who occasionally refer to themselves as white are under-a-quarters (which also reflects the fact that under-a-quarters make up 75 percent of enrolled Choctaws). It is not uncommon, however, for quarter-or-mores to racially self-identify as white. Skin color appears to be an important factor governing this practice. Most such self-identifiers are light-skinned, and none (that I have observed) are full-blood. In Kalichito, as elsewhere in the Choctaw Nation, Choctaws occasionally refer to themselves as white in interethnic contexts, that is, in contexts in which whites and/or blacks are present. They also sometimes do so in Choctaw-only contexts.[31] Racial self-identification as white is so common among Choctaws throughout the Choctaw Nation that one year Chief Roberts mailed a letter to the homes of all enrolled Choctaws instructing them to identify their race as Indian, not white, on the U.S. census.

Periodic Choctaw self-identifications as white can be explained in part by the history of the identity constructions and processes described above. Choctaws who lived through the period during which Jim Crow laws were in effect, for example, are keenly aware of the fact that most of them experienced white privilege, even in cases in which they or other Choctaws were placed at the margins of white identity or were accorded only honorary whiteness. In addition, most Choctaws acknowledge that most of them—most of the time—are treated as whites by the larger, non-Indian society. This is not to say that many Choctaws did not or have not experienced prejudice and discrimination against Indians. Prejudice against Indians has a long and unbroken history in Oklahoma and has probably affected all living Choctaws who have ever resided in the state.

Periodic Choctaw self-identifications as white are not what they may seem to non-Choctaws. Rarely are they denials of Choctaw identity. The larger, non-Indian society treats the categories of white (or black) and Choctaw as mutually exclusive. In general, Choctaws do not. Partial explanation is found in constructions of Choctaw identity that derive from the tribe's prestatehood past, constructions that have had a profound impact on contemporary constructions of Choctaw identity.

The principal idea that underpins what can be termed "the older Choctaw rhetoric" on identity and belonging is that "Choctaw" is a political affiliation, specifically a nationality. It is not a race. A Choctaw can thus assert a racial identity as white (or black) without compromising his or her political identity as Choctaw. In this connection, Choctaws construct the categories of white (or black) and Choctaw as overlapping and compatible. A Choctaw can thus be a Choctaw whose race is white, a Choctaw can be a Choctaw whose race is black, and a Choctaw can be a Choctaw whose race is Indian. This reality is probably part of what Pesantubbee means when she notes that Choctaws affiliated with Choctaw churches (a category of Choctaws that contains a disproportionately high number of quarter-or-mores) "have maintained a strong identification with their culture [that is, their identity as Choctaws] yet remained very much a part of the dominant white American culture and Christian church" (1994: 21). Many Choctaws decouple race and nationality. Many see themselves as part of a multiracial nation—the Choctaw Nation—just as they also see themselves as part of the multiracial nation that is the United States.

This is not to say that ideas about "blood" and race, derived from the larger, non-Indian society, have not had an impact on contemporary constructions of Choctaw identity. They have. Indeed, the older Choctaw rhetoric includes artifacts of other ideologies—ideologies of blood and race—that the Choctaws borrowed from the larger, non-Indian society and incorporated into their understandings of Choctaw identity well before the late-twentieth-century era of Choctaw nation building. Instead of replacing existing constructions of Choctaw as a nationality with this "new" notion of "blood," however, Choctaws added a notion of Choctaw "blood" to their understandings of Choctaw as a nationality. In other words, they came to see themselves as Choctaws not simply on the basis of their political and social ties to and citizenship in the Choctaw Nation but also on the basis of their Choctaw "blood" (see Sturm 2002 for a detailed look at a similar phenomenon among the Oklahoma Cherokees).

It is not clear when the Choctaws made this modification. When the tribe's leaders passed laws during the nineteenth century that institutionalized citizenship in the Choctaw Nation by naturalization (see chapter 2), they were clearly expressing and reinforcing the tribe's construction of Choctaw as a nationality. But during this period Choctaw leaders also passed laws that limited the political rights of these naturalized citizens, prohibiting them, for example, from holding certain elected political positions, such as Choctaw chief. The incorporation of a notion of Choctaw "blood" into the larger construction of Choctaw as a nationality—which may have occurred during this period or during the century prior—may help explain these laws. The reason that Choctaws did not grant full citizenship rights to their naturalized citizens may have been because these individuals lacked Choctaw "blood." On the other hand, during this period Choctaw "blood" was certainly not a criterion for full citizenship rights in the tribe. Choctaw (male) leaders limited the citizenship rights of women with Choctaw "blood," and, in fact, accorded Choctaw women fewer citizenship rights in the tribe than they did naturalized male citizens (or males who lacked Choctaw "blood").

What is clear is that, for about two centuries, Choctaws have understood that the category "white" is a racial category. In other words, the older Choctaw rhetoric does not deny the existence of race. Instead, it rejects the racialization of Choctaw identity and insists upon Choctaw-defined identity constructions that derive from the tribe's pre-twentieth-century past. The older rhetoric, which constructs Choctaw as a nationality and decouples race and nationality, is an example of the ways by which Indian nations have become sites for the complex articulation of different constructions of race and identity, constructions that find their origins in the larger, non-Indian society, as well as in Indian societies themselves. This social fact was first identified by Circe Sturm (2002), who developed an analytic framework with which to better understand this important aspect of American Indian experience and identity.

During the twentieth century, another popular rhetoric among Choctaws began gaining currency and currently exists alongside the older Choctaw rhetoric. Also representing constructions of race and identity that have been imported from the larger, non-Indian society and have been given their own redefinition and reinterpretation, the newer Choctaw rhetoric is articulated mainly by the younger generations of Choctaws, but it also has currency among some other Choctaws. Its defining feature is its clear and sometimes explicit construction of "Choctaw" or "Indian" as a race. Dozens of times I observed Choctaws articulating the old rhetoric, then several days later, the newer. When I pointed out the inherent contradictions of the two and asked them to explain their appropriation of both (rather than simply one or the other), many simply shrugged their shoulders.

Among those who expressed to me their discomfort with the coexistence of these two, contradictory sets of identity constructions were members of the political faction discussed in chapter 4 that was defined by blood quantum (one-quarter or more Choctaw "blood"). At least a half-dozen members of this approximately two-hundred-member group told me that they thought that the rhetoric that made "race" a part of Choctaw identity should be made to define modern Choctaw identity. The older Choctaw rhetoric, they felt, should be discontinued. Many of the Choctaws who felt this way were full-bloods. While the newer rhetoric currently competes with the older rhetoric as a basis for defining Choctaw identity, the older rhetoric is still the primary one through which Choctaws understand and make sense of their Choctaw identity.

The Resurgence of a Public Choctaw Presence

Today Choctaw identity in Kalichito, as was described earlier, is foregrounded. Locally, both Choctaws and non-Choctaws are patently aware of who is and is not a Choctaw, a striking difference from that which existed during the greater part of the twentieth century. The kinship networks that link Kalichito's Choctaws to Choctaws elsewhere in southeastern Oklahoma (and beyond) are apparent—they are no longer "hidden ties"—and formalized relations among Choctaws, that is, relations of shared citizenship, are a part of local public knowledge. Often the Choctaw residents of Kalichito are treated not simply as individuals. In the local non-Choctaw imaginary, behind each Choctaw looms the tribe, which today is understood by most southeastern Oklahomans to be a powerful sociopolitical and economic force in the region. In these ways Choctaw experience in Kalichito has come full circle.

The post-1970s rise in public expressions of the tribe's presence in the town has played a critical role in effecting this transformation in the public experience and identity of Kalichito's Choctaws. The many public expressions of the tribe's presence in Kalichito are assertions of continued Choctaw survival in a community that has long contested the Choctaw identity of its Choctaw residents. Forced to confront these expressions, including the tribal travel plaza, on a daily basis, the non-Choctaws of Kalichito are forced to confront the tribe. In so doing, they are forced to confront the town's identity as a Choctaw town and the region's identity not merely as southeastern Oklahoma but as the Choctaw Nation.

Of the many present-day public expressions of Choctawness in Kalichito, the travel plaza is perhaps the most potent. This is partly because it more clearly and powerfully articulates the meanings of contemporary Choctaw identity than do some of the other ways that the tribe has become an everyday presence in the town, such as tribally supplied homes, food, and holiday gifts. The Kalichito project stands for Choctaw sovereignty, self-determination, strength, and independence. In contrast, many other visible expressions of the tribe's presence, expressions which also are about sovereignty and self-determination but which center on benefits, are often misread and misunderstood by local whites. Local whites frequently point to these other public expressions when they present their argument, which they often do, that Choctaw identity is exclusively about benefits.

Latching onto a construction of contemporary Choctaw identity as entirely instrumental, some non-Choctaws in Kalichito have been resisting the efforts of Choctaws to regain local public recognition of their Choctaw identity. According to local Choctaws, this resistance on the part of non-Choctaws to public Choctaw identity assertions and to the expansion of tribal control in the region helps explain the frequency with which I encountered negative stereotypes of Choctaws in Kalichito. Non-Choctaws have stepped up their expressions of prejudice against Indians since the 1970s, according to some Choctaws. An assessment of white-Choctaw relations in the early 1950s by historian J. D. Morrison, a white man who lived in the Choctaw Nation and studied the Choctaws, provides some support for this contention, the hyperbole of his statement notwithstanding. Several decades prior to the tribe's resurgence in the late twentieth century, Morrison remarked in 1952, "intermarriage has continued so generally [in the Choctaw Nation] that practically all vestiges of prejudice between the white and red races has disappeared from the area" (Morrison 1987: 131).

Conclusion

When I began pursuing questions about the impact of the Kalichito project and about community experience and identity in small-town Choctaw Nation, I encountered a striking difference in the relationship that the Choctaw tribal government and the people of Kalichito were forging with the Kalichito project. Choctaw tribal leaders and bureaucrats showed a marked preoccupation with the tribal level. For them, the Kalichito project was in the first instance about generating tribal revenues for programs and services and about reducing unemployment. As tribal leaders had predicted, the Kalichito project made and continues to make only a tiny contribution to total tribal revenues. Even so, the project is valued as a bread-and-butter tribal business that also facilitates the expansion of the tribal economy into new and different sectors. The project is celebrated for making a contribution, defined as modest, to the goal of Choctaw economic self-sufficiency.

Kalichitoans, in contrast, tend to view the project's impact as significant, even profound. When asked to identify how, specifically, the new tribal travel plaza has affected their community, the Choctaw residents of this small, impoverished, and job-hungry town almost always focused on the fact that the project created a number of highly prized nonfactory jobs in their town, jobs that have significantly improved the financial situation and quality of life for many of the town's residents. However, as the Choctaws in this community are also well aware, the new tribal travel plaza is much more than simply a new business that brings jobs into the community and struggling families out from under the poverty line. On an everyday basis, the Kalichito project makes visible the enduring presence of the Choctaw people and their continued survival as Indians and as a tribe. More specifically, the project facilitates Choctaw efforts to reclaim their town as a Choctaw town and reassert Choctaw-defined constructions of identity. In these and other ways, the project helps counter nearly a century of local efforts to assimilate Choctaws and a much longer history of federal efforts to destroy tribes by assimilating their members into white society.

A critical part of this chapter explored some of these efforts to assimilate Choctaws, efforts that occurred during the twentieth century in one small town in the Choctaw Nation. "Racial projects," as Biolsi notes, "are always local" (2004: 415). Following Oklahoma statehood in 1907, the white-defined "racial project" that was pursued in Kalichito had as its goal the legal and symbolic redefinition of Kalichito as a white town. Using data from interviews and archival research, I reconstructed the history of this town, showing how whites developed and deployed what Biolsi (2004), utilizing Foucault, terms "technologies" of "stating," "classifying," and "spacing," with and without the use of force. The story of this race-making project is a story about the construction of whiteness (and processes of conferring "honorary whiteness") in a context in which the greatest threat to the success of the project was posed not by the presence of blacks in this community, as the actions and rhetoric of whites suggest, but rather by the enduring presence of Indians in this town and in the Choctaw Nation. In the years just prior to the conception and implementation of the project, whites had illegally acquired much of the land in the Choctaw Nation, and their lawmakers in Washington DC had broken a U.S.-Choctaw treaty, the Treaty of Dancing Rabbit Creek, to raze the structures with which Choctaws were exercising their sovereignty, thereby facilitating the seizure of Choctaw land. During the mid-twentieth century, as the whites in Kalichito continued to carry out their race-making project, they were probably unaware that the Choctaws in their community were still resisting and rejecting the central feature of their project: the erasure of Choctaw distinctiveness. They were also probably unaware that Choctaws were steadfastly holding on to core principles of Choctaw-defined constructions of Choctaw identity that predate statehood and possibly even removal, constructions that today still form the bedrock of Choctaw identity. Last, whites were almost certainly unaware of the fact that the 1970s would bring about the beginning of the process of their race-making project's glorious unraveling, a story that is the larger story of this chapter.

This chapter has probed local-level reconfigurations of power and realignments of control over both resources and people. I have focused on the reconfigurations and realignments that have followed in the wake of the reconstitution of the Choctaw tribe in the 1970s, rearrangements that derive part of their meaning and import from early-twentieth-century efforts to make, unmake, and remake social relations. The next chapter addresses what is essentially the same set of issues—reconfigurations of power and realignments of control over both resources and people—but at the regional, state, and national levels. In addition, the analytic focus shifts from the relations of citizenship that bind together enrolled Choctaws and link them to the tribal government to the relations of diplomacy that create interfaces between the Choctaw tribal government, on the one hand, and the Oklahoma state and U.S. federal governments, on the other.

6. "We Don't Believe That Claim Is Valid"

Choctaw Sovereignty Assertions and the Water-Rights Conflict of 2001

At a regular session of the Choctaw Nation Tribal Council in the summer of 1992, tribal councilman Charley Jones reported on his recent trip to France. Representing the Choctaw Nation, Mr. Jones said that he was one of seven "ambassadors" from "various Indian nations" with whom the French government "wished to renew their friendship." "We were given a royal reception. . . . We were received by diplomats, dignitaries and industrialists," Jones told the council and the Choctaw citizenry. "The French government paid for everything." To honor the Choctaws for their contributions to France during the eighteenth century, he continued, the French presented the Choctaws with a tract of French land.

Mr. Jones paused as he looked at his fellow council members, then surveyed the audience with his eyes. Stiffening in his seat, he added that, at one point during the trip, he slipped into a French bank to cash a check. "I didn't have my passport on me, and they would not accept any other [form of] I.D. I [then] pulled out my tribal membership card. They cashed the check immediately." For a few seconds, the council sat motionless. Then multiple-term council members Bertram Bobb and Ted Dosh, together with my own councilman, Perry Thompson, raised their eyebrows and nodded their heads in approval. Speaker of the Tribal Council Randle Durant cleared his throat and let out a short, soft chuckle. They were impressed by behavior that, it was said, indicated that the French government and the French people treated the Choctaws and other Indian tribes as "full-fledged nations." Most noteworthy for many of the council members, I later learned, was the incident at the bank: the teller, it appeared, regarded Mr. Jones's tribal membership card as a passport of a sovereign nation. For Choctaw activist and lawyer Scott Kayla Morrison, with whom I discussed Jones's account of his experiences over coffee in a small restaurant in Talihina, the councilman's account revealed that "France regarded U.S. Indian tribes not as a 'domestic dependent nations' [as the United States has long been accustomed to defining tribes], but [rather] as nations on par with the United States!"

With Jones's words still heavy in the air, from my seat in the tribal council house I exchanged glances with several other Choctaw citizens. I also looked around the room. Like Mr. Durant, many of us were smiling. We, too, were pleased that the French appeared to be seeing our tribe the way that many of us Choctaws often see ourselves. "If the French people can do this," said one Choctaw citizen after the meeting, "why is it so difficult for the American people to do it?" This man, I assumed, was referring primarily to many of his non-Indian neighbors, who often resist the rhetoric that constructs our tribe as a nation. Other segments of the non-Indian American population use the rhetoric themselves. For example, during the years that I worked for the Bureau of Indian Affairs (1994–95, 2000), dozens of times I heard Washington-based non-Indian politicians, staffers, and lawyers refer to our tribes as nations. In fact, it seemed to me that, at least in their interactions with the BIA, which is staffed almost entirely by Indians, most of these individuals took every opportunity to refer to our tribes as nations. This is not to say that they, like the French according to Jones, constructed U.S. tribes as fully independent nations, separate and autonomous from the United States. The vast majority, in fact, did not. The term "semisovereign" was often used to describe the political status of U.S. tribes.

Although dangerous politically because it can be used to deny that tribes have the potential to exercise full sovereignty, the term "semisovereign" is important from an anthropological perspective because it hints at the current slippage between the rhetoric of American Indian tribal sovereignty that is practiced by many Indians and the reality of that sovereignty. Current tribal sovereignty rhetoric, a rhetoric that some Indian peoples have been using since at least the early 1700s, asserts a structural equivalence in the global political arena between American Indian tribes, on the one hand, and nations such as Colombia, Japan, and Switzerland, on the other. It is a rhetoric in which we refer to our tribes as nations, and the memberships of our tribes as our citizenries. A political statement, this rhetoric is believed to accelerate what many of us refer to as our decolonization process. It is also, however, descriptive of an empirical reality, foregrounding the social, political, and legal fact that sovereignty is a critical feature of contemporary, as well as historical, U.S. Indian tribes.

Building upon the discussion in the last chapter, which addressed, among other things, the tribe's "domestic" policy and the high priority given to economic development, this chapter turns to Choctaw "foreign" relations, policy, and diplomacy in order to more fully explore the realities, as well as the rhetoric, of Choctaw tribal sovereignty and the relations of diplomacy that create interfaces between the Choctaw tribal government, on the one hand, and the Oklahoma state and U.S. federal governments, on the other. What is the content and character of these diplomatic relations? How, specifically, do the Choctaw tribal government, the Oklahoma state government, and the federal government experience these interfaces?

I probe these broader questions by describing and analyzing a conflict that involved all three of these governments. Only the Choctaw, Oklahoma-state, and U.S. federal governments were implicated or involved in the conflict from 1974 to 1990, after which point a municipal government, a consortium of municipal governments, and later the Chickasaw Nation became involved. In the 1990s the consortium of municipal governments, which was based in Texas, offered four hundred million dollars for 130 million gallons of southeastern Oklahoma water per day for one hundred years (*Oklahoman*, August 10, 1997: 10), bringing to a head a long-standing disagreement between Oklahoma and the Choctaw Nation over who owns this water and representing the first time that "the water wars that raged in the west have . . . crossed Oklahoma's borders" (Helton 1998: 979). On November 14, 2001, the state and the Choctaw and Chickasaw tribes agreed on a draft of a negotiated settlement of this conflict, a settlement that was widely expected to become the basis for a tribal-state compact. Since 2001 the draft settlement, which at the time was imbued with great historical significance, has lost nearly all of its public import. The reason: the water lessors (Choctaw Nation, Chickasaw Nation, and Oklahoma) and the proposed lessee (the consortium of municipal governments in Texas) could not agree to the terms of a water lease. Specifically, the lessee failed to offer what the lessors considered a fair price for the water, and the lessee insisted upon receiving reliable water storage (either in existing lakes or through the construction of new reservoirs) rather than relying, as the lessors insisted, on available river flows (Choctaw Nation, January 9, 2002).[1]

Prior to the breakdown of these negotiations, Oklahomans had focused their attention on the series of negotiations over water rights that had culminated in the 2001 Choctaw-Chickasaw-Oklahoma draft settlement. An important artifact of a failed political trajectory in Oklahoma that had as its goal a large-scale lease of Indian water, this settlement stated, among other things, that the Choctaw and Chickasaw Nations were entitled to half of the proceeds from a prospective lease of water within their tribal homelands (37.5 percent for the Choctaws, 12.5 percent for the Chickasaws); Oklahoma was entitled to the other half. During the month in which it was announced that the parties had agreed to a draft settlement, the state's major newspaper had asked, "Could water be as integral to Oklahoma in the 21st century as petroleum was in the 20th?" (Oklahoman, November 25, 2001). Given that the water in question was located entirely within the borders of the Choctaw and Chickasaw Nations, and given that "Indian water rights are generally paramount to rights perfected under state systems" (Helton 1998: 981), how was Oklahoma able credibly to claim during the negotiation process with these tribes any share at all of the proceeds from a prospective water lease, much less as much as half of the proceeds from such a proposed lease?

The story of this turn-of-the-twenty-first-century government-to-government battle over water rights brings to the fore three critical aspects of tribal sovereignty. The first is the construction of tribal sovereignty as "a bundle of inherent rights," rights that tribes insist derive from their long-standing status—a status that predates the arrival of Europeans—as nations with inherent sovereignty (see Wilkins and Lomawaima 2001). Tribal leaders often point out that the sovereign rights of tribes are either explicitly or implicitly enshrined in treaties, the U.S. Constitution, federal Indian policy, and federal law. Tribal water rights in particular have been extensively negotiated and defined by and through the U.S. courts. In providing an overview of the body of Indian water law and identifying the primary water issues with which Indian country is dealing, as well as in describing Choctaw involvement in the conflict described in this chapter, the concept of tribal water rights, as will be seen, is central, bringing into relief the salience of the bundle-of-inherent-rights aspect of tribal sovereignty in tribal, state, and federal diplomatic relations.

A second aspect of tribal sovereignty, an aspect that shaped much of the conflict over water in southeastern Oklahoma, is that tribal sovereignty operates in a landscape populated by multiple, overlapping, and competing sovereignties (see especially Biolsi 2005; Wilkins and Lomawaima 2001). As Jessica Cattelino (2004) has pointed out, when tribes exercise their sovereignty, they often do so not in isolation from but rather in relation to these other sovereignties, specifically in relation to the sovereignty of state governments and the federal government. The patterned mesh of interrelationships within which tribal sovereignty exists helps define a third critical aspect of tribal sovereignty that is laid bare by the conflict discussed in this chapter: like other sovereignties, tribal sovereignty has important processual components. When tribes, states, and the federal government spar over who has control over certain resources, a process of moves and countermoves is set into motion. For a good many conflicts in Indian country, these moves and countermoves cardinally define tribal sovereignty as a process of negotiation (Clara Sue Kidwell, personal communication; see also Cattelino 2004). The conflict over water in southeastern Oklahoma provides a potent example of this.

At the center of the conflict over Choctaw water was the Choctaw-Oklahoma dyad. The course and nature of the conflict described here thus speaks to tribal-state relations more generally, an area of "international" relations in which friction and hostility often predominates. "States have often presented the tribes with the greatest threats to their sovereignty and resources," O'Brien explains (1989: 290). States are opposed to tribal sovereignty, and continue to threaten the very "existence of indigenous nations," asserts Porter (1997: 92). State abuses against tribes are many (see Wilkins and Lomawaima 2001: 178–79 for a good summary of these abuses) for reasons that include "ignorance concerning tribal rights, jealously over tribal resources, and prejudice against Indians" (O'Brien 1989: 290). States also frequently perceive the efforts of tribes to develop their economic base as threatening (Meredith 1993). Tribes resent the fact that, among other things, "states have often acted as if they were the political superiors of Indian nations" when, in fact, the U.S. courts have acknowledged the status of tribes as higher than that of states (Wilkins and Lomawaima 2001: 179; O'Brien 1989). By the end of the twentieth century, there were few signs of improvement in tribal-state relations (see, for example, Johnson and Turner 1998). Rather, during the 1990s these relations continued to deteriorate (Wilkins and Lomawaima 2001).

I begin by outlining the legal landscape that frames tribal water rights in the United States and by providing a perspective on some of the ways Indians have experienced water-rights issues and conflicts. I then address at length one of the key precipitating events of the conflict over Choctaw water: the building of Sardis Lake Reservoir. This extensive discussion is followed by a detailed look at the actions and perspectives that helped define the course and nature of the conflict over Choctaw water. Tacking back and forth between, on the one hand, the social field that state leaders occupied in their Oklahoma City epicenter, and, on the other, the tribe's base for strategizing in the Choctaw Nation, I explore the rhetoric of state and tribal leaders and identify some of the driving forces and conditions that shaped the positions of the state and the tribe. My treatment of the state's position includes an overview of the key characteristics and uses of water, together with the problems associated with water, in Oklahoma. This background is essential to understanding the perspectives of state leaders, lawmakers, and bureaucrats on the conflict. It is also, however, important in helping situate the conflict and Choctaw water itself in a larger regional context.

As will be seen, great clarity and consistency characterized the Choctaw tribal government's position and involvement in the conflict. In contrast, Oklahoma state leaders pursued different courses of action at different points in time, and endured serious intragovernmental problems that compromised their ability to effectively address important issues, including water issues. The story of the Choctaw tribe's involvement in the conflict is thus remarkably straightforward, and the story of the state's involvement, remarkably convoluted. Adequately addressing the state's involvement, in particular, required considerable space.

My findings with respect to the state's involvement underscored the necessity of conducting field research in what is sometimes called "the supralocal domain," that is, the domain that exists at a remove from the group being studied but which impacts—often significantly—that group. If I had "not investigated but assumed" "the character of the larger-scale, the supralocal domain" and addressed the supralocal domain "without direct study" in accordance with anthropological conventions (Moore 1987: 730), I would have missed much. Specifically, I would have seriously overestimated the degree to which state actions and perspectives were coherent, unified, coordinated, and consistent. I also would have grossly underestimated the level of hostility and resistance on the part of the Oklahoma state government to Choctaw water rights.

Three things are striking about the modern battle over tribal water described in this chapter. The first is the extent of Oklahoma's resistance to recognizing Choctaw water rights and the related arrogance of many Oklahoma state leaders, which is most apparent in the event of the building of Sardis Lake but is also an unmistakable feature of the conflict over ownership of southeastern Oklahoma water. Most states in the American West received a basic education in Indian water rights at least a generation ago and have long discontinued their overt expressions of hostility to tribal water claims. Also striking about this story is what it suggests about the comparative efficiency and effectiveness of the Oklahoma state government and the Choctaw tribal government. Much popular and scholarly attention has been given to problems in the performance of contemporary tribal governments. Charges of corruption, favoritism, despotism, and inefficiency are common. Yet in the story told here, a picture of a not-so-upstanding state government emerges alongside a tribal government that during the water-rights conflict displayed courage, charisma, intelligence, and a remarkable ability to quickly and efficiently mobilize support from within and without. This social fact helps explain a third striking thing about this story: the choice that many non-Indian residents of the Choctaw Nation made to side with the tribe rather than the state during the conflict.

To document the story of Choctaw water during the late twentieth and early twenty-first centuries, I observed and collected information from state officials in Oklahoma City, especially from state-government bureaucrats at the Oklahoma Water Resources Board. I also spent time conducting field research in the Choctaw Nation among tribal officials and among Choctaws and non-Choctaws living in the conflict's primary battleground, the Kiamichi Valley. Several brief journeys to other parts of the Choctaw Nation, to north Texas, and to western Oklahoma helped round out my research into this seminal Choctaw sovereignty assertion.

Water and Tribes

Winters v. U.S. (1908), hereinafter referred to as *Winters*, affirmed that tribes' rights to water derive from the doctrine of reserved rights, a doctrine best explained and analyzed in Wilkins and Lomawaima (2001). The reserved-rights doctrine holds that tribes have retained sovereignty over all rights not explicitly taken away by treaty, by federal law, or by the U.S. Supreme Court. Such rights "can include a property right, such as the right to hunt, or gather, or fish; or a political right, such as the power to regulate domestic relations, tax, administer justice, or exercise civil and criminal jurisdiction" (p. 119). Universally described as "the foundation of all Indian water law" (Lopach et al. 1998: 125), the *Winters* decision states that tribes have reserved rights to water sufficient to develop and maintain vibrant, growing economies on tribal homelands, even if this leaves non-Indians with little or no water (see especially Williams and Montoya-Lewis 2000). Subsequent case law has found that "sufficient water" means at least enough water to service all "practicably irrigable acreage" in a tribal homeland (*Arizona v. California* [1963]), but that tribes may put their reserved water to any use that enhances the economic viability of their reservations (McGuire 1991). Tribal reserved rights to water are land based. Often, they are implied in specific reservation-creating treaties, as is the case with the Choctaws. When reservation water is insufficient, however, which is not the case with the Choctaws, *Winters* states that tribes have rights to water outside tribal boundaries. Two critical features of tribal reserved rights are that they are federally protected, and they are not subject to state law or state regulation (Wilkins and Lomawaima 2001).[2]

McCool notes that "water [is] a symbol to Indians of their determination to remain Indian and preserve their traditional homelands" (1987: 254). Toward these ends, what is sometimes described as the *Winters* doctrine has become "an important political tool" for tribes and "has functioned effectively as a core around which Indian claims, hopes and activity have revolved" (p. 254). This is especially important in the present day: "For most of our nation's history," explains Burton, "the struggle was over land; the most severe and protracted conflicts today concern water" (1991: 2). According to law professor Taiawagi Helton (1998), *Winters* and related decisions have created a context in which the U.S. courts now presume the existence of tribal reserved rights to water, limiting tribal-state water disputes to, for example, issues of the quantity and use of water. The question, Burton (1991) adds, is no longer whether the courts will recognize tribes' reserved rights to water but rather how much water constitutes their entitlement.

Unfortunately, the history that led up to the current condition of tribal water-rights recognition has been difficult and often perplexing for tribes. Regardless of whether Indian water-rights claims have been settled by the parties themselves (as was occurring in the Choctaw case until the early

2000s), by the courts, by the U.S. attorney general, or by the BIA, settlements have been "situation-specific" and "haphazard," and, until recently, nineteenth- and twentieth-century federal policy with respect to tribal water rights was not "coherent, coordinated [or] evenly applied, [presenting] serious problems of fairness" between and among tribes (Burton 1991: 124–25). More generally, water-related legislation in the United States "typically is piecemeal and ad hoc," and water development and administration, "disjointed," reflecting a non-Indian American policymaking process characterized by iron triangles, distributive politics, logrolling, and vote trading (McCool 1987: 60, 99). This has exacerbated the problems tribes have faced in obtaining the water to which they are entitled.

The center of disputes over tribal water rights has been and continues to be the arid west, where conditions of water scarcity have shaped the content and outcome of water conflicts that involve tribes. Conditions of water scarcity have helped make such conflicts primarily about tribes acquiring sufficient water, which generally means supplementing reservation-based water resources with off-reservation water. The water-use issues of tribes in this region reflect this reality: water for consumption rather than, for example, for industry or tourism, is a focus of tribal water-rights disputes, even in cases in which tribes lease or plan to lease (i.e., sell for designated periods) some of their *Winters*-rights water to off-reservation communities.

Despite the fact that tribal water rights are not subject to state law, the legal framework that western states have devised for the relative dearth of water in their region has impacted tribal water-rights settlements, often to the detriment of tribes. Western-state water law is based on the "prior appropriation" system, which bases water rights on date of first use, assigns specific quantities of water to users, and makes prior use(s) of water a basis for future use(s) (see Kahrl 1978). Although in the context of the prior-appropriation system "tribes have been largely successful in establishing the seniority of their claims" (Burton 1991: 125), often they have been induced to accept specific quantities of water and restrictions on the uses to which they can put their water. For example, in 1968 the Navajos accepted a water-rights settlement that accorded them such a small quantity of Colorado River water that the settlement is now being renegotiated (Weinberg 2000). In the 1980s the Fort Peck Assiniboine and Sioux Tribes, the Pima, the Ak Chin, and other tribes accepted settlements remarkable not simply for their quantification of tribal water but also—and more strikingly in their cases—for the regulations placed on tribal use of that water, especially in the area of water leasing to non-Indian communities (Lopach et al. 1998; Burton 1991). Disturbingly, quantifications of tribal water—which the Carter administration held up as the answer to the "problem" of tribal water-rights in the arid west—limit the economic development options of tribes. This is a serious legal and moral problem. *Winters*, for example, states that tribes are entitled to enough water to create economically viable, even economically vibrant, reservation homelands, but in many cases tribal water-rights settlements have accorded tribes too little water to realize this goal. The water-use restrictions of many tribal water-rights settlements are equally problematic, as they interfere with the sovereignty of tribes over their water.

Much less popular and scholarly attention has been given to tribal water-rights conflicts in water-rich areas, which include the eastern United States, the Pacific Northwest, and even eastern Oklahoma, with the Pacific Northwest being the hub of tribal water-rights activity in water-rich areas. Significantly, the water-rights claims of tribes in these areas tend to stress issues of water for economic development rather than, for example, water for consumptive use. A good number of tribal water-rights cases in the Pacific Northwest, for example, have involved the protection or development of tribal fisheries and lakes that foster tourism. Fisheries and recreational-use lakes on Indian reservations in the Northwest have long experienced threats from non-Indian-owned structures, especially from hydroelectric facilities, which impede the instream flow of key tribal watercourses (Burton 1991). The conflict described in this chapter reflects the emphasis given in water-rich areas to water for tribal economic development. Choctaw and Chickasaw national leaders sought affirmation of their water rights in part to generate capital, through water leasing, for new tribal businesses.

Tribal water-rights conflicts in water-rich areas also differ from conflicts elsewhere in the country in that, in water-rich areas, such conflicts tend to focus on existing reservation-water resources rather than off-reservation water. Some such cases address issues of the pollution or contamination of tribal water by non-Indians (see below). Less frequently, they involve questions of the ownership of particular watercourses or lakes on reservations, especially on reservations or tribal homelands that were subjected to allotment. The most notable of these is what the BIA, the interested tribes, and others describe as the Arkansas riverbed cases. In the 1970s the U.S. Supreme Court found that the Cherokee, Choctaw, and Chickasaw tribes of Oklahoma, not the state of Oklahoma, owned the beds of a key commercial river that traverses their tribal homelands (see, for example, *Choctaw Nation v. Oklahoma*, 397 U.S. 620, 631 [1970]; see also Roberts and Kidwell 1980). Also at issue in the Arkansas riverbed cases was the inadequate federal stewardship of this tribal property, an issue that is common not only in tribal-water cases but also, more generally, in cases involving tribal resources. The conflict documented in this chapter reflects the focus given in water-rich areas to water within tribal boundaries: the conflict was limited to water in the Choctaw Nation (and ultimately also the Chickasaw Nation). Exceptions to the reservation-based nature of tribal water-rights conflicts in water-rich areas include the successful defense by the Confederated Tribes of the Warm Springs Reservation of their rights to water from the Columbia River, north of their reservation in central Oregon. This tribe's water-rights settlement affirmed the tribe's entitlement to a share of profits from a hydroelectric facility (White 1990).

Several patterns in the content of tribal water-rights conflicts are common to tribes in both water-rich and water-starved areas. The most disturbing is the pollution and/or contamination of tribal water by non-Indian structures on or near reservations. Examples include the contamination, which takes place on their reservation, of Navajo water resources by Peabody Coal in the Southwest, and the pollution of tribal fisheries by off-reservation hydroelectric facilities in the Pacific Northwest. In tribal water-rights cases across the United States, tribes seek affirmation of their right to clean water and adequate measures to safeguard the quality of their water. Here the Choctaw case represents an exception: there exists almost no pollution or contamination of southeastern Oklahoma water, an important feature of Choctaw water that has heightened its attractiveness to potential lessees.

The Choctaw case documented below also departs from general patterns of tribal experience with water in the extent to which the Choctaws were able to escape the imposition of legal constraints on their pursuit of water leasing, also known as water marketing, and the extent to which water leasing was a part of the Choctaws' water development plans. In the Choctaws' 2001 draft settlement, none of the water affirmed as Choctaw tribal water was banned from use in leasing or otherwise unduly restricted in the area of leasing, and Choctaw leaders said that, aside from making numerous water- and sewer-system improvements, their water development plans would probably involve only water leasing. (The Choctaws announced that water-leasing revenues would help fund not only new tribal businesses but also new roads, hospitals, and clinics.) Williams and Montoya-Lewis (2000) describe water leasing as a new frontier for tribes, a terrain that is so uncharted that, in their view, tribes may even have to go to court to win the right to engage in water leasing. Recognizing, however, that the tribal right to lease water is implied in the reserved-rights doctrine, they assert: "Tribes that are not able or have no need to develop their water rights on their reservations, but that would benefit from the economic resources resulting from the lease of those water rights, should be able to further the economic development of their reservations by alternative uses of their water rights" such as water leasing. Indeed, it is in part through "creative water leasing," they add, that "tribes can become leaders in effective water resource management" (p. 27). Law professor Taiawagi Helton describes water leasing as both groundbreaking and a tribal sovereignty assertion that is of broad significance for tribes. "The marketing of water is one of the most important aspects of the reserved rights doctrine today," he declares (1998: 1002).

Although tribal water-rights conflicts often address issues outside of the domain addressed in *Winters*, the *Winters* case has been important, even critical, to tribes in their centuries-old effort to obtain, use, and control their own water. *Winters* has helped make possible a dramatic improvement since 1900 in the legal ability of tribes to exercise their sovereignty over water. *Winters* has also helped affirm the federal trust responsibility over tribal natural resources more generally. In the end, however, two things deserve mention. The first is the fact that "relatively little water has been diverted under *Winters*; in contrast, the federal government has spent literally billions of dollars and has stored, diverted, and delivered millions of acre-feet of water under the aegis of state water law" (McCool 1987: 185). The second is that most tribes still have "far less legal and functional control over reservation water resources than do neighboring governmental jurisdictions" (Burton 1991: 33).

The Building of the Sardis Lake Reservoir

The most important precipitating event of the turn-of-the-twenty-first-century conflict over Choctaw water began in 1974. That year, the state of Oklahoma contracted with the Army Corps of Engineers to dig a large

hole at the foot of the Jackfork and Wolf mountains in the middle of the
Choctaw Nation. The hole became the Sardis Lake Reservoir, a state project to control area flooding and to provide water to cities and towns outside
of the Choctaw Nation. The construction of this reservoir attests to the
historic fact that "the state [Oklahoma] has been using tribal water since
its creation, without regard for tribal interests," and under the assumption that it owns the water (Helton 1998: 1000). In the early 1990s, when
a prospective lease of southeastern Oklahoma water brought to a head
conflicting claims to the water, Oklahoma state officials used the Sardis
Lake Reservoir to buttress their argument that Oklahoma had sovereignty
over all the water involved in the lease. Several state employees and dozens of non-Indians who lived in Oklahoma City told me that the state
alone should acquire all of the water-lease revenues in part because it had
made possible the commoditization of much of the region's "excess" surface water. In the absence of Sardis Lake, several of them explained, the
water that was slated to be leased in the 2000s would have continued to
flow south, out of the Choctaw Nation, and eventually into the Gulf of
Mexico (see also *Oklahoman*, February 7, 1993).

The water structure that played such a large role in the conflict over
Choctaw water spans 13,610 acres, 15 by 8 miles at its broadest. Its 117
miles of shoreline define an intricate network of inlets and peninsulas
that in 2001 helped make the structure the top bass-tournament fishing
lake in Oklahoma. Created by a rolled earthfill dam that is 14,138 feet
long and rises 81 feet from a valley floor to a maximum height of 101 feet,
Sardis Lake Reservoir is located in the Choctaw Nation's Kiamichi Valley,
an area that is about 60 to 80 miles long and 50 to 60 miles wide. A place
of frequent Bigfoot sightings, legends of buried gold coins, and specters
of giant black panthers and mountain lions, the valley is home to about
25,000 people, approximately 3,000 of whom are Choctaws. It is a place
of stunning physical beauty, particularly in the fall when the Kiamichi
Mountains that help define the valley are ablaze with the golds, reds, and
oranges that clothe its deciduous trees. Valley folk either string themselves
out along the highways and byways that wind through the mountains, or
they cluster in small communities and towns. The largest of these population centers totals less than 6,000. The valley is located in the central
part of the Choctaw Nation, about fifty miles north of Kalichito.

When I spoke with valley residents about "the building of Sardis," as
it was put, dozens of middle-aged Choctaw men spoke fondly of the project. "We had good work—oh, yes, we sure did—when Sardis was bein'

dug," explained fifty-five-year-old Lester McGee from the shack in which he lived alone. About forty minutes earlier, Lester's sister, Angela, who lived five miles to the south, had brought me to his home at the end of an infrequently used dirt road in the Potato Hills area of the valley. Weaving through overgrown scrub while dodging six or eight chickens, we had arrived with several sacks of groceries for Lester. His delay in coming out to greet us had worried Angela, but her anxiety quickly turned to relief when he intercepted us on the path just west of his home. At about the midpoint of our visit, this bearded, dark-haired man began to talk about his work history. His construction job with the Army Corps of Engineers, he insisted over a ham sandwich and a Coke, was one of the best he had held during the forty years that he had held odd jobs. Interviews with at least a half-dozen other Choctaw men, all of them poor, yielded similar pronouncements. Again and again, Choctaw men heralded the "high pay" and "regular work" that the project brought to the area during the late 1970s and early 1980s. Few expressed resentment of the project.

This was not the case for many Kiamichi Valley Choctaw women with whom I spoke, including one who was a local leader. Many expressed anger and sadness when they shared with me their remembrances of the lake's construction. A focus of their accounts was the inundation of the town of Sardis when the reservoir was filled in 1983. A farming and ranching community, Sardis was home to 350 people at the height of its population, many of them Choctaws (*Oklahoman*, November 18, 1977: 97). During the late 1800s and early 1900s, when Sardis was known as Bunch Town, it had two blacksmith shops, two grist mills, a saloon, and several churches (*Oklahoman*, November 18, 1977; WPA Indian-Pioneer History Collection, interviews with Green Bohanon, b. 1882, and Tandy Anderson, b. 1875). In the mid- to late twentieth century, the town sported a school, a post office, and Brown's Grocery (*Oklahoman*, November 18, 1977: 97). As it has done elsewhere, as part of the construction of the reservoir the Army Corps of Engineers bought from the town's residents their land, which was purchased for up to $750 an acre, and most of their homes and buildings (*Oklahoman*, October 20, 1997: 1; November 18, 1977: 97). Some displaced residents moved several miles to what was expected to become lakefront property; others simply relocated. Some families moved to Durant, the current headquarters of the Choctaw Nation; another, to Henryetta (*Oklahoman*, November 18, 1977: 97). One individual moved as far as Alaska (*Oklahoman*, November 5, 1978: 214). On August 3, 1978, the residents of this part of the valley voted, purportedly 300 to 8, to have the lake renamed Sardis in honor of the old town, requiring the destruction of a number of freshly painted "Clayton Lake" signs (*Oklahoman*, January 4, 1981: 1–2; July 26, 1978).[3]

Choctaw women also decried the relocation of Choctaw graves from lands that eventually became part of the lake bottom. In 1980 the Corps announced plans to move graves from as many as twenty private cemeteries to make way for the lake (*Oklahoman*, November 20, 1980: 19). The disturbance of the "resting places" of these loved ones was traumatic, said several Choctaw women, and "filled us with tears." Women told me that then, as now, they grieved not only for the dead who were Choctaw, white, and black but also for the 1,000-year-old graves of Caddo Indians, who had inhabited the area prior to the Choctaws' relocation in the 1830s. Such feelings of loss were shared by some Indians who lived outside the area. One Choctaw woman living in Oklahoma City, for example, raised the issue of the relocation of graves when we discussed the water conflict; she described this as "one of the worst parts of the entire [conflict]." In addition, in 2003 the Caddo Tribe, then headquartered fifty miles west of Oklahoma City in Binger, filed a notice of debt against the Corps for what they described as the "desecration" of ancient tribal "burial grounds" that had been flooded during the construction of Sardis Lake and other eastern Oklahoma reservoirs (*Oklahoman*, August 22, 2003: 1).

Many Choctaws describe the state's act of building the reservoir as a violation of Choctaw tribal sovereignty. The lake was not built on tribal land; but because it was built on land that lay within the boundaries of the Choctaw Nation, it was incumbent upon Oklahoma to at least consult with and gain the consent of the Choctaws prior to the project's construction. The impoundment of Choctaw water considerably strengthened this imperative, not simply suggesting but mandating the negotiation of tribal-state agreement prior to the construction. The basis for the Choctaws' claim to the water is the reserved rights to water implied in the act that created the tribe's postremoval homeland, the Treaty of Dancing Rabbit Creek (Helton 1998; *Oklahoman*, April 29, 2001: 8). Per the terms of this treaty, the Choctaws acquired the entire southern one-third of what is now Oklahoma, roughly double the area that is encompassed by present-day Choctaw tribal boundaries. In 1830 U.S. officials underlined the intended permanence of this homeland by providing the tribe with a patent

to the land rather than, as was done with most other Indian tribes, placing the land in trust. The United States also agreed never to include the
new tribal territory in any state. The other Five "Civilized" Tribes also
received patents to land they acquired during their removal treaties, and
treaty-based promises that their homelands would never be included in
any state. At least one legal scholar has opined that these unusual treaty
terms may provide the basis for a different status of Five Tribes' water,
entitling the Five "Civilized" Tribes not only to their reserved water but
also to the water that exceeds these rights (Helton 1998). In most cases,
water that exceeds tribes' reserved water reverts to the state(s) in which
the tribe is located.

A hypothetical example exposes the incomplete federal respect that
was given to Choctaw tribal property rights and sovereignty during the
nine-year period during which Sardis Lake was built. If a nation such as
Iraq had crossed the border into Turkey and dug a hole with which to capture water to pipe back across the border to the Iraqi city of Mosul, the
incident would surely have been regarded as a violation of Turkey's sovereignty, prompting the notification of Turkey's military and the filing of
an action with the United Nations. The United States and other nations
would probably step in to defend Turkey against this sovereignty violation. The Sardis Lake project engendered no such response, despite an
explicit obligation on the part of the federal government to defend Indian
tribes against encroachments upon their sovereignty by the United States
and others. As O'Brien points out, "Protecting tribal property is the most
clearly defined and important aspect of the government's trust relationship [with tribes]" (1989: 262). Under the supervision of the Department
of the Interior and with the assistance of the Department of Justice, the
BIA is expressly responsible for defending Indians' reserved water rights
from non-Indian encroachment under state water law (Burton 1991). In
the Choctaw case, neither a lack of federal knowledge about the construction of the Sardis Lake project nor a lack of clarity about the federal
responsibility to intervene existed as a possible justification for the federal inaction. The federal government itself built the project. Also, it had
been taken to task several decades earlier for failing in its responsibility
to safeguard tribal resources during the implementation of the Pick-Sloan
Missouri Basin Program, a massive water project begun in 1944. After the
completion of this program, both the Department of the Interior and the
Department of Justice were severely criticized for failing to fully protect

and defend Indian rights and property (McCool 1987). In an ethnography of the Paiutes of the American Southwest, Knack (2001) exposes the specific way by which Paiute water rights during the first half of the twentieth century were inadequately protected. At the local and federal levels, BIA agents were aware of and generally supportive of the federal mandate to protect Indian water-rights, but poor record keeping, high levels of BIA staff turnover, bureaucratic miscommunication, and conflict within the BIA about how best to procure Paiute water conspired to leave unclaimed a significant portion of the tribes' reserved water rights.

The federal government did more than simply fail to protect Choctaw water in the 1970s and early 1980s; it facilitated Oklahoma's impoundment of this tribal resource by loaning Oklahoma the money for the project and by constructing the project. The builder was the U.S. Army Corps of Engineers, described as "one of the oldest and most successful agencies in the federal executive branch" (McCool 1987: 20). The Corps was established in 1802 as an autonomous unit of the Department of War, now the Department of Defense, in the Department of the Army (p. 94). In 1977 when the building of Sardis Lake was well under way, the Corps had as many as 292 ongoing projects, nearly four times as many as had the Bureau of Reclamation (BOR), an agency with a similar mission (p. 206). It is worth noting that, over time, the Corps has come to be seen as a southern and eastern states' organization; the BOR, as an agency for the dry western states (p. 251). The Corps is often said to have engendered "less conflict with Indian tribes than the BOR" (p. 179), but neither is known for its respect for tribal sovereignty and self-determination.

Not only did the Sardis Lake project violate Choctaw sovereignty but also, as was mentioned earlier, it destroyed thousands of acres of farm- and ranch land and forced the relocation of Choctaw graves. The flooding of Indian land is not unusual when the Corps or the BOR build water projects on or near Indian reservations. In 1965 the completion of a Corps reservoir flooded 10,000 acres of the Allegany reservation of the Seneca Tribe, leaving only 2,300 acres flat enough for use and forcing the relocation of one-third of the reservation's members (O'Brien 1989; see also McCool 1987). Earlier that decade, two Navajo villages were destroyed by flooding from the federally built Navajo Dam (Weinberg 2000). The Pick-Sloan Missouri Basin Program, mentioned earlier, authorized the construction of 107 dams by both the Corps and the BOR beginning in the mid-1940s. This program flooded one-fourth of the Fort Berthold reservation of the

Mandan, Hidatsa, and Arikara Nation (McCool 1987). Five different Sioux reservations were also flooded in the dam constructions, requiring the relocation of over one-third of the residents of these reservations and the destruction of nearly 90 percent of the tribes' timberland, 75 percent of their wild game, and their best agricultural lands (McCool 1987).

When water projects are built by non-Indians in Indian tribal home-lands, it is also not unusual for Indian graves to be relocated, as occurred during the Sardis Lake project. The Corps reservoir on the Seneca tribe's Allegany reservation, for example, required the relocation of three thousand Indian graves (O'Brien 1989), and an entire Kaw tribal cemetery was relocated in the mid-1970s when the Corps built Kaw Reservoir in Oklahoma (*Oklahoman*, October 20, 1997: 1). In the early 1990s, plans were being laid for the disposition of Tohono O'odham human remains from the future site of a BOR project on the tribe's San Xavier reservation, a project that was the chosen mechanism to implement a 1982 water-rights settlement act (McGuire 1991).

"We Don't Believe That Claim Is Valid": An Introduction to Oklahoma State Perspectives on the Conflict

When I was conducting my field research, state leaders were preparing to pump out of the Choctaw Nation water that they were impounding in Sardis Lake, and the Choctaws were contesting this presumption of absolute state sovereignty over southeastern Oklahoma water. My research among state leaders and workers, especially among state bureaucrats at the Oklahoma Water Resources Board, exposed two central features of the state's position on who owns southeastern Oklahoma water. The first was the state's steadfast refusal, which continued long after an agreement had been reached on a Choctaw-Chickasaw-Oklahoma draft settlement, to concede that Choctaw (as well as Chickasaw) rights to this water even exist. The second was the fact that the state chose to ground its claim in the history of water problems that have plagued and continue to plague Oklahoma, a history that, according to the state, provided justification for Oklahoma to seize Sardis Lake water—irrespective of the question of whether tribal water rights exist—in the name of the public good. My discussion of this second key feature of the state's perspective on the conflict requires not only a detailed look at water problems statewide, specifically the water problems on which the state focused, but also a basic map of existing water resources and uses within state boundaries.

In defending its right to extract water from the Choctaw Nation, the state pointed out that Sardis Lake was a key component of the Water Conveyance Project, a large-scale state water project that aims to correct the water "imbalance" between the eastern and western halves of Oklahoma by piping eastern Oklahoma water—first from Sardis Lake and later from other eastern Oklahoma lakes—to western Oklahoma and Oklahoma City. State leaders believed that, to carry out this project, it was necessary for Oklahoma to exercise sovereignty over all Sardis Lake water. The Choctaws did not have rights, according to the state, to even a portion of southeastern Oklahoma water in the name of their tribal reserved rights. This legal position did not contradict Oklahoma state water law, already "in disarray" as a result of its legal history of attempted reconciliations of the riparian and prior-appropriation systems (Helton 1998: 986). Oklahoma state water law does not recognize the water rights of the Indian tribes within its borders (Helton 1998: 986; *Oklahoman*, August 10, 1997: 10A), which is not on its face problematic or even unusual, as Indian reserved water rights exist outside of state water law. What is unusual, particularly given Oklahoma's status as a state with a large Indian population, is that state officials do not readily acknowledge either Indian reserved water rights or the related fact that state law cannot alter such rights, which are classed as federal property rights (Helton 1998; Williams and Montoya-Lewis 2000). As late as 2001, Duane Smith, executive director of the state agency that manages Oklahoma water, publicly asserted that the Chickasaw and Choctaw nations have "no legal claim to the natural resources." About the Choctaw claim to ownership of the water specifically, he said to reporters, "We [simply] don't believe that claim is valid" (*Native American Times*, October 2001). Fewer officials from western states, in contrast, have continued in their denial of the existence of tribal reserved rights to water (Helton 1998: 981). For example, McGuire noted that "virtually no one in the legal community in Tucson denied that [the Tohono O'odham] had a claim to the water"; rather, the issue focused on "how best to make restitution to the Indians" (1991: 144). It should be pointed out that the present-day acknowledgment by western states of the reserved water rights of Indian tribes does not imply that officials in those states understand the nature of Indian reserved rights. For example, a spokesperson for the Arizona Farm Bureau described a Tohono O'odham water-settlement bill in the 1980s as "a raid on *Arizona's* water supply" (emphasis mine; McGuire 1991: 145).

In explaining and justifying the state's position in the conflict, Oklahoma leaders and lawmakers framed Oklahoma's longstanding water problems as sufficient cause for the state to exercise absolute sovereignty over Sardis Lake water. The water problems of the state, state officials correctly pointed out, begin with the fact that Oklahoma's western half, which lies in the American Great Plains and is blanketed by mixed prairie grass, gets too little water, resulting in problems of drought; while eastern Oklahoma, which is covered with timber and forms the easternmost swath of the Eastern Woodland region of the United States, gets too much water, creating problems of flooding. Some parts of western Oklahoma average as little as sixteen inches of rain per year; some parts of eastern Oklahoma, as much as fifty-six (USGS Water-Supply Paper 2375, n.d.). The problems to which these realities give rise can be great. This is especially apparent when these problems are viewed historically. Between 1929 and 1933, for example, western Oklahoma, among other parts of the state, was devastated by the Dust Bowl, an event of drought-induced major soil erosion that prompted the exodus of as many as 400,000 people, or one-sixth of Oklahoma's population, from the state (Gatch 1998b). Only ten years after the official end of this drought, western Oklahoma again was the primary victim of a major drought. This drought, later dubbed the Drought of '51, lasted for seven years, placing western Oklahoma municipal water supplies in critical condition for nearly a decade (USGS Water-Supply Paper 2375). Western Oklahomans were suffering through the Drought of 1995–96, identified as one of the most severe in state history, when I was conducting my fieldwork. A brief visit I made to the region exposed a "rhetoric of water scarcity" that resembled that of the arid American Southwest as described by McGuire (1991).

Eastern Oklahoma's water problems, problems of which both state and Choctaw leaders are well aware, are arguably no less acute. Since 1955 nearly thirty of Oklahoma's major disaster declarations have involved flooding, predominantly in Oklahoma's eastern half.[4] During the 1970s and 1980s the city of Tulsa in the state's northeastern quadrant led not only the state but also the United States in the number of flood declarations (USGS Water-Supply Paper 2375, n.d.). In 1981 an especially dramatic flood occurred in parts of the Choctaw and Chickasaw nations: eighteen inches of rain fell in thirty-six hours, causing more than $23 million in damages. Today, as in the past, submerged river crossings—often called "flooded passes"—are a significant problem in eastern Oklahoma. Flooded passes regularly strand residents. They also cause tens of thousands of dollars of losses per year by preventing farmers and ranchers from transporting agricultural products and livestock to market.

A brief overview of the comparative water resources of western and eastern Oklahoma provides a perspective on the possibilities that eastern Oklahoma water presents to relieving the water problems of both halves of the state and a greater appreciation of the dire condition of the supply of water relative to its demand in western Oklahoma. As is the case in much of the American southeast, high levels of precipitation in eastern Oklahoma help make surface water plentiful. Lakes, streams, rivers, and natural springs are not only abundant but also generally clean, clear, and safe (USGS Water-Supply Paper 2400, n.d.). Consequently, eastern Oklahomans draw only minimally on their groundwater reserves, the largest of which, the Antlers aquifer, spans nine counties in the Choctaw and Chickasaw nations (USGS Water-Supply Paper 2275, n.d.). Western Oklahomans, in contrast, use groundwater for most of their needs. The region has some streams, but they are unsuitable for use as public water supplies due to high concentrations of dissolved minerals (USGS Water-Supply Paper 2400, n.d.). Western Oklahomans draw most of their groundwater from the High Plains aquifer in the northwestern part of the state, the single largest source of groundwater in the state, and the Rush Springs aquifer in the west-central part (USGS Water-Supply Paper 2275, n.d.). Since 1929 western Oklahoma's water problems have been exacerbated by the region's success in utilizing new methods to increase wheat yields (Gatch 1998b). Intensive irrigation is now the primary use to which water is being put in western Oklahoma, a method that has helped make this part of the state one of the most productive wheat-producing regions in the world (USGS Water-Supply Paper 2275, n.d.; Water-Supply Paper 2400, n.d.).[5]

To date, the increased demand for water in western Oklahoma has been met almost entirely by increasing aquifer withdrawals. In the early 2000s, 90 percent of irrigation water in Oklahoma derived from aquifers.[6] Three hundred seventy-five million gallons of water per day is withdrawn from the High Plains aquifer, which has dropped its water levels one hundred feet in some areas. The water levels of the Rush Springs aquifer in the west-central part of the state and the Dog Creek-Blain aquifer in the southwestern corner have also suffered significant declines. Seventy-nine million gallons of water a day is pumped from these two aquifers, contributing to a recent fifty-foot drop in the water levels of each (USGS

Water-Supply Paper 2275, n.d.). These alarming facts, together with the loss in human life and property that result from water problems in the state, provide a perspective on why the state felt justified in their extraction of Choctaw water. The state, it was often said, was acting in the public good, and because of this, the state should be accorded absolute sovereignty over the water in the Choctaws' homeland.

The OWRB and State Water-Rhetoric

Expressly responsible for worrying about Oklahoma's water problems is a state agency, the Oklahoma Water Resources Board (hereafter referred to as OWRB). During the conflict over southeastern Oklahoma water, the OWRB emerged as a key player and mouthpiece for the state. Created in 1957 during the Drought of '51, the OWRB helped found an era that sharply increased the level of state control over water in Oklahoma, ostensibly to fulfill the ambitions of a handful of state leaders who sought not simply to address but to solve the state's water problems. These leaders, and eventually also the OWRB staff, were almost certainly inspired by the massive water projects of the Bureau of Reclamation (BOR), which included the giant and "powerfully symbolic" Hoover, Glen Canyon, and Grand Coulee dams built between 1930 and the early 1960s, structures that quickly became "metaphors for the entire American experience" (McCool 1987: 82). The Sardis Lake project was conceived during what has been described as "the glory years of the big dam era" (p. 220), and the contract to build the lake was obtained two years prior to the 1976 collapse of the first BOR dam (the Teton Dam), a well-publicized event that damaged the symbolic power of the metaphor and hurt the poster-child image of the BOR (pp. 82–83).

The OWRB had 101 employees in 2000, almost all of whom were non-Indian. In this the OWRB mirrors Oklahoma state government as a whole. Only about 4,000 (just over 6 percent) of the 65,000 Oklahoma state-government employees are Indians (Carney 1998). The OWRB is one of about 360 Oklahoma state boards and commissions. Together these entities exercise "considerable administrative authority" over state affairs and help render the modern Oklahoma state government as "very fragmented" (Carney 1998: 116).[7] In this respect the Oklahoma state government contrasts sharply with the highly centralized Choctaw tribe which vests the chief executive with considerable power (see chapter 4).

The owrb's present-day responsibilities include water-project development, public-relations management, and providing administrative and technical leadership on water issues. During the initial part of my research, the agency was headquartered in downtown Oklahoma City across the street from the Alfred P. Murrah Federal Building, the site of the bombing of April 19, 1995. Several owrb staff were among the 168 killed in the blast, which occurred during my fieldwork.

In the summer and fall following the bombing, the owrb helped organize the Oklahoma Governor's Water Conference, an event held in November that brought into sharp relief state perspectives on the Choctaw water conflict. During the event, which was held in Oklahoma City at a swank uptown hotel, the Choctaw Nation's Sardis Lake was heralded as a critical piece of the Water Conveyance Project, despite the fact that, as will be seen later in this chapter, several years earlier, problems repaying the federal loan for Sardis Lake had virtually tabled this plan for the reservoir. It was clear during the conference that the idea of ending the state's unhappy history of devastating droughts and debilitating floods had captured the imagination of state leaders. "Moving Oklahoma's water from where it is to where it's needed" is our goal, declared Gary Sherrer, then executive director of the owrb, in a conversation I had with him at the conference. With Mr. Sherrer and others, I was privy to dozens of conversations during the conference in which state officials talked about moving my tribe's water, including but not limited to the water in Sardis Lake, to Oklahoma City or arid western Oklahoma.

This talk of where to send my tribe's water was a buzz that I heard at all points of the conference and was not limited to closed-door meetings of the state's top lawmakers. In a speech given during the water conference, for example, Glen Johnson, then Speaker of the Oklahoma House of Representatives, spoke eagerly and openly about the Water Conveyance Project. This project would "maximize our resources!" he exclaimed, "and put 'em where they'll do the most good!" Even then governor Frank Keating gave a ringing endorsement of the project at the conference. His enthusiasm about the plan was palpable, prompting him to exclaim in a speech, "We're [Oklahoma is] on the threshold of greatness. . . . We're on the verge of great things!" Unlike most others at the conference, however, Keating followed his endorsement with a note of caution: "[But] we [do] need to handle Sardis in a common-sense way," he said. "The agenda is growth."

The governor admitted to being particularly pleased by the prospect of using southeastern Oklahoma water to help attract more industry to the state's metropoles (see also *Oklahoman*, April 29, 2001: 8).

The Choctaw Response

As a Choctaw who supported tribal control of the water, I often winced at the expressions by state leaders and bureaucrats of the state's position and rhetoric about the water, particularly when such statements included bald-faced denials of the existence of Choctaw water rights, as they often did. My inquiry into the way my tribe responded to the state's claims and actions was much less jarring. This inquiry began in 1992, three years before I began my fieldwork, when I happened to attend the tribal council meeting at which tribal leaders first told the Choctaw public about the impending water conflict. On a hot Saturday morning on August 8, 1992, I sat in the Choctaw tribal council house, less than five miles from Sardis Lake, waiting for my tribe's monthly council meeting to begin. After the opening Christian prayer (a regular feature of Choctaw tribal council meetings that reflects the tribe's immunity to U.S. rules regarding the separation of church and state), Speaker of the Tribal Council Randle Durant said that the council should talk about the possibility of the tribe claiming ownership of southeastern Oklahoma water. The announcement was described as the first to the Choctaw public. I later learned that tribal leaders had been talking with the state about issues of ownership and control over our tribe's water for nearly two years (*Oklahoman*, August 10, 1997: 10).

Speaker Durant began by announcing that, together with Director of Tribal Development Wilma Robinson and "all the tribe's attorneys," he had just returned from Oklahoma City where he had discussed "the issue of the water" with the owrb "in a room filled with attorneys." He then explained what the issue of the water was. "Congress never took away the tribe's water rights!" he exclaimed, raising his eyebrows as he adjusted his bolo. "All the water belongs to us! We own all the water of southeastern Oklahoma, including the reservoirs and the Arkansas river bed![8] That water . . . well, we told them [the owrb] that the Choctaws' water was more valuable than gas or oil!" He spoke deliberately and passionately. At least two council members complained that they had never been told anything about what they termed a "secret meeting" with the state, or about the Choctaws' challenge to state control of tribal water.

One council member gruffly dismissed the idea of challenging the state on this issue. Showing a fundamental misunderstanding of the meaning of tribal reserved rights to water, he said, "The state would never give us the water!" The audience sat in silence.

The Choctaws officially asserted their sovereignty over the water in November of 1997 (*Oklahoman*, November 6, 1997: 20). Joining them in such an assertion were the Chickasaws, who had acquired a one-fourth interest in Choctaw land and mineral rights through a nineteenth-century treaty (see chapter 3). "The tribes have been quiet all this time," explained attorney L. V. Watkins, who assisted the tribes in preparing their case, "because the water has stayed here. But if it goes outside the tribal boundaries, they have to speak up" (*Oklahoman*, August 10, 1997: 10). "This water is our birthright," Choctaw leaders explained (*Shawnee News-Star*, January 12, 2002). "The state [doesn't] have the right to [appropriate] the water" (*Indian Country Today*, October 25, 2000). Anticipating possible objections to the tribes' claims, Choctaw Nation attorney Bob Rabon announced, "Even though some of the tribal lands have been sold to non-Indians through allotment, tribal water rights are implied and can't be removed" (*Oklahoman*, November 6, 1997: 20). The tribes said that if their water rights continued to be violated, they would have no choice but to sue Oklahoma (*Indian Country Today*, October 25, 2000).

In asserting their sovereignty over the water, Choctaw leaders delivered to state legislators "A Guide to Indian Water Rights in Oklahoma," a position paper by Attorney Watkins that argues that tribes own the rights to about 85 percent of the state's water. They also provided copies of the treaty upon which Choctaw tribal ownership of the water is based and copies of the U.S. patent that the Choctaws received for the land. Said attorney Watkins about these supporting documents, "We asked them (state officials) for one piece of paper that documented their claim to the water. To this date, we haven't received one" (*Oklahoman*, August 10, 1997: 10A). Among those who were as ruffled about the Choctaws' sovereignty assertion as were state legislators was the mayor of Oklahoma City. The tribes claimed ownership over water that includes two of Oklahoma City's primary reservoirs, reservoirs that together provide as much as one-half of Oklahoma City's water (*Oklahoman*, August 10, 1997: 10A; November 14, 2001: 2).

From the day in 1992 that tribal leaders told the Choctaw citizenry of the possibility that the tribe might make a major sovereignty assertion,

Speaker Durant, Chief Roberts, and Assistant Chief Greg Pyle began edu-
cating the tribe about the tribe's rights, the illegality of the state's actions,
and the urgency of the Choctaws taking action in light of the Oklahoma
Water Conveyance Project and the impending seizure and removal of Choctaw water. During my fieldwork in the mid-1990s, all of which occurred
while Hollis Roberts was still chief but while Greg Pyle, then assistant
chief, was exercising leadership in key areas, I was struck by how remarkably focused and concerted were these tribal-government efforts. Tribal
leaders identified the first targets for "tribal water-rights education" as
tribal lawmakers and employees, with the idea that this then 1,500-member
group would become a force for the broader dissemination of information
to the Choctaw public. Speaker Durant coordinated the effort among the
tribal council. He convened special meetings about the water, and when
it became clear that additional education was necessary, he held at least
two mandatory meetings for council members. Durant required that the
tribal council read government studies and master technical information
about lake water levels, "safe yields," water-delivery systems, and other
topics. Many times he told the council that, with so much at stake in the
conflict, it was critical that all council members were "on the same page"
and could "present a united front" to state officials.

At the same time, Speaker Durant, Chief Roberts, and Assistant Chief
Pyle promoted a general awareness about and knowledge of the conflict
among tribal employees. In tribal staff meetings, tribal employee gatherings, and even at an office birthday party for a tribal program administrator, Durant, Roberts, and Pyle gave critical information about the
basis for the Choctaws' claim, the tribe's expected strategy, and the status of the conflict. Several times I observed these leaders electrify crowds
of tribal employees with their words about the water. Before long, a consensus of strong support for this seminal sovereignty assertion had developed within the Choctaw tribal state, and tribal employees had emerged
as effective "point persons for the Choctaw public about the water issue,"
as Durant put it.

In watching tribal employees interact with one another and with other
Choctaws, I was struck by the extent to which their talk about the conflict was marked by deeply soulful disclosures. For example, once when
I was hunting with about six tribal employees, one of them mentioned
the water conflict. In response, another looked at his gun, then out at the

horizon. "That water . . . that water is more valuable than gas or oil!" he declared proudly but with a hint of sadness, echoing the words and affect of Speaker Durant. "And it's rightfully ours!" said another, waving his arms in a symphony of righteousness and triumph lined with exasperation. Without a transition of any kind, the conversation then turned to the early poststatehood period of our tribal history, during which non-Indian Oklahomans appropriated most of our land. As is common in conversations among Choctaws, my companions exchanged expressions of sorrow and loss over this dispossession. At the same time, they affirmed their deep-seated distrust of the state of Oklahoma, a key player in the dispossession that followed allotment. The conversation points to an important fact about my tribe's response to the conflict over the tribe's water: the conflict centered on the attempt of non-Indian Oklahomans to appropriate a Choctaw tribal resource, and, as such, it exposed wounds from the past that are still in the process of healing. Such wounds are a part of the embodied experience of possibly every Choctaw.

Almost entirely through word of mouth, the tribal state effectively raised awareness about the conflict among the tribal citizenry. This was not difficult in the Kiamichi Valley, where talk of the conflict was frequent and where many citizens actively sought information from the tribal state. In other parts of the Choctaw Nation, it was clear that, through "point persons" in the tribal state and through other means, many Choctaws acquired a basic understanding of the conflict and were able to speak knowledgeably and intelligently about it. For example, one day in Poteau, a city of about eight thousand in the northeastern part of the Choctaw Nation, I visited a seventy-one-year-old Choctaw elder. In a pair of old metal chairs, I sat with her on the porch of a white 1940s farmhouse, now part of a city neighborhood. For most of my visit, we sat in silence, a feature of visiting that is not unusual when Choctaws, particularly younger Choctaws, visit with tribal elders. The woman's occasional comments focused mainly on the approaching front, the familiar rolling-in of dark-grey storm clouds from the upper eastern part of the sky. Absorbed by the unfolding drama, I had settled deep into my seat when she brought up what she described as "the Sardis Lake situation." By building the lake, she declared, Oklahoma was "most definitely not trying to help all of its citizens," including the Choctaws (as state officials were arguing). Rather, the state was trying "to take advantage of a weaker government and people"; that is, they were trying to take advantage of the Choctaw government and citizenry. It was one of the few times that I saw this lady express anger. Several weeks later, I overheard two straight-backed businessmen in neatly pressed suits, both of whom I knew to be Choctaws, discussing the conflict as they poured their morning coffee at a convenience store near Broken Bow in the southeastern part of the Choctaw Nation. One of them decried the state's actions. Donning thick dark-rimmed glasses, he remarked to his companion that, without permission, the state had built a project that aimed to profit by and from stripping the Choctaws of one of their most valuable resources. By claiming the water, he continued, the tribe was simply defending itself against a stronger, more powerful government. The other man nodded as he took his first sip of morning coffee.

By 2001 the Choctaw tribal government was using full-page newspaper ads, door-to-door solicitors, and public meetings to promote tribal sovereignty over the water to all southeastern Oklahomans, Choctaws and non-Choctaws alike. Tribal control of the water, said tribal leaders to southeastern Oklahomans, would bring "an unprecedented economic boon to the region." The tribe sponsored dinners to which they invited journalists, bankers, and county commissioners. They also hired Tommy Thomas, a former legislator, to promote public acceptance of a large-scale water lease that would still leave "plenty of water for Oklahoma's needs" and would permit "tens of millions of dollars [to] flow into southeastern Oklahoma" (*Daily Ardmoreite*, December 10, 2001). "The tribes are very sensitive," said Choctaw chief Greg Pyle in 2001, "to concerns that we might make some kind of deal that is harmful to southeast Oklahoma or that we and the local areas will not be properly compensated for our water resources" (*Oklahoman*, November 14, 2001: 2). During my fieldwork in the mid-1990s, some southeastern Oklahomans, including Choctaws, were expressing anxieties about a large-scale water lease, but these anxieties had not yet become the basis, as they did in the early 2000s, of a small but organized effort to oppose the leasing of Choctaw Nation water.

Several times mention was made by tribal leaders and Choctaw citizens of the support that other Oklahoma tribes were giving to the Choctaw tribe in their pursuit of this water-rights claim, regardless of the issue of whether the Choctaws planned to lease or not lease the water. Johnson and Turner (1998) correctly note that tribal divisions, especially broad divisions between eastern Oklahoma tribes and those in western Oklahoma, often undermine tribal political unity in Oklahoma, but in late 1995 when I was conducting my field research, Oklahoma tribes were sufficiently alarmed by the then recently proposed federal tribal-program cuts that most had united under the leadership of Tyler Todd of the Cheyenne-Arapaho Tribe to form a political action committee of Oklahoma tribes (see *Oklahoman*, December 13, 1995: 16). Though this alliance was forged to pursue action in Washington DC, it created a moment of goodwill and sisterhood among Oklahoma tribes from which the Choctaws benefited enormously in their much more local struggle. Of course, it helped that the Choctaws were pursuing a claim considered groundbreaking in terms of Indian water rights in the state. If the Choctaws won their claim, it was often noted, it was possible that all but 15 percent of the water in the state would come under tribal control (see *Oklahoman*, November 6, 1997).

Such a development, if it came to pass, would help rectify the problem in Oklahoma—in practical, not legal terms—of the relative disempowerment of tribes vis-à-vis the state, a problem in which there has not been significant improvement, according to Johnson and Turner (1998), since Oklahoma statehood in 1907. "The Native American presence in Oklahoma politics," they contend, "is decidedly limited in the present day" (p. 102). Pointing to American Indian service in state legislatures as one barometer of Indian political influence and power, Wilkins (2002a) implicitly concurs. Between 1997 and 1999, he claims, there was only one Indian who served in the Oklahoma state legislature. However, as he also points out, according to the Democratic National Committee, American Indians are a "significant swing vote" in Oklahoma (p. 199). And conflicts such as the one described in this chapter, as well as the turn-of-the-twenty-first-century conflicts in Oklahoma over tribal sales of motor fuels and over tribal gaming, have already allowed tribes to make up some of the ground that they lost when Oklahoma became a state at the turn of the twentieth century.

Problems in Implementing the Water Conveyance Project

Although as late as 1995 some state leaders and lawmakers were strongly suggesting that the conveyance of Sardis Lake water under the Water Conveyance Project was imminent, several years earlier in the early 1990s the state legislature had actually voted not to carry through with these plans but rather to sell Sardis Lake water to the highest bidder and thereby make literally hundreds of millions of dollars off of Choctaw water. Fiscal and ethical irresponsibility on the part of the state help explain this action. In contracting for the lake's construction, the state incurred a debt that it could not—or perhaps simply did not want to—repay, and in seeking solutions to this problem, they chose to abandon the moral obligation they had taken on in their public justification of the project: their commitment to build the reservoir in order to help both flood-besieged southeastern Oklahomans and water-starved western Oklahomans. On their own terms, then (that is, notwithstanding the legal and moral problems of assuming that they could build the lake and use Choctaw water in the first place), the state's actions with respect to Sardis Lake were reprehensible. Co-conspirator in the production of such an outcome was a serious breakdown in the functioning of the Oklahoma state-government political process, as will be seen.

In 1983, as Sardis Lake literally was being filled, Oklahoma sent the federal government $450,000, the first of fifty annual loan payments for building the lake (*Oklahoman*, February 7, 1993: 12). Five additional payments followed in the 1980s (p. 12). Between the late 1980s and the early 1990s, the state failed to make as many as seven payments on the loan (*Oklahoman*, November 6, 1997). By 1993, it was $2.3 million behind in its payments, and the state legislature had voted not to pay anything more on the loan (*Oklahoman*, February 7, 1993: 12). At that point, the state was still reeling from substantial losses in tax revenues that derived from the collapse of the energy industry in 1982, when oil prices dropped from over thirty dollars a barrel to less than twenty dollars a barrel. Prior to the collapse, 29 percent of state government had been funded by the gross production tax on oil; by the mid-1990s, the amount had plunged to 7 percent (Humphreys 1998). State legislators pointed out that selling southeastern Oklahoma water could lessen the financial problems brought on by this unfortunate event, as well as by other events that had been either within or beyond the control of the legislature.

A breakdown in the political process of the state government contributed to the state's decision to sell Choctaw water, a breakdown that stymied the attempts of state leaders and bureaucrats to lay the groundwork for the conveyance of Sardis Lake water and prompted the throwing up of hands that characterized the legislature's vote to sell the water. Despite meeting many times about the matter, the governor, on the one hand,

and the state legislature, on the other, were never able to reach an agreement on who should receive southeastern Oklahoma water. In addition, state legislators could not agree among themselves on this matter. In the mid-1990s, Governor Keating was arguing that Sardis Lake water should go toward "growth." By growth, he meant industry, specifically the idea of bringing more industry to Oklahoma from outside the state's boundaries. In a speech in 1995 that I attended, he described the recent visit of a group of Korean businessmen from Seoul and an unrelated event several months earlier in which a company called Micron had rejected Oklahoma as the site for its new plant. For both groups of businessmen, "the availability of water, good water," Keating explained, "was a big consideration." These two incidents helped convince him, he said, that water is "the key to the state's economic growth."

During the 1980s, significant opposition to the governor's proposed plan for southeastern Oklahoma water developed within the state legislature. By the 1990s this opposition had become entrenched. Some state lawmakers, most of them from western Oklahoma, argued that southeastern Oklahoma water should go toward the support of existing, not prospective, industries. Specifically, they argued that wheat-field irrigation should be the priority. The coalition they organized focused on mobilizing their constituents in western Oklahoma and securing the support of some of the state's most prominent organizations. One of these was the Oklahoma Cattlemen's Association. During my field research, I asked the executive director of this association, Jarold Callahan, why his group endorsed the coalition. Politely, he said, "Well, you see, [poor] wheat crops hurt cattle prices." Though the coalition effectively protested the adoption of a water policy that was metropolitan directed (and governor supported), most if not all coalition members were hamstrung by constituents who demanded that they win for their home districts unreasonably large amounts of the water, cutting out other western Oklahoma communities if necessary. State lawmakers chose to resolve this impasse not by effective use of the political process but rather by giving up on the plan for Sardis Lake, particularly in the context of the possibility that substantial profits could be realized from selling the water.

By 1996 the federal government was issuing threats that it planned to sue Oklahoma for nonpayment of the loan. State leaders responded by sending in a payment of just over a half-million dollars. That next year, they appropriated and paid twice that amount from the state's rainy day fund, bringing the total payments on the loan to almost $4.5 million, and the balance on the loan to approximately $38 million (*Oklahoman*, November 6, 1997: 20). As these last-ditch efforts to avoid defaulting on the loan were being made, some state leaders were secretly investigating the question of approximately how much money could be got from selling the water. "Informal talks" with Texas on the matter appear to have begun as early as 1990 (*Oklahoman*, August 10, 1997: 10; April 29, 2001: 8). Before century's end, the default was official. Oklahoma was sued for nonpayment of the loan (*Indian Country Today*, October 25, 2000; *Oklahoman*, November 6, 1997: 20).

The work of obtaining and evaluating bids from prospective buyers of the water thus began in earnest for the state. Two entities emerged as frontrunners in the competition for the valued resource: the Oklahoma City Water Utilities Trust (OCWUT) and the North Texas Water Agency (NTWA). The OCWUT announced that it had enough water to serve its 165,000 households and businesses through 2035, but that expected population growth, together with conservative city planning, suggested that the city's water supplies be augmented (*Oklahoman*, April 29, 2001: 8). The OCWUT offered to pay off the federal loan for Sardis Lake and reimburse the state for past payments. In addition, it would pay the state $40 million for the water rights to Sardis Lake. Short-term increases in customer water bills would pay for the new water source. The city did not say how much water, beginning in about 2035, that it expected to extract from the lake. By all accounts, though, the amount was expected to be modest. Here it should be pointed out that, statewide, Oklahomans consume 360 billion gallons of surface water per year, 3.2 billion gallons of which are used in the Kiamichi Basin area (*Daily Ardmoreite*, December 10, 2001; *Oklahoman*, April 29, 2001: 10A). Five hundred billion gallons of water per year flow over a dam at Hugo Lake (a lake that catches the overflow from Sardis Lake) and into the Red River, where the water becomes contaminated by minerals (*Oklahoman*, April 29, 2001: 10A; *Indian Country Today*, October 25, 2000).

The other serious bidder, the NTWA, a consortium of municipal governments in north Texas, wanted a specific quantity of water, 130 million gallons per day, from Sardis Lake and nearby Hugo Lake (also in the Choctaw Nation), beginning as soon as possible and continuing for a period of one hundred years. For this the NTWA offered as much as $400 million, a portion of which would go to paying off the federal loan and reimbursing

Oklahoma for past loan payments (*Oklahoman*, August 10, 1997: 10). By the early 2000s the Texas group had expanded to include the Dallas–Fort Worth area, and was representing as much as 25 percent of Texas's population. This expanded group declared an interest in not simply Kiamichi River Basin water but also a river basin just east of it (also in the Choctaw Nation). For 20 million additional gallons of Choctaw Nation water per day, the group increased the original offer by $100 million (*Oklahoman*, April 29, 2001: 8, 10A; November 14, 2001: 2). Both Jim Couch, director of Oklahoma City's Water and Wastewater Utilities Department, and Carl Reihn, executive director of the NTWA, told me that they were well aware of the conflict over who owned this water and that it mattered not at all whether the water was got from the state or the tribe. They simply wanted the water.

The State or the Tribe? Local Perspectives on the Conflict

A half decade before the occurrence of the event that some thought signaled the end of the Choctaw-Oklahoma conflict over water—the negotiation of the 2001 draft settlement—I spent several months in the conflict's epicenter, the Kiamichi Valley, exploring the perspectives of both Choctaws and non-Choctaws on the conflict. I listened carefully to dinner-table discussions, conducted interviews, and attended four public hearings that were held in the valley about the water.[9] Most important and unexpected was my finding that local, public support for either the state or the tribe did not fall along Choctaw/non-Choctaw lines. I had expected to find significant support for the state's claim among non-Choctaws, and significant support for the tribe's claim among Choctaws. Instead, I found overwhelming support for tribal control of the water among both Choctaws and non-Choctaws. My consultants were clear, and some of them were strident, about the reason: their view of the state of Oklahoma. Both Choctaws and non-Choctaws contended that the interests of the state were directly opposed to those of southeastern Oklahoma. The state was committed to exploiting southeastern Oklahoma to benefit Oklahoma City and Tulsa, many of them explained. The continued growth of the state's metropoles depended upon the seizure of southeastern Oklahoma water. Such a seizure also helped ensure the continued economic underdevelopment of southeastern Oklahoma, they continued, which would facilitate future extractions of southeastern Oklahoma resources by the state. The Choctaws, in contrast, were committed to making southeastern Oklahoma a better place to live and work, Choctaws and non-Choctaws alike told me. "Economic development," dozens proudly pointed out, "is one of the tribe's highest priorities." Echoing popular opinion in the valley, a white farmer told me that, regardless of whether the Choctaws chose to use the water as a carrot to attract more industry or lease it to generate capital for tribal economic development (or both), southeastern Oklahomans were sure to share in the bounty. On the other hand, "if the state won the water," he continued, "well, you know what would happen—we [in southeastern Oklahoma] would see nothin'!" As is evident in my data, southeastern Oklahomans are well aware of the fact that, especially since World War II, Oklahoma City and Tulsa have experienced rapid growth, and rural Oklahoma, continued population decline. It is clear that this reflects a decline in agriculture and mining and an increase in manufacturing, services, and government (Gatch 1998b). The extent to which state policies and prejudices have been a factor, however, is still unclear. Between 1980 and 1990 Oklahoma City grew by almost 10 percent. In 1994 its population was 463,030, the largest in the state (Jenks 1998).

Longstanding regional grievances with the state, together with the state's fiscal and ethical irresponsibility with respect to the Sardis Lake project, informed the staunch opposition I encountered in the valley to state control of the water. In addition, the antipathy that I found in the valley (and in other parts of southeastern Oklahoma) toward the state of Oklahoma reflected what has been described as the general tendency of Oklahomans "to be skeptical about [state] government and politicians" due in part to "the state's ongoing experience with political corruption" (Johnson and Turner 1998: 2). "From the first days of the new state," Johnson and Turner explain, "there have been ethical and legal problems in the political system. . . . Few states can match Oklahoma's ongoing problems with corruption" (p. 2). Southeastern Oklahoman distrust of the state was at a high point when I was conducting my research. Two years earlier in 1993, then governor of Oklahoma David Walters had pled guilty to violating state campaign law after a protracted FBI and grand jury investigation in which he was accused of selling state jobs, violating campaign contribution laws, and attempting to cover up these crimes (p. 17). The fact that the Choctaw conflict was about water no doubt buttressed local non-Indian opposition to state control (and support of tribal control). Elsewhere in the United States, metropolitan areas have leached the water supply of rural areas, soaking up an enormous quantity of water to the detriment of their rural counterparts (see McGuire 1991).[10] In the small

Indian tribe of Isleta Pueblo, for example, water for farming is important and increasingly threatened due to proximity of Albuquerque, which is rapidly depleting the area's aquifers (O'Brien 1989). Equally if not more disturbing, Weinberg argues that "the future growth of the region's [the American Southwest's] booming super-developed sprawl is virtually predicated on the surrender of Navajo water rights" (2000: 18).

The OWRB and the governor's office were aware of southeastern Oklahoma's antipathy toward the state and the threat that this posed to state-controlled water management. Gary Sherrer, OWRB executive director in the mid-1990s, was a non-Indian who had been reared in the Kiamichi Valley in a community called Snow, less than ten miles from Sardis Lake. His father, Leonard, had served as Snow postmaster from 1940 to 1982, and his mother, Florida, had been a clerk in the local store. In October and November of 1995, on behalf of the OWRB, Mr. Sherrer organized a series of public hearings in the valley about the water. At the same time, the Oklahoma governor's office launched a campaign to promote tourism in the valley and southeastern Oklahoma as a whole. On November 8, 1995, I watched Governor Keating kick off the campaign by addressing a crowd of valley residents from the porch of the Clayton Country Inn five miles from Sardis Lake. Describing southeastern Oklahoma as the "jewel of Oklahoma," he announced a renewed "state commitment to development in this part of the state." Valley residents countered these and other overtures on the part of the state with resistance. OWRB's public hearings, for example, yielded what was described as "a number of angry questions" about a wide range of topics.

Elsewhere in the state, I encountered significant non-Indian public support for the state's claim (see also *Oklahoman*, November 25, 2001: 8). In 2002 many such supporters formed a group called "One Nation." Based in Oklahoma City, the group's stated purpose is to "raise public awareness of the growing threat to our state's economic future posed by the unprecedented expansion of the power of the Native American tribes" (NativeTimes.com, June 30, 2004; www.onenationok.com). One Nation, which includes members of the Southern Oklahoma Water Alliance, a group formed in 2001 that is based in the southeastern part of the Choctaw Nation, explicitly opposes tribal water rights (*Idabel McCurtain Daily Gazette*, May 4, 2003). After the terms of the draft settlement were revealed, spokespersons for this group, as well as for the Oklahoma Family Farm Alliance and Oklahoma Sierra Club, posted a paper on a Web site in which they argued: "The Choctaws and Chickasaws form 3% [of Oklahoma's population]. How can the Oklahoma Water Resources Board possibly justify a giveaway of HALF the potential revenues for a water sale as a bribe for this small population?" (emphasis in the original).[11]

The 2001 Draft Settlement

About five hundred miles away on a Montana reservation in the mid-1990s, another Indian tribe, the Blackfeet Tribe, were asking themselves the same question about their own tribal water-rights conflict with the state as were the Choctaws and Chickasaws. The question was, Which of two options should the tribe(s) choose to resolve their claims? As is the case for most tribes involved in turn-of-the-twenty-first-century water-rights conflicts, for the Blackfeet, as well as for the Choctaws and Chickasaws, the two options were the same: litigate, or pursue a negotiated settlement.

Until the mid-1980s litigation was "by far the preferred method of tribes for settling Indian water-rights disputes," and negotiation, the preferred method of most states (Burton 1991: 49; McCool 1987). In fact, during the 1970s and much of the 1980s most tribes actively resisted non-Indian pressures to negotiate rather than litigate (McCool 1987). During the 1980s, however, tribes began to "fare less well in litigation" over water rights due in large part to an increasing orientation toward states' rights in the U.S. Supreme Court (Burton 1991; see also Wilkins and Lomawaima 2001). Court decisions on tribal water rights since the mid-1980s have been characterized as "more consistently anti-Indian than in any other realm of resource management" (Burton 1991: 45, n. 53). This has forced tribes to reevaluate their preference for litigation.

Despite the shift in favor of states in water-rights litigation that involves tribes, states still prefer negotiation. For states, "one of the greatest limitations to [litigation] is cost," McCool explains. "The states simply cannot afford the prolonged and complex trials" (McCool 1987: 246). States are also spooked, he adds, by the "open-ended nature of Winters Doctrine rights" and "the uncertainty created by [the *Winters*] doctrine" (pp. 245–46). By the late 1990s Oklahoma had made clear its preference for a negotiated settlement with the Choctaws and Chickasaws. "We feel we ought to try to compact with the tribes," said Duane Smith of the OWRB; "we should not be litigating." State leaders pointed out that their willingness to settle with the two tribes did not at all imply that the state was herewith acknowledging the existence of Choctaw and Chickasaw water rights. "We don't need to have a stance [on tribal ownership of water rights]," the governor's chief of staff, Howard Barnet, insisted. "We're trying to reach a settlement; not to answer [that] question" (*Native American Times*, October 2001). The OWRB explained that Oklahoma planned to simply "set aside" the question of who owns the water during their negotiations with the Choctaws and Chickasaws, focusing instead on such issues as the administration of water rights and water-quality standards. If the tribes and the state were to continue to fight over who owns the water, the OWRB's Duane Smith continued, the parties might never reach agreement about the more important issues of managing the water. "If the water is properly managed," he said, "why should we fight over who owns it?" (*Oklahoman*, November 6, 1997: 20).

On November 14, 2001, it was announced that agreement on a draft settlement had been reached between the state of Oklahoma and the Choctaw and Chickasaw nations. Under the terms of the draft settlement, the state, on the one hand, and the Choctaw and the Chickasaw nations, on the other, would evenly split the revenues from leasing southeastern Oklahoma water.[12] The Choctaws would get 37.5 percent; the Chickasaws, 12.5 percent. Significantly, the draft settlement stated that all of the state's share was to be spent on economic development in southeastern Oklahoma. A board of southeastern Oklahomans, with only limited representation on the part of the state, would decide how, specifically, to spend the state's share. In addition, the duty of administering water-quality standards for the water was to be the state's, and the tribes agreed to waive their claims to all existing water rights issued by Oklahoma, including Oklahoma City's rights to two reservoirs that had been clouded by the tribes' claim. Last, the draft settlement accorded Oklahoma City a limited amount of Sardis Lake water to meet the rise in demand that would come from the city's expected population growth during the first half of the twenty-first century.

Why and how did the tribes assent to the recognition, in a public and "international" forum, of their entitlement to only half of the revenues from the leasing of water within their tribal homelands? The draft settlement mandated that the other half of the revenues be used to fund economic development in the Choctaw and Chickasaw nations, but these monies would have been funds over which the tribes would have had no direct control. Moreover, the tribes' assent to surrender a portion of revenues from water leasing carried with it the possibility of weakening the tribes' hand in future negotiations oriented toward clarifying their (and/ or the state's) water rights. Why might the Choctaws and Chickasaws have agreed to such a draft settlement?

Law professor Larry Echo-Hawk provides some insight into these questions. Specifically evaluating the option of litigation for the Choctaws and Chickasaws in this water-rights claim, in 1997 Echo-Hawk characterized the option of litigation for the two tribes as "a risky proposition" because "it can be an all-or-nothing shake of the dice" (*Oklahoman*, November 6, 1997: 20). "Or," he added, through litigation "you can come up with a court decision that doesn't provide the answers to settle the needs of the people involved" (p. 20). Pointing to his experiences in Idaho, a state for which he served as attorney general and later as chief counsel for the Shoshone tribe, Echo-Hawk described negotiated settlements as the best way to resolve tribal water-rights conflicts. We in Idaho "avoided an expensive legal battle over water rights," he explained, through a five-year process of tribal-state negotiations during which both the state and the tribe "compromised on who would use, regulate and sell the water" (p. 20). However, as the draft settlement between the Choctaw and Chickasaw nations and the state of Oklahoma suggests—a settlement that fortunately was not legally institutionalized—negotiation may not be the "all-or-nothing shake of the dice" that litigation often is, but it carries the risk—in the spirit of "compromise"—of forcing from the party with the stronger claim concessions that are too great when evaluated in terms of the merits of that party's claim. At the negotiating table, a fifty-fifty water-rights split between the state, on the one hand, and the Choctaw and Chickasaw tribes, on the other, may appear to be a fair way of reconciling the polar opposite positions of the state and the tribes on the question of the ownership of southeastern Oklahoma water. But when the settlement terms are evaluated in terms of the relative strength of the legal positions of the parties, such an agreement is revealed as not just unreasonable but also unjust.

There is no doubt that the Choctaws and Chickasaws were aware of the fact that both forums for the settlement of tribal water-rights conflicts in the United States—the courts and the negotiated-settlement process—jeopardized the affirmation of their full water rights. The tribes began steering a course that forced them to choose between what they knew to be two imperfect alternatives. The course that they ended up pursuing, however, was not forced upon them. It was a course that they themselves chose to take. In 1997 Oklahoma state environment secretary Brian Griffin even suggested that a negotiated settlement was the tribes' idea: "The tribes are proposing," he said, "that we create a compact similar to what we did with the motor fuels tax exemption" (*Oklahoman*, August 10, 1997: 10A). Both the Choctaw and the Chickasaw nations publicly explained this position. Choctaw tribal attorney Bob Rabon said, "Both parties [the tribes and the state] understand that [the conflict] is not [one] that needs to be litigated. It would take years, and in the meantime, there's valuable water not being exploited as it should be" (*Oklahoman*, August 10, 1997: 1). "What we are trying to do," Chickasaw governor Bill Anoatubby added, "is head off a major conflict that will tie-up water rights in southeastern Oklahoma" (*Native American Times*, October 2001).

After much careful thought and deliberation, the tribes chose the forum that offered them the least chance of losing all of their water rights. In the negotiations, the tribes sought an affirmation of their entitlement to water within their boundaries. Possibly even more important from their perspective, they also sought a guarantee that, if they chose to lease their water, all revenues from such a lease would be spent in their tribal homelands. For these things, they expressed a willingness (1) to give up tribal control of over half of the leasing revenues to which they are entitled, and (2) to donate some water to Oklahoma City. The tribes' willingness to make such sizeable concessions speaks to the sense of urgency that the leaders of both tribes feel about the need to create new jobs and businesses in their homelands. For years, Choctaw and Chickasaw leaders have expressed alarm about the massive out-migration of their youth. Almost daily, middle-aged Indians and elders bemoan the dearth of jobs in the area and the consequent flight of their children and grandchildren to the cities. The children and grandchildren themselves shake their heads and say, "What can we do? There are no jobs here." The decisions of the tribes to pursue their water-rights claim and participate in talks to help resolve conflicts pertaining to their water rights and to a prospective lease of Indian water were oriented toward addressing this and other problems. Through this process, the tribes affirmed their sovereignty and sought affirmation of their rights to acquire much-needed capital for tribal economic development through water leasing. By pursuing a settlement, a settlement that at the time they expected to serve as the basis for a tribal-state compact, they attempted to secure this capital for the immediate future, that is, for the current generation of Choctaw and Chickasaw youth. The creation of not simply economically viable but economically vibrant tribal homelands, they no doubt were hoping, would then possibly lie within reach.

In the early 2000s, when the water lessors (Choctaw Nation, Chickasaw Nation, and Oklahoma) and the proposed lessee (NTWA) could not agree on the terms of a water lease, the compacting process that aimed to resolve some of the conflicts over Choctaw and Chickasaw water was halted. The 2001 Choctaw-Chickasaw-Oklahoma draft settlement never became a tribal-state compact. When I spent some of the summer of 2005 in the Choctaw Nation, some Choctaws told me that they were confused and uncertain about what had happened with the Choctaw-Chickasaw-Oklahoma water compact. They said that they were aware that the agreement between the water lessors and the proposed lessee fell through when the lessee (NTWA) failed to offer a fair price for the water. They also showed a general awareness of their chief's and assistant chief's response to the NTWA offer. In a 2002 press release, Choctaw chief Greg Pyle had announced, "The Tribes have always contended that if an agreement could not be reached that was good for southeast Oklahoma and the Choctaw and Chickasaw Nations, we would walk away from the negotiating table. This water is our birthright and if we can't negotiate a water deal that ensures our future growth and prosperity, there will be no deal at all." To this statement, Assistant Chief Mike Bailey had added, "To some degree, I think all involved parties are disappointed that we have reached this point. The sale of water from Oklahoma could have been one of the most historic occurrences since statehood" (Choctaw Nation, January 9, 2002).

In 2005, however, the reasons why the pursuit of a tribal-state compact had also been halted were less clear to Choctaw civilians. Two shared with me their theories. One said that he thought that it was Oklahoma who had stopped the compacting process. "They didn't want us [the Choctaws] to have the water [i.e., have state recognition of Choctaw tribal water rights]," he said. Another Choctaw speculated that the Choctaw and Chickasaw tribes had stopped the process. She said that she thought that both the Choctaw and Chickasaw leadership had simply realized, later, that they had not gotten as good a deal in the compact negotiations as they could have received.

During the summer of 2005, I found little evidence in the Choctaw homeland of the small but organized effort to oppose a large-scale water lease that had begun during the mid-1990s when I was conducting my field research and had reached its height in the early 2000s. In the mid-1990s, I found that most of those who opposed such a lease were non-Indian (but a few were Choctaws). More important, I found that these individuals had adopted such a position primarily because they strongly supported slow to negative economic growth in southeastern Oklahoma. Some members of this category of southeastern Oklahomans were senior citizens who had migrated to the Choctaw Nation when they had retired from blue-collar jobs in Oklahoma City, a migration that, they said, enabled them to stretch their meager monthly retirement checks. They feared that economic development would raise their cost of living and thus lower their standard of living. Others were owners of mom-and-pop stores who feared that economic development would bring into the area more Wal-Mart stores and other national chains, forcing the mom-and-pop stores out of business. According to some Choctaws, still others who opposed a water lease were marijuana farmers. Marijuana farmers (who by all accounts were numerous in the central part of the Choctaw Nation) were said to oppose economic development because they assumed that it would bring to the region increased surveillance of people and property.

Conclusion

The conflict over water in the Choctaw tribal homeland—an event that began in 1974 and that reached what many thought was a conclusion in 2001—archives a shift in relations of diplomacy between the state of Oklahoma and the federal government, on the one hand, and the Choctaw tribal government, on the other. Five years prior to the event's inception in 1974, the Choctaws were facing the termination of their trust relationship with the U.S. government and thus a future in which, in federal terms, they would no longer exist as a tribe. Both the Oklahoma state and U.S. federal governments were well aware that their diplomatic relations with the Choctaw tribal government would end if the tribe were terminated, and continue if the legislation were repealed. The Choctaw termination legislation was indeed repealed—before it was scheduled to take effect—but as late as four years after its repeal the Oklahoma state government, together with the U.S. Army Corps of Engineers, took actions that disregarded their obligation to enter into diplomatic relations with the Choctaws in affairs involving resources within the Choctaws' homeland. By building a structure with which to extract water from the Choctaw Nation, the state and federal governments created conditions that demanded interfaces with the Choctaw tribal government, but they ignored (or perhaps even denied the existence of) this imperative. For twenty-two years of the conflict involving Choctaw Nation water, diplomatic relations between the state and federal governments, on the one hand, and the Choctaw tribal government, on the other, over who owns the water in the Choctaw Nation were virtually nonexistent. During this part of the conflict, the content and character of state and federal actions were cardinally defined by the assumption of absolute state and federal sovereignty over the water within Choctaw tribal boundaries.

The Choctaw tribal nation building that had only just begun when the state and federal governments began building Sardis Lake in 1974 was nearly complete in the mid-1990s, permitting the Choctaws to substantially redefine their diplomatic relations with the Oklahoma state and U.S. federal government—in part by and through their participation in the water conflict described in this chapter. By challenging the state's assumption of absolute sovereignty over this water and engaging in a protracted battle to negotiate their water rights, the tribe resisted the efforts that were made earlier in the conflict to render their tribe not simply impotent but invisible. By the 1990s the Choctaws—like other U.S. tribes, as Biolsi points out—were increasingly managing their interfaces with other sovereigns in terms of "an assumption of coequal sovereignty, not nested, hierarchical sovereignty or a relationship of scaled sovereignty" (2005: 246). Choctaw participation in the water conflict illustrates this broader phenomenon.

In an odd way, the history of Choctaw-Oklahoma-federal relations of diplomacy that is archived in the history of the water conflict—a history of relations defined first by Choctaw disempowerment, disrespect, and marginality, and later by Choctaw empowerment, self-determination, and inclusion—is inscribed in the draft settlement that many believed would bring an end to a longstanding tribal-state water conflict. From a tribal perspective, the 2001 draft settlement—which was the last expression of a very active phase of Choctaw-Chickasaw-Oklahoma negotiations over water rights—is both strikingly regressive and remarkably progressive. The recognition given to Oklahoma in the settlement of the right to as much as one-half of the proceeds from a lease of Choctaw and Chickasaw water is regressive. In fact, it is disturbingly reminiscent of some of the tribal water-rights agreements of the early twentieth century, agreements that were later deemed manifestly unfair and were consequently renegotiated.

However, in terms of its water-use provisions, especially its provisions for the use of water for tribal economic development, the 2001 Choctaw-Chickasaw-Oklahoma draft agreement is remarkably progressive. In the arid west, the focus of scholarly and popular attention to tribal water rights, tribes have historically struggled to secure water simply for subsistence, and the vast majority of such tribes emerge from water-rights conflicts with agreements that restrict their use of water for economic development. This is especially true in the "new frontier" area of water leasing. Located in a water-rich area with sufficient water (in their view) to accommodate new tribal businesses and industries, the Choctaws made no secret of the fact that they planned to allocate most of the water for tribal economic development, specifically for water leasing. In the end, the tribe agreed to a deal that placed no restrictions on their ability to water lease. In terms of its respect for the right of tribes to use their water in whichever ways they deem best, the 2001 draft settlement provides a model for future tribal-state water settlements.

Using a conflict that revolved around a type of tribal reserved rights—tribal water rights—that has received a great deal of tribal, legal, and popular attention but very little scholarly attention, in this chapter I have brought to the fore an aspect of tribal sovereignty of which tribes and lawyers are well aware but which is often overlooked by others, particularly by the larger non-Indian population. This aspect of tribal sovereignty derives from the fact that, even when particular tribal rights, such as tribal water rights, appear legally well established, tribes must often negotiate—with other sovereigns—their right to exercise these rights. Often, it is not until tribes submit certain of their rights to review by other sovereigns and make these rights products of negotiations with other sovereigns that tribes are able to legitimately exercise these rights. In the course of these negotiations, many such tribal rights tend to be regarded by interested non-Indian sovereigns as merely rights-claims. The recognition—or in many cases, the re-recognition—of these rights as rights is an artifact of a bargaining process. As can be seen in the Choctaw case described above, the process is a process that is sometimes humiliating for tribes, and it is a process that too often warps and perverts the rights that tribes claim inhere in federal law, case law, and treaties.

7. Conclusion

This book has explored one of the most important and inspiring eras in the history of the Choctaw Nation, the era of tribal nation building that began in the late twentieth century. I have addressed questions about how, specifically, this era was forged, how it unfolded, and the ways by which it has realigned and reconfigured relationships in and beyond the Choctaw Nation. As was seen, tribal rebuilding began rather modestly with the actions of a few poor, urban-migrant Choctaws. Less than two decades later, it had burgeoned into a large-scale social and political project that was being led by an experienced and talented politician, Hollis Roberts, and was affecting the lives of hundreds of thousands of individuals, both Choctaws and non-Choctaws. With this rebuilding, the Choctaws completed a cycle of rupture and rebirth that broadly structured the history of our tribe during the twentieth century and has defined Choctaw history, as was seen in chapter 2, since the late 1500s. With the most recent rebuilding, our tribal government has taken steps to break the cycle of rupture and rebirth by insulating the tribe against the most pernicious effects of a future federal effort to again dismantle Choctaw corporate structures and to again disrespect tribal sovereignty. By building tribal businesses that today fund more than 80 percent of Choctaw tribal programs and services, our tribal government has eliminated our tribe's dependence on the funds it receives in partial fulfillment of federal treaty obligations to Indian tribes. In so doing, Choctaw tribal leaders have lessened the threat that a federal discontinuation of these funds would pose to Choctaw tribal survival.

This modest but important realignment of the relationship between our tribe and the federal government is but one of the ways the nation building of the late twentieth century has been reconfiguring relationships. Another, equally important reconfiguration, a reconfiguration that lies at the core of the nation-building project, has been the reconfiguration of Choctaw identity and belonging. In order to reconstitute the tribe and help legitimize its status as a nation, tribal leaders reinstated the relations of citizenship that had defined Choctaw belonging during the nineteenth century, relations that formally tie Choctaws to one another and to a tribal government. In the late twentieth and early twenty-first centuries, these relations of citizenship have reinscribed ideas of Choctaw nationhood, fueled Choctaw nationalism, redefined the ways Choctaws negotiate their relations with one another, and fostered the development of a politics of inclusion and exclusion based on whether one is or is not a tribal citizen.

In the context of the era of Choctaw nation building that produced this critical reconfiguration, the relationship between rank-and-file Choctaws and the tribal government has undergone important shifts. The Choctaw nationalism that precipitated tribal rebuilding was forged as part of a resistance movement led by Choctaw youth activists in the late 1960s, a movement that sought and achieved the repeal of a federal law that set a date for the termination of our tribe's trust relationship with the U.S. government. Especially in the 1960s but also through the greater part of the 1970s, the goal of tribal survival and empowerment was almost entirely a grassroots Choctaw initiative. It is worth noting that, in the course of forging a Choctaw nationalism, youth leaders and other activists promoted an inclusive definition of Choctawness. As was seen, the youth and other rank-and-file Choctaws made self-identification as Choctaw, not legal documentation of Choctaw belonging, a primary basis for determining who was and was not a Choctaw.

After the elimination of the threat of tribal termination and the restoration of our tribe's right to select our own leaders, it was Choctaws at the periphery of formal tribal political power, not those at the core, who led the effort to build new political institutions and expand old ones. Choctaws positioned outside the tribal bureaucracy defined goals that included adding legislative and judicial branches to the tribal government and reopening the tribal rolls that had been closed since the turn of the twentieth century. Chief Harry J. W. Belvin and others at the emerging center

resisted both of these efforts in favor of the status quo, which vested all
tribal-government powers in the executive and which recognized only
Dawes enrollees (who were a significant base of Chief Belvin's support)
as uncontested Choctaw citizens. As a result, Belvin was voted out of office. Grassroots Choctaws replaced him with a new chief, David Gardner,
whom they expected to carry out goals that they themselves had defined.
Eight years later in 1983, more than three thousand Choctaws formally
participated in deciding criteria for tribal citizenship, in determining
how many individuals would serve on the tribal council (and whether
representation would be based on population and/or on geography), and
in identifying the geographic boundaries that would define the reconstituted Choctaw tribal homeland.

In Hollis Roberts the reconstituted tribal citizenry found a strong executive who brought tremendous focus, clarity, and intensity to the mission
of Choctaw tribal rebuilding and empowerment, but did so at a cost—at
the cost of broad citizen participation in nation-building processes. Roberts dramatically expanded the tribal government, spearheaded an ambitious program of tribal economic development, and significantly increased
the amount and net worth of the tribe's assets. He took full advantage of
new opportunities for tribal empowerment created at the federal level—
including, for example, the opportunity to compact federal Indian monies—in order to create a wide array of tribal programs and services and
secure much greater Choctaw control over tribal affairs. In part to encourage Choctaws to enroll in the tribe, he limited participation in tribal
elections, attendance at some tribally sponsored events, and eligibility for
tribal programs and services to Choctaws who held tribal membership
cards, hardening the boundaries around the tribe and promoting a comparatively narrow definition of Choctawness. In addition, he emphasized
the role of Choctaw citizens as tribal subjects, not as co–decision makers.
Under Roberts's leadership, the new community centers built in all parts
of the Choctaw Nation became sites almost entirely for social events, not
for structured citizen participation in determining the course of nation
building. Under Roberts's leadership, a primary way Choctaws practiced
their citizenship was by participating in tribal elections.

A tribal election that occurred near the end of Roberts's remarkable
political career brought to the fore a set of citizen assessments and critiques of how his administration had been constructing its relations with
the citizenry and defining the nature of the citizenry's horizontal ties

with one another. By pointing to the need for more opportunities for citizen participation in tribal governance, the challenger in the race for chief, Doug Dry, suggested that the tribal government was exercising too much control over nation building relative to the citizenry. He also claimed that one way that the tribal government was managing its relations with citizens was by calibrating tribal citizenship, treating some categories of citizens, namely under-a-quarters and Choctaw Nation residents, as more deserving of tribal citizenship than others. During the electoral season, some Choctaws negotiated their relationships with one another and with the tribal government by claiming that the relations of citizenship should be relations of equivalence and equality, or by suggesting that tribal-government relations with citizens should be relations of impartiality. Others supported a calibration of tribal citizenship, but only if the existing arrangement was revised or rearranged. A radical faction of the quarter-or-more group, for example, claimed that quarter-or-mores, not under-a-quarters, should receive preferential treatment from the tribal government and should in other ways be accorded a privileged status vis-à-vis other Choctaws. In contrast, some members of the Oklahoma City–based absentee group, OK Choctaw Tribal Alliance, supported the eradication of hierarchies of citizenship based on blood quantum but a continuation of those based on residence—despite the fact that, as absentees, they would remain disadvantaged by this arrangement. Still others negotiated their relations with one another and with the tribal government by treating the ways the Roberts administration was managing its relations with citizens and crafting Choctaw citizenship as a small price to pay for the building by this administration of a strong, effective, and efficient new tribal political order. These and other perspectives of rank-and-file Choctaws emerged from and through the mobilization of the citizenry into different political groups during the electoral season, a mobilization and contingent reconfiguration of Choctaw relationships that together constitute a key way Choctaws have been negotiating their tribal citizenship in the immediate aftermath of the tribe's reconstitution.

Particularly when placed in the context of the history of how the tribe was rebuilt, these citizen assessments of how the Roberts administration was constructing and managing the ties of Choctaw tribal citizenship are revealing of a tension that may be a general feature of nation building. In the Choctaw case and probably other cases, the origins of this tension

can be traced to the act—which for the Choctaws took place at the beginning of the era of tribal rebuilding—in which grassroots leaders and activists delegated a duty to what Weber terms a staff. This duty was that
of implementing objectives that had been developed at the grassroots
level, and the staff that was charged with carrying out this duty for the
emerging citizenry was the then tiny Choctaw tribal bureaucracy. From
the moment that this delegation took place, the tribal staff experienced
the pull of an imperative that derived from its identity as a bureaucracy—
the bureaucratic imperative of expanding the powers and scope of control
of its bureaucracy. Thus began a struggle between grassroots Choctaws
and the emerging center for creative control over the course of planned
social change. As was seen, Choctaws positioned outside the tribal bureaucracy managed to retain creative control over tribal rebuilding during the late Belvin administration, as well as during the Gardner administration, which together spanned the greater part of the 1970s. But by the
early Roberts administration in the early 1980s, the tribal bureaucracy
had accrued so much power by building new structures that Choctaws
outside the core of formal tribal political power were no longer able to determine or even substantially shape tribal policy and the trajectory of the
new political order. The actions and rhetoric of the citizenry during the
1995 electoral season, described in these pages, thus provide a view of a
grassroots population that had lost control of the design of the new order,
particularly of the design that was structuring not only the formal vertical ties between the tribal government and the citizenry but also the
horizontal ties between citizens as individuals. During the 1995 electoral season, rank-and-file Choctaws from diverse socioeconomic, racial,
and rural/urban backgrounds struggled to make sense of the design that
the center had created and evaluate that design in terms of broader ideas
about who and what they, as a tribe, wanted to be during the twenty-first
century. As Dombrowski (2001: 110) points out, the tribal disputes and
disagreements that non-natives often interpret as evidence of a hopelessly
factionalized Native American society are often, among other things, expressions of a community in search of itself.

Grassroots Choctaws did not reach a consensus on the question of how
best to redesign the ties of tribal citizenship or even on the question of
what, if anything, was problematic about the way the center had designed
these ties. In fact, the electoral season ended with Choctaws assuming
vastly different political positions on these matters. Even so, the loudest

and probably the most poignant note was struck by the call for Choctaws at both the center and the periphery to reorient and restructure tribal ties in terms of the values of equality, impartiality, mutual tolerance, respect, and celebrations of difference and diversity. Although this call, made by a number of Choctaws, probably had little impact on Roberts, it seems to have deeply affected his running mate, Greg Pyle, who later became chief when Roberts was imprisoned two years after he won the election. From the day Pyle took office, he has worked to combat prejudice and discrimination within the tribe, treat quarter-or-mores and under-a-quarters equally, and promote tribal policies that accord absentees and Choctaw Nation residents equal rights to tribal resources. If the citizenry were to approve a referendum that would extend tribal citizenship to Choctaws who can demonstrate proof of Choctaw belonging but who cannot meet current tribal membership requirements, progress would be made toward developing a more inclusive definition of Choctawness, a definition of Choctawness that is in greater accord with that with which the nation-building era began. In so doing, healing could begin of the wounds that derive from the division of the Choctaw population into the categories of the enrolled and the unenrolled, or—as Choctaw Nation communities often refer to the latter—the "Choctaws but not enrolled."

The event of the building of a tribal economic-development project in a Choctaw Nation community—another event that was explored in some depth in these pages—was striking in the extent to which Choctaws ignored or repressed the decades-long struggle for control of the new order between Choctaws within and Choctaws outside of the new tribal bureaucracy. As was seen, the ongoing tension between these two categories of Choctaws dissolved as both rank-and-file Choctaws and the tribal government joined forces to promote local public acceptance of a new tribal economic development project in a predominantly non-Choctaw community and encourage the non-Choctaws in this community to view Choctaw tribal rebuilding as a set of sociopolitical and economic transformations from which non-Choctaws, too, would benefit, despite their noncitizenship in the new order. The building of the tribal travel plaza fostered positive, cooperative relations between grassroots Choctaws and the tribal government partly because local, rank-and-file Choctaws tended to view the project as a response by their leaders—as it was in part, as was seen—to the demands of the tribal citizenry for jobs. For many of the new jobholders and their kin, the desired outcome of these jobs was achieved: a dramatic improvement in the quality of life and level of economic security of dozens of Choctaw families. Tribal bureaucrats, in turn, were pleased with the economic success of the project, which depended in part on the willingness and ability of local Choctaws to provide the tribal government with high-quality job performances.

The project's new jobs provided openings for the layering of a different type of formal relationship—the relationship of employer and employee—onto existing government-citizen relationships, expanding and diversifying the linkages between Choctaws and the tribal government and increasing the extent to which new jobholders and their kin tied their personal fortunes to the fortunes of the tribe. While new jobholders and their kin experienced a wedding of their personal economic empowerment to tribal empowerment, both they and other Choctaws in this community found tribal empowerment to be a key to their local social and political empowerment. As was seen, after the dismantling of most Choctaw formal political structures and the allotment of most of the tribe's land at the turn of the twentieth century, whites in this community developed and implemented a racial project that attempted to legitimize white control and ownership of the town—and of Choctaw land—by trying to erase the Choctaw identity of the Choctaws in this town. Through the creation of a variety of structures, structures that I describe in some detail, local whites shoehorned local Choctaws into the racial categories of "white" and "black." Choctaws resisted by continuing to assert their identity as Choctaw, but the violence and brutality of the racial project limited the contexts in which such assertions were made, relegating the sites of this resistance to the private, domestic sphere and to semiprivate, Choctaw-only contexts. In the wake of the reconstitution of the tribe and the local erection of a project that is a potent symbol of the continued existence of the Choctaw tribe, Choctaws in this town found in the tribal government a powerful partner in their ongoing efforts to reinstitute their Choctaw identity in public (interethnic) contexts and reclaim the Choctaw identity of their town.

By building new institutions in the communities within its boundaries, formal leaders have been extending the reach of the tribal nation into these communities and thus carrying out a central imperative of nation building. Such acts of the vertical entrenchment of the tribal government have been complicated by the fact that the Choctaw Nation is a nation within a nation. The reconstituted tribal citizenry is interspersed

among the citizenry of another nation, the United States, and Choctaws
are, of course, citizens of both of these nations. In conditions defined in
part by the coexistence of two citizenries within a single political space,
tribal leaders have pursued strategies of accommodating those who live
within tribal boundaries but who are not Choctaw. Instead of ignoring or
contributing to an escalation of the anger and resentment that many non-
Choctaws feel about tribal rebuilding, tribal leaders expend time, money,
and other resources trying to assuage the fears of the non-Choctaws who
live within tribal boundaries, foster relationships of trust and coopera-
tion with them, and persuade them that tribal rebuilding is in large part
about improving the quality of life for both Choctaws and non-Choctaws
who live in the Choctaw Nation.

The fact that the Choctaw Nation is part of the United States and that
Choctaws are U.S. citizens has made some aspects of tribal rebuilding—
including and perhaps especially the vertical entrenchment of the tribal
government—both easier and more difficult. In conditions characterized
not only by plural citizenship but also by overlapping citizenship, tribal
leaders are able to argue that the rearrangements that are a part of tribal
rebuilding are rearrangements that permit a marginalized, rural population of Americans—both Choctaw and non-Choctaw—to share in the
American Dream. At the same time, tribal leaders and all Choctaws remain vulnerable to the charges of local non-Choctaws, as well as the
larger, non-Indian American population, that tribal citizenship is dis-
pensable and superfluous because tribal citizens are U.S. citizens. The
vulnerability of the Choctaws to becoming a target of such attacks has
been exacerbated by the long-standing efforts of many non-Indians to racialize Indian identity. Many non-Indians, for example, continue to believe the myth that racial distinctiveness is a criterion for maintaining
Indian tribal identity. This myth persists despite the historical fact that
U.S.-tribal relations were founded on the principle of the political, not racial, distinctiveness of American Indian tribes. It also persists despite the
fact that, contrary to popular belief, the U.S. Bureau of Indian Affairs does
not require a minimum blood quantum for recognizing an individual as a
member of a federally recognized tribe. Instead, the U.S. government rec-
ognizes as Indian all those whom federally recognized tribes recognize as
their tribal citizens. As a matter of federal law and tribal law, tribes have
exclusive jurisdiction over determining their citizenries.

During the water conflict of 2001 the Choctaws faced another, powerful myth that disrespects Choctaw sovereignty—a myth-claim embraced

by the state of Oklahoma that maintained that, upon statehood, the Choctaws and other tribes in Oklahoma lost their water rights. In stepping
forward to claim and defend their rights to the water within their tribal
homeland, the Choctaws encountered a state government that not only
had assumed absolute sovereignty over this water since statehood but
also had taken action, beginning in the early 1970s, to remove this water
from the Choctaw Nation. In challenging the state on this critical matter, the Choctaw tribal government also took on the federal government.
As was seen, beginning in the 1970s the U.S. Army Corps of Engineers
provided the state of Oklahoma with the necessary financial and technical support to carry out this plan, despite the fact that the federal government is explicitly charged with safeguarding tribal resources from
being appropriated, without tribal consent, by American states and non-
Indian individuals.

Even though Choctaw rights in this case appeared legally well established, the Choctaws were required either to engage in diplomatic relations with the state or to confront the state in the U.S. courts for recognition of these rights as rights. This fact, which in large part defined the
battle itself, was revealing of the fact that such negotiations are a critical aspect of tribal sovereignty. Looking closer at the conflict, it was seen
that other critical aspects of tribal sovereignty include the bundle-of-
inherent rights construction of tribal sovereignty, an aspect of tribal sovereignty of which tribes tend to make extensive use, together with the
set of constraints and opportunities that are produced by the reality that
tribes operate within a political space inhabited by multiple and overlapping sovereigns. With respect to this structured set of relations within
which tribes negotiate their sovereignty, the Choctaws have, since the
tribal rebuilding of the late twentieth century, achieved some success in
their efforts to upset the arrangement that governed these relations during the greater part of the twentieth century. For example, during the
mid-1970s both the state of Oklahoma and the U.S. Army Corps of Engineers took actions with respect to water that suggest either that they
hardly took note of the Choctaw tribal presence and existing Choctaw
water rights or that they decided they need not take this tribe and this
tribe's rights seriously because the tribe was so weak politically. Two decades later, at sites at the interface between the Choctaw tribal government and the Oklahoma state and U.S. federal governments, the Choctaws reclaimed their former identity as a sovereign that could not easily

be dismissed. Partly by and through the water conflict (but also as part of a much broader Choctaw tribal effort), Choctaw tribal leaders reinstantiated the tribe as a formidable political presence in the south-central part of the United States.

With respect to their relations with other sovereigns in this political landscape, the Choctaws have considerably strengthened their hand. Their political power and potential far exceeds that which existed at the outset of the era of tribal nation building and appears to be moving closer to that which was envisioned by the Choctaw youth activists in the late 1960s. Some of the conditions that contribute to the tribe's power and potential, such as a marked increase in tribal revenues and an expansion in the number and type of specialists (such as lawyers) who are employed by the tribe, are not surprising. Others are somewhat less expected. Two examples help illustrate this. First, since the late tribal nation-building period, Choctaw tribal leaders have been engaging in diplomatic relations with the state and federal governments as representatives of a tribal citizenry that, since the late 1990s, has exceeded 100,000, all of whom are U.S. citizens and most of whom are Oklahoma state citizens. The fact that tribal leaders formally represent a constituency to whom the Oklahoma state and U.S. federal governments are beholden means that there exists for state and federal leaders an additional political cost of alienating Choctaw tribal members: votes. This condition, which gives tribes a small but important advantage in their diplomatic relations with non-Indian sovereigns, did not exist until recently, as Choctaws were not U.S. citizens, as was seen in chapter 2, until the early twentieth century.

Another unexpected condition, an emerging condition, has also been strengthening the tribe's hand in its present-day diplomatic relations with other sovereigns: the capacity of the non-Choctaw population of southeastern Oklahoma to enhance and increase Choctaw political power. Choctaw tribal leaders, as was seen, have enjoyed a modicum of success in their efforts to frame the new tribal political order as an order to which non-Choctaws living in the Choctaw Nation would do well to give their loyalties when a choice is required, as it was during the water conflict, between supporting the Choctaw tribal government and supporting the Oklahoma state government. In tapping the political potential of this population to augment Choctaw tribal authority and influence, tribal leaders have made political use of the fact that the Oklahoma state government has privileged the economic development of its metropoles over its rural

areas, whereas the commitment of the Choctaw government to developing southeastern Oklahoma is unquestioned by non-Choctaws, as well as
by Choctaws, living in the Choctaw Nation and is an objective that en-
joys strong public support in southeastern Oklahoma. At the same time,
tribal leaders have also made political use of the fact the Oklahoma state
government has experienced serious problems of corruption and misman-
agement not only in the past but also very recently, whereas the Choctaw
tribal government has created a wide range of social-welfare programs, generated a number of successful tribal businesses, and in other ways established a regional reputation as a highly efficient and effective organization.
Non-Choctaw support for increasing the political power of the Choctaw
tribal government, particularly vis-à-vis the Oklahoma state government,
is an additional and unexpected source of legitimacy and political influence for the Choctaw Nation, a source that has already strengthened the
tribe's hand at least once—in its relations with the Oklahoma state government during the water conflict—and may continue to do so in future
Choctaw diplomatic relations with non-Indian sovereigns.

The story of tribal rebuilding and empowerment told in this book is a
uniquely Choctaw story, a story that reflects the tribe's history, the unique
personalities of its grassroots and elected leaders, and the particular social
and political context of the Choctaws' southeastern Oklahoma homeland.
At the same time, the story of Choctaw tribal nation building is part of
a much larger story, a story of tribal nation building that has been radically transforming most of Indian country during the late twentieth and
early twenty-first centuries. Many of the elements of this broader story
exhibit striking similarities. Across Indian country, tribal governments
have undergone rapid expansion, tribal membership has been bureau-
cratized and used to harden the boundaries of tribes, tribal governments
have made tribal economic development one of their highest priorities,
and tribes have reconfigured their relationships with state governments
and with the federal government. These structural rearrangements, reconfigurations of social and political relationships, and canalized goals
have been substantively remaking Indian identity in this country. This
book has offered a view of the ways by which the Choctaws have participated in these localized processes, what these processes have produced in
and beyond the Choctaw Nation, and what this has meant for both Choctaws and non-Choctaws in Oklahoma.

Notes

1. Introduction

1. I use the terms *tribal nation, tribe,* and *Indian nation* interchangeably to refer to American Indian entities with whom the United States has what U.S. leaders term a "government-to-government relationship." It is common for American Indian leaders and their citizens, together with U.S. leaders, to refer to such political entities as "tribes" ("American Indian Tribe" is, in fact, a specific legal category). It is also common for the U.S. president, members of Congress, and others to refer to such politico-legal entities as "tribal nations," "Indian nations," or even "nations," as I learned during the many months that I spent working at the Bureau of Indian Affairs in Washington DC. In this book, I use these and other terms in accordance with their meanings and usages in the local, regional, and national ethnographic contexts that I am trying to describe, setting aside questions as to whether these politico-legal entities meet the definitions of "tribe," "nation," or "society" that appear in the literature of anthropology, sociology, and political science.

2. Tribal bureaucrats claimed that at no point was Roberts's portrait in the tribal capitol ever covered.

2. The Journey Has Been Long and Hard

1. There are two principal Choctaw creation stories. Both were recorded by non-Indians during the nineteenth century. The first is the one that opens this chapter, chronicling the journey of the Choctaw people to present-day Mississippi from "a distant country far to the west" following a pole (*fabussa*) (Swanton 1931: 11; see also Debo 1934). In some accounts, only Chahta leads the people; Chikasa, progenitor of the Chickasaw people, is absent. The second principal Choctaw creation story asserts that the Choctaws emerged from the mound of *Nanih Waiya* itself, a mound that is said to have been thrown up by "a superior being" to gen-

erate "the red people" (Swanton 1931: 201; Champagne 1992, 2001). The mound in both stories corresponds to an actual mound in present-day Mississippi (Halbert 1985d [1899], 1985e [1901b]).

2. Kidwell and Roberts point out that, in addition to Choctaw burial customs, the Choctaw practice of flattening the foreheads of their infants by placing weights on their faces as they lay in their cradleboards "drew the attention" of Europeans visiting the area (1980: 5).

3. Of course, some matrilineages that were termed *iksas* may not have crosscut Choctaw society at all, and undoubtedly some clans did not enjoy wide geographic representation in the nation. See Champagne (1992) for additional information.

4. According to White (1983), there was also significant settlement in "the uplands." Some Choctaws clearly preferred to live in the uplands, settling there even when "stream terraces" were available. White also argues that in the late 1700s or early 1800s, settlement shifted to what he calls the borderlands. Kidwell and Roberts point out that some eighteenth-century Choctaw villages spanned "areas as long as three miles long and a mile wide" (1980: 13).

5. Mooney points out that the politically autonomous entity that was called the *okla* "may have consisted of a single town, or a large town and its associated dependencies, or an association of towns which constituted a division" (1997: 8). *Okla* exercised a high degree of political autonomy at least until the period right before removal when their power and authority was subsumed by the larger political unit of the division or district (Mooney 1997; White 1983).

6. White (1983) notes that eighteenth-century chiefs maintained a monopoly of control over the gun, greatly affecting the extent to which they exercised control over certain categories of persons, particularly warriors. He also argues that the very "nature" of Choctaw redistribution changed during this time. Scarce European goods, as well as food, began being channeled to a "select group of kinsmen and followers" (p. 46).

7. It is often asserted that during the eighteenth century the war chief was not a permanent position. Rather, a man was appointed to the position when it was perceived that there was a need (e.g., Galloway 1995). Given that the Choctaws were at war for most of the eighteenth century, however, it is possible that the position was maintained almost without interruption.

8. Even Swanton (1931), who tends to exaggerate the importance of farming among the Choctaws of the eighteenth and early nineteenth centuries, includes evidence that suggests that some Choctaws hunted and gathered exclusively. Kidwell (1995), White (1983), and Hudson (2001) have brought to light the importance of hunting and hunters, particularly as compared to settled farmers, among the Choctaw during this period. It is also important to note that Choctaws who engaged in farming consumed a great deal of fish, game, nuts, and berries, which together may have made up as much as one-third of their diets (see also Mooney 1997).

9. There is some evidence that suggests that the authority of the chiefs over their people may have been quite strong. White, for example, cites an account

from 1716 that claims that the Indians had "a very exact subordination and great respect for their chiefs whom they obey spiritedly" (1983: 39).

10. Sometimes there were as many as one hundred on each team (Swanton 1931).

11. Kidwell and Roberts argue that the well-known rebellion of the mid-1740s was "sparked by a sexual assault upon the wife of Red Shoe, a chief already leaning toward the English" (1980: 11).

12. American trading houses were instruments of a government-sponsored arrangement called the "factory system" that was designed to run European traders out of business (Kidwell 1995; Plaisance 1954).

13. Carson explains, "Unlike the Creeks and Cherokees, where market intrusions gave rise to class divisions and bitter socioeconomic strife, among the Choctaws bonds of kinship and the long-standing political relationship between chiefs and commoners militated against the formation of new class lines. Instead, the old tensions between chiefs took on new guises" (1999: 71).

14. The Treaty of 1820, known also as the Treaty of Doak's Stand, contained provisions for the establishment of the Choctaw lighthorse (Baird 1972; Kidwell 1995). Champagne notes that the northeast district created a lighthorse of ten "to enforce the collection of debts and to execute the law regularly" (1992: 149).

15. For information about the relocation of Choctaws from Mississippi to Indian Territory in the late nineteenth and early twentieth centuries, see Kidwell 1995; Wade 1985 [1904]; and Howard and Levine 1990.

16. For the purposes of determining the distribution of coal and other royalties between the governments of both tribes, it was later determined that the Chickasaws, outnumbered four to one by the Choctaws, had a one-fourth interest in the Choctaw-Chickasaw Territory.

17. The six Choctaw towns were McAlester, Hartshorne, Haileyville, Krebs, Alderson, and Lehigh.

18. This bill failed in the tribe's House of Representatives (Debo 1934).

19. U.S. Senator Charles Curtis, who directed the Senate committee that drafted the act, was a Kaw/Osage Indian who later served as vice president of the United States under Herbert Hoover (Strickland 1980; Getches, Wilkinson, and Williams 1998; Brown 1931).

20. By tribe, the number of Cherokees "by blood" totaled 36,619; Chickasaws "by blood," 5,659; Muscogee Creeks "by blood," 11,952; and Seminoles "by blood," 2,141 for a total Five Tribes population of 75,519 (Debo 1940).

21. Allotments made to Choctaw citizens "by blood" ranged from 160 to 4,165 acres (Morrison 1987; Debo 1940).

22. Per the Supplemental Agreement of 1902, 433,950 acres of land rich in coal and asphalt deposits were reserved from allotment. In 1906–7, upon the order of the Department of the Interior, the Indian Service reserved from allotment an additional 1,373,324 acres of land that was rich in timber. The total number of acres that was corporately held and that remained in trust was thus 1,807,274. By

the terms of the Atoka Agreement, these lands were held jointly for the Choctaw and Chickasaw tribes, and per the treaty of 1837, Choctaws were to receive three-fourths of the profits from their sale, and the Chickasaws, one-fourth.

23. Baird states that the 1908 legislation alone released from federal supervision as much as 63 percent of allottees of the Five "Civilized" Tribes (1990).

24. Choctaw and Chickasaw freedmen were prohibited from sharing in the proceeds from the division of the tribal estate.

25. The nine that have been identified as Choctaw are William A. Durant, Benjamin Harrison, Victor Locke Jr., Thomas Hunter, James Dyer, Edgar A. Moore, Hiram Impson, Virgil Tinker, and Harry J. W. Belvin (Wright 1951).

26. In November of 1907, members of the Five Tribes captured three of the seven positions in the U.S. Senate and House of Representatives that were reserved for Oklahomans. Robert L. Owen, a Cherokee, became one of the first two Oklahoma state senators, and Charles Carter, a Chickasaw, became one of the first five Oklahomans in the House of Representatives. Owen and Carter began what became an almost continuous Indian presence representing the state of Oklahoma in the nation's capitol during the first half-century of Oklahoma's existence (Wright 1951; Baird 1990). Owen served continuously as U.S. senator from 1907 to 1925, and in the November elections of 1919 he received the highest vote of any candidate for office in Oklahoma (*Albion Advocate*, December 6, 1918). Charles Carter, too, was a popular politician, winning reelection several times (Debo 1940). In 1915 W. W. Hastings, a Cherokee, joined Carter in the House and was several times reelected. During Oklahoma's first fifty years, N. B. Johnson, a Cherokee, was elected justice of the Oklahoma Supreme Court, as was Earl Welch, a Chickasaw. From 1928 to 1932, Jessie R. Moore, who was a Chickasaw, was elected to and served as clerk of the Oklahoma Supreme Court. In 1950 Chickasaw William H. Murray was elected governor of Oklahoma (Wright 1951; Baird 1990).

27. Enrollment in church-run schools fluctuated. For example, between 1921 and 1925, the student body of Goodland Indian School jumped from eighty to two hundred due solely to the fund-raising efforts of School Superintendent Bailey Spring, who was himself a Choctaw (*Kiamichi Valley News*, September 11, 1925).

28. Children who inhabited the category of unrestricted or who were of less than one-quarter Indian "blood" often were required to pay tuition (Lomawaima 1994).

29. In 1955 when Wheelock Academy was closed, approximately fifty-five girls were transferred to Jones Academy. From 1955 to the present, then, Jones Academy has been a coeducational boarding dormitory (Samuels 1997).

30. For example, W. A. Durant, described by Hertzberg as "a Choctaw who had long been a leading member of the Oklahoma legislature," was elected the first vice president of SAI at the SAI conference in 1915 (1971: 137).

31. Oklahoma tribes were exempted from the IRA. The OIWA, passed two years after the IRA, provided Oklahoma tribes with most of the same opportunities provided to other tribes by the IRA. The OIWA, Cohen explains, "offered

[Oklahoma] tribes a new statutory structure for their existing tribal governments" (1982: 775 n. 54). It authorized tribal organization "in a manner similar to the IRA" and extended to tribes that organized under its provisions "any other rights or privileges secured to an organized Indian tribe under the [IRA]" (p. 775). Among the "distinctive provisions" of the OIWA, particularly as compared to the IRA, was the provision authorizing "cooperative associations for business purposes" (p. 775 n. 54).

As many as seventy-seven tribes outside of Oklahoma rejected the IRA, for reasons that included a lack of enthusiasm among tribal members for the democratic, representative form of government promoted by the IRA (and the OIA) and the threat that an IRA "reorganization" posed to the continued autonomy of local Indian groups (e.g., bands), groups that might have been assimilated into larger groups (e.g., tribes) had they "reorganized" under the IRA. Though neither of these two reasons likely explains the rejection of the OIWA by the Five Tribes, it is likely that integrationist sentiment does not fully explain the responses of the Five Tribes to the OIWA.

Wright characterizes Oklahoma tribes in general as "conservative in taking advantage of [the OIWA]." Between 1937 and 1942, she explains, only eighteen comparatively small groups in Oklahoma reorganized under OIWA (Wright 1951: 25; see also Philp 1977; Strickland 1980). By the mid-twentieth century, however, fifty-one tribal and credit associations had been chartered (Strickland 1980; Wright 1951).

32. Serving as both chiefs and presidential appointees prior to Belvin were Green McCurtain, 1906–10; Victor M. Locke Jr., 1911–18; William F. Semple, 1918–22; William H. Harrison, 1922–29; Ben Dwight, 1930–37; and William A. Durant, 1937–48 (Wright 1951).

33. In 1958 alone, which was the year prior to the Choctaw legislation, as many as forty-eight rancherias in California were terminated (Nies 1996).

3. "Because We Were Proud to Be Choctaw"

1. Kidwell and Roberts (1980) note that the federal relocation program affected hundreds of Choctaws, who were relocated not only to Oklahoma City but also to Tulsa, Dallas, Los Angeles, and other cities.

2. See Howe (2001) for numerous references in her novel *Shell Shaker* to Choctaws who left the Choctaw Nation in the twentieth century, seeking work.

3. The vote was 1,668 to 1,329 (McKee and Schlenker 1980).

4. One of the youth movement's early members told me that, due to Mr. Brown's advanced age, he had misremembered this story. The consultant claimed that Mr. Brown had been visited by a clergyman, a man whose name this consultant could not recall, who had presented Mr. Brown with a letter alluding to the imminent termination of the Choctaw tribe. The consultant said that he could remember nothing else about the letter and was unaware of its current whereabouts.

5. The BIA did restrict eligible candidates for chief to males, and it restricted eligible candidates and voters to those who had been enrolled by the Dawes Com-

mission more than forty years earlier as Choctaws by blood ("Regulations Governing the Election of Candidates for Appointment as Principal Chief, Choctaw Nation, Oklahoma," January 30, 1948, Section X—Choctaw Elections, OHS Research Division).

6. All four of these tribes were "restored" in 1979 (Waldman 1985: 194).

7. There existed (and continue to exist) Indian churches in Oklahoma City, as well as in Choctaw Nation, through which Brown, other grassroots Choctaw leaders, and candidates for tribal office have organized and campaigned. An example of one of these church organizations in an urban area is All Tribes Faith of Oklahoma City, which appears to have been a major arena for the political mobilization of Choctaws in the early 1980s (Oklahoma City Council of Choctaws 1981).

8. During the period in which their mobilization of Choctaws was at its height, two new highways in southeastern Oklahoma were completed, facilitating the youth's efforts to penetrate even the most remote areas of the Choctaw Nation. The year 1969 saw the opening of Talimena Drive, a major road that runs east-west through the eastern part of Choctaw Nation, which had long been plagued by poor roads (Spears 1991: 134). The following year the southern section of the Indian Nation Turnpike, which runs north-south through Choctaw Nation, was completed (interview with Mary Kay Audd, Oklahoma Turnpike Authority, October 24, 1995).

9. The bureau's concern focused primarily on those urban Indians whose ties with their tribes were weak and who, partly because of this, supported tribal termination (George Roth, personal communication).

10. Another important event in modern Choctaw history also occurred in 1970: in *Choctaw Nation v. State of Oklahoma* (397 U.S. 620), the U.S. Supreme Court ruled that the Cherokee, Chickasaw, and Choctaw nations owned the beds of the Arkansas River from Fort Smith, Arkansas, to Muscogee, Oklahoma.

11. It should be noted that, as individuals (rather than as collectivities), Indians participated in state and local relief programs decades before the 1960s. For example, in 1930 some Oklahoma Indians qualified for and received help in the amount of two to five dollars per week from the Oklahoma State Drought Relief Committee (Quinten 1967: 41). Moreover, Quinten writes that, as a population, Oklahoma Indians received "extensive benefits from a large national relief program" in 1931. They received surplus wheat and flour from the Federal Farm Board, he explains, and used clothing from the U.S. Army. That year Indians also received seed loans from the Department of Agriculture. In April of 1931, the Red Cross, which had been feeding approximately 3,000 Indian families, was instructed "to give no more aid to Indians" (pp. 41–42). Beginning in the 1960s, some non-BIA federal agencies earmarked funds for Indians and offered Indian programs as part of the larger set of programs they administered (Roth 1997).

12. The 1971 board of commissioners consisted of Reverend Joe Reed, Jimmy Going, Bentley Beams, J. A. Campbell Jr., and Walter B. Hall. Interviews revealed that C. Wilson James and Charlie Jones also made important contributions to the

building of the Choctaw Housing Authority. It is worth noting that at the time of my research, according to Mr. Batton the Choctaw Nation Housing Authority was still operating as a de jure state agency. Beginning in 1983, the tribal council assumed the position of the authority's board of commissioners.

13. Note that Roth (1997) addresses only the 1960s.

14. The booths are also a way that Oklahoma City Choctaws raise public awareness about their urban organization. Money is raised by selling "Indian tacos." One member of the organization told me that the idea of selling Indian tacos can be traced back to a supper that took place at an Indian church at First and Villa in Oklahoma City during the 1970s. A Navajo woman who had married an Oklahoma Indian brought a dish called "Navajo tacos." Church members found the tacos so delicious that, when the idea for selling food at the fair came up, it was proposed that the Navajo tacos be served under the name "Indian tacos."

15. For more information about the charges and Roberts's trial, see the *Choctaw Vindicator*, July 1997; *Denison Herald* (Denison TX), June 11, 1995; *Daily Ardmoreite* (Ardmore OK), June 12, 1995; *Muskogee Daily Phoenix* (Muscogee OK), June 15, 1995; and *Oklahoman* (Oklahoma City OK), June 11, 1995; September 5, 1995; October 4, 1995; October 11, 1995; January 18, 1996; July 9, 1996; July 15, 1996; September 30, 1996. I attended Roberts's trial.

16. Among the Choctaws involved in the suit were Randy Jacobs and Jimmy Sam. At the same time, Oklahoma City Choctaw Charles Brown filed a separate suit challenging the election of Hollis Roberts as principal chief. Brown argued that Roberts's election to the position of chief following the death of David Gardner did not meet with the terms and criteria set forth in the Constitution of 1860. Note that the Choctaw tribal council also was referred to during this period as the general council (*Bishinik*, August 1978).

17. The twelve districts were carved out of ten and a half counties of southeastern Oklahoma: the counties of LeFlore, Latimer, Atoka, Pushmataha, Choctaw, McCurtain, Haskell, Pittsburg, Bryan, Coal, and half of Hughes. The district that includes Coal and Hughes counties together elects one council member, and LeFlore and McCurtain counties each elect two council members.

18. The ratification of the new constitution and the election of tribal officers may have taken place at the same time.

19. This includes 40,000 acres that were being held in trust by the U.S. government for individual Choctaws (Faiman-Silva 1997).

20. For example, one significant land acquisition was a 230–acre pine plantation on ranch property in Tuskahoma (Faiman-Silva 1997). Most of the new land was acquired after 1991; that year, Choctaw tribal trust land totaled only 11,453 acres (Roberts 1991).

21. Prior to the founding of *Bishinik* in 1978, there existed a tribal newspaper/newsletter called *Hello Choctaw*. This publication was started in 1975 (Littlefield 2001; Kidwell and Roberts 1980).

22. Choctaw casinos are located in Durant, Pocola, Idabel, Broken Bow, Grant, McAlester, and Stringtown.

4. "Tomorrow Is the Day YOU Are Chief"

1. *Denison Herald* (Denison TX), June 11, 1995; *Daily Ardmoreite* (Ardmore OK), June 12, 1995; *Muskogee Daily Phoenix* (Muscogee OK), June 15, 1995; *Oklahoman* (Oklahoma City OK), June 11, 1995; July 5, 1995; October 4, 1995; October 11, 1995; January 18, 1996; July 7, 1996; July 15, 1996; September 31, 1996.

2. *Choctaw Vindicator*, July 1997.

3. Note that absentees are not absentees as the term is defined in the non-Indian American political system. Instead of requiring that a voter demonstrate an intention to reestablish residence in the political district in which his or her vote will be cast, the Choctaw tribal government (and, following the tribal government, the Choctaw citizenry) defines absentees simply as Choctaws who are nonresidents of the Choctaw Nation.

4. Only once during my research did my friendships with members of opposing groups pose problems. In the late spring and early summer of 1997, two years after the 1995 election, supporters and opponents of Chief Roberts were brought together for the chief's trial on sexual assault and sexual abuse charges in the U.S. federal courthouse in Muscogee. When I spoke to Chief Roberts in a courthouse hallway or sat with his supporters in the courtroom, the chief's opponents expressed some resentment toward me. In the mornings or during breaks when I chatted with Roberts's opponents on the courthouse steps or shared a cup of coffee with one of them in the courthouse snack room, I was accused by "the chief's people" of "siding with the enemy." During the tribal elections of 1995, however, there were no events of which I was aware that brought members of the most politically salient groups into the same physical space, and members of these different groups appeared to have little contact with one another. My interactions with them, then, occurred largely in separate social—but not political—spheres. Some of these social spheres were new; others predated the electoral season or represented combinations of older social configurations. On many days, I did not venture into the social spheres of any one of these organized groups, seeking instead to listen to voters unaffiliated with these groups when they aired their views about the election in their homes or in public places, such as in restaurants, sale barns, or tribal community centers.

5. Northeastern Oklahoma, which is the contemporary Cherokee homeland, is the most Republican part of the state (Hardt 1998a). Regarding the state as a whole, Hardt (1998b) points out that the average presidential vote in Oklahoma from 1960 to 1996 was 55.3 percent Republican while the national average is 48.1 percent. It should be pointed out that since statehood the Oklahoma legislature has been majority Democrat every year except 1920 and 1921 (Hardt 1998b).

6. Wilkins (2002a) points out that in Indian country there exists a variety of types of legislative bodies, including tribal councils, general councils, business committees, legislatures, and boards of directors.

7. O'Brien (1989) notes that the Isleta Pueblo executive even selects the legislative branch. Wilkins points out that there is "great variety" in the executive in

Indian country, with some tribes having presidents and others having governors, chairpersons, spokespersons, chiefs, or principal chiefs (2002a: 141).

8. Wilkins (2002a) points out that not all tribes elect the supreme executive by popular vote. In some cases, members of the tribal council elect the executive.

9. According to the Cherokee Nation of Oklahoma, on November 18, 2005, the enrolled membership of their tribe totaled 258,229. Currently, the Navajo Nation is the largest tribe in the United States. In December of 2005, Navajo Nation communications director George Hardeen told me that Navajo tribal members totaled "around 300,000."

10. The question of why, during the same time period, the Choctaws and the Cherokees pursued diametrically opposed informal hiring policies is an interesting question, a question first posed to me by anthropologist Orin Starn and one that deserves attention.

11. She is referring to the annual Choctaw Nation Labor Day Festivals. For more information on the origins, content and significance of this regular event, see chapter 3.

12. In 1980 national newspapers reported that a black/white "race riot" had erupted in Idabel after a fifteen-year-old black youth, William Henry Johnson, was shot to death in the parking lot of a white nightclub. Helping fuel the black response to the murder was a rumor that Johnson was hung on a fence by his assailants.

13. Of course, there are some tribes in which relations between the tribal police and the tribal citizenry must be described as poor. Much popular attention has been given to the difficulties of such relations among the Oglala Sioux Tribe of the Pine Ridge Reservation (see, for example, Crow Dog and Erdoes 1990). In 1975 a study found that tribal members on Rocky Boy's reservation viewed their tribal police as "agents of raw power rather than enforcers of the law" and that the police were used to silence members' criticism of tribal government (Lopach et al. 1998: 149).

14. As mentioned in chapter 3, Brown ran for Choctaw chief in 1978. Hollis Roberts defeated him by only 339 votes. Roberts received 1,668 votes to Brown's 1,329 (McKee and Schlenker 1980).

15. This contrasted with what I observed in the Choctaw Nation, where by all accounts conversations in Choctaw are infrequent.

16. Sandra Faiman-Silva (1997) states that the number of Choctaw language speakers is about 730. Kidwell (2004) places the number at close to 5,000.

17. Several full-bloods who lived in the Choctaw Nation told me that they took offense at the suggestion that they themselves were somehow more "authentic" than other Choctaws. For example, they expressed frustration and resentment at those who assumed that a Choctaw full-blood was knowledgeable about Choctaw culture and history simply because he or she was a full-blood. (Those who made such assumptions included Indians as well as non-Indians, and Choctaw citizens as well as noncitizens.) For reasons that are unclear, Alliance members who were migrants tended not to take offense at these associations and constructions. They seemed simply to accept them as the basis of their authority.

18. About a dozen Choctaws claimed that Roberts sabotaged the businesses and business dealings of his opponents, prevented his opponents from receiving certain benefits and entitlements by virtue of their status as Choctaws, and even arranged for his opponents to suffer physical harm. See LeAnne Howe's novel *Shell Shaker* for additional insight into the perspectives of those who make such claims.

19. See, for example, "Oneida Nation Evictions Highlight Rift within Tribe," indianz.com, accessed October 29, 2003. Indianz.com is a product of Noble Savage Media, LLC, and Ho-Chunk, Inc. Based on the Winnebago Reservation in Nebraska with an office in Washington DC. See also www.oneidasfordemocracy.com, accessed November 7, 2003. Site owned by Oneidas for Democracy, Oneida NY.

20. It is not uncommon in Indian country for Indians living within their tribal homeland to argue either that tribal benefits and services should be restricted to those who live within the tribal homeland or that tribal homeland residents should get priority for these benefits and services over those who live off the reservation or tribal homeland.

21. Absentees remain populations of minor political significance in some tribes. Northern Arapahoes, for example, refer to their absentees as "one-day Indians" who come to pick up their per capita check each month, then leave, participating not at all in the institutionalized sharing network that is part of the bedrock of tribal politics (Fowler 1982).

22. In the late 1990s, 32 percent of quarter-or-mores, or about 8 percent of the total Choctaw citizenry, were full-bloods (Faiman-Silva 1997).

23. Dry ran many advertisements and letters to the editor in local newspapers. He also tried unsuccessfully to obtain a copy not simply of the list of all registered Choctaw voters, which he received at the time he filed his candidacy for the position of chief, but also of their contact information. When the tribal government declined his request, he appealed to the Bureau of Indian Affairs, which replied that it could not and would not intervene in the internal affairs of a sovereign Indian tribe.

24. Sturm (2002) found that "fuller-blood" Oklahoma Cherokees also "invoked a racial ideology" that asserted that Cherokee identity is a question of blood quantum. In so doing, these individuals, like the members of the radical faction of Choctaw quarter-or-mores, informally challenged the rules for membership in their tribe, rules that do not require a minimum blood quantum for tribal membership.

25. Sturm points out that 10 percent of the membership of the Cherokee Nation live in these communities. She also points out that 21 percent of the Cherokee citizenry are more than one-quarter "blood quantum" (2002).

26. Roberts's long tenure in office was also an important factor that helped determine the breadth and scope of the power and influence he exerted, as Circe Sturm reminded me in a personal communication.

27. Roberts was able to bank on the absentee vote for reasons that include the fact that it is not uncommon for an absentee to have little contact with Choctaws living in the Choctaw Nation and the fact that candidates for elected office in our tribe are not given a list of the names and contact information of voters.

5. "The First of Many Good Things to Come"

1. In an effort to further protect the confidentiality of my consultants, I have also disguised some of the details of this town. In addition, some of the stories presented in this chapter were collected from individuals who lived in communities near, not in, Kalichito.

2. These evaluations of the relative performance of the Kalichito travel plaza were made in 1998.

3. The number of new jobs created by the Kalichito travel plaza was typical of the number of new jobs that Choctaw tribal travel plazas tend to generate. For example, travel plazas were opened in the towns of Stringtown and Poteau in the early 2000s. Together with a nearby tribal travel mart, the first such tribal business was said to have created between forty-five and fifty new jobs; the second, thirty jobs (*Bishinik*, February 2003). Two years earlier, in 2001, the opening of a new tribal travel plaza created thirty new jobs (*Bishinik*, July 2001).

4. "Economic Research Service, United States Department of Agriculture: County-Level Unemployment and Median Household Income from Oklahoma," www.ers.usda.gov/Data/Unemployment/RDList2.asp?ST=OK, accessed March 11, 2003. Site owned by the U.S. Department of Agriculture Economic Research Service, Washington DC.

5. See quickfacts.census.gov/qfd/states/40/40023.html, accessed March 21, 2003. Site owned by the U.S. Department of Commerce, U.S. Census Bureau, Suitland MD.

6. "Population of Counties—Oklahoma: 1920–1990," www.ancestry.lycos.com/home/free/censtats/okcens.html, accessed May 21, 2003. Site co-owned by Ancestry.com and Lycos.com, Orem UT.

7. The Choctaws use a modified form of the Indian preference clause of the BIA and IHS. The BIA gives employment preference to American Indian and Alaska Native candidates who meet the U.S. Secretary of the Interior's definition of Indian, which, with a few exceptions, is limited to enrolled members of federally recognized tribes.

8. In the early 2000s, the Choctaw tribal leadership began "softening" the tribe's Choctaw preference policy. More non-Choctaws are now being hired as the tribal leadership (1) has recognized, from past experience, that large numbers of "political appointees" in the Choctaw tribal government carries with it certain disadvantages and problems; (2) has placed a higher value on the job qualifications and job skills of candidates for tribal employment; and (3) believes that the American Indian tribes that are the most successful economically are those with weak to nonexistent Indian preference policies (that is, as Chief Pyle explained, "that they hire the best people for the job").

9. It is worth pointing out that, throughout Indian country, thousands of non-Indians and unenrolled Indians directly benefit from tribally sponsored job creation, as well as from BIA and IHS jobs. In the Choctaw Nation, this is because most Indian families contain at least one non-Indian or unenrolled Indian, a de-

mographic reality that is not uncommon on tribal homelands throughout the United States. For example, Fowler notes that on the Wind River reservation "almost every Arapahoe household included some members who were not enrolled in the tribe" (1982: 228).

10. Some even questioned whether the jobs had even been created.

11. See www.ers.usda.gov/Data/Unemployment/RDList2.asp?ST=OK, accessed March 11, 2003. Site owned by the U.S. Department of Agriculture Economics Research Service, Washington DC.

12. Recipients make payments on these homes, typically for twenty-five years, of not more than 15 percent of their adjusted gross income, according to Choctaw Nation Housing Authority employees. At the end of the period of payments, the home and the land on which it sits is deeded by the tribe to the family. In the mid-1990s, the average Indian home cost the Choctaw Nation $63,000 to build, according to tribal officials, and the minimum monthly payment was $40. All home sites are required to be at least one acre in size. A three-bedroom Indian home offered 1,250 square feet of living space; a four-bedroom, 1,450.

13. Bobbi did not think her chances of getting enrolled were good. She explained that she thought her ancestors were in Arizona when the Dawes Roll was being compiled.

14. On average, this constituted sixty-six food items per family member. In the mid-1990s, more than six thousand Choctaw families were taking advantage of this program, according to tribal officials.

15. It is worth noting that Kalichito's Choctaws also take advantage of day care (for their [enrolled] children aged six weeks to twelve years), educational scholarships, clothing allowances, job training and placement programs, and burial assistance.

16. Evidence suggests that poverty has been a defining feature of experience in Kalichito since at least the early poststatehood period. Kalichitoans whom I interviewed, however, distinguished between what they described as "the poverty of the past" and "the poverty of today." They claimed that in the past, community members made sure that everyone always had at least something to eat and a place to sleep.

17. As an enrolled Choctaw, I promote a revision of our tribal citizenship laws (laws, it should be remembered, that are entirely within Choctaw jurisdiction) that would permit Choctaws who cannot meet the narrow requirement of lineal descent from an ancestor listed on the Dawes Rolls to become members of our tribe on the basis of other criteria.

18. There are other Choctaws with phenotypes that are stereotypically African American who are not enrolled. The history and experience of members of this category among the Oklahoma Cherokees have been explored by Circe Sturm (2002).

19. In the WPA Indian-Pioneer History Collection's interview with Paul Garnett Roebuck, Mr. Roebuck does not state the date of the birth of this black baby,

who was his father. He does, however, note later in the interview that his father was twenty-six years old when black slaves were freed. The black baby, then, must have been born in 1839. The interview with Roebuck also reveals that the small Choctaw plantation or farm was owned by a Choctaw man who was three-fourths Choctaw and his wife, who was one-half Choctaw. Information on early Choctaw burials was found at www.rootsweb.com/~okgenweb/cemetery/cem-online/roebuck.html (site funded and supported by Ancestry.com, Inc., Orem UT).

20. One of the Choctaw citizens was a citizen by marriage, not by blood (see chapter 2 for a discussion of the meanings of these two statuses).

21. In the early 1920s, there were three successive crop failures, leading many in and around Tali to default on loans (Imon 1977). This may have affected the size of the population, as well as the spirit of Kalichito as perceived by the reporter in 1926.

22. Black experience was shaped by these features but not entirely defined by them. For example, I knew of no Choctaw without apparent black ancestry who had been forced into the category of "black" on the basis of his or her status as a farm laborer.

23. Quinten (1967) points out that before the Great Depression (1929–33), cotton picking in the Choctaw Nation often paid as little as seventy-five cents a day.

24. At least some members of the town probably received supplies from the nearby town of Tali. They may also (or alternatively) have ordered supplies from such mail-order companies as Sears, Roebuck and Company in Chicago and O. L. Chase Mercantile Company in Kansas City, Missouri, as did one Choctaw in a nearby town (I. A. Billy Collection, box 2, folder 2, OHS Research Division).

25. Choctaws probably helped define these categories: the law that implemented the above article was House Bill 365, and the first speaker of the Oklahoma House of Representatives was a Choctaw (see chapter 3).

26. The racialization of Indian identity suits white interests and black political goals. Racializing tribal identities serves the goal of legitimizing white control of Indian land because it denies tribal sovereignty. Many blacks conspire with whites in this strategy not only because they have adopted white definitions of Indian identity but also because racializing Indians serves the political goal of many blacks of allying with other racialized American groups.

27. Between 1832 and 1955 when it was in operation, Wheelock Academy for Girls was able to educate only a fraction of the total population of Indian girls from southeastern Oklahoma. There were only about one hundred girls attending the school in the 1950s, for example (Herndon n.d.). In 1932 principal teacher Mrs. Agnes Orcutt stated that, although Wheelock had "no specified academic entrance requirements," "before pupils are accepted certain other requirements are considered; such as, distance from the nearest public school, degree of Indian blood, parents living or dead and available funds to continue education elsewhere" (p. 36).

28. The hospital was built in Talihina for the treatment of tuberculosis. In 1919 a state hospital for non-Indians was established, the Oklahoma State Tuberculosis Hospital, and it was located near the Indian hospital (Peck 1963).

29. At no point in Choctaw history has there ever been a minimum blood quantum requirement for tribal membership (see chapters 2 and 3). Yet Choctaws working at the Talihina Hospital before the 1980s told me that, as regards health care, the practice locally was to limit care to those with a blood quantum requirement of at least one-quarter. This was part of a larger IHS initiative of limiting Indian health care to those whom Choctaws term "quarter-or-mores," an initiative that was successfully challenged by the Cherokee Nation in 1977 (see Sturm 2002) and other tribes in later years (see, for example, Finger 1991).

30. The Eastern Band of Cherokee Indians provides health services not only to all enrolled members but also to all first-generation descendants of enrolled members.

31. The presence (or absence) of full-bloods in these Choctaw-only contexts does not appear to affect Choctaw racial self-identifications as white. In other words, such assertions are only rarely made as a way for under-a-quarters to draw boundaries between themselves and full-bloods. This is not to say that under-a-quarters do not draw and maintain boundaries between themselves and full-bloods (or full-bloods with respect to under-a-quarters); they do, but they do so in other ways.

6. "We Don't Believe That Claim Is Valid"

1. The NTWA ended up offering only $174 million for the water.

2. Wilkins and Lomawaima (2001) argue that tribal reserved rights will be vulnerable to state and federal attack until, or unless, tribally reserved rights attain a status comparable to the Tenth Amendment. About tribal reserved rights to water in particular, McCool (1987), too, sounds a note of caution, pointing out that *Winters* is case law and has never been blessed by explicit congressional approval.

3. Prior to the construction of the reservoir, there existed a small lake nearby that was and still is called Clayton Lake.

4. See www.state.ok.us~owrb/vars/wfl.html, accessed March 1, 2002. Site owned by the Oklahoma Water Resources Board, an agency of the State of Oklahoma, Oklahoma City OK.

5. Irrigation is also the primary use to which water is put in most of the American West, a region in which irrigated agriculture accounts for as much as 85 percent of water use (Burton 1991).

6. See www.state.ok.us/~owrb/vars/wfl.html (details in note 4 above), accessed March 1, 2002.

7. Curiously, since its creation the OWRB has comparatively little power on paper. State law vests local government, not state government, with responsibility for planning and responding to droughts and other water-related problems. Virtually the only way that the state, through the OWRB, actually "manages" the state's water resources, affecting water use and distribution in practical terms, is through a permit program that the OWRB runs. This program issues licenses to companies to drill water wells for nondomestic uses. Other than this licensing program, the state's direct, on-the-ground involvement in the actual water prob-

lems of specific communities is limited to times when the governor declares a state of emergency, prompting the Oklahoma Civil Defense Agency to organize and coordinate responses among such agencies as the owrb and the state health department. By organizing the building of Sardis Lake, the owrb was overstepping its authority; but because some cities and towns have severe water problems and few resources, some may have welcomed this transgression.

8. The reference to the Arkansas river bed refers to a dispute resolved in *Choctaw Nation v. Oklahoma*, 397 U.S. 620, 631 (1970), mentioned earlier in this chapter. This suit was one of a set of suits that involved the question of whether the Choctaw, Chickasaw, and Cherokee nations, on the one hand, or Oklahoma, on the other, owned the navigable portions of the Arkansas River in eastern Oklahoma. The U.S. Supreme Court ruled that the title to the beds had passed to the Indian nations "since the beds were not specifically excluded in the [treaty-based] grants to the Indians and since questions regarding treaties with Indian nations are to be resolved in favor of the Indians" (90 S CT 1328–1346). Since the 1970 decision, issues related to Choctaw (as well as Chickasaw and Cherokee) rights to the Arkansas River bed and the inadequacy of federal stewardship of this tribal property have been and continue to litigated. In fact, all matters related to the dispute had still not been resolved as late as the late 1990s. "That is not the fault of the tribes," Chickasaw Governor Bill Anoatubby has explained. "We have contended for a century that the riverbed and adjacent lands belonged to us. Had the federal government as our trustee protected our property from the beginning this would not be happening" (*Oklahoman*, December 12, 1997: 1).

9. In investigating the local water politics that emerged out of the dispute that is the subject of this chapter, I identified and interacted with valley residents whom I eventually sorted into an informal typology of fourteen different (but overlapping) categories of persons, an informal typology that I developed to better understand the views of residents toward the dispute and the proposed water lease, as well as to test my own conclusions. Members of the following seven categories tended to tell me that they opposed the lease of the water, but, like members of other categories, they also tended to tell me that they supported tribal control of the water. They were (1) those who had built moderately priced to expensive homes on the Sardis Lake waterfront; (2) those who had built their livelihoods around the lake; (3) those who did not have running water in their homes but who happened to live near Sardis Lake; (4) retirees who had migrated to the area from Oklahoma City and elsewhere; (5) farmers and ranchers who had declared an interest in continuing to farm or ranch; (6) those who owned grocery stores or dime stores in the valley; and (7) those who grew marijuana commercially. Like members of these categories, other categories of valley residents tended to tell me that they supported tribal control of the water, but unlike members in the above seven categories, they tended to tell me that they supported a large-scale lease of the water. They were (1) elected tribal representatives; (2) the unemployed and underemployed; (3) parents and grandparents of young children; (4) workers who sought

better or different jobs; (5) farmers and ranchers who told me that they wanted to get out of farming and/or ranching; (6) local business leaders (nonretail); and (7) return migrants (nonretirees).

10. Some cities, such as Tucson, have been especially aggressive in pursuing tribal water (McGuire 1987).

11. See http://oklahoma.sierraclub.org/chapter/watersale/myths_and_truths. htm. Site owned by the Sierra Club, Oklahoma Chapter, Oklahoma City OK.

12. It should be pointed out that the settlement addressed tribal water rights not only to the Choctaw Nation's Kiamichi Basin, Little River Basin, and Upper Mountain Fork River Basin but also in the Chickasaw Nation (to the immediate west of the Choctaw Nation) (*Oklahoman*, April 29, 2001: 10A). A total of more than twenty counties in Oklahoma and the area along the Kiamichi River Basin were affected (*Indian Country Today*, October 25, 2000), an area from which more than two trillion gallons per year of untapped water crosses Oklahoma state and Choctaw and Chickasaw tribal boundaries (*Daily Ardmoreite*, December 10, 2001). Among other things, this expansion of the scope of this water-rights conflict increased the interest of the Chickasaws in the conflict, an interest that heretofore had been limited by the one-fourth interest in Choctaw land and mineral rights that the Chickasaws had acquired in the nineteenth century.

Works Cited

Primary Sources
Archival Sources

Bureau of Indian Affairs, Washington DC.
        Files of the Office of Tribal Government Services. Five Civilized
        Tribes Files.
Oklahoma Department of Libraries, Oklahoma City Archives and Records
        Division.
        MS-8, vol. 1. Agency Files of Inter-tribal Council of Five Civilized
        Tribes. Minutes of the Inter-tribal Council of the Five Civilized
        Tribes. Minutes of Meetings, 1951–55.
Oklahoma Historical Society, Research Division, Oklahoma City.
        Choctaw National Records (Microfilm Roll CTN 53)
        Final Rolls of the Five Civilized Tribes
        I. A. Billy Collection
        Peter J. Hudson Collection
        Section X—Choctaw Elections (1923–83 and undated–1995)
        WPA Indian-Pioneer History Collection

Other Documents

Choctaw Nation. May 18, 2002. "The Commemorative Trail of Tears Walk."
        Brochure printed and mailed to all Choctaw enrollees.
———. January 9, 2002. "Press Release." Announcement of the halting of water-
        lease negotiations between the Choctaw Nation, the Chickasaw
        Nation, and Oklahoma, on the one hand, and the North Texas Water
        Authority, on the other.
———. July 8, 1995. "Election Results."
———. 1983. "Constitution of the Choctaw Nation of Oklahoma."

———. 1973. "[1860] Constitution of the Choctaw Nation." In A. R. Durant, *Constitution and Laws of the Choctaw Nation together with the Treaties of 1837, 1855, 1865 and 1866*, 5–29. Wilmington DE: Scholarly Resources. First published in 1894 by John F. Worley, Dallas TX.

Dry, Douglas. May 22, 1995. Doug Dry to enrolled Choctaws.

———. 1995. "Vote for Responsible Government, for Accountability, for Doug Dry Choctaw Chief." Campaign literature of Douglas Dry.

Pyle, Gregory E. April 3, 2003. Chief Gregory E. Pyle to enrolled Choctaws.

———. August 13, 2002. Chief Gregory E. Pyle to enrolled Choctaws.

———. February 5, 2002. Chief Gregory E. Pyle to enrolled Choctaws.

Roberts, Hollis E. June 7, 1995. Hollis E. Roberts to Choctaw voters.

———. June 1995. Hollis E. Roberts to enrolled Choctaws.

———. 1995. "Chief Hollis Roberts: A Proven Leader." Campaign literature of Hollis Roberts.

———. 1991. "Hollis E. Roberts: Choctaw Chief." Flyer printed for 1991 Choctaw Chief campaign.

Robinson, Wilma, Laura Ketchum, Lisa Easterwood, et al. 1995. Robinson, Ketchum, Easterwood et al. to enrolled Choctaws. Letter mailed to all enrolled Choctaws and signed by 131 female tribal employees urging Choctaws not to believe the charges of sexual assault and sexual abuse being made against Roberts.

Secondary Sources

Adair, James. 1968. *The History of the American Indians, Particularly Those Nations Adjoining to the Mississippi, East and West Florida, Georgia, South and North Carolina, and Virginia*. New York: Johnson Reprint. Reprint of the 1775 edition.

Agnew, Brad. 1980. *Fort Gibson, Terminal on the Trail of Tears*. Norman: University of Oklahoma Press.

Aldrich, Gene. 1973. *Black Heritage of Oklahoma*. Edmund OK: Thompson.

Alfred, Gerald R. 1995. *Heeding the Voices of Our Ancestors: Kahnawake Mohawk Politics and the Rise of Native Nationalism*. Oxford: Oxford University Press.

Amin, Samir. 1997. "The Nation: An Enlightened or Fog-Shrouded Concept?" *Research in African Literatures* 28 (4): 8–18.

Anderson, Benedict. 1983. *Imagined Communities: Reflections on the Origin and Spread of Nationalism*. London: Verso.

Baird, W. David. 1990. "Are the Five Tribes of Oklahoma 'Real' Indians?" *Western Historical Quarterly*, February 1990: 5–18.

———. 1972. *Peter Pitchlynn: Chief of the Choctaws*. Norman: University of Oklahoma Press.

Barsh, Russel Lawrence. 1994. "Indian Policy at the Beginning of the 1990s:

The Trivialization of Struggle." In *American Indian Policy: Self-Governance and Economic Development*, ed. Lyman H. Legters and Fremont J. Lyden, 55–69. Westport CT: Greenwood.

Barth, Frederik. 1967. "On the Study of Social Change." *American Anthropologist* 69: 661–69.

Bee, Robert L. 1982. *The Politics of American Indian Policy*. Cambridge MA: Schenkman.

Berthrong, Donald J. 1992. "Struggle for Power: The Impact of Southern Cheyenne and Arapaho 'Schoolboys' on Tribal Politics." *American Indian Quarterly* 16 (1): 1–24.

Biolsi, Thomas. 2005. "Imagined Geographies: Sovereignty, Indigenous Space, and American Indian Struggle." *American Ethnologist* 32 (2): 247–59.

———. 2004. "Race Technologies." In *A Companion to the Anthropology of Politics*, ed. David Nugent and Joan Vincent, 400–417. Malden MA: Blackwell.

———. 2001. *"Deadliest Enemies": Law and the Making of Race Relations on and off Rosebud Reservation*. Berkeley: University of California Press.

———. 1992. *Organizing the Lakota: The Political Economy of the New Deal on the Pine Ridge and Rosebud Reservations*. Tucson: University of Arizona Press.

Blanchard, Kendall. 1981. *Mississippi Choctaws at Play: The Serious Side of Leisure*. Urbana: University of Illinois Press.

Bordewich, Fergus. 1996. *Killing the White Man's Indian: Reinventing Native Americans at the End of the Twentieth Century*. New York: Doubleday.

Brown, Loren N. 1944. "The Appraisal of the Lands of the Choctaws and Chickasaws by the Dawes Commission." *Chronicles of Oklahoma* 22: 177–91.

———. 1931. "The Dawes Commission." *Chronicles of Oklahoma* 9: 71–105.

Burton, Lloyd. 1991. *American Indian Water Rights and the Limits of the Law*. Lawrence: University of Kansas Press.

Bushnell, David I., Jr. 1985. "The Choctaw of Bayou Lacomb, St. Tammany Parish, Louisiana." In Peterson, *Choctaw Source Book*, 1–37. First published in 1909 as "The Choctaw of Bayou Lacomb, St. Tammany Parish, Louisiana," Smithsonian Institution, Bureau of American Ethnology, Bulletin 48.

Carney, Sharon J. 1998. "The Oklahoma Bureaucracy." In Markwood, *Oklahoma Government and Politics*, 111–26.

Carson, James. 2001. "The Choctaw Trail of Tears." In Haag and Willis, *Choctaw Language and Culture*, 288–91.

———. 1999. *Searching for the Bright Path: The Mississippi Choctaws from Prehistory to Removal*. Lincoln: University of Nebraska Press.

Carter, Kent. 1999. *The Dawes Commission and the Allotment of the Five Civilized Tribes, 1893–1914*. Orem UT: Ancestry.com.

Cash, Joseph H., and Herbert T. Hoover. 1971. *To Be an Indian: An Oral History*. New York: Holt, Rinehart and Winston.

Cattelino, Jessica. 2004. "High Stakes: Seminole Sovereignty in the Casino Era." PhD diss., Department of Anthropology, New York University.

Center for Demographic Policy. 1990. "The Demographics of American Indians: One Percent of the People: Fifty Percent of the Diversity." Washington DC: Center for Demographic Policy.

Champagne, Duane. 2001. "The Choctaw People Resist the Treaty at Dancing Rabbit Creek." In Haag and Willis, *Choctaw Language and Cultures*, 280–87.

———. 1992. *Social Order and Political Change: Constitutional Governments among the Cherokee, the Choctaw, the Chickasaw, and the Creek*. Stanford CA: Stanford University Press.

Chatterjee, Partha. 1993. *The Nation and Its Fragments: Colonial and Postcolonial Histories*. Princeton NJ: Princeton University Press.

Choctaw Nation Housing Authority. 1971. "Report, Housing Authority of the Choctaw Nation of Oklahoma under Harry J. W. Belvin." Report in possession of the relatives of the late Randy Bailey.

Claiborne, John Francis Hamtramck. 1880. *Mississippi, as a Province, Territory, and State: With Biographical Notices of Eminent Citizens*. Jackson MS: Power and Barksdale.

Clarkson, Gavin. 2002. "Reclaiming Jurisprudential Sovereignty: A Tribal Judiciary Analysis." *University of Kansas Law Review* 50: 473–521.

Codere, Helen. 1966. *Fighting with Property: A Study of Kwakiutl Potlatching and Warfare, 1792–1930*. Seattle: University of Washington Press.

Cohen, Felix. 1982. *Handbook of Federal Indian Law*, 1982 ed. With an introduction by the Board of Authors and Editors. Charlottesville VA: Michie / Bobb-Merrill.

Cornell, Stephen. 1988. *Return of the Native: American Indian Political Resurgence*. Oxford: Oxford University Press.

Cornell, Stephen, and Joseph P. Kalt. 1992. "Reloading the Dice: Improving the Chances for Economic Development on American Indian Reservations." Cambridge MA: Harvard Project on American Indian Economic Development.

———. 1991. "Where's the Glue? Institutional Bases of American Indian Economic Development." Cambridge MA: Harvard Project on American Indian Economic Development.

Cotterill, R. S. 1954. *The Southern Tribes: The Story of the Civilized Tribes before Removal*. Norman: University of Oklahoma Press.

Crow Dog, Mary, and Richard Erdoes. 1990. *Lakota Woman*. New York: Grove Weidenfeld.

Cushman, H. B. 1999. *History of the Choctaw, Chickasaw, and Natchez Indians*, ed. Angie Debo. Norman: University of Oklahoma Press. First edition published in 1899.

Debo, Angie. 1951. "The Five Civilized Tribes of Oklahoma: Report on Social and Economic Conditions." Philadelphia: Indian Rights Association.

———. 1940. *And Still the Waters Run: The Betrayal of the Five Civilized Tribes*. Princeton NJ: Princeton University Press.

———. 1934. *The Rise and Fall of the Choctaw Republic*. Norman: University of Oklahoma Press.

Deloria, Vine, Jr., and Clifford M. Lytle. 1984. *The Nations Within: The Past and Future of American Indian Sovereignty*. New York: Pantheon.

———. 1983. *American Indians, American Justice*. Austin: University of Texas Press.

DeRosier, Arthur H. 1970. *The Removal of the Choctaw Indians*. Knoxville: University of Tennessee Press.

———. 1959. "Pioneers with Conflicting Ideals: Christianity and Slavery in the Choctaw Nation." *Journal of Mississippi History* 21: 174–89.

Dombrowski, Kirk. 2001. *Against Culture: Development, Politics, and Religion in Indian Alaska*. Lincoln: University of Nebraska Press.

Doran, Michael F. 1976. "Antebellum Cattle Herding in the Indian Territory." *Geographical Review* 66: 48–58.

———. 1975. "Population Statistics of the Nineteenth Century Indian Territory." *Chronicles of Oklahoma* 53: 492–515.

Dudley, C. E. n.d. "Days Gone By." Photocopied manuscript in possession of Oklahoma Historical Society Library, Oklahoma City.

Durant, Randle. 1979. *Foot Steps of the Durant Choctaws*. Phoenix AZ: Randle Durant.

Dye, David H. 2001. "Southeastern Iconography." In Haag and Willis, *Choctaw Language and Culture*, 261–66.

Edmunds, R. David. 1984. *Tecumseh and the Quest for Indian Leadership*. Boston: Little, Brown.

Edwards, John. 1932. "The Choctaw Indians in the Middle of the Nineteenth Century." *Chronicles of Oklahoma* 10: 392–425.

Eggan, Fred. 1966. "The Choctaw and Their Neighbors in the Southeast: Acculturation Under Pressure." In *The American Indian: Perspectives for the Study of Social Change* by Fred Eggan. Chicago: Aldine.

———. 1937. "Historical Changes in the Choctaw Kinship System." *American Anthropologist* 39: 34–52.

Faiman-Silva, Sandra. 1997. *Choctaws at the Crossroads: The Political Economy of Class and Culture in the Oklahoma Timber Region*. Lincoln: University of Nebraska Press.

———. 1993. "Decolonizing the Choctaw Nation: Choctaw Political Economy in the Twentieth Century." *American Indian Culture and Research Journal* 17 (2): 43–73.

———. 1984. "Choctaw at the Crossroads: Native Americans and Multina-
    tionals in the Oklahoma Timber Region." PhD diss., Department of
    Anthropology, Boston University.

Fast, Phyllis. 2002. *Northern Athabaskan Survival: Women, Community, and
    the Future.* Lincoln: University of Nebraska Press.

Ferguson, Bob. 1962. "A Choctaw Chronology." Photocopied manuscript in
    possession of Nashville Chapter, Tennessee Archaeological Society,
    Nashville.

Finger, John R. 1991. *Cherokee Americans: The Eastern Band of Cherokees in
    the Twentieth Century.* Lincoln: University of Nebraska Press.

Fite, Gilbert C. 1949. "Development of the Cotton Industry by the Five Civ-
    ilized Tribes in Indian Territory." *Journal of Southern History* 15:
    342–53.

Fixico, Donald L. 2000. *The Urban Indian Experience in America.* Albuquer-
    que: University of New Mexico Press.

———. 1986. *Termination and Relocation: Federal Indian Policy, 1945–1960.*
    Albuquerque: University of New Mexico Press.

Foreman, Carolyn Thomas. 1956. "The Light-horse in the Indian Territory."
    Chronicles of Oklahoma 34: 17–44.

Foreman, Grant. 1989a. *The Five Civilized Tribes: Cherokee, Chickasaw, Choc-
    taw, Creek, Seminole.* Norman: University of Oklahoma Press.

———. 1989b. *Indian Removal: The Emigration of the Five Civilized Tribes of
    Indians.* Norman: University of Oklahoma Press.

———. 1928. "Early Post Offices of Oklahoma." *Chronicles of Oklahoma* 6 (1):
    4–25.

Foster, Morris W. 2001. "Choctaw Social Organization." In Haag and Willis,
    Choctaw Language and Culture, 250–54.

———. 1991. *Being Comanche: A Social History of an American Indian Com-
    munity.* Tucson: University of Arizona Press.

Foucault, Michel. 1979. "On Governmentality." *Ideology and Consciousness* 6:
    5–26.

———. 1977. *Discipline and Punish: The Birth of the Prison.* New York: Pan-
    theon. First published in 1975.

Fowler, Loretta. 1982. *Arapahoe Politics, 1851–1978: Symbols in Crises of
    Authority.* Lincoln: University of Nebraska Press.

Fried, Morton H. 1975. *The Notion of Tribe.* Menlo Park CA: Cummings.

Galloway, Patricia. 1995. *Choctaw Genesis, 1500–1700.* Lincoln: University of
    Nebraska Press.

Galloway, Patricia, and Clara Sue Kidwell. 2004. "Choctaw in the East." In
    Handbook of North American Indians, vol. 14: Southeast, ed. William
    C. Sturtevant, 499–519. Washington DC: Smithsonian Institution.

Garroutte, Eva Marie. 2003. *Real Indians: Identity and the Survival of Native
    America.* Berkeley: University of California Press.

Gatch, Loren C. 1998a. "The Political Economy of Oklahoma: An Overview." In
    Markwood, *Oklahoma Government and Politics*, 39–64.

———. 1998b. "Taxing and Spending in Oklahoma." In Markwood, *Oklahoma
    Government and Politics*, 193–210.

Gellner, Ernest. 1983. *Nations and Nationalism: New Perspectives on the Past.*
    Ithaca NY: Cornell University Press.

Getches, D., D. Rosenfelt, and C. Wilkinson. 1979. *Federal Indian Law.* St. Paul
    MN: West.

Getches, D., C. Wilkinson, and R. Williams. 1998. *Federal Indian Law,* 4th ed.
    St. Paul MN: West.

Gibson, Arrell Morgan. 1971. *The Chickasaws.* Norman: University of Okla-
    homa Press.

———. 1965. "The Choctaws: The Story of a Resourceful Tribe in its Oklahoma
    Home--*Yakni Achnukma,* the Good Land." *Sooner Magazine* (July):
    24–29.

Gluckman, Max. 1958. *Analysis of a Social Situation in Modern Zululand.*
    Rhodes-Livingston Papers, no. 28. Manchester: Manchester Univer-
    sity Press.

Godelier, Maurice. 1978. "Infrastructures, Societies, and History." *Current
    Anthropology* 19: 763–71.

Graebner, Laura Baum. 1978. "Agriculture among the Five Civilized Tribes,
    1840–1906." *Red River Valley Historical Review* 3: 45–60.

Graebner, Norman Arthur. 1945a. "The Public Land Policy of the Five Civilized
    Tribes." *Chronicles of Oklahoma* 23: 107–18.

———. 1945b. "Pioneer Indian Agriculture in Oklahoma." *Chronicles of Okla-
    homa* 23: 232–48.

Haag, Marcia. 2001. "A History of the Choctaw Language." In Haag and Willis,
    Choctaw Language and Culture, 276–79.

Haag, Marcia, and Henry Willis, eds. 2001. *Choctaw Language and Culture:
    Chata Anumpa.* Norman: University of Oklahoma Press.

Halbert, Henry S. 1985a. "The Choctaw Creation Legend." In Peterson, *Choc-
    taw Source Book,* 267–70. First published in 1901 as "The Choctaw
    Creation Legend," *Mississippi Historical Society Publications* 4:
    267–70.

———. 1985b. "District Divisions of the Choctaw Nation." In Peterson, *Choc-
    taw Source Book,* 375–85. First published in 1901 as "District Divi-
    sions of the Choctaw Nation," *Alabama Historical Society Publica-
    tions* 1: 375–85.

———. 1985c. "Funeral Customs of the Mississippi Choctaws." In Peterson,
    Choctaw Source Book, 353–66. First published in 1900 as "Funeral
    Customs of the Mississippi Choctaws," *Mississippi Historical Society
    Publications* 3: 353–66.

———. 1985d. "Nanih Waiya, the Sacred Mound of the Choctaws." In Peterson, *Choctaw Source Book*, 223–34. First published in 1899 as "Nanih Waiya, the Sacred Mound of the Choctaws." *Mississippi Historical Society Publications* 2: 223–34.

———. 1985e. "Okla Hannali; or, the Six Towns District of the Choctaws." In Peterson, *Choctaw Source Book*, 146–49. First published in 1893 as "Okla Hannali; or, The Six Towns District of the Choctaws," *American Antiquarian and Oriental Journal* 15: 146–49.

Hardt, Jan C. 1998a. "Interest Groups and Political Participation in Oklahoma." In Markwood, *Oklahoma Government and Politics*, 173–92.

———. 1998b. "Political Parties and Elections in Oklahoma." In Markwood, *Oklahoma Government and Politics*, 151–72.

Harmon, Alexandra. 1998. *Ethnic Relations and Indian Identities around Puget Sound*. Berkeley: University of California Press.

Harris, LaDonna. 2000. *LaDonna Harris: A Comanche Life*, ed. H. Henrietta Stockel. Lincoln: University of Nebraska Press.

Helton, Taiawagi. 1998. "Indian Reserved Water Rights in the Dual-System State of Oklahoma." *Tulsa Law Journal* 33: 979–1002.

Herndon, Toru Wilson. n.d. "Wheelock--Through the Years." Photocopied manuscript in possession of Muscogee Area Office, Bureau of Indian Affairs.

Hertzberg, Hazel W. 1971. *The Search for an American Indian Identity: Modern Pan-Indian Movements*. Syracuse NY: Syracuse University Press.

Herzfeld, Michael. 1992. *The Social Production of Indifference: Exploring the Symbolic Roots of Western Bureaucracy*. Oxford: Berg Publishers.

———. 1991. *A Place in History: Social and Monumental Time in a Cretan Town*. Princeton: Princeton University Press.

———. 1985. *The Poetics of Manhood: Contest and Identity in a Cretan Mountain Village*. Princeton NJ: Princeton University Press.

Hightower, Michael J. 1984. "Cattle, Coal, and Indian Land." *Chronicles of Oklahoma* 62: 4–25.

Hittman, Michael. 1973. "Factionalism in a Northern Paiute Tribe as a Consequence of the Indian Reorganization Act." In *Native American Politics: Power Relationships in the Western Great Basin Today*, ed. Ruth M. Houghton, 17–32. Reno: Bureau of Governmental Research, University of Nevada.

Hobsbawm, Eric, and Terence Ranger, eds. 1983. *The Invention of Tradition*. Cambridge: Cambridge University Press.

Holmes, Jack D. L. 1985. "The Choctaws in 1795." In Peterson, *Choctaw Source Book*, 33–46. First published in 1968 as "The Choctaws in 1795," *Alabama Historical Quarterly* 30 (1): 33–49.

Howard, James H., and Victoria Lindsay Levine. 1990. *Choctaw Music and Dance*. Norman: University of Oklahoma Press.

Howe, LeAnne. 2001. *Shell Shaker*. San Francisco: Aunt Lute.

Hudson, Charles. 2001. "Daily Life in the Southeastern Forest." In Haag and Willis, *Choctaw Language and Culture,* 255–57.

Humphreys, George G. 1998. "Public Policy." In Markwood, *Oklahoma Government and Politics,* 227–48.

Hunke, Naomi Ruth. 1986. *B. Frank Belvin: God's Warhorse.* Birmingham AL: New Hope.

Imon, Frances. 1977. *Smoke Signals from Indian Territory,* vol. 2. Wolfe City TX: Henington.

———. 1976. *Smoke Signals from Indian Territory.* Wolfe City TX: Henington.

Innes, Pamela. 2001. "The Life Cycle from Birth to Death." In Haag and Willis, *Choctaw Language and Culture,* 245–49.

Jackson, Deborah Davis. 2002. *Our Elders Lived It: American Indian Identity in the City.* DeKalb: Northern Illinois University Press.

Jackson, Jason. 2003. *Yuchi Ceremonial Life: Performance, Meaning and Tradition in a Contemporary American Indian Community.* Lincoln: University of Nebraska Press.

Jenks, Stephen S. 1998. "Municipal and County Government in Oklahoma." In Markwood, *Oklahoma Government and Politics,* 221–26.

Johnson, Richard R., and Alvin O. Turner. 1998. *Oklahoma at the Crossroads.* Dubuque IA: Kendall Hunt.

Josephy, Alvin M., Jr. 1971. *Red Power: The American Indians' Fight for Freedom.* New York: McGraw-Hill.

Kahrl, William L., ed. 1978. *The California Water Atlas.* Sacramento: State of California General Services, Publication Section.

Kersey, Harry A. 1996. *An Assumption of Sovereignty: Social and Political Transformation among the Florida Seminoles, 1953–1979.* Lincoln: University of Nebraska Press.

Kidwell, Clara Sue. 2004. "Choctaw in the West." In *Handbook of North American Indians,* vol. 14: Southeast, ed. William C. Sturtevant, 520–30. Washington DC: Smithsonian Institution.

———. 2001a. "Choctaws and Missionaries." In Haag and Willis, *Choctaw Language and Culture,* 309–12.

———. 2001b. "Choctaw Schools." In Haag and Willis, *Choctaw Language and Culture,* 306–8.

———. 1995. *Choctaw and Missionaries in Mississippi, 1818–1918.* Norman: University of Oklahoma Press.

Kidwell, Clara Sue, and Charles Roberts. 1980. *The Choctaws: A Critical Bibliography.* Bloomington: Indiana University Press.

Knack, Martha. 2001. *Boundaries Between: The Southern Paiutes, 1775–1995.* Lincoln: University of Nebraska Press.

Knight, Oliver. 1953. "Fifty Years of Choctaw Law, 1834 to 1884." *Chronicles of Oklahoma* 31: 76–96.

Knight, Vernon James, Jr., and Vincas P. Steponaitis, eds. 1998. *Archaeology of the Moundville Chiefdom.* Washington DC: Smithsonian Institution.

Kurtz, Donald. 2001. *Political Anthropology: Paradigms and Power.* Boulder CO: Westview Press.

Lambert, Michael. 2002. *Longing for Exile: Migration and the Making of a Translocal Community in Senegal, West Africa.* Portsmouth NH: Heinemann.

Lambert, Valerie. In press. "Choctaw Tribal Sovereignty at the Turn of the Twenty-first Century." In *Indigenous Experience Today,* ed. Orin Starn and Marisol de la Cadena. Oxford: Berg.

———. In press. "Political Protest, Conflict, and Tribal Nationalism: The Oklahoma Choctaws and the Termination Crisis of 1959–1970." *American Indian Quarterly.*

———. 2001a. "Choctaws in Oklahoma: Government." In Haag and Willis, *Choctaw Language and Culture,* 300–305.

———. 2001b. "Contemporary Ritual Life." In Haag and Willis, *Choctaw Language and Culture,* 317–21.

———. 2000. "Native Spiritual Traditions and the Tribal State: The Oklahoma Choctaws in the Late Twentieth Century." In *Spirit Wars: Native North American Religions in the Age of Nation-Building,* ed. Ronald Niezen, 156–60. Berkeley: University of California Press.

Libecap, Gary D. 1989. *Contracting for Property Rights.* Cambridge: Cambridge University Press.

Littlefield, Daniel F., Jr. 2001. "Choctaw Newspapers." In Haag and Willis, *Choctaw Language and Culture,* 313–16.

———. 1980. *The Chickasaw Freedmen: A People without A Country.* Westport CT: Greenwood.

———. 1979. *Africans and Creeks: From the Colonial Period to the Civil War.* Westport CT Greenwood.

Leach, E. R. 1954. *Political Systems in Highland Burma: A Study of Kachin Social Structure.* London: G. Bell and Son.

Lees, William B., and Heather N. Atherton. 2001. "Urban and Rural: New Life in the West." In Haag and Willis, *Choctaw Language and Culture,* 296–99.

Levine, Victoria Lindsay. 2004. "Choctaw at Ardmore, Oklahoma." In *Handbook of North American Indians,* vol. 14: Southeast, ed. William C. Sturtevant, 531–33. Washington DC: Smithsonian Institution.

Lomawaima, K. Tsianina. 1994. *They Called It Prairie Light: The Story of Chilocco Indian School.* Lincoln: University of Nebraska Press.

Lopach, James J., Margery Hunter Brown, and Richmond L. Clow. 1998. *Tribal Government Today: Politics on Montana Indian Reservations.* Niwot: University Press of Colorado.

Lowie, Robert H. 1920. *Primitive Society.* New York: Boni and Liveright.

McCool, Daniel. 1987. *Command of the Waters: Iron Triangles, the Federal Water Development Program, and Indian Water.* Berkeley: University of California Press.

McGuire, Thomas R. 1991. "Indian Water Rights Settlements: A Case Study in the Rhetoric of Implementation." *American Indian Culture and Research Journal* 15 (2): 139–69.

McKee, Jesse O. 1971. "The Choctaw Indians: A Geographical Study in Culture Change." *Southern Quarterly* 9: 107–41.

McKee, Jesse O., and Jon A. Schlenker. 1980. *The Choctaws: Cultural Evolution of a Native American Tribe.* Jackson: University Press of Mississippi.

McLoughlin, William G. 1974. "Red Indians, Black Slavery and White Racism: America's Slaveholding Indians." *American Quarterly* 26: 367–85.

Markwood, Christopher L., ed. 1998. *Oklahoma Government and Politics.* Dubuque IA: Kendall Hunt.

Martini, Don. 1986. *Chickasaw Empire: The Story of the Colbert Family.* Ripley MS: Don Martini.

Mankiller, Wilma. 1993. *Mankiller: A Chief and Her People: An Autobiography by the Principal Chief of the Cherokee Nation.* New York: St. Martin's.

Means, Russell. 1995. *Where White Men Fear to Tread: The Autobiography of Russell Means.* New York: St. Martin's.

Meredith, Howard. 1993. *Modern American Indian Tribal Government and Politics.* Tsaile AZ: Navajo Community College Press.

Mihesuah, Devon Abbott. 2005. *So You Want to Write about American Indians? A Guide for Writers, Students, and Scholars.* Lincoln: University of Nebraska Press.

———. 2003. *Indigenous American Women: Decolonization, Empowerment, Activism.* Lincoln: University of Nebraska. Press.

———. 2000. *The Roads of My Relations.* Tucson: University of Arizona Press.

Miller, Bruce G. 2001. *The Problem of Justice: Tradition and Law in the Coast Salish World.* Lincoln: University of Nebraska Press.

Miller, David Reed. 1978. "Charles Alexander Eastman, Santee Sioux, 1858–1939." In *American Indian Intellectuals: Proceedings of the American Ethnological Society,* ed. Margot Liberty. St. Paul MN: West.

Mills, Lawrence. 1924. *Oklahoma Indian Land Laws.* St. Louis: Thomas Law.

Miner, H. Craig. 1989. *The Corporation and the Indian: Tribal Sovereignty and Industrial Civilization in Indian Territory, 1865–1907.* Norman: University of Oklahoma Press.

Mooney, Timothy Paul. 1997. "Many Choctaw Standing: An Archaeological Study of Culture Change in the Early Historic Period, Archaeological Report No. 27." Jackson: Mississippi Department of Archives and History.

Moore, Sally Falk. 1989. "The Production of Cultural Pluralism as a Process." *Public Culture: Bulletin of the Project for Transnational Cultural Studies* 1 (2): 26–48.

———. 1987. "Explaining the Present: Theoretical Dilemmas in Processual Anthropology." *American Ethnologist* 14 (4): 727–36.

———. 1986. *Social Facts and Fabrications: "Customary" Law on Kilimanjaro,
    1880–1980*. Cambridge: Cambridge University Press.

Morgan, James F. 1979. "The Choctaw Warrants of 1863." *Chronicles of Okla-
    homa* 57: 55–66.

Morgan, Lewis Henry. 1870. *Systems of Consanguinity and Affinity of the
    Human Family*. Washington DC: Smithsonian Institution.

Morrison, James D. 1987. *The Social History of the Choctaw Nation: 1865–1907*,
    ed. James C. Milligan and L. David Norris. Durant: Choctaw Nation
    of Oklahoma.

———. 1954. "Problems in the Industrial Progress and Development of the
    Choctaw Nation, 1865 to 1907." *Chronicles of Oklahoma* 32: 70–91.

Mould, Tom. 2003. *Choctaw Prophecy: A Legacy of the Future*. Tuscaloosa:
    University of Alabama Press.

Nagel, Joanne. 1996. *American Indian Ethnic Renewal: Red Power and the
    Resurgence of Identity and Culture*. Oxford: Oxford University Press.

Nash, Manning. 1989. *The Cauldron of Ethnicity in the Modern World*. Chi-
    cago: University of Chicago Press.

Neely, Sharlotte. 1991. *Snowbird Cherokees: People of Persistence*. Athens: Uni-
    versity of Georgia Press.

Nicholas, Ralph W. 1965. "Factions: A Comparative Analysis." In *Political Sys-
    tems and the Distribution of Power*, ed. Michael Banton, 21–61. New
    York: Tavistock.

Nies, Judith. 1996. *Native American History: A Chronology of the Vast
    Achievements of a Culture and Their Links to World Events*. New
    York: Ballantine Books.

Noley, Grayson. 2001. "Foreword: Choctaws Today." In Haag and Willis, *Choc-
    taw Language and Culture*, ix–xiii.

———. 1979. "Choctaw Bilingual and Bicultural Education." In *Multicultural
    Education and the American Indian*, 25–39. Los Angeles: American
    Indian Studies Center, University of California.

Nugent, David. 2004. "Governing States." In *A Companion to the Anthropol-
    ogy of Politics*, ed. David Nugent and Joan Vincent, 198–215. Malden
    MA: Blackwell.

O'Brien, Greg. 2002. *Choctaws in a Revolutionary Age, 1750–1830*. Lincoln:
    University of Nebraska Press.

O'Brien, Sharon. 1989. *American Indian Tribal Governments*. Norman: Univer-
    sity of Oklahoma Press.

Oklahoma City Council of Choctaws, Inc. 1981. *English to Choctaw Diction-
    ary*. Oklahoma City: Oklahoma City Council of Choctaws, Inc.

Oklahoma State Advisory Committee to the U.S. Commission on Civil Rights.
    1974. "Indian Civil Rights Issues in Oklahoma."

Ong, Aihwa. 2004. "Citizenship." In *A Companion to the Anthropology of
    Politics*, ed. David Nugent and Joan Vincent, 55–68. Malden MA:
    Blackwell.

Park, Mary C. 1987. "Thumbnail Sketches of Choctaw Chiefs." Photocopied manuscript in possession of Three Valley Museum, Durant OK.

Pauketat, Timothy R. 2001. "The Ancient Ones." In Haag and Willis, *Choctaw Language and Culture*, 241–44.

Peck, Henry L. 1963. *The Proud Heritage of LeFlore County: A History of an Oklahoma County*. Van Buren AK: Argus.

Peebles, Christopher S. 1983. "Moundville: Late Prehistoric Sociopolitical Organization in the Southeastern United States." In *The Development of Political Organization in Native North America*, ed. Elizabeth Tooker, 183–98. Philadelphia: American Ethnological Society.

Perdue, Theda. 2003. *"Mixed Blood" Indians: Racial Construction in the Early South*. Athens: University of Georgia Press.

———. 1998. *Cherokee Women: Gender and Culture Change, 1700–1835*. Lincoln: University of Nebraska Press.

Pesantubbee, Michelene. 2005. *Choctaw Women in a Chaotic World: The Clash of Cultures in the Colonial Southeast*. Albuquerque: University of New Mexico Press.

———. 1994. "Culture Revitalization and Indigenization of Churches among the Choctaw of Oklahoma." PhD diss., Religious Studies, University of California at Santa Barbara.

Peterson, John H., Jr., ed. 1985. *A Choctaw Source Book*. New York: Garland.

Philp, Kenneth R. 1977. *John Collier's Crusade for Indian Reform, 1920–1954*. Tucson: University of Arizona Press.

Plaisance, Aloysius. 1954. "The Choctaw Trading House, 1803–1822." *Alabama Historical Quarterly* 16: 393–423.

Planning Support Group of the Bureau of Indian Affairs. 1973. "The Choctaw Nation: Its Resources and Development Potential, Report No. 213." Washington DC: U.S. Government Printing Office.

Porter, Robert B. 1997. "Strengthening Tribal Sovereignty through Government Reform: What Are the Issues?" *Kansas Journal of Law & Public Policy* 7 (2): 72–105.

Prucha, Francis Paul. 1985. *The Indians in American Society: From the Revolutionary War to the Present*. Berkeley: University of California Press.

Quinten, B. T. 1967. "Oklahoma Tribes, The Great Depression and the Indian Bureau." *Mid-America: An Historical Review* 49: 29–43.

Rawick, George P., ed. 1941. *The American Slave*, vol. 7: *Oklahoma and Mississippi Narratives*. Westport CT: Greenwood.

Richardson, Jane. 1940. *Law and Status among the Kiowa Indians*. New York: Augustin.

Roth, George. 1997. "The BIA Program for Building Tribal Governments under Phileo Nash and James Officer, 1961–1966." Paper presented at the Society for Applied Anthropology Meetings on the panel "Building Tribal Governments in the 1990s." Seattle WA.

Rusco, Mary Kiehl. 1973. "Indian Tribal Governments in Nevada." In *Native American Politics: Power Relationships in the Western Great Basin Today*, ed. Ruth M. Houghton, 88–97. Reno: Bureau of Governmental Research, University of Nevada.

Sait, Edward McChesney. 1938. *Political Institutions, A Preface*. New York: D. Appleton-Century.

Samuels, Wesley, and Charleen Samuels. 1997. *Life and Times of the Choctaw Original Enrollees*. Published and distributed by Wesley and Charleen Samuels.

Schneider, David M. 1968. *American Kinship: A Cultural Account*. Englewood Cliffs NJ: Prentice-Hall.

Shkilnyk, Anastasia M. 1985. *A Poison Stronger Than Love: The Destruction of an Ojibwa Community*. New Haven CT: Yale University Press.

Simpson, Philip M. 1998. "The Oklahoma Judicial System." In Markwood, *Oklahoma Government and Politics*, 127–50.

Skaggs, Jimmy M. 1978. *Ranch and Range in Oklahoma*. Oklahoma City: Oklahoma Historical Society.

Smith, Bruce D., ed. 1978. *Mississippian Settlement Patterns*. New York: Academic Press.

Smith, Calvin C. 1975. "The Oppressed Oppressors: Negro Slavery among the Choctaw Indians of Oklahoma." *Red River Valley Historical Review* 2: 240–53.

Smith, M. G. 1974. *Corporations and Society*. London: Gerald Duckworth.

Smith, Paul Chaat, and Robert Allen Warrior. 1996. *Like a Hurricane: The Indian Movement from Alcatraz to Wounded Knee*. New York: New Press.

Spaulding, Arminta Scott. 1967. "From the Natchez Trace to Oklahoma: Development of Christian Civilization among the Choctaws, 1800–1860." *Chronicles of Oklahoma* 45: 2–24.

Spears, Sarah Singleton. 1991. *Yesterday Revisited: An Illustrated History of LeFlore County*. Poteau OK: Poteau Daily News and Sun, LeFlore County Newspapers Limited Partnership.

Spicer, Edward H. 1969. *A Short History of the Indians of the United States*. New York: D. Van Nostrand.

Spier, Leslie. 1925. *The Distribution of Kinship Systems in North America*. University of Washington Publications in Anthropology, vol. 1, no. 2. Seattle: University of Washington Press.

Spoehr, Alexander. 1947. *Changing Kinship Systems: A Study in the Acculturation of the Creeks, Cherokee, and Choctaw*. Anthropological Series, Field Museum of Natural History 33, no. 4. Chicago: Field Museum of Natural History.

Steiner, Stan. 1968. *The New Indians*. New York: Dell.

Steponaitis, Vincas P. 1983. *Ceramics, Chronology, and Community Patterns: An Archaeological Study at Moundville*. New York: Academic Press.

———. 1978. "Location Theory and Complex Chiefdoms: A Mississippian Example." In *Mississippian Settlement Patterns,* ed. Bruce Smith, 417–53. New York: Academic Press.

Stremlau, Rosemarie. 2005. "Cherokee Families: Cultural Resilience during the Allotment Era." PhD diss., Department of History, University of North Carolina at Chapel Hill.

Strickland, Rennard. 1980. *The Indians in Oklahoma.* Norman: University of Oklahoma Press.

Sturm, Circe. 2002. *Blood Politics: Race, Culture, and Identity in the Cherokee Nation of Oklahoma.* Berkeley: University of California Press.

Swanton, John R. 1985. "An Early Account of the Choctaw Indians." In Peterson, *Choctaw Source Book,* 53–72. First published in 1918 as "An Early Account of the Choctaw Indians," *American Anthropological Association Memoirs* 5: 51–72.

———. 1932. "Choctaw Moieties." *American Anthropologist* 34: 357.

———. 1931. *Choctaw Social and Ceremonial Life.* Washington DC: Smithsonian Institution, Bureau of American Ethnology.

———. 1911. *Indian Tribes of the Lower Mississippi Valley.* Bureau of American Ethnology Bulletin 43. Washington DC: Government Printing Office.

Tambiah, Stanley J. 1986. *Sri Lanka: Ethnic Fratricide and the Dismantling of Democracy.* Chicago: University of Chicago Press.

Tax, Sol. 1955. "Some Problems of Social Organization." In *Social Anthropology of North American Tribes,* ed. Fred Eggan, 3–32. Chicago: University of Chicago Press.

Thompson, Bobby, and John H. Peterson Jr. 1975. "Mississippi Choctaw Identity: Genesis and Change." In *The New Ethnicity: Perspectives from Ethnology,* ed. John W. Bennett, 179–96. St. Paul MN: West.

Thompson, James Matthew. 1962. *Leaders of the French Revolution.* New York: Barnes and Noble.

U.S. General Accounting Office. 2001. "Indian Issues: Improvements Needed in Tribal Recognition Process. Report to Congressional Requesters." GAO-02-49.

U.S. Geological Survey. n.d. "National Water Summary--Oklahoma--Ground Water Resources." U.S. Geological Survey Water-Supply Paper 2275.

———. n.d. "National Water Summary 1988–1898--Floods and Droughts: Oklahoma." U.S. Geological Survey Water-Supply Paper 2375.

———. n.d. "National Water Summary 1990–1991--Stream Water Quality: Oklahoma." U.S. Geological Survey Water-Supply Paper 2400.

Wade, John William. 1985. "The Removal of the Mississippi Choctaws." In Peterson, *Choctaw Source Book,* 397–426. First published in 1904 as "The Removal of the Mississippi Choctaws," *Mississippi Historical Society Publications* 8: 397–426.

Waldman, Carl. 1985. *Atlas of the North American Indian.* New York: Facts on File.

Warrior, Robert Allen. 1995. *Tribal Secrets: Recovering American Indian Intellectual Traditions*. Minneapolis: University of Minnesota Press.

Watkins, John A. 1985. "The Choctaws in Mississippi." In Peterson, *Choctaw Source Book*, 69–77. First published in 1894 as "The Choctaws in Mississippi," *American Antiquarian and Oriental Journal* 16: 69–77.

Weinberg, Bill. 2000. "Water Wars." *Native Americas: Hemispheric Journal of Indigenous Issues* 17 (2): 16–27.

Wesson, Cameron B. 2001a. "Choctaw Houses and Public Buildings." In Haag and Willis, *Choctaw Language and Culture*, 267–71.

———. 2001b. "European Contact and Trade." In Haag and Willis, *Choctaw Language and Culture*, 272–75.

———. 2001c. "The Origins of Maize." In Haag and Willis, *Choctaw Language and Culture*, 258–60.

White, Richard. 1983. *The Roots of Dependency: Subsistence, Environment, and Social Change among the Choctaws, Pawnees, and Navajos*. Lincoln: University of Nebraska Press.

White, Robert H. 1990. *Tribal Assets: The Rebirth of Native America*. New York: Henry Holt.

Williams, Nudie E. 1981. "Black Men Who Wore the Star." *Chronicles of Oklahoma* 59 (1): 83–90.

Williams, Susan M., and Raquel Montoya-Lewis. 2000. "Federal Indian Water Rights." *Native Americas: Hemispheric Journal of Indigenous Issues* 17 (2): 20–27.

Willis, William S. 1957. "The Nation of Bread." *Ethnohistory* 4: 125–49.

Wilkins, David E. 2002a. *American Indian Politics and the American Political System*. Boulder: Lanham, Rowman and Littlefield.

———. 2002b. "Governance within the Navajo Nation: Have Democratic Traditions Taken Hold?" *Wicazo Sa Review* 17 (1): 91–121.

Wilkins, David E., and K. Tsianina Lomawaima. 2001. *Uneven Ground: American Indian Sovereignty and Federal Law*. Norman: University of Oklahoma Press.

Wood, Peter H. 1989. "The Changing Population of the Colonial South: An Overview by Race and Region, 1685–1790." In *Powhatan's Mantle: Indians in the Colonial Southeast*, ed. Peter H. Wood, Gregory A. Waselkov, and M. Thomas Hatley, 35–103. Lincoln: University of Nebraska Press.

Wright, Alfred. 1828. "Choctaws: Religious Opinions, Traditions, Etc." *Missionary Herald* 24: 178–83, 214–16.

Wright, Muriel H. 1951. *A Guide to the Indian Tribes of Oklahoma*. Norman: University of Oklahoma Press.

———. 1930. "Early Navigation and Commerce Along the Arkansas and Red Rivers in Oklahoma." *Chronicles of Oklahoma* 8 (1): 65–88.

Index

Winners of the North American Indian Prose Award

Boarding School Seasons: American Indian Families, 1900–1940
Brenda J. Child

*Listening to Our Grandmothers' Stories: The Bloomfield Academy
for Chickasaw Females, 1852–1949*
Amanda J. Cobb

Northern Athabascan Survival: Women, Community, and the Future
Phyllis Ann Fast

Claiming Breath
Diane Glancy

Choctaw Nation: A Story of American Indian Resurgence
Valerie Lambert

They Called It Prairie Light: The Story of Chilocco Indian School
K. Tsianina Lomawaima

Son of Two Bloods
Vincent L. Mendoza

All My Sins Are Relatives
W. S. Penn

Completing the Circle
Virginia Driving Hawk Sneve

Year in Nam: A Native American Soldier's Story
Leroy TeCube

Lightning Source UK Ltd.
Milton Keynes UK
UKOW02f1651100616

276027UK00001B/30/P